DIZNEY LAND

By Way Of Military Escort

Dennis Novicky

Copyright © 2020 Dennis Novicky
All rights reserved
First Edition

NEWMAN SPRINGS PUBLISHING
320 Broad Street
Red Bank, NJ 07701

First originally published by Newman Springs Publishing 2020

Some of the characters names may have been changed to protect their identity.

ISBN 978-1-64801-787-2 (Paperback)
ISBN 978-1-64801-788-9 (Digital)

Printed in the United States of America

Preface

Before you venture across the border…

Within these pages, my true everyday character is revealed by quoting lines from movies and TV shows I have watched; music I possess; and quotes from family members and historical figures. I have inserted the quotes to help create a little humor amongst this true tragedy to dissipate some of my emotional stress and depression from the story.

Before you glance at the footnotes to reveal the origin of the quotes, try figuring it on your own; though to your disadvantage, my family members are the only ones who have a good chance recognizing all the embedded quotes. Good luck and thank you for reading my story!

The Day We Crossed the Border

Day 1

Our trip started on May 10, 2017, from Southern Missouri. Brenda, my girlfriend, and I were driving to our timeshare in Loreto, Baja California Sur state, Mexico for a seven-day vacation. We planned to do some exploring during our four-day journey to our destination, also extend our vacation during the return trip home by exploring some national parks in Arizona. I don't consider us to be timeshare people. Just the word "timeshare" symbolizes rich, pretentious people sitting poolside being served Mai Tais, being waited on hand and foot all in an artificially man-made controlled environment. For us, a timeshare is just a place to sleep and use as a base camp between our adventures in the great outdoors.

Two days after leaving home, we arrived at the border town of Calexico. We made a quick stop to exchange some of our money over to pesos, which at the time was an exchange rate of 17.80 pesos to one US dollar. Crossing the border into Mexicali Baja, California, Mexico was a prolonged process due to the number of vehicles wanting to cross. While patiently sitting idle in the middle lane of congested cars, I saw two young men holding hands, crouched down and swiftly scurrying between traffic. The oldest man led them right next to our truck, where he looked over his left shoulder with a fearful glance, though acted as if he knew what he was doing; most likely, this was not his first grand escape from "The Mexicali Blues."[1] He had obviously found a flaw in border security and was sneaking his accomplice across the border entrance into the USA. It's a good plan; why would US security personal be looking for illegals walking the opposite direction of the incoming traffic into Mexico. With so much chaos going on, it was easy for the two men to cross the border undetected.

So that was another two people added to the roughly 11 million illegal immigrants in the US. Who needs a border wall when you can simply walk across the border in broad daylight? Even with multiple security cameras and Border Patrol Agents (BPA) with dogs, they still manage to slip in the country. Besides, "Those damn Mongolians would tear down my shitty (city) wall anyway."[2] So instead of building an expensive boarder wall, we could just build a cheap crosswalk making it more convenient for the influx of intruders.

Upon crossing the border, we were directed to a building across the street. We purchased a visa allowing us to enter the country and extend the duration of our stay, which reminded me to buy a map before leaving town.

I am old-school and prefer a real map, not a GPS (dumb, dumb). I prefer to get a visual of my entire route and destination before heading out to see all the optional routes to take. This way, I can learn how to get there and retain the knowledge on how to get home without relying on a GPS or Google map. I've realized that a GPS will not always give the best route to follow that compliments my driving tendencies, also my memory is just as reliable as an electronic gadget that needs to be charged. Case in point: Years ago I made my first trip to the Craters of Moon national park in Idaho to partake in CRF (Cave Research Foundation) survey expedition, where I met up with a small group of men in far reaches of the park and did so without a GPS or map. Days later upon completion of our project, I headed back to town following a fellow caver, who stopped his vehicle a few minutes later to ask me, "Can I follow you? My cell phone doesn't have a signal."

---

[1] Song by Grateful Dead.
[2] *South Park*, TV show.

With that in mind, after driving in Mexicali for five minutes, we saw a Walmart on an overpass and decided to get a map. I could see the store but getting there would prove to be interesting. The store was on the right side of the bridge, but the exit was on the left side, and of course, we were in the wrong lane to exit, and because of the heavy traffic, merging over was not an option. I could not achieve a U-turn because the median consisted of a concrete curb, so we had to drive a quarter of a mile to turn around. With all the one-way roads, unfamiliar road signs, and unyielding traffic, I found myself getting aggravated and started driving a little aggressively just to blend in with chaotic traffic. In less than one mile, I did an illegal U-turn, failed to yield, ran a stop sign, did an unlawful lane change while speeding, and cut someone off. Just when the store was in sight, surprise, surprise, surprise, flashing lights appeared in my rearview mirror. Only ten minutes into the country, and I was getting pulled over by the police! I was trying to figure out which one of the many traffic infractions they were pulling me over for, or were they going to write me up for all of them.

Two young policemen walked up to my truck window, and one of them politely said something in Spanish to which I replied, "No Española." In broken English, he repeated that was I pulled over for not wearing a seat belt. Really? In the States, I never use a seat belt and have never been pulled over for that infraction. I was relieved there was no mention of the long list of traffic violations I had committed. I figured he would want to see my driver's license, so being a bit proactive, I handed it to him. He studied the identification with a look of confusion then displayed it to his partner.

They had a brief conversation between them, then in a courteous tone, asked, "Which branch of the military were you in?"

I said, "The army." But how did he know I was ex-military?

Instead of handing him my driver's license, I gave him my veteran's card by mistake. A mistake that turned out to be very beneficial for me. As it turns out, he had also been in the service of the Mexican military, which prompted some friendly small talk between us and created a more relaxed encounter.

He informed me that I would have to go to a different town to pay a fine. Brenda and I deliberately looked at him with a confused expression as he tried to explain, in broken English, the details of what to do. We just kept shaking our heads and saying we did not understand what to do. He kept looking at his partner for help in translating what we needed to do, but he did not speak any English and was no help at all.

Eventually the respectful police officer just gave up trying to explain his instructions, then said, "You are free to go, and you need to use your seat belt."

I thanked him, and away we went. As we were driving away, Brenda told me, "You are one lucky son of a bitch." Who knew my luck would soon run out, or would it?

Regrettably, Walmart didn't have a map, but we successfully made it out of town and into the open countryside with no more issues. We drove south on Highway 5 for about two hours, when the road began to run close to the shore of the Sea of Cortez. We came upon a section of highway that had a narrow gravel road heading east directly into the sea. As I was driving past the side road, I said to Brenda, "We should go explore that road." She eagerly agreed, so we turned around and headed back to investigate the area.

Brenda and I had long been infected with the exploring disease. We always wanted to explore around the corner, down or up a hill, and what was at the end of a road, making for some unexpected fun adventures.

Brenda and I were in our fifties and had been a couple for eight years after meeting on eHarmony. Our online introduction was a near-perfect match. We share a lot of the same interests, viewpoints, likes, dislikes, and beliefs. We also have the same views toward the big things during this time in our lives—we both said no thanks to the financial burden of being in debt, the daunting task of raising children, or the misguided energy used to take care of a pet.

The first thing that caught my attention while searching through website photos of potential matches were the number of women displaying their cleavage, caked-on makeup, or cradling a pet. Such pictures instantly produced a first impression of what they thought was important to themselves and to the viewer of their photo. Most of the views were followed by my finger tapping on the delete key. Then I came across Brenda's photo of her standing ten feet off the ground in a large eucalyptus tree somewhere in Australia—the only realistic photo I came across within the three months of searching for someone to fill the void in my life. Sometimes a picture is worth a thousand words!

Brenda is semi-retired, and I operate my own drywall business, which gives us the freedom to pack up the truck and take frequent trips out of town, state, or country. Our passion is derived toward adventures in the great outdoors requiring less greenback ($), not because we're strapped for cash, but adamantly refuse to piss our money away on worthless material things. We firmly believe—it's what you do in your life, not what you own! This line of thinking has resulted in allowing me to brag on time well spent away from work. There are two thousand work hours in a year, of which I have worked an average of six hundred hours per year for the last five years and still managed to have hundreds of adventures, compiled with a thousand stories to tell, and do not plan on slowing down anytime soon!

Even after what happened on this particular adventure, we both still love our travels that free us from the confines of home.

Salt road leading into the Sea of Cortez

We took a hard-right turn on the access road, leading to the horizon, though without a map, we were unclear of our destination. There was a vehicle so far away from us that we could not tell if it was a car or truck, even its color was obscured. The road base consisted of big boulders filled with gravel and dirt and only wide enough for one vehicle to travel it at a time. The tide must have been low because the seabed was exposed for thousands of feet. We drove a few hundred feet, stopped, exited the truck, and walk around a little bit to explore the unique landscape. The seabed looked cool; it had a four to a six-inch layer of sea salt that seemed to go on forever into a distant abyss.

We walked out about fifty feet onto the semi-dry seabed and observed many different stages of formations in the salt layers. Some looked like it was still in a thick liquid form, while other areas had a crystal-like crust forming on top, producing some stunning configurations, especially with the sunlight hitting the crystalized salt formations on both sides of the road. There were signs of the salt being harvested from plots that were 15'×10' and went on for hundreds of feet running parallel to the road. After exploring the area for a while absorbing all nature's glory, we hopped back in the truck and started driving further down the road. We drove over a mile but had to suddenly stop near the other vehicle we saw earlier, as the sea had cut a wide, deep trench across the road. It's a good thing we had to stop because if not, I would have delayed our trips' main objective by going further, and the end of the road was nowhere in sight.

The route must have veered off to the north at about seven miles out, because I could barely make out the silhouette of the road before it dropped off the horizon disappearing into a distant mirage. Being well over a mile from the shoreline, we were able to get an incredible visual of our surreal surroundings, making it hard to believe we were surrounded by the Sea of Cortez with water levels at only about six inches deep. Of course, we had to get out and do some more exploring in this unusual landscape. Brenda was walking on the salt-encrusted shallow water looking for more salt features, when suddenly one of her legs sank into a hole up past her knee. She instantly went into panic mode while frantically asking me to help her to get out, not knowing if the rest of her body would sink deeper into the hole. Clearly, the salt layer was not strong enough to hold her weight, giving her a drenched right leg and a funny visual for me. I had to laugh as it was kind of funny, but at least she was okay as I helped her out of the hole. After Brenda's failed miracle of walking on water, we gazed upon the vast emptiness of the sea with great wonder; how does an endless void of visual stimulation seduce us to ponder its beauty? Upon our departure, I had to back the truck up over a thousand feet, just to find a suitable spot to turn the truck around, even then it was a little spotty as the banks of this road were soft and steep. The possibility of getting stuck in the Sea of Cortez watching the high tide roll in would be most disconcerting.

Back on the main highway, we drove until an hour before dark then stopped at a campground facing the Sea of Cortez, in the small town of San Felipe. The campground was small and well maintained, with nine-foot cinder block walls on three sides of the park supplying plenty of privacy and security within the walls. The internal privacy of the park was nonexistent due to the small campsites placed close to each other, accommodating space for only one vehicle with a picnic table. So it was a good thing that very few people were camping there that night, giving us ample space to roam freely. The table had an elevated porch-like structure eight feet above it, equipped with a rooftop that could be used for a tent or extra sitting to view the sea.

While preparing something for dinner, I heard Brenda laughing off in the distance. I looked up as she was walking out of the bathroom while attempting a conversation with a park employee. He spoke a few words in Spanish then received Brenda's chuckling response of "I thought that was the women's restroom!" I don't think he understood English, as there was no reply except for the confused smile on his face. In her defense, some of the bathrooms in Mexico are not well marked, also this particular bathroom wasn't equipped with urinals, only a concrete trough at the back wall.

After dinner, we crawled into the back of my pickup truck to go to sleep. My eight-foot truck bed is equipped with a camper shell containing a full-size Tempur-Pedic mattress on an eleven-inch elevated platform, which is great for allowing storage underneath along with small shelving on one side of the truck bed, which I constructed. I prefer sleeping in my truck on my Tempur-Pedic mattress than in a nasty hotel room with uncomfortable beds and stale air. Most times, we go to places where there are no hotels or people, so the truck with the camper shell is very convenient and comfortable for us, though more so for me than Brenda. Time for bed, as it has been a busy and long day.

Day 2 in Country

In the morning, we had an early, light breakfast to be the first two people enjoying a peaceful walk on the beach. Our early arrival was met with the sun on our faces as we looked out to the sea, hearing the seagulls and watching the gentle waves lapping the beach. We walked for about ten minutes and came upon an old abandoned fishing net fifty feet from the shoreline where a seagull was trying to pull a nine-inch fish free from the tangled webbing. It was apparent the bird had been working at this task for a while, and even though the net was winning the battle, the bird was able to get bits and pieces of the fish. With the bird trying to pull the fish free, the net would move, so the bird kept backing up to keep better leverage of freeing the fish from its captor. That bird was determined to get a free meal, though with us watching this epic battle between the living and the dead, the seagull became spooked and flew away. For now, score one for the dead and zero for the living.

Thirty feet away from the netting was a big mound of rock outcroppings at the shoreline, it was 50'×50'×8' high. With it being low tide, we were able to see all the interesting features in the very porous rock and large cavities for sea life to hide in during high tide. I did not see any sea life due to all the old tattered fishing nets, which were covering eighty percent of the outcropping with trash caught up in the netting and crevices. It was disturbing to see this natural beauty in such a mess, where acceptance of neglect is the norm and self-responsibility no longer exist. When I see garbage like this, it makes me think about the T-shirt I designed that says, "Are you lazy or stupid? Pick one!"

After a short exploration of this area, we started walking back to the campsite, when Brenda began picking up sea glass along the way.

Sea glass is just old broken pieces of glass that the motion of the sea has smoothed the sharp edges over a long period. The smoother the glass usually means that it is older. Some people collect the sea glass to make necklaces and bracelets.

When two men showed up on the beach, Brenda went to see what they were doing, while I continued looking for sea glass. They were looking for clams in the shallow pools of water left behind from low tide. On our way back, we walked closer to the beach wall and buildings, which revealed areas of littered trash, and not from the high tide; it was left behind from people visiting the beach. Lazy or stupid, pick one! After we arrived back at the campsite, we loaded up the truck and "Moved to Beverly, Hills that is."[3]

We were still going south on Highway 5 for about three hours when we came upon a bridge that was about a hundred feet above the valley floor. While driving across it, one could look down on the Sea of Cortez, which had a secluded beach nestled between the two rock canyon walls. Of course, I had to turn around and go back to check it out, though reaching the elusive beach would be a slight challenge. There was a very steep, rough dirt road leading down to the valley floor. It appeared to be an old abandoned construction site road when the bridge was being built, of which I call old goat trails, but was doable for my 1991 half-ton GMC 4×4. Brenda wasn't sure about us driving down the precarious hill and displayed a nervousness. She usually says one or more of the following, "You won't make it, you should not try it, are you sure you will make it, or it looks too dangerous." My reply to her is always, "How many times have I killed you?" (with my driving).

We made it down with ease and parked under the shade of the bridge, then laid out a blanket and enjoyed a peaceful lunch. This area must be hard for people to get to, as there was very little trash here and few signs of recent human activity.

After lunch, we walked down to the beach, where we were once again all by ourselves. On days like this, it's easy to forget there are over seven billion people on my planet. Within a few minutes of

---

[3] *Beverly Hillbillies*, TV show.

walking the shoreline, we came across these strange bugs that looked like a cross between a cockroach and a beetle. They moved very fast together in unison, and when you would get close to them, they would scurry away to another rock or object to hide behind. They all stayed close together and moved like a school of fish or a startled flock of birds. The bugs were about one-fourth-inch long and moved in groups of a hundred or so and were interesting to watch them go from rock to rock, trying to avoid being seen as we walked by.

Prehistorical looking bug

Traversing closer to the cliff wall, the stones on the beach were getting larger, and so too were the bugs. The bigger the rock, the bigger the bugs, no small bugs on big rocks, no small rocks with big bugs. While approaching the big boulders, we discovered the bugs were three inches long and no longer assembled in groups, making it easier for us to sneak up on them, allowing for a much better visual of their prehistoric-looking features. Even though they were captivating to study, we weren't brave or dumb enough to touch the dangerous-looking creatures.

I found a correlation between humans and these bugs from beaches I visited in Mexico, more people fewer bugs, more bugs fewer people. I have been on many beaches in Mexico and never seen these bugs as big as the ones on this secluded beach—a unique experience I will truly never forget!

After twenty more minutes of rock hopping, boulder climbing, and wildlife gazing, we went back to the truck and four-wheeled it up the goat trail with ease. This little adventure would have been missed altogether if we just drove across the bridge at 60 MPH. You never know until you go!

We drove for about two hours when suddenly the pavement just ended. What the hell, where did the road go? After driving a hundred feet on the detoured section, we ended up on a rough dirt road that was used mostly by road construction vehicles. We became slightly worried as no road signs were informing us that we were still traveling on Highway 5. Brenda was more concerned than me as she thought the desolate goat trail wouldn't take us to Highway 1. My only concern was the extra time it would take to get to our destination. Her Dumb, Dumb (GPS) said a highway existed here even though there was not, and the nearest road leading to Highway 1 was over an hour and a half away in the opposite direction! Damn Walmart for not having a map. At least the treacherous road was heading south, so how bad could it be?

Well, it was slow-going forever and our top speed was between twenty and thirty miles per hour. Every time I tried to go faster, we would hit a rough spot in the road, causing the truck to bounce all over the place, trying to knock my fillings out of my teeth. According to Google Maps, this is the only main road on the northeast side of the Baja. Therefore, it gets used a lot, made apparent by all the discarded tires alongside the road. In the last two days, I had seen well over two hundred discarded tires strewn about, especially in areas far from any towns. Apparently, some people carry a spare tire that is not mounted on a rim. When they get a flat tire that can't be repaired, they replace the tire, leaving the damaged one alongside the road and creating a vast graveyard of tire corpses.

During our bumpy ride, we encountered areas of the dirt road crossing over construction sites of a new highway project. Securing my confidence, we would eventually run into Highway 5. The different stages of the unorthodox construction site were sporadic. It did not make any sense compared to how road construction is done in the States. There were completed bridges in the middle of nowhere connected only by goat trails, and small sections of the highway were partially finished throughout the sixty miles or so of the project. To gain relief from the constant jarring, we defied barricades by driving around or over mounds of dirt to gain access to the smooth sections of the unfinished highway. It was obvious from the tracks in the dirt that others had blazed the trail before us, by doing the same.

After about two hours of driving on the dirt road, when we finally ran into Highway 1. Yeah! The highway was only a two-lane, but much better than driving on the goat trail from hell. It was time to put the pedal to the metal and make up for some lost time and did so until one hour before dark. I found a dirt road that went from the main road into a cactus-filled wilderness in search of a place to camp for the night. We did not have to drive very far before coming upon a little area to pull off the dirt road. This led us another three hundred feet into a vast cactus field before parking under the stars to conclude our evening.

Our campsite was awesome! It had mountains in the far distance, to the east and west. We were surrounded by fields of cactus, with no artificial light or man-made structures to be seen anywhere. Allowing us a wonderful view of the night sky and permitting us to enjoy this majestic beauty.

Camping area

Unfortunately, the only reason we were able to venture off the dirt road into the secluded wilderness, was from a small blazed trail that people made to use the area for dumping their trash. Is there no escape from mankind's madness?

It was interesting to see all the different types of cactus in the area and finding such a wide variety of plants that had adorned thorns. While walking around exploring the area, we had to be careful not to get stuck with the sharp spines that seemed to be on most of the plant life. Making it hazardous and not a good idea to journey outward while wearing flip-flops and shorts. Our daily walks into the wilderness usually involved a little prick for poor Brenda, who was constantly getting poked and not in a good way.

It was well past dinnertime, so I dug out a hole in the sand for a fire pit to cook some burgers on the grill. While sitting on the tailgate enjoying our meal, we watched the full moon rise through the outstretched arms of a large cactus. Birds were flying from one cactus to another, finalizing their nightly routine. Another good day ended with the moon and stars as our personal night light, followed by a *very* peaceful night's sleep.

Day 3 in Country

In the early morning, we watched the majestic sunrise ascend the mountaintops, had a quick breakfast, and headed out down the highway. Most of the drive was uneventful, except for routinely trying to avoid roaming farm animals of goats, cows, horses, and donkeys on the road, commonly occurring in areas far from the towns. Most of the time, the malnourished livestock moved slowly across the road, displaying no concern of getting out of our way. The extreme heat and lack of food supply in their environment seemed to give them a discouraging attitude; they were not going to be rushed by a two-ton vehicle.

We arrived in Loreto at noon, followed by driving twenty more minutes south, arriving at the condominium at two o'clock in the afternoon. I won't bore anybody with our week of vacation time photos of "This is Pebbles waving hello, this is Pebbles waving goodbye."[4] Instead, I'll just give a quick synopsis of what we did for the week:

  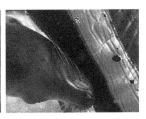

Rock Face in hill   Snorkling with Sea Lions   Sea Lion playful bite

Snorkeled with sea lions in the Sea of Cortez where we were chased and bitten by the playful varmints, a day hike into the deep

---

[4] *The Flintstones*, TV show.

wilderness where we found an abandon baby goat, hiked to a secluded beach and snorkeled where we found thirty stingray carcasses, a lengthy exploration day where we went to see the second oldest church in Baja California in San Javier, a short hike on the condominium trail where we met up with a rattlesnake, and let's not forget the mind-numbing shopping trips to the tourist traps requiring a bullet to my temple. I have a creed, if it doesn't make me money, feed or entertain me, I have no use spending money on worthless crap that will inevitably end-up in a garage sale or landfill.

One thing that was consistent with all our day trips into the wilderness was the discouraging amount of trash. Whether walking a mile away from a road or many miles from civilization, we saw discarded water jugs and bottles on the ground. Proving my point: a water bottle weighs more when empty than full because humans will carry a full eight-pound jug of water into the wilderness for many miles, but not an empty four-ounce jug for ten feet upon their exit.

Trash in the middle of nowhere

Day 10

Let us fast forward to May 19, 2017, the day that profoundly changed my life. We left the condominium at 11:00 a.m., filled up the gas tank in Loreto, and began our long journey back home. Thirty minutes north of Loreto, I was just getting into my fast driving mode of passing cars, anxious to start making some good time to our next camping destination, when I saw a military checkpoint straight ahead. I was not concerned about having our truck searched, for we had gone through four different military checkpoints while in Mexico, with little to no searching of our truck.

When we pulled closer to the checkpoint, I could see there were a few vehicles in front of us and noticed the soldiers were doing a more thorough search than normal of every vehicle. *Oh Shit!* Some people say when you are in danger, you should either fight or take flight. Unfortunately, those two options are not realistic when soldiers are present and carrying automatic weapons. So I chose option number three—do nothing and hope for the best.

There are only a handful of controversial actions I have committed during my life, of which I have not revealed to anybody. However, this moment requires one of those secrets to be told—an admittance of my own lazy and stupid judgment, which could have been averted in only *five seconds!*

That morning at the condominium, I was loading the back of the truck with our luggage, coolers, and gear. I grabbed some smaller items to put up front in the cab and began rearranging my portable Bose speakers that I keep on the floorboard just in front of the truck seat, where I noticed my nine-millimeter handgun under the driver's seat behind one of the speakers.

Many may ask, "What the hell is wrong with you? Guns are illegal in Mexico!" Yeah, no shit, I know! I have an excuse for why. Though there was no real justification for having that gun in my truck. Excuses are like assholes; everybody has one and they all stink. Don't get me wrong I'm usually not this reckless, maybe more arrogant, if anything. It's only Mexico, who the hell cares. Like Albert Einstein said, "Only two things are infinite, human stupidity and the universe, but I'm not sure about the latter."

While I can admit to myself when I'm at fault, the true test of my character is the admission to others of my guilt. Later, a friend of mine asked if I had noticed the signs at the border that read "no guns." I felt like responding to his slightly sarcastic question with a smart-ass answer. Still, I kept my composure with a polite reply. I really did not feel like going into much detail in explaining myself to anyone, so I was vague with my answer by only mentioning something about forgetting the gun was in the truck.

After thinking about that conversation for a few days, it festered in my mind. I realized that having the gun in the truck may have been more deliberate on my part than I was willing to admit. My convoluted logic at the time seemed to be sound and justified. We had plans to explore the countryside, which did not involve being around tourists or very many people. For me, an enjoyable day consists of not seeing any humans at all. Some of my journeys have been quite successful in doing so!

Which brings me back to the subject of the gun. I realized we would be traveling far away from the safety of our condominium fortress and avoid most of the tourist traps. Mexico has a murder rate that is off the charts. It is five times higher than in the United States. Some places in Mexico have a higher murder rate than in Detroit, New Orleans, St. Louis, and Chicago combined. Not to mention the corrupt police and out of control crime rate, especially against tourists. With this in mind, I did not want to play the odds and chance being one of those dreaded news stories of an American couple gone missing, abducted, robbed, raped, or murdered in a foreign country.

With our travel tendencies, we could possibly end up in the wrong place at the wrong time, so I snuck a gun into Mexico, who gives a shit! It's Mexico, not a church social! At least there would not be a TV reporter covering the story on our demised trip into Mexico. Questioning why we went to a dangerous country, left the safety of our condo, went on a hike in the middle of know where, or went out after dark? All of which could have ended in a much worse outcome than possession of a handgun charge! Now, do you see my arrogance? But isn't it more arrogant entering Mexico wearing blinders expecting everything will be peaches and cream? Remember, chance favors the prepared mind!

Back to the moment when I held that nine-millimeter in my hand. I said to myself, "I should hide this in back of the truck—no, I will do it later," then placed it back under the seat cradled in a blue Frisbee, though later never came. It would have only taken five seconds to tuck away the gun under some camping gear deep into the back of the truck. Some may ask, "Wouldn't the soldiers have found the gun anyway?" No. We went through all the other checkpoints, including this one last week. I noticed vehicles with less cargo were searched more thoroughly than ones that were full of cargo. Our truck was packed full of gear for camping, backpacking, scuba diving, caving, and rock climbing along with a full-size mattress, coolers, and luggage. We were truly prepared for any outdoor adventure that came our way, oh, and don't forget about the Frisbee under the seat cradling the 9mm.

At various checkpoints, when a soldier did take the time to search our vehicle, they would raise up the camper shell door, only slightly lifting up a corner of a blanket or move a small item to see what was underneath it. Previous checkpoints had only required us to drive by slowly. The soldiers did not appear to have the motivation to complete a two-hour search of all our tightly packed gear in ninety-degree temperatures, while wearing full combat gear and only making about one hundred dollars a week; who would?

While I was waiting behind other vehicles in line, a state of panic was brewing internally. Externally I tried to appear calm since there was absolutely nothing I could do about it anyway except to see how all this played out. When I pulled forward, a soldier walked over to my window and said something in Spanish.

Clueless, I handed him our passports and said, "No, Espanola." He gestured for us to get out of the truck. As we proceeded to do so, another soldier began searching the cab of the truck on the passenger side. He soon caught my peripheral vision when he began searching on the driver's side. He quickly found my six-inch survival knife in the side pocket of the driver's door, pulled the knife out of the sheath to inspect the blade just before placing it back in the truck. After that, he immediately searched behind the speaker to find the nine-millimeter handgun underneath the seat of the truck!

Oh Shit! I instantly became overrun with an intense fear, realizing I was truly in a world of trouble, with no viable options in gaining a favorable outcome. The extreme amount of sheer dread deep within my gut would have been crippling if I were a weaker man. My state of internal panic was quickly diverted while witnessing the soldier nonchalantly clearing the gun's chamber and magazine to count the bullets.

I was quite surprised at his calm demeanor in handling the firearm as it was a common daily occurrence finding a weapon in somebody's vehicle. There was no Hollywood drama, as seen on TV. No drawn or cocked weapons, somebody telling me to put my hands up, or taking me to the ground and handcuffing me. Hell, they did not even search me! So in the back of my mind, I was thinking maybe this situation wouldn't be as bad as I had anticipated, encouraging my unjustified relaxed sensation.

During the inspection of the gun, a guard called for a colleague (Charles) who spoke English to assist with translation. He only spoke broken English and had difficulty asking if I had a permit, which I did manage to understand. I quickly responded, "Of course I do!" I opened my wallet, pulled out my carry and conceal permit, and handed it to him even though I knew a Missouri permit was good as toilet paper here in Mexico. I knew he was asking for some type of legal document from Mexico. Still, I hoped by showing them I was a legal gun owner in the USA, it might smooth things over a little bit, which it did to an extent by confusing them. They were at a complete loss on how to proceed with the newly acquired information, along with my innocent display of overconfidence. Charles was having difficulty translating and understanding the validity of my permit. We were fortunate enough to find a woman passing through the checkpoint who spoke adequate English and was willing to help with translations.

After exchanging introductions and thanking her for helping us, Maria quickly began conversing with the soldiers. It soon became made apparent by Maria that this kind of ordeal had never happened before at this checkpoint. The higher-ranking military personnel were clueless about what to do. They had to call headquarters to find out what the procedures were. Even though Maria was helpful, she was mostly a bearer of bad news. After talking to a military officer, she relayed to us, "This is a big problem, having a 9 mm handgun is a federal crime!"

Oh shit! That does not sound good! Fight or flight? I'm still sticking with safe option number three for now, though the phrase "Big problem" was a bit disconcerting!

Maria also informed us that we might be able to see a judge today, fill out some forms for a temporary permit, pay a fine, and be on our way. This gave me false hope that option number three might produce a favorable outcome. I thought the severity of a federal crime in Mexico could not possibly be rectified by only paying a fine.

Charles had to frequently walk back and forth to a building two hundred feet away, where he obtained pertinent information to relay to us. Due to mass confusion within the military, the ability to make a decision was slow going, which had them awaiting phone calls from officials at headquarters. We were standing around for twenty minutes only to realize nobody truly knew what to do with us.

It is comical that the military's only task is to search vehicles for two things, drugs, and guns. They had already found 50 percent of their objective yet were completely clueless about protocol and how to proceed. The irony is they still hadn't searched the back of my truck, which would have yielded them a batting average of one thousand by finding Brenda's unlabeled pharmaceuticals. Hell! We could have been smuggling three illegals under the bed, fifty pounds of cocaine, and a bag full of cash with nobody being the wiser, or better yet a case of 9mm handguns.

After about twenty-five minutes of Maria patiently helping us with translations, her husband walked over to us and told her it was time for them to leave. Just before doing so, she relayed the last bit of information that Charles gave her... I would be driving my truck with Brenda and a soldier who speaks English, escorted by a military vehicle to La Paz five hours away. Where we were to see a judge, though there was no mention of being arrested, and I did not ask.

Soon after Maria's departure, Charles escorted Brenda and me to a small food shack next to the guard's hut, which mainly sold chips, candy bars, and drinks. The crude shack was constructed of plywood with a dirt floor. It was almost like a fort that children would build in their back yard, though kids today would require a Google search before attempting such an endeavor. He had us sit at a short bench in the shade of the shacks canopy where we were to wait until the military was ready to escort us to La Paz. Charles kept repeating, "No problem," trying

Checkpoint's food shack

to ease Brenda's state of panic, which was at this point not too bad and began to ease, but that would soon change from bad to worse.

As we sat on the bench, Charles walked away, leaving us supervised by a very young armed guard. His demeanor was not standoffish, or defensive, but more of a calm and relaxed posture. He admitted to only knowing a few words in English, so there wasn't much verbal interaction between us. Charles returned ten minutes later to inform us it would be another twenty minutes before leaving, and a slight dialogue began to emerge between the four of us. Charles was polite, friendly and tried to keep the conversation alive, but had difficulty finding the correct English words to use. After a failed attempt from his partner for help, Brenda suggested retrieving our translation book from the truck, to which he responded, "No problem." Allowing her to go unescorted to the truck seemed utterly odd to me. Wasn't my vehicle a part of a crime scene, or at least a role in an investigation? Either way, Brenda can now release the three illegals we had hiding under the mattress and have them carry the contraband away with them.

Charles thumbed through the book, searching for the elusive words. The book was more for translating phrases, so he gave up and handed it to the other guard, who appeared to have more patience with the confusing book, or maybe he was just trying to kill some time.

The four of us were able to have some limited small talk, which put Brenda and I a little at ease. When the subject of our vacation arose, I mentioned our encounter with a rattlesnake, and we had a video of it on our GoPro. I asked if it was okay for Brenda to retrieve it from the truck, and without hesitation, Charles said, "Yes, no problem." Once again, she was off to the truck unescorted. She soon returned with the camera in hand, showing them the video, which was taken three days earlier while we were walking on a dirt road at the condominium's property.

During our stroll, Brenda damn near stepped on the snake! It had failed to use its rattle to warn her of its presence. I took advantage of the opportunity at being around a calm snake, placed the camera about six feet in front of the snakes' original direction of travel. I went four feet behind the snake to motivate it toward the camera. Fortunately, there was no need to agitate it forward. I think the snake was drawn to the little flashing red light on the video camera because it moved directly toward the light while using its tongue to pick up the elusive scent. Luckily, the snake's curious movements were caught on video up close and personal. It was so cool to watch the video with the rattlesnake slithering right up to the camera lens flicking its tongue.

The two young men were in amazement, watching the video. From their strong impression and squeamish reactions, I gathered they were not comfortable being around snakes, even the ones displayed on a tiny screen.

After waiting around for another twenty minutes, a higher-ranking soldier walked over to us and gestured with his hand it was time to go, so we followed him over to my truck thirty feet away. We met up with five other soldiers standing there, which looked like a gathering for my going away party. I quickly realized it wasn't a going-away party, for it resembled more of an arresting party. Appearing that everybody was invited to watch the show, and the only thing missing from this strange spectacle were clowns and balloons.

As soon as my rights were being read to me, Brenda's panic button was pushed and instantly became extremely upset. She was thinking they were going to arrest her as well. She was so distraught that her face turned blood red, and her eyes full of a nightmarish fear while crying uncontrollably. Brenda and I were standing nine feet apart with a few soldiers in between us, so I was unable to go over and comfort her. Being forced to witness her in so much pain made me feel ashamed for putting her in this avoidable situation.

The devastating pain in my heart made it impossible for me to even look at her. Especially knowing there was absolutely nothing I could do to ease her torment. How in the hell could I possibly put the sweetest woman I have ever known in this outrageous predicament? Fortunately, there were a couple of soldiers standing alongside Brenda trying to calm her down. They kept telling her, "You are not getting arrested, don't worry, no problem." All of it was in broken

English, which took a while to finally ease her mind and stop her crying.

During the next few minutes, more soldiers arrived, increasing the spectators threefold. They seemed to be coming out of the woodwork like cockroaches to watch this circus. It was odd to witness so many soldiers appearing since there were only three or four soldiers outside at various checkpoints at any given moment. Just how many? Well, two with Brenda, one reading my rights in Spanish, one translating, one supervising the reading of the rights, three taking video with their phones, four or five just watching the show, and most likely somewhere off in the distance a captain, an assisting captain and a "Major ready to assist the captain if the captain needed the majors' assistance."[5] So how many is that? "I don't know, kid, a bunch!"[6]

As an officer read me my rights in Spanish, Charles relayed them to me in English from a printout sheet. Even though he did a pretty good job reading from it, he had trouble with the pronunciation of some words, so he allowed me to view the paper and read along with him. When they finished reading my rights, I had to sign some forms in triplicate, stating I understood what was just read to me. I don't remember a damn thing about what my rights were, except they were three times longer than the Miranda Rights in the USA.

I figured a foreigner in Mexico probably didn't have many rights anyway and was not enforced with diligence. In the back of my mind, I thought of news stories of Americans in trouble with foreign military, none of which ended in a happy ending. Regardless, I was not concerned about being mistreated or feared for my safety from the friendly and courteous soldiers. They were obviously just following orders from headquarters and did not have a dog in the fight; they were just doing their job.

Soon after crossing the Ts and dotting the Is on all the paperwork, all the spectators dispersed from this one ring short of a circus. Brenda and I along with a very young soldier named Robert hopped into my truck, then waited there for ten minutes while noticing a

---

[5] *Mash*, TV show.
[6] *Badder Santa*, movie.

guard carrying a small box that had been taped shut with an excessive amount of duct tape covering the entire surface of the box; it's safe to say that I will never see that 9mm again. Then he and three other soldiers loaded into their Humvee and proceeded to escort me off to jail. Guess its official! I am a prisoner of Mexico driving myself to jail accompanied by an unarmed soldier, finding it hard to comprehend how inconceivable this is and regret rolling the loaded dice, which has drastically altered my destination and now must "Go directly to jail, do not pass go, do not collect $200."[7]

Brenda and I ended up leaving the checkpoint at about 2:00 p.m. escorted by four soldiers in a military Humvee manned with a fifty-caliber machinegun mounted on top. It seemed a bit of an overkill, the display of power over the likes of two dangerous criminals as ourselves. What our young unarmed passenger failed to realize was he was traveling with someone who still had access to that six-inch survival knife that a curious soldier placed back in my truck upon inspection.

I truly felt screwed from this dire situation that I had absolutely no control over. So much so, that during most of the drive, I kept quiet with a very somber demeanor, as the guilt of my actions had overtaken my thought process, stripping me of the privilege of amiable speech of which I did not deserve to display. My reserved behavior was a concern for Brenda's worried state of mind.

When Brenda was trying to communicate her concerns to Robert. Most of his replies consisted of "No problem," like a parrot with a limited vocabulary that had absolutely no comprehension in the meaning of the phrase or how it affects others. Robert displayed empathy when he told Brenda she was not going to be arrested while reiterating "no problem." If that were true, why didn't they let her drive the truck and throw my ass in the Humvee? Eventually, she calmed down enough to pull out her phone to video the Humvee escorting us and attempt some small talk with Robert. However, most of it was limited due to his lack of the English language.

---

[7] Monopoly game.

Continuing to follow the Humvee down the two-lane highway, I was amazed at the high rate of speed it was traveling. We were aggressively passing every vehicle we came upon with speeds of at least 20 mph over the speed limit. Even when the road signs displayed a decreased speed limit, their foot remained heavy on the gas pedal. There were moments when I was behind other vehicles waiting for the opportune time to pass, which expanded our distance from the Humvee. This action made Robert take notice and gestured for me to pass vehicles that were in front of us, though his display of impatience might have been a mistake.

I put the pedal to the metal and started driving more aggressively, keeping a closer distance to the Humvee and passing vehicles in a more limited time and space. Robert became fearful, and I caught sight of him stepping on the imaginary brake pedal, which is only activated when Brenda uses it. Of course, Robert was not familiar with my driving skills and little did he know I drive with "slight" aggression all the time on back roads in the States, with a three-page driving record of infractions to prove it! So this style of driving is just another day at the races. I could not figure out why the military was driving like they were responding to a five-alarm fire and failed to ask Robert what their big hurry was. Unfortunately, I found out days later it assisted in a bad outcome for me!

After a couple of hours burning up the pavement, the Humvee pulled off the road onto a dirt shoulder and stopped. I pulled up behind them, wondering what they were doing, we were literally in the middle of nowhere with no man-made structures anywhere. Then it dawned on me; this scene resembles a Hollywood mobster movie set in the vast emptiness of a desert, where a disloyal gangster finds himself getting buried in the loose soil.

I turned to Brenda and Robert and asked with a sarcastic tone, "Is this where they take us out into the wilderness and put a bullet in the back of our heads?" No shit! Under all this stress, I still have not lost my witty, dry sense of humor.

Robert grinned and quickly responded with, "No, No!" It was just a pee break, not a Mexican military execution, lucky us!

After watering the gravel, we hopped back into our vehicles and proceeded to dial it up to "Ludicrous speed."[8] It was quite obvious why Brenda did not utilize mother nature's man-friendly bathroom and waited until we reached our destination. However, the exceeding long trip eventually had her saturated bladder painfully yearning for a bathroom. We were driving for about another hour, passing everything in sight, including gas stations. The soldiers did not stop at a gas station; instead, they met up with another military Humvee in a small town where they siphoned fuel from a ten-gallon plastic jug. Yeah, I'm not kidding! Not sure if we are watching a poorly funded military refueling station or a Mexican NASCAR pit crew; their time was a little slow even though they did not take on fresh tires. Only NASCAR enthusiasts will know what that means. It was inevitable on this exceedingly long trip; the Humvees would get low on gas. My truck, on the other hand, did not need gas, as it has a thirty-gallon tank and gets at least twice as much mileage as a Humvee. Though just as painful on the wallet to fill up as gas was close to four dollars a gallon, calculating to $120 to fill up.

A helpful side note for would-be travelers to Mexico: Purchasing fuel at a gas station is a gamble on whether you get ripped off from the misfortune of having a dishonest attendant working the gas pump. They will not clear the gas pump gauges from the last customer's purchase before pumping your gas, thus pocketing the extra money you paid for the total purchase. Brenda and I think we were ripped off at least once. Between the language barrier, peso to dollar conversion, and how much to tip the attendant, one tends to be distracted from always checking to see if the gauges started at zero, and to increase in confusion, their analog pumps are not capable of reading past 999 pesos. Which had me cautious when saying, "Fill it up," as it would require over 2,000 pesos to do so. Most of the time, the attendants had to write down the peso amount on a piece of paper, restart the pump in order to fill my tank, then add the two amounts for my final tally. After being in Mexico for a while, I began observing the gas station attendants' activities more diligently!

---

[8] *Spaceballs*, movie.

After the Hummer was finished sucking down fuel, the two pit crews had a few words together, then loaded up and headed down the highway. We were now being escorted by a Humvee in front and one behind us with double the firepower, with the capability of taking out this dangerous American tourist if the situation presented itself. This is no longer looking like a "No problem, pay fine" type of escort! It's safe to assume our vacation was officially over!

At 7:30 p.m., we finally dropped out of warp speed ending up in the city of La Paz, a population of two hundred thousand. In 2014, Brenda and I were here snorkeling with the whale sharks in the Sea of Cortez. The whale sharks are approximately twenty to thirty feet long; they are neither a shark nor a whale, but the largest fish to feed on the smallest life forms in the ocean, of plankton, krill, and fish eggs.

We went with a tour group out of Cabo. We were able to snorkel with the whale sharks for over an hour, an exceptionally long excursion considered by the tour guide. While floating in slightly choppy water, Brenda was a good distance away began yelling to get my attention. "Dennis behind you, behind you!" I slowly turned around and, to my surprise, was a twenty-five-foot whale shark with its four-foot-wide open mouth heading straight for me.

At first, I was not concerned about being in any danger, as these lackadaisical fish are non-aggressive and swim at a slow pace. Their throats are only the size of a grapefruit, so there was no chance of getting swallowed by the giant fish. They have three thousand match head size teeth, which don't get utilized because of their preferred diet. My first reaction was to instantly start recording with my GoPro. Assuming this big fish would eventually turn to avoid me, confident I'm not on its lunch menu.

Whale sharks eat while slowly moving forward opening and closing their large mouth. While sucking in massive amounts of seawater, they filter out tiny food sources through their built-in filter system within its gills. The whale shark repeated this process, closing the gap between us quicker than I was comfortable with. So I slowly tried to move out of its direction of travel hoping not to startle the gentle giant while keeping the camera steady on target. As this enormous fish drew nearer, the physics of my possible encounter began to play out, quickly transforming my amazement into heightened anxiety! How much volume of water could this fish suck into its large mouth, and at what force, and at what proximity would I be before accidentally getting sucked in? Also, what intensity would the fish exert the unwanted object from its mouth? Despite processing this information in a fraction of a second, my reaction time had suddenly disappeared.

The force generated from the massive amount of water getting displaced from the big fish, nullified the energy I was exerting in trying to escape the inevitable encounter. Even with well equipped with scuba fins, I found my face within inches of the enormous whale sharks' mouth, close enough to view the detailed coloring on its lips! What the hell! Was this fish blind or interested in using those baby teeth on a convenient noontime snack? I completely freaked out, arms and legs flailing, loud moans and groans coming from the snorkel tube while frantically trying to avoid a head-on collision with the unyielding creature.

My GoPro video shows a perfect interpretation of my complete state of panic. The last clear shot viewable was the giant fish lips followed by a massive amount of bubbles from my uncontrollable thrashing, thereby making it totally impossible to see anything else on the video. We never made any physical contact, and my big spotted friend did not seem to mind the intrusion into its personal space.

In conclusion, it was an exceptional day ending with an excellent video and a lifelong experience. Unfortunately, I was about to embark on an epic journey that didn't have the luxury of a GoPro video!

After driving ten minutes in town, we turned off the main road onto a side street. We drove alongside an ancient prison surrounded by a twenty-foot-high concrete wall, equipped with thirty-foot guard towers at each corner. With the decreased speed, I was able to get a good visual of the tower guards brandishing automatic weapons also guards standing across the street in front of the courthouse carrying shotguns. My freak out level now intensified, contemplating if this was indeed to be our destination, notably when our forward progress slowed to a crawl!

South Prison Wall

To my horror, we ended up parking right next to the backside corner of the prison, thirty feet away from one of the prison's towers. As I stepped out of the truck, a sobering thought emerged while standing there among scattered trash in the shadows of a riddled pockmarked Mexican prison wall, this ominous destination damn sure wasn't in our vacation brochure!

The soldiers displayed confusion about where I should park the truck. They had me move it a few feet over from where I originally parked, then had me hop back in and drive it ten feet further from the road. Only to be moved again by a soldier a minute later. Just like at the checkpoint, there seemed to be multiple debates being carried out on how to conduct this dysfunctional circus. After the truck's final resting place was settled, they all stood around in the parking lot for a few minutes displaying what seemed to be a constant state of confusion on how to proceed. Eventually, four soldiers casually escorted Brenda and me across the street to the city jail. Just inside the entrance was a security guard standing next to a baggage X-ray machine and metal detector similar to what you find in an airport.

After going through the X-ray and metal detector machine, Brenda and I patiently stood at a check-in counter, watching more confusion commence between the military and office personal. However, by this time, Brenda was in no mood to stand around waiting on their indecisiveness, as her enlarged bladder was in total control of her next destination. We interrupted their unproductive debate and desperately asked where a bathroom was. While they were staring at us with total confusion, Brenda focused her attention on the female personnel in the room. Using creative body language to

DIZNEY LAND by Way of Military Escort

help explain what she wanted, which induced a quick understanding of her game of charades from the woman.

When Brenda returned from her bathroom break, the military men took us back outside to the jails compound parking area; for what? Who knows! Maybe they are waiting for a printout manual from Ringling Brothers on how to properly run this circus. They left us standing there with no explanation in the presence of one guard who didn't speak a word. We just stood there on the sidewalk watching the grass grow.

It was reassuring to see they had parked my truck inside the safety of the jails compound area. Relieving my worries about all the expensive gear in the back of the truck, which is undoubtedly more valuable than what the truck was worth. My fear of the contents disappearing was a big concern, especially after driving through La Paz, witnessing so many houses and commercial buildings with barred windows and doors. Surrounded by tall cinder block walls with metal entry gates and atop some of the walls were barbwire, metal spikes and broken glass embedded in concrete. I honestly cannot remember noticing any house without some sort of wall or fence surrounding it. Only the poorest of the poor seemed to have no walls or fencing, although what would you steal from someone who has nothing? I don't know if they live this way as a result of fear for their lives, fear of losing their possessions, or both. The final question is, is there that much crime to justify living in their fortress of locked cages.

I feel incredibly fortunate to live in an area where my truck keys never leave the ignition while parked at home. We don't lock our house at night, or even when we go out for the whole day. We don't have a fence, wall, guard dog, or security system, but we do own a shotgun, 302 rifle, 22 rifle, and a 25 handgun, minus a 9 mm. If you feel the need to approach our property, do so at your own risk, as the sign out front reads, "We don't dial 911." I may be going to jail today, but it appears the people of La Paz already live in their own prison every day; what about you?

In the meantime, twenty minutes had passed when three soldiers returned and escorted us back into the building. They relinquished us over to the jail personal who took Brenda and me down a long hallway to a doctor's office, which could explain why we were standing outside for so long, most likely awaiting the doctors' arrival. A doctor? One would ask, "Why?" I didn't have a clue!

Upon entry, we were greeted by an older gentleman wearing a doctor's uniform who attempted to be social. Still, the language barrier quickly thwarted any chance of friendly interaction. He began asking questions pertaining to our personal information, name, address, height, weight, etc. However, he had difficulty verbalizing himself, which painfully slowed the process to a snail's pace. The doctor's evaluation became more arduous when he started asking questions about our medical history. He soon realized the task at hand was going nowhere fast, so he left the office and returned with Robert to assist with translations.

While the doc was asking Brenda about her medical history and current ailments, I suddenly became aware that the only reason we are getting questioned by a doctor is that they were processing us for an overnight stay in a jail cell. Until now, everybody had been telling us that Brenda was not going to be arrested. Regrettably, I concluded it was all a big fabrication of misinformed individuals. I don't think Brenda recognized her freedom was about to abruptly come to an end. I didn't have enough courage to inform her of our impending sleepover. All I could do was sit there waiting for this demoralizing torment to play itself out.

The doc had Robert ask us if we had been mistreated by the military, or if we had any suicidal thoughts. He had no problem translating our simple responses. He did have trouble with technical words in the medical field, which, in his defense, was completely understandable as translating medical lingo is probably not in his vocabulary. After painfully watching this slow process drag on, I spoke up, "Why not use Google translate?" The doc was already in front of a computer typing in our answers, so why not simplify this unproductive process?

I'm not a big fan of telling someone to "Google it" or being told to do so for myself, for it only reveals our own inadequacy of knowledge. Though I was exposed to A trough Z Google during the seventies before it was even conceived, when my mother would reply to us siblings in search of knowledge, by saying "Look it up in the encyclopedias." For you young readers who don't have a clue what encyclopedias are "Google it" (conveyed with sarcasm).

Even after the almighty Google was involved with our dilemma, there still was some confusion with the doc's ability to acquire the correct information from the internet. Robert, being a bit more proficient in front of a computer screen, assisted by getting in the driver's seat. I kept my answers to their questions short and without detail to speed up this ordeal. Besides, their questions were just a formality to a process that probably holds no real importance anyway. Brenda, on the other hand, was overloading their translating ability with a way too much detailed information concerning medical history and present ailments. However, the longer we sat in the doc's office, the less time we would be spending in a jail cell. Trust me when I say it's more advantageous to be stuck in a dentist chair or watching golf than being confined in an 8'×10' jail cell.

When the doc was finally finished with us, two office personnel showed up and escorted us toward the back-door exit. As I asked myself why we were going back outside, somebody spoke up from the far end of the hallway and turned us back around toward the direction we just came from. I was beginning to think total confusion is the norm around here.

We ended up in a small corridor containing an eight-foot fold-out plastic table with a couple of chairs, low budget cabinets, and an array of shelving. Also, standing in the hallway were three young staff members, one woman and two men, one of whom spoke fluent English. He was well dressed and very cordial, apparently brought in this evening to help with translating. At this point, Robert and the military appeared to have vacated the area.

The translator asked us to sit at the table and fill out some forms, which were a repeat of information we already relayed to the doc and military. Before having a chance to complete them, a staff member brought us some dinner along with something to drink. Unfortunately, I'm not a fan of Mexican food and a picky eater, so my consumption of the unsavory meal was minimal, not to mention it tasted and smelled nasty. Brenda will eat just about anything and had no trouble with the cuisine, especially after not having lunch or dinner.

While we were eating, a staff member walked over and wanted Brenda to go into an adjacent room to get fingerprinted. I eagerly stood up and volunteered to go first, allowing Brenda to finish her meal. I was more than happy to get away from poking at my undesirable dinner. This act of poking at my food brought on a clear recollection of when I was a child. Finding myself night after night sitting at the dinner table for hours, the result of me adamantly refusing to eat my vegetables.

I was fingerprinted many years ago in the States for a misdemeanor filed by my crazy ex-wife, so I'm familiar with the process, or so I thought! The man performing the task did not speak English, which raised the difficulty level in this activity, but more so for Brenda than I. She has never been fingerprinted and possesses a spotless criminal record, but by no means innocent as she may appear. I sometimes find myself following her lead by crossing over a fence or boundary signs that read keep out or no trespassing. To say he only fingerprinted me would be an understatement. The procedure consisted of old school technology by pressing my fingertips in an ink-soaked pad, then pressing them one at a time onto a sheet paper designed for filing the recorded prints. He repeated the process for each hand four times; first four fingers together, then my thumb, palm, and finally the pinky finger side of the hand, which for some reason was all done twice for both hands. So if I were to get crazy and go on a crime spree in Mexico, I certainly would wear gloves.

When Brenda finished dipping her fingers in the jailors' ink, they took us to a room one door over where comical confusion encountered intense fear. I knew by entering through the security door that the next stage of our journey wasn't going to be very pleasant for Brenda. The door made of metal had a sliding bolt latch that was made to be locked with a padlock with a little metal sliding window. It's safe to say we were not entering the employees' lounge, and soon obtained a visual of where we will be resting our heads for the night!

The 12'×22' foot room containing three jail cells on the left, one of which housed an old man that looked like he had done an all-night drinking binge. To the right was a small interview room next to this was a sizeable two-way mirror on the right wall. Resembling the military checkpoint, the room was filling up with show-goers quickly. At one point, there were six other people in the room with us, four men, two women, all young adults, not counting the old man in the middle cell who probably wished he had some popcorn while watching the show.

None of the staff members were dressed in any style of uniform, so it was impossible for me to figure out who was in charge, or even in control of all this mass delirium. The only person in some sort of uniform was the jailor who was the only one not involved with all the chaotic chatter which filled the room. His only job appeared to be opening and closing the metal security door for all the foot traffic continuously coming and going.

Everything attempted by the staff members in the room resembled an employee's first day on the job, mirroring the military's on-the-job training. Imagine being at a grade school play, and you know how the storylines should be performed. Still, it's hard to follow as it's going horribly wrong, and even though you feel uneasy because your child is on the stage, you still want to laugh, as it's funny but can't or shouldn't.

I genuinely believe our presence at the Mexican jail had set a precedent that day. One of the first things they asked us while in the room was, "Has anybody read your rights?" We had been there for almost two hours, and they waited until that moment to ask us that question. I responded, "Yes, but not to Brenda. The military said she was not going to be arrested."

This is where the shit hits the fan! I'm not quite sure what they said to her next, but it damn sure was not pleasant. She instantly began crying and sobbing while saying, "I have never been arrested before. I am a good person!" She began to repeat herself, followed by a sorrowful whimpering, "I've never seen jail bars, I don't even know anything about the judicial system back home, I'm a good person!"

In my entire life, I have never witnessed a person's face so freakishly blood red as hers at that moment; it was insanely scary, no exaggeration! If I were to take a pin and poke her face, it would have exploded into a million pieces! Once again, the pain in my heart for Brenda continued to grow more out of control. Will she ever be able to forgive me?

One woman was trying to calm Brenda down, and began to get upset and started to cry along with Brenda. Meanwhile, all the other parrots in the room kept squawking, "No problem, don't worry, it will be okay, no problem, no problem!"

Witnessing Brenda this way triggered a memory of when we were in Jamaica on a cruise a few years ago. She had been dealing with health issues for quite some time, and somebody told her to try using marijuana to ease her ailment. So one day while walking in the town of Falmouth, Jamaica visiting local shops, we came upon a paraphernalia shop. The man working there fits the stereotypic description of a Jamaican to a tee, with loose colorful clothing, dreadlocks, and a strong distinguishable Jamaican accent. Brenda went inside and bought a unique pipe and was invited by the clerk into the back room, where he gave her a small amount of Ganja (weed).

Long story short, the night before departing from the ship heading to a US port, we were packing our luggage when Brenda contemplated stuffing the Ganja in her suitcase. I instantly spoke up and adamantly said, "No way in hell, I'm not doing jail time for you or anybody else!" So she left the wacky weed in a dresser drawer for a maid to find and maybe have a little party of her own. Well! I, mister macho man, was talking out his ass, because after witnessing Brenda in her extreme state of distress in that Mexican jail. Not only would I do time, but I would also take a bullet for her!

By the way, when we were waiting in the US customs line at the port, a drug-sniffing dog checked our luggage. So I should be congratulated for eliminating jail time for at least one of us then; you're welcome!

After the staff was able to calm Brenda down a little, they read her rights and asked if we had anything in our pockets. Little did they know I could have said, "Excuse me while I whip this out."[9] Then proceed to reveal my survival knife. They all waited until now to search us for contraband or potential weapons two hours after our arrival, which seemed totally bizarre to me!

After I emptied my pockets, they searched me more thoroughly, leaning me against a wall with legs spread for a pat-down. A staff member relieved me of personal items, 6,000 pesos, Chapstick, belt, phone, eyeglasses, placing them all in a manila envelope and sealing it closed. For those not familiar with jail protocol, if I wear wearing shoes, they would have taken my shoelaces to keep me from hanging myself or strangling others. Oddly enough, Brenda was spared the indignity of a pat-down. She was only asked to empty her pockets, relying on the honor system not to smuggle anything into the jail; strange, is it not?

One of the guards retrieved a camera and handed us an 8'×10' sheet of paper, which had our personal info written on it, name, age, height, etc. We took turns standing at the back wall for our mug shots while holding the paper in front of us.

When our low budget photo shoot was over, they made a phone call to the US consulates office in Mexico for us. However, being well past nine o'clock at night as they had no luck getting in touch with anyone. They were determined to allow us our one phone call and took us across the hall to use their phone in the office. So we could contact a family member and let them know about our predicament. In essence, this also turned into a problem twofold. Problem #1. These days, nobody needs to remember phone numbers, unlike the days with rotary phones when everybody knew all their friends and family's numbers by heart. Brenda asked a staff member if I could get my phone back to retrieve some phone numbers, which we did. Problem #2. There was confusion between the staff on how to dial out of the country and after many failed attempts, they finally just gave up. Fortunately, Brenda was able to leave a voice mail with the US consulates office informing them of our unfortunate situation. She left our names with contact phone numbers of our daughters,

---

[9] *Blazing Saddles*, movie.

which gave us some comfort knowing someone knew we were being held in a Mexican jail.

After receiving a bottle of water that I had asked for, I finished using Mexico's telecommunication service. The staff took us to the interview room across from the jail cells to take our statements and fill out more forms. The small 6'×10' room was sectioned in half with a 4' high partition wall in the center of the room with a glass panel extended all the way to the ceiling. There was one chair on each side of the partition and a door at each end.

For me to read and sign more forms, I needed to borrow Brenda's glasses, which for some odd reason they did not confiscate from her. Three staff members were still utilizing the young man for our translator, who relayed their request of a short statement from us explaining the actions of our crime. I informed them about my carry and concealed permit for the gun and that I just forgot the gun was under my seat. I hadn't touched it in almost a year, and Brenda had no knowledge that the weapon was in the truck. It was more convenient to say, "I forgot" than justify why I had a 9-millimeter handgun in the truck while eliminating complete responsibility of guilt.

In a distressed voice, Brenda said essentially the same thing, evoking a comforting response from them—that she would most likely be released but would have to wait until tomorrow after speaking to the public defender and prosecuting attorney.

Every time a staff member spoke to Brenda, they genuinely seemed concerned that she was distraught. They were diligent in consoling her, which continuously ensued the "no problem" phrase. It appeared this hypnotic phrase, and their sincere willingness to comfort her began to calm and ease her anxiety.

When the staff was finished taking our statements, they took us to the jail cells. The jailor opened a cell door, and as Brenda and I started to enter, he stopped us while saying something in Spanish and shaking his head no. It did not take a Spanish linguist to understand the jailor wanted us in separate cages. This saddened my already shattered heart, knowing I would not be able to comfort my baby tonight!

The jailor put Brenda in a cell to the right of an old man, and I, to his left. The 7'×10' cell was encased by three concrete walls and an entrance barred from floor to ceiling. All furnishings were stripped of all movable hardware from the toilet seat, sink, and shower. There was a concrete bunk bed complete with foam mats and as a bonus, a roll of toilet paper. I hope that paints a vivid picture of this unfurnished guest room, which certainly makes for easy inspection on inventory day.

After the jailor locked the cell door with a padlock, he proceeded to show me how the shower worked. I was to bang the bolt latch against the cell door, so he could hear it from the adjacent room. Alerting him to return and open a water valve next to my cell door allowing water to flow from the headless shower spout. The same process was required to flush the toilet, except there was a foot pedal for the jailor to step on, which flushed all three toilets at the same time. No directions were needed for the sink as the water remained on at a slow trickle all day then turned off during the night. After effectively demonstrating the jails plumbing system, he left the room then returned with a toothbrush and a small tube of toothpaste for Brenda and myself.

The next and last time I saw the jailor that night was when he returned to flush all the toilets and turn on two large halogen lights that were so intense and bright that a 747 jet could have landed. I have no idea why the jailor seemed to be trying to burn our retinas at bedtime. I can sleep while the lights are on, but Brenda has problems falling asleep with just a glow from a night light. Because of this, she did not fall asleep until five in the morning, and I had some trouble sleeping throughout the night as well, but I can't imagine why! Could it be the insanely bright lights, a cold cell with no blanket, no pillow, or a thin foam sleeping mat on concrete? Maybe that the love of my life is confined two cells over in a freaking Mexican jail because of me? The only reason I slept as much as I did was utter complete mental and emotional exhaustion.

At two o'clock in the morning, Brenda quietly called to me through the cell walls to ask if I was awake. I was. She proceeded to tell me that my daughter Kathleen and Summer (Brenda's daughter) had been notified of our disastrous situation.

"*What?*" I responded in a confused tone. "How?"

"I texted them," she said, "and let them know what has happened to us."

Once again, "*What?*" Did Brenda's jail cell come equipped with a computer and internet that I was not aware of, or does she have an inside connection with the jailor? She snuck my phone into her jail cell and had been texting family members during the night and supplying them with pertinent information. She also gave them the US consulate's phone number to call for more details.

I was genuinely impressed at Brenda's fortitude while under extreme duress—being able to sneak a phone into a Mexican jail, how awesome is that? Apparently, after she retrieved phone numbers from my cellphone in order to place a call from the jails landline, she never gave it back to the staff, and they never asked. Yeah! Their mass confusion had inadvertently helped us score a phone. However, if I had known Brenda was so cleaver in the smuggling business, I would have had her sneak a hacksaw into the jail, or maybe a 9mm. Yes, it's a little funny!

I found out later that Brenda had to shield her activities by facing away from the security camera, while sending text messages and taking pictures of our public defenders' business cards. What was not funny was my daughter's reply despite the urgency of Brenda's text. "What do you want me to do about it?" was her response. That, my friend, is the last thing a father wants to hear from his offspring! A smart-ass response from us would have been "Send lawyers, guns, and money—the shit has just hit the fan!"[10]

The day's events wrapped up our tenth day of summer vacation. All jokes aside, those five seconds still weigh heavy on my mind with an inescapable sense of shame!

---

[10] Warren Zevon song.

Day 11 in Country

Second day in jail

@@@It was seven o'clock Saturday morning when I was suddenly awakened by the sound of a flushing toilet, only two feet from my face. The jailor had extinguished the runway lights making the room predominantly darker, even with the intensity of the daylight sun. Crazy, I know! I proceeded to force myself out of bed though I don't know why; the new day has absolutely nothing to offer but secluded confinement!

The jailor returned with breakfast in a Styrofoam take-out box and some type of orange-flavored drink. Despite not remembering what the lackluster meal consisted of, I do know very little of it found its way into my digestive system, along with the over-sweetened drink, which was impossible for me to consume. Because I'd been cutting down my sugar intake and hadn't had a soda in over ten years, one sip of the glucose concoction puckered my face like a baby taking nasty medicine.

After abstaining from my first Mexican breakfast in a jail cell, I was still a little tired and board out of my freaking mind. I laid back down, though sleeping for any lengthy amount of time was totally out of the question. As the bed was uncomfortable, resulting in a lot of tossing and turning on hard concrete due to the thin sleeping mat. It dawned on me to retrieve the other mat from the upper bunk and double my comfort level. The tattered mat lacked a protective cover revealing about sixty little divots in the foam in rows of ten and in a uniform square. It obviously was picked at by someone counting their unfortunate days spent in this mind-numbing cage. I can't begin to imagine being stuck in here for two months! That poor bastard!

By having two sleeping mats, I was able to fold one of them a foot over itself and use it as a pillow, allowing me to gain a little more sleep in comfort. While in and out of consciousness, I heard the old man in the middle cell bang on his cell door, soon to have the jailor arrive and turn on the water for a shower. Motivating me to crawl out of bed and use the toilet, then sat back down on the edge of the bed and thought, what can I do now besides absolutely nothing!

I can tolerate solitude with great ease, but the boredom of doing nothing would end up driving me completely crazy. Relieving, some of the monotony by conversing with my neighbor was not an option as he kept to himself and spoke no English. I felt ashamed talking to Brenda, who was two cells over. The only thing I should be saying to her is, "I'm sorry," which fails to rectify this FUBAR (Fucked Up Beyond All Repair) situation.

When sitting on the bed had lost its thrill, I went to the door and hung out there for a while. Doing nothing is still the same thing as doing nothing somewhere else, so I started pacing the floor to help elevate some of the boredom and receive a little exercise in the process. Unfortunately, it didn't take long before feeling like a caged animal, as the small cell was not suitable for a proficient walk. It appeared as if I were just psychotic with nervous energy. Within five minutes of restlessly pacing the floor, I began thinking about the sudoku puzzle that I had been working on for the last two days before my incarceration. Wishing I had a pen and paper to draw out the layout of the grid and numbers.

Yes, I complete the puzzles in ink and remember the whole layout by heart. Instead of mimicking all the zombies on this planet who have an idiot phone surgically implanted in their hands and faces glued to the hypnotizing screen, all while their brainwashed minds slowly turn to jello, I *actually* exercise my brain muscles by working on "Super Tough Killer Sudoku" puzzles! "I fear the day that technology will surpass our human interaction, and the world has a generation of idiots." Another profound quote from Albert Einstein.

These puzzles are not equipped with helpful starter numbers. Instead, there are random amounts of highlighted connected boxes with a small number in the upper corner of the boxes when added together must produce the sum shown in the clue. Like regular Sudoku one through nine can only be used in each row and grid square with no repeating numbers. It may sound complicated, and it is, it is just hard to explain. There is absolutely no guessing in Killer Sudoku as the number of possible number configurations is 6.6×10/21, which calculates to a sum with twenty-one place values.

Even though there wasn't a pen or paper in the cell, I did have access to toilet paper and water to pull a MacGyver. I rolled pieces of toilet paper into three-inch-long sticks, dabbing them with a small amount of water while shaping them into numbers. This kept their form after drying, and I patiently repeated this process one through nine for a total of eighty-one times. I shit you not, plus a handful of tiny balls for making the grid layout. I was quite proud of my ingenuity as the numbers turned out damn good while in a jail cell, which induced anticipation in working on the puzzle and giving my mind a temporary escape from the overwhelming boredom.

After the numbers finished drying, I placed one of the foam mats back on the top bunk, then partially folded the other up against the wall allowing for a comfortable sitting area while working on the Sudoku. I attempted to decipher the puzzle for two days straight with no luck and began to think I might have two numbers inverted. Either way, it was nice to stay busy and keep my mind preoccupied.

During the creation of the toilet paper masterpiece, I was interrupted by the jailor bringing lunch, who handed me a Styrofoam box sideways through the bars. I asked for some agua (water) and he soon returned with water in a small eight-ounce clear plastic cup. I instantly knew that I would be milking this drink for a while, as there is no way in hell, I'm getting a refill of the swill coming from the sinks tap. I was starving and hoped the food was more tolerable this time, but once again, I was unsuccessful in forcing down a Mexican meal of tortilla and beans, and only found the bread roll to be edible.

Soon after completing my unwanted diet regiment, the jailor returned and took Brenda and me into the interview room. Awaiting there for us was a room full of people, three men and two women who all were well dress and appeared to be in their mid-thirties. The group consisted of Irvin, our public defender and a woman as his assistant, a younger woman as the interpreter and, a prosecuting attorney who also had an assistant. The tiny room resembled a contest for how many people could fit inside a phone booth.

Once again, we were asked for personal information and to fill out more forms. However, before proceeding, I asked for my glasses to be returned, after which our interview officially began. Irvin was corrigible, displayed concern for us and spoke very little English. He relied heavily on the translator to relay all our comments to the participants in the room, while his assistant wrote everything down. He only wanted the basic facts about our case, and tomorrow would come back to talk about my defense strategy for the pretrial. After listening to my spiel, he told Brenda he would speak to the judge concerning her noninvolvement with the gun, which should secure her release.

During the conversation, the translator told Brenda, "No problem" and reiterated she most likely would be released sometime tomorrow. It was followed by a confident agreement by others of her impending freedom. This fantastic news lifted some of the heavy weight off my heart; the most crucial agenda was getting Brenda released from this depressing environment. Maybe I deserve to be here, but her tender heart should have never been anywhere near this kind of torment!

When the inquiry was over, Irvin gave me a large folded business card containing my case number and his name with a phone number, though any pleasantries between us during our departure elude my memory. As Brenda and I entered the other room, Hector, who appeared to be the prosecuting attorney's assistant, asked if we needed anything.

I said, "Yes, two blankets from my truck."

He replied, "Oh, are you cold?"

"No, we need them at night when we go to sleep." The ceiling area of the room and jail cells were constructed with an open-air skylight system, effectively producing cold temperatures in the cells during the nighttime, hence the request for the blankets.

Hector spoke adequate English, and the friendly young man did not seem to mind helping us, even though he is technically the enemy of my savior. Before leaving the area, he had to ask a staff member if it was okay for us to have the blankets from our truck, then asked for my permission allowing him to retrieve them. I replied, "Yes, no problem." No problem? Did that damn parrot just land on my shoulder? As Hector began to walk away, I added, "Also two pillows, please, thanks!" Upon his return with the items, we thanked him with much appreciation. However, I was surprised they allowed Brenda to receive her blanket without first questioning her about the suspicious characteristics of the quilt. The unique blanket is weighted with little pellets sewn between the lining. It is made to help people who have trouble sleeping due to various medical problems. Due to all the extra weight throughout the blanket, picking it up with only one hand would allow the rest of the unclutched material to drag on the floor behind you as if a small child incapable of carrying an adult size blanket.

Back in the cell, I continued to work on the sudoku puzzle while killing more time, which was extremely beneficial at eliminating most of my boredom. Brenda made good use of her time by doing yoga, which has helped her with balance and flexibility. Within an hour of rearranging little toilet paper numbers on a grid of white dots, the jailor showed up at my cell door and handed me a portable landline phone.

With a confused expression, I held it to my ear, wondering who it could possibly be. "Hello?"

To my surprise, the voice on the other end introduced himself as Edger from the US consulates office in Mexico City. He was calling to check up on us and let us know he has contacted some of our family members informing them of our predicament. His friendly voice expressed concern for my welfare by asking if I was being treated okay and if I needed anything. I assumed there was little he could do for me, so I kept our conversation short, though I did mention Brenda needed her daily medicine. His amiable reply was genuine with a, "I will see what I can do about getting her medicine."

After thanking him and saying our goodbyes, I handed the phone back to the jailor, who then gave it to Brenda and let her talk to Edger for a while.

When she was done talking with Edger, and the jailor had left the room, Hector showed up and asked Brenda, "What medicine do you need?" She wanted her daily thyroid medication along with other pills. She began telling him where they were located inside the truck, he again asked for permission to enter our vehicle. Regrettably, he was only allowed to give her the sleeping pills, due to it being the only bottle with a label. The staff is not authorized to provide unlabeled pills to anybody in jail.

The rest of the day and into the evening was painfully uneventful, as the only thing that absorbed some of the never-ending boredom was Sudoku, poking at my dinner and finding out Brenda drank dirty tap water from the sink. I thought she knew not to drink tap water while in Mexico, guess she knows now but had to learn the hard way while in an inhospitable environment. My poor baby!

It was apparent this day was coming to an end as the airport security, aka jailor, had just turned on the intense runway lights. It must be time for our nighttime siesta or a flight to St. Louis. I can dream, can't I?

Day 12 in Country

Third day in jail

What the hell! Another morning abruptly awakened by that irritating alarm clock of a jailor flushing the toilets! I must have been in a deep sleep because the noise completely startled the hell out of me, inducing a fearful reaction that quickly turned to anger for the jailor, waking me up in such a rude and unpleasant manner.

My fearful reaction was comparable to many years ago during my marriage of my now ex-wife Helen. She had recurring nightmares in the middle of the night and would wake up screaming at the top of her lungs, convinced an intruder was standing over her, ready to attack her. She would suddenly cry out my name in total fear as if she was expecting me to protect her from the phantom intruder. I instantly would wake up yelling her name in a complete state of panic frantically searching for the lamp switch in total darkness. My first instinct was to comfort her, though holding a hysterical woman in the darkened bedroom would require a great deal of convincing that I was not the intruder. So with the intense fear I was experiencing, my priority would be to find a light source first and foremost. Only then was I able to calm her down, which always took a few seconds, convincing her everything was okay. It invariably took longer for my heart rate to slow down back to normal than it did for her to fall back to sleep. For many years during these terrifying awakenings, I slept with a night light on or cracked the door open, letting some ambient light into the room, thereby giving her a visual confirmation there was not a scary bogeyman in the bedroom.

Honestly, most of my anger toward the jailors' rude intrusion stemmed from a horrific event some twenty-five years ago. When

Helen woke me up in the middle of the night in a terrifying state of panic, yelling, "Dennis wake up! *The house is on fire!*" I think I was out of the bed before she even finished her outburst. I instantly ran across the hall to our daughter's bedroom and grabbed Kathleen, who was seven at the time, and took her outside into the cold winter weather. Within a fraction of a second, I was back inside the burning house to retrieve our two boys from the downstairs bedroom at the far end of the house. In the short amount of time, it took to return to the house, the stairway was engulfed entirely with thick black smoke, making it impossible to reach their bedroom, consequently creating a death sentence for all three of us on our way back through. Without hesitation, I quickly ran back outside while shutting the door behind me, which ended up being a catastrophic mistake. I ran to the basement door only to discover going this route was also a death trap, as the smoke forced a hastily retreat where I once again shut the door. I thought by closing the doors, it would help keep the fire from accelerating out of control by eliminating its oxygen source.

My last and only option in saving the boys from this inferno was to go rescue them through their bedroom window, by the time I reached their basement window, Helen had already broken out the glass. She was kneeling in front of the window, yelling for them to stay in their beds so she could find them more easily and get them out of the burning house. Upon arriving at the distressing scene, I dove headfirst through the small window, face-planting on the concrete floor five feet below. I found the room to be in complete darkness due to the extremely thick billowing smoke eliminating my visibility to zero.

Knowing the layout of the room, I went directly to their beds and grabbed our three-year-old Austin from the lower bunk, swiftly handed him through the window to Helen. I then grabbed our five-year-old Christopher from the top bunk, turned around to repeat the process, but the intensity of the smoke had increased so dramatically that there was no longer a visible exit! I immediately started sliding my left hand across the wall, searching for that little 1 1/2'×2' window opening out of the fiery furnace. That is why one of my fingerprints no longer exists on my left hand. The intense temperature of the smoke heated the bare concrete wall so much that it *Literally* began melting the skin off my hand. It probably only took three to five seconds to find our escape to freedom, *but god damn it*, it felt like an eternity! Though I really don't remember feeling any pain or being fearful for our lives, there was absolutely no time for indecisiveness or panic. Just pure focus accompanied by massive amounts of adrenaline to save my family!

After handing Christopher to Helen, I climbed out through the window, which still held some shards of glass protruding from the metal frame. I once again proceeded to slice my completely naked lacerated body as a fireball followed me out of the inferno! Not sure if I was on fire, I rolled around on the cold ground to extinguish myself if I were. *Pure focus!*

We lived in the Ozarks of Missouri and our house was in the backwoods, away from emergency responders and without access to a phone. I realized the quickest way to get help was to retrieve it myself. With my adrenaline still pumping throughout my veins, I ran to the truck and jumped in, a benefit of leaving the keys in the ignition and drove ¼ mile to a neighbor's house. I grabbed a coat from the truck and wrapped it around my waist, then banged on their front door while yelling for help. The people living there had a daughter who is mentally challenged, and that's who answered the door, looking dazed and confused while I was speaking to her. Time was essential, so I quickly hopped back into the truck and sped away like a madman to my sister-in-law's house (Kat) a little farther down the road. It was a good decision to leave, because a badly burned naked man dripping in blood with skin dangling from his hands frantically screaming at a retarded girl in the middle of the night could not possibly have a quick or peaceful resolution, especially if her father came to the door.

Kat must have heard the spinning of my tires and flying gravel while I was speeding into her driveway because she met me at her front doorstep in a confused state of panic. As we were hurriedly entering her house, Helen and the kids arrived in our other vehicle. By now, my adrenaline level had dropped tremendously, and I began shaking uncontrollably along with excruciating pain; I was going into shock. From that moment forward, all I could feel was an extreme burning sensation, so Kat put me in the shower to cool off. The water instantly made me start shivering as if I were freezing to death. This is understandable as I had suffered third-degree burns on sixty percent of my body, robbing me of insulation value for my skin. Thereby making any degree of water temperature painfully difficult to tolerate.

After frantically exiting the frigid shower, Kat wrapped me up in a white sheet and had me sit in a living room chair to wait for the arrival of the ambulance. It seemed to be a short wait though my recollection of events from here on begins to get fuzzy. I remember walking to the back door of the ambulance, but not the drive to the helicopter or the flight to the hospital, I just remember a glimmer of a woman saying she was going to put a tube down my throat to help me breathe.

The only clear memory I had next was waking up in a hospital bed hooked to wires and tubes in every orifice while being held down by restraints. They were required due to my attempt at getting out of the bed, still hooked to life support, a byproduct of the drugs that were pumping through my veins, making me have wild hallucinations.

A nurse asked, "How long do you think you have been here?" I thought two or three days; "No," she replied, "It's been a week."

That's then when I found out my survival was so bleak that Helen actually said her goodbyes while I was in an unconscious state, which must have been a living hell for her. She did receive some relief days later, when a nurse said to her, "He must be very strong-willed and a fighter to still be alive." Could this be the reason for my survival from a life-ending tragedy with only partial lung damage?

Days after my awakening, I found out Austin and Christopher were also admitted into the hospital, though Austin had already been released. Christopher was not as fortunate he was in the burn patient ward across the hall from me. I failed to realize he was in that bad of shape while we were at Kat's house. Other than the obvious chain of events that brought Christopher to the hospital, the most detrimental was the closing of the entry doors and breaking the glass out from the boys' bedroom window. Therefore, giving only one source of oxygen to feed the fire, which had sucked the smoke and fire through the boys' bedroom like a vacuum. This, in turn, exposed Christopher's tiny lungs to the inescapable terror at a more rapid rate while trapped on the top bunk closer to the ceiling and thick smoke.

Despite being in the hospital for about three weeks, my pain was nowhere near as dreadful as Helen's! During the fire, while I was running around searching for a safe path to the boys' bedroom, Helen was attempting to go through their window multiple times. Still, her efforts were thwarted by the thick billowing smoke, and after each retreat, she told them, "Stay in bed, I'm coming to get you!" Yet her actions never materialized. To some, it might not sound too upsetting because, after all, I was able to get the boys out of the burning house. However, her spoken words of rescue and her fearful restricted movements had completely shattered her heart, spirit, and mind. Two weeks after her failed rescue attempt, she sat by Christopher's bed in the hospital, while watching him take his last breath eight days after his fifth birthday due to lung failure. Two words, "overwhelming devastation!"

I truly believe this was the beginning of the end of our marriage, which ended up lasting twenty-six years. As it consumed her mind for many years, trying to deal with the tragedy while blaming herself for his death, which is far from the truth! That night before the fire, when she was cooking dinner, the smoke detector started beeping, so I removed the battery to silence the noise of which has been done many times before. Yet it only takes one time of forgetting to place the battery back in the detector that will drastically change your life forever! What would it have taken to prevent the loss of our home and save Christopher's life by putting that nine-volt back into the smoke detector? Maybe *five* seconds!

So being stuck in a Mexican jail is truly just an insignificant setback compared to the severe hardships life can hand you. That's why I always say, "Stop your whining and crying and rub some dirt on it, it could always be *worse!*" As I have the scars and skin grafts on my back and ass to prove it! Only in sweet death will we no longer cry!

After missing my early morning flight to St. Louis and avoiding most of the disappointing breakfast. I worked on the Sudoku puzzle for a while, letting my mind escape into deep thought, which was interrupted by a maid cleaning the area and the middle jail cell. The old man had been released from it earlier and never returned. She finished with her chores and left the room smelling of an overpowering aroma of industrial cleaner. The jailor showed up and transferred Brenda to the middle cell right next to mine; how nice. Sometimes in life, the smallest action produces the most profound result!

At about 10:00 a.m., the jailor returned and took us to the interview room, waiting there was Irvin, his assistant and interpreter. They were there to discuss my defense for the preliminary trial, to determine if there is enough evidence against me to take this case to trial. Also, to find out if bail will be granted. Brenda was informed she was going to be released from jail sometime later today. They were waiting on some paperwork signed by the judge, and of course, "no problem" was mentioned a couple of times during their reassurances. Yeah! It was great news and relieved my worrying concerns for her. However, she did appear to have doubt in her eyes of the impending release and failed in displaying any joy. Further into our interview, Irvin began discussing my defense strategy for the pretrial, which were as follows:

> Tourists visiting our condo in Loreto who routinely visit Mexico.
> No criminal record.
> Having a permit to carry a gun.
> Gun was not used in a crime.
> Had proof of ownership.
> Forgot the gun was in the truck.
> Workingman with his own business.
> Willing to pay fine.

Irvin was quite optimistic toward the outcome of the preliminary trial and confident I would most likely make bail, which was probably going to be a couple hundred dollars. Oddly enough, the trial was going to be held at eight o'clock tonight due to a Mexican statute stating. When someone gets arrested, they must be seen by a judge within a certain amount of time. From the sound of it, they were cutting it real close to violating my rights, which explained the late-night pretrial on a Sunday. When our meeting came to an end, I realized nobody said "no problem" about my pretrial, inducing my concern. This phrase has been continuously used by everyone we had met, ultimately trying to convince us everything was going to be okay until now! Should I be relieved or worried and try to escape from this jail before the trial, though El Chapo I'm not, or am I?

El Chapo (Joaquin Loera) is a well-known Mexican drug lord and former leader of the Sinaloa Cartel. He escaped from a Mexican prison, and in only twelve minutes from doing so was on a private airplane to freedom. One could say he had a lot of connections and, more importantly, a massive amount of money. I, on the other hand, do not have those crucial assets to support a jailbreak. However, I do possess an enormous amount of tenacity and a unique ability to squeeze through small and tight spaces. Escaping from this jail cell most definitely crossed my mind from day 1 upon my arrival.

Yesterday while sitting on the top bunk working on Sudoku, I looked up toward the ceiling. I noticed there were sizable gaps of spacing between the glass blocks embedded in the walls of the cupola, revealing a flaw in the security of the jail. A cupola is a small dome underneath a larger dome meant for ventilation. This instantly sparked my interest in devising an escape plan if or when my situation became more direr than expected. Concerned someone could be watching me through the two-way mirror while looking upward, I tried to be inconspicuous by taking short glances at the cupola's layout. The cupola's dimensions were 4'×7' and 1 ½' tall extending to a height of about 14' from the floor. The two long opposing walls were open to the outside environment with glass blocks spaced at different intervals throughout, which appeared too small for me to squeeze through. However, the gap on the far end of the cupola looked big enough for me to fit through.

I'm only 140 pounds of a slender build and do not require much space to squeeze through a small hole, besides, I have been in tighter spaces than the one that appears from up above. I do a massive amount of spelunking (caving) involving many precarious and dangerous passages. I only need an 8"×14" opening to squeeze into a cave's virgin passage, 7"×13" if my life depended on it. There have been many occasions I was the first human on this planet of 7.5 billion to enter a hidden underground chamber of majestic beauty. All by slithering through small holes not much bigger than my caving helmet, and I have GoPro videos to confirm my insanity. I feel extremely fortunate to be able to express, "There have been more men on the moon than places I have stood in my underground world, which contains fewer footprints than the surface of the moon!" It is truly a moment of pure euphoria!

The next question would be, how do I ascend to the fourteen-foot ceiling? Simple! The jail was constructed with a design flaw, or more so with bad mathematic skills. One and a half feet down from the ceiling of the cupola is a five-inch-wide ledge, more than enough room to pull myself up. I can achieve one-arm pullups, so this obstacle would be manageable, especially with the opposing wall only four-feet away to wedge my feet against. The concrete bunkbed is five-foot-high, almost directly underneath one end of the cupola. I can stand flat-footed and reach a height of seven and a half feet, so by doing the math, it adds up to a total of fourteen feet. If I missed judged the ceiling height by one foot, that still puts the ledge at only twelve inches above my reach. Some say, "White men can't jump."[11] But one foot is more of a hop, and if I need assistance in my ascent, there was a fourteen-inch column protruding from the wall next to the bed, which could be used to grab or wedge my feet against. This climb would be much easier than some of the free climbs I have performed in caves, which is achieved without the assistance of rope or climbing gear.

If I were to execute a successful escape, it would have to be conducted late night or early morning, by taking a page from the movie Alcatraz by shaping a body figure under my blanket. I would have to utilize the extra bed mat to pull apart pieces of the foam-forming them into the required shapes. As an added benefit to my plan is

---

[11] Movie starring Woody Harrison.

that the jailor has seen me sleep with a blanket pulled up over my ear while laying on my side. To further obstruct his view, I sleep in the bottom bunk with my head facing the opposite end of the door.

Like most plans, there are flaws and calculated risks—first, the chance of the jailor looking through the two-way mirror at the exact moment while climbing up the wall. Completing the task at two in the morning would increase the odds in my favor. Certainly, the jailor would not be interested in watching me sleep, especially if he's more concerned about his own REM (Rapid Eye Movement) sleep.

The second issue would be the logistical nightmare following my escape of no money, no phone, connections, or passport while being hampered by the language barrier in an unfamiliar environment with no clue on where to go. Retrieving the phone from Brenda would eliminate most of those complications, or at least make them more manageable. The third and most important issue was I couldn't escape until Brenda gets released, which would be sometime later that day. My court time was eight o'clock tonight, which might negate my return to this cell and slam shut my window of opportunity twofold. In La Paz in May, it does not get dark until nine thirty to ten o'clock, eliminating my advantage of having the cover of darkness during my departure from the jails compound. Also, the jailor would not be asleep, increasing the odds of him seeing me attempting to escape. After evaluating my options and calculating the risk to reward, I decided to leave jailbreaker off my resume for now and continue to stay with option number three to see how this all plays out. Besides, Irvin was confident I would make bail, though we will wait and see!

It's time to eat, what's for lunch? Who cares! All I remember is eagerly accepting two bread rolls from Brenda and saving one for dinner. If I continue to live the lifestyle of Mahatma Gandhi, there will be no need to plan an escape; I'll just slip down through the shower drain.

The rest of the prolonged dull day consisted of glancing at the clock on the wall, slowly ticking down toward the eight o'clock hour. While inadvertently placing toilet paper number 9's upside down or 6's right side up, as the creator did not distinguish them between the two.

A break in the action arose at 5:22 when the jailor entered the room with a few other people and told Brenda she was free to go. She appeared a little subdued, still not convinced she was being released, so they had to show her the paperwork confirming it was official.

With absolutely no display of relief from her newfound freedom, she walked over to my cell, handed me her pillow along with a cup of that glucose-filled orange-flavored drink. She leaned in to kiss me goodbye while whispering in my ear, "Your phone is in the pillowcase," then proceeded to exit the room with the others. Even though I was utterly relieved by her newfound freedom, my happiness quickly faded as I stood with hands clutched to the cold steel bars watching Brenda walk down the hallway disappearing from my sight. As the jailor closed the security door, leaving me to ponder, Now I'm truly all alone.

I found out later the jail did not release our truck to Brenda. She was told to come back Monday and sign some forms to retrieve it, and yet again hearing, "No problem," though ended up being total bullshit! This created a massive amount of unimaginable problems which could induce someone to pull out a 9mm and start shooting!

Brenda was allowed to retrieve all my personal items they confiscated on Friday, including my passport. I could not believe the Ringleader permitted her to have the most essential document one could own while in a foreign country! Instantly My risk/reward of escaping had increased in my favor. I now have a phone, access to my passport, 6,000 pesos and a connection to someone on the outside, although for now, waiting to make bail would still be the safer bet.

After all the commotion died down, I repeated my routine with the hope of finishing the Sudoku puzzle anticipating the short arm of the clock approaching number eight. It may sound strange, but I barely thought about the impending trial, or what outcome waited for me oddly possessing a calm attitude toward the whole ordeal. Immersing myself in Sudoku helped keep my mind preoccupied. Why worry about something that is entirely out of my control? All I could do was place little toilet paper numbers in the correct configuration, wondering if anybody else has ever done this in a Mexican jail, certainly not!

It was almost eight o'clock that night when the jailor showed up and unlocked my cell door; it was time for court. He gestured for me to gather my personal items and follow him. I quickly scooped up all the numbers and tiny balls and placed them in a paper cup, then put it on the sink to leave for the maid. I can't imagine what will be running through her mind after finding a cup full of toilet paper numbers. I put the toothbrush and paste in my pocket, grabbed the two pillows and blanket, then headed out of the cell.

As we entered the corridor, three-armed security officers were waiting for me, who were sharply dressed in uniforms. They appeared to have more authoritative power than anybody I have encountered thus far. They handcuffed my wrist with my arms in front of my torso, allowing me to carry the two pillows and blanket, and YES, the phone is still in one of the pillowcases, which is bizarre. It could have been dangerous contraband with nobody being the wiser; it's almost comical! But these Three Stooges were far from any type of comic relief or confusion like their counterparts who were more direct, precise, and purely professional.

The three men wasted little time shuttling me into the back seat of a pickup truck parked in the jail's garage. They drove out of the garage into the compound where the officer in the front passenger side, stepped out and opened a large solid metal gate leading to the side street. At the moment we began to drive away, I wondered how long I would have to endure this uncomfortable sensation of being transported to a Mexican courthouse in handcuffs. Before having a chance to finish that thought, we had already arrived at our destination only 200 feet away from the jails parking lot gate.

We entered the courthouse parking garage by driving under the building, drove past an armed guard holding a shotgun, then went a short distance around a corner and parked. The drive was shorter than the walk to and from the truck, which seemed unnecessary driving instead of walking to a building that shared an adjoining wall with a walk-in entrance literally only 100 feet apart from each other. Still, maybe they were following protocol to the letter. When our incredibly short road trip was over, the three men escorted me through a basement door of the courthouse building, which looked brand new, very clean, well maintained and more modernized than the structure of the jail. The officers walked me down a ramp, turned the corner to the right and went down a wide hallway forty feet to a large holding cell. They handed me off to three security personnel waiting there for my arrival.

These three young men looked to be in their mid-twenties, resembling their counterparts' professionalism of being clean-cut and sharply dressed in uniforms with polished boots.

After putting me in the cell and removing the handcuffs, one of the security guards politely addressed me and in a friendly manner asked in broken English, "What are you in jail for?"

"Possession of a handgun," I replied.

"No problem, pay fine and go home."

Sounds good to me, hope it turns out to be that easy. A few minutes later, while the security guard was standing twenty feet away talking with fellow coworkers, he slightly raised his voice to grab my attention. He asked, "Why are you in Mexico?" My one-word response, "Vacation," was met with a snicker by both of us, to which he replied, "Nice vacation, ha-ha!" I concluded our interaction by saying "Crazy American!"

Within five minutes of sitting on the bench, an older man wearing a suit and tie entered the cell, with a friendly greeting, introduced himself as Oscar. He was a court-appointed liaison who was there to make sure I was being treated well.

Oscar must have had access to my medical file and read I was allergic to gluten because he asked with a concerned tone, "Can I get you something to eat that is gluten-free?" I figured it would be impossible to acquire something gluten-free at eight o'clock at night on a Sunday, so I told him not to worry about it. His next thoughtful offer, "How about a couple of hotdogs?"

But for some dumb ass reason, I said, "No, thanks." I may be allergic to gluten though eating it will not make sick or even ruin my day. What the hell was wrong with me? I was starving! My nature is not to inconvenience anybody by asking for help. More times than not, I can rectify a problem or task on my own, which may be challenging to accomplish at times, it's usually simpler to do it myself, "simpler" not to be confused with easier.

Just before leaving, Oscar said, "If you need anything, let me know." I thanked him and wondered as he walked away if I would ever see him again. In these circumstances, it is hugely beneficial to have someone like Oscar willing to help. I should consider myself fortunate he offered some hotdogs from the dinner menu and not the lunch special of a North Korean beating.

Soon after Oscars' departure, the security guards had me leave my personal items in the cell and escorted me upstairs to the courtroom. Where apparently, the staff was not ready for my arrival. The guards turned me around to exit the room then placed me into a 4'x6' cell adjacent to the courtroom. So far today, I have seen more bars than the town drunk who has lost all ability to go home.

Within two minutes of waiting in the small cage, a woman showed up introducing herself as Angelica, the court-appointed translator for my trial. She looked to be in her early forties, casually dressed, five feet six inches tall, slightly above average build and weight, spoke English exceptionally well. She, as with other people during my dealings in Mexico did not reveal her last name, or I failed to remember. She was very friendly and seemed to have a genuine concern for my well-being, easing what little anxiety I was feeling at that moment. Angelica appeared pressed for time as she spoke hurriedly, informing me of what was to be expected in the court's proceedings, how to conduct myself within the courtroom, and how to address the judge. Just before anxiously walking away, Angelica said she would return in a few minutes with my lawyer. She would help translate pertinent information the lawyer needed to relay before the trial begins.

Angelica soon returned with a smartly dressed young woman who introduced herself as Karla, my lawyer. I thought to myself, "Who the hell is this?" I saw my lawyer Irvin ten hours ago. I'm confident he was a man or did he have a recent sex change and waited until now to show off her pretty new dress. However, I think it was a pants suit, but what the hell is the difference when my freedom is on the line! Oh, it gets better! Karla had difficulty speaking what little

English she knew, failed to bring an assistant or a translator and never explained the change in lawyers.

This morning while in the interview room, you couldn't swing a dead cat around without hitting a lawyer, translator, or assistant, now when it's most important to have an excellent support team by my side, they send someone incapable of communicating with me. Karla couldn't rely on Angelica to translate our personal interactions during the trial, because she was the courts-appointed translator not ours. Therefore, I would be in a Mexican courtroom charged with a federal crime while sitting next to a non-English speaking attorney. How could this possibly be good for me?

During their explanation of the do's and don'ts, Karla did not want me to mention anything to the judge about having possession or any subjects pertaining to the gun, thoroughly confusing the hell out of me. When I spoke with Irvin this morning, there was no discussion related to Karla's request in any shape or form, which left me totally in the dark. As the two women headed back into the courtroom, I felt extremely unsettled putting my fate in the hands of a lawyer that I had just met, nor a clue in her defense strategy!

It was shortly before eight thirty, when the three guards escorted me into the courtroom and sat me down at a table seated next to Karla, across the aisle from the prosecuting attorney who was fortunate enough to have an assistant.

The first disturbing thought that went through my brain while sitting next to Karla was, "You have got to be fucking kidding me!" She was reading my case file and writing down notes from what looked like a lawbook minutes before court was in session. At least she was studying my record before the trial started. Well, that's not entirely true; she continued to periodically research the lawbook and examine my case file during the court's proceedings. Why did she wait until the last minute to do her homework in class and not complete it on the school bus, just like the rest of us?

Just before the judge entered the courtroom, I was directed to put on headphones to listen to Angelica's translations of the court's proceedings. She had difficulty keeping up with the pace of the courts vernacular while trying to translate it into English, and with the speed at which it was spoken. Consequently, making it difficult for me to grasp certain statements, and of course, there was nobody to elaborate with on matters I did not understand.

At eight-thirty, this circus commenced in grand form. When the prosecuting attorney (Antonio) read from the military's arrest report, my jaw hit the floor with total disbelief. I instantly became agitated while listening to the bile spewing from his mouth! I don't know if he was quoting from a military report, or creating his own bullshit interpretation? Either way, it painfully boggled my mind beyond any comprehension, making it impossible to just sit there listening to the fabricated report and not say a word.

I gestured to a staffer seated behind a desk for a pen, then received a sheet of paper from Karla to begin writing down every lie spilling from Antonio's mouth to have a list of untrue statements to use in our rebuttal argument. Imagine my utter frustration in being totally powerless over my own destiny! By not being able to lean over to my non-English speaking lawyer and voice all my concerns, especially after realizing she was completely unaware of the falsified statements and failed to address any of the detrimental issues.

The only factual comments that came out of that puppet's (Antonio) mouth was "Dennis Novicky, 9mm Handgun and nineteenth of May 2017." Yet everything else was just false, you might as well press the delete key. I had an irresistible urge to get up out of my chair and go punch him in his stupid face! Yes, one could say I was very perturbed!

First, let's get this straight! As I revealed to both lawyers the day before, yes, I had a handgun under my truck seat, and yes, I admit it's my own fault. So why would Antonio lie about the facts and throw salt into an open wound when he had an admittance of guilt from a defendant? Two reasons came to mind: one, he was just a vindictive hard-ass, or maybe he was unsure of the legality of his case against me. He must have felt forced to secure his victory by fabricating the actual chain of events. Who fucking knows!

The first lie to hit the judge's ears when the prosecutor was reading from the military report was that I gave the military consent to the search the truck, which was total bullshit. The two soldiers involved spoke not a word of English, therefore eliminating any understanding of verbal communication between us. I may have assumed they were going to search the truck, I never consented to it. Second: One of the soldiers said he could see the handgun from looking through the passenger window prompting their search of the vehicle. Two things wrong with that statement; if the gun were visible, they wouldn't need consent to search the truck. Also, it would be physically impossible to see the gun from any vantage point from outside the vehicle, the 9mm being cradled in a Frisbee under my seat behind the portable speaker. Third: The Military personally drove me from the checkpoint to La Paz at a slow rate of speed to keep me safe, also stopped somewhere to get something to eat. This blatant lie instantly raised my aggravation level again and forced my hand to pick up the pen once more. No! I was not a passenger in their freaking Humvee; I have the video to prove the contrary and where in the hell was I when we were getting something to eat.

At that moment, I did not understand what possessed someone to fabricate irrelevant information pertaining to a handgun case until the prosecutor continued reading from the misleading report stating that driving slowly, stopping to eat and the extremely long distance between the military's checkpoint and La Paz is what delayed my timely arrival to the jailhouse. Antonio was trying to diminish the fact that my civil liberties were violated due to the excessive amount of time it took them to process me at the jailhouse from the time of my arrest, which took eight hours, apparently, this is unacceptable by Mexican law.

The bogus report sounded like someone was trying to cover their ass, brought on by the militaries' inability to make a decision promptly at the checkpoint. Which explains the warp speed we were driving from the inspection station as they were trying to make up for the lost time. If I would have known pushing the pedal to the metal was going to assist in a prosecutor's case against me in a trial. I would have taken my foot off the accelerator and drove like a little old lady going to church.

After Mr. Puppet Man (Antonio) was finished reading the military's report, he babbled on about my questionable character. He began to attack me on a personal level by mentioning something about the gun and said, "I was old enough to know better!" *No shit*, he actually spoke those words in a courtroom? So if I were younger and did not know any better, would they let me go free? What a dumbass! I wonder if it took twelve years of college for Antonio to get a law degree and graduate last in his class? I'm sure his moronic statement could not possibly be quoted from any law book. Though it did remind me of when I was a child and our dad would tell us, "You kids are old enough to know better" and, "The older you get, the dumber you get." Well, I guess he called that one right.

Puppet Man continued to lay it on thicker and heavier as he went. He went on to say, possession of a 9mm handgun is allowed to be carried by military personal only and is a felony punishable by a maximum prison sentence of ten years with a minimum of three years. What did he just say? *Ten years*, you must be fucking kidding me! Internally I was in panic mode and driven by fear to start thinking about making bail and getting the hell out of this crazy-ass country no matter what it takes!

After hearing the Puppet Man's last shocking statement, I pretty much tuned him out and stopped paying attention to Angelica's translations. While sitting there thinking that all the courtroom theatrics was a big waste of time, as they yammered on, I had a sense of calm come over me. I actually had a slight smirk on my face from my previous thought, knowing there is no way I'm coming back to this courtroom to possibly face a ten-year prison sentence or even three years. Once out on bail, I will be gone like a cool breeze!

It was well over an hour when Mr. Puppet finished with his spiel, trying to convince the judge that the case needed to go to trial. The judge then addressed the court by monotonously repeating the entire court proceeding we just listened to for well over an hour. His lengthy rhetoric definitely did not sound any better after hearing it for the second time.

When the judge finished with his tiresome spiel. Karla commenced presenting our defense to the court. However, within minutes of her opening remarks, my disgust was diverted from Puppet Man to the person on my right and went from bad to worse the more she spoke. For starters, when I talked to Irvin this morning about my defense strategy for the preliminary trial, it certainly did not sound like the same strategy! What was coming out of Karla's mouth was *not even close!*

The sales pitch Karla was conveying to the judge sounded like she was trying to dismiss my guilt on minor technicalities. First: By mentioning the illegal search of the truck, even though she was utterly oblivious of the facts that transpired during that event. That might be a solid defense back in the States, but not here in Mexico. Secondly: I did not know that having a 9mm handgun in Mexico was a federal crime. Thereby trying to convey my logic that you can carry one in the USA when accompanied by a permit. She subsequently based her defense on that I knew the gun was in the truck, but not the severity of the criminal intent. She then went way off the subject of firearms by mentioning laws relative to hunting rifles being allowed in Mexico. Still, it made absolutely no sense to me as it had no correlation to my case.

Thirdly: The excessive amount of time it took from my arrest to my arraignment (booking) was a violation of my rights. She explained this to the judge without any of the detailed knowledge I possessed about factual information that took place with the military. Once again, I could not convey any of the pertinent information to her. So out of frustration from her feeble, confusing and weak defense, I reached for the pen jotting down some notes in hopes of rectifying some of the issues that were bothering me.

When Karla finished addressing the court with her nonsensical defense. The judge once again proceeded to recap everything she had just said, and yes, it sounded just as ridiculous coming from his mouth as it did from hers. Upon the completion of the judge's reiterated spiel, he asked if there was something I wanted to say to the court. I didn't know if it was standard procedure for him to ask that question or if he was motivated by me taking notes during the proceedings. Either way, before I had a chance to respond, Karla leaned over and whispered in my ear, I was not to mention anything about the gun. This, in turn, reluctantly prompted a modification to my notes, diminishing the severity of my grievances!

While reading from my notations of the military's incorrect statements, I realized that by not being able to speak about the illegal search of the gun, left me with minor technicalities that could not possibly help me in any way. At least I felt justified in making the court aware of the false report, also the questionable motivation behind the prosecutor who read from the military's story.

There was no response from the judge after I voiced my concerns, only a calling for a short recess. I motioned for Angelica to approach our table and ask if she could translate to Karla my trepidation toward the changed defense strategy and to inquire about my bail. Before Angelica responded, I proceeded to graciously thank her for helping me, which was met with an enthusiastic reply, "No problem, I'm happy to help!" She informed me that Irvin and Karla changed the defense strategy at the last minute because they thought it would have a more beneficial outcome.

Karla waited until *now* when the preliminary trial is over halfway through to tell me! I would have to strongly disagree with their new hair-brained strategy. However, the only person's opinion that really matters is the man behind the bench wearing a black robe. My understanding of Karla's altered approach was basically telling the judge I was aware of the gun in the truck. Also, the court should have leniency by setting me free all because of some minor technicalities. It seems to me it would only irritate the judge knowing a guilty defendant was trying to avoid justice by utilizing dubious tactics, as opposed to someone asking for leniency from the court who is admitting a degree of guilt. My incompetent defense team (of one) did not disprove any evidence against me in this preliminary trial! This only showed that I was a spineless worm attempting to squirm out of a crime, "Go team worm, go!"

Angelica was acquiring information from Karla concerning my bail when the sound of the squawking parrot emerged amongst their discussion. Karla looked at me with a confident gesture and said, "No problem!" Prompting Angelica to elaborate her translation that, "Getting bail should be no problem." *Awwk!* Hearing the over-excited bird lowered my aggravation level. Especially after sitting through the dreadful courtroom proceedings for hours listening to Puppet Man ramble on about a ten-year prison sentence.

When the judge returned, he began summarizing whether the prosecutor had proven his case against me, who, in short order, accepted all the evidence Antonio had presented to the court; which did not sound good for me, but that was to be expected. Next, the judge recapped Karla's defense in the same manner, yet he totally disagreed with everything she stated in my case; this, too, was to be expected. From the moment of Karla's weak rebuttal, I knew she did not have a chance in hell of winning this case and the judge would have been entirely braindead to buy what she was selling.

After shooting down Karla's defense, the judge concluded there was enough evidence against me to go to trial, so he asked Antonio for a trial date, who replied, "Sixty days from today." The judge asked Karla if that was okay with her; she turned and looked at me for an agreement of the sixty days.

I said, "Absolutely not!" I thought to myself, *if* I stay here in Mexico until the trial date, there is no way I'm going to wait two months in doing so! Karla revised the counteroffer to thirty days, which I accepted. She pleaded to the judge that waiting here in Mexico for sixty days would put a financial burden on Brenda and me, for we wanted to resolve this matter as quickly as possible. The prosecutor refused the shorter time frame due to being very busy and would not have enough time to prepare for the trial. However, the judge disagreed and scheduled the trial date thirty days from today. Score one point for team worm!

As the judge was wrapping up for the evening, or should I say early morning, Karla interjected at the last second inquiring about getting bail. Which prompted him to confer with the prosecutor on Karla's motion, and of course, Mr. Puppet Man wanted bail to be denied. He rambled on with something about me being a US citizen facing a ten-year prison sentence who could afford to leave the country and would be a flight risk. Well, he called that one right!

Karla's argument for bail mainly consisted of; it was my legal right to be allowed bail and should not be denied because I was a US citizen. When she finished with her plea, the judge asked if I had anything to say concerning the matter. I told him I could financially afford to stay in Mexico for thirty days while resolving this matter. Then added something entirely out of context, "I don't care for Mexican food, so I do not want to stay here longer than needed." Sounds crazy I know. I stated it with a slight chuckle, but I don't think anybody else was amused.

The reason I mentioned my financial stability to the judge was due to the conversation I had with Irvin yesterday morning. He was adamant about me informing the judge that I could afford a lengthy stay in Mexico, also Brenda and I periodically visited our condominium in Cabo San Lucas, which might just alleviate the judge's concern of me leaving the country prematurely.

Unfortunately, to my complete surprise, Karla's and my statements fell upon deaf ears, as our motion for bail was emphatically denied by the ill-natured judge! What the hell just happened? My cocky smirk had instantly been wiped from my face. It was quickly replaced with utter disbelief and fear as dreadful thoughts of a ten-year prison sentence became more plausible with the lack of bail! Where is that god damn parrot now, squawking *"No problem?"*

The judge justified the reason for denying my bail as mainly based on my citizenship of the USA and my possession of money, which could motivate me to be a flight risk. If circumstances were altered and I was a poor Mexican, would the judge then grant bail, and if so, how would a penniless man acquire 20,000 pesos? All I know right now is I'm spending at least thirty more days in lockup, damn! Time to search for a competent lawyer or revisit an escape plan! ASAP!

While keeping my disgusted rage for Karla locked up internally, I lost focus during the last few moments of the trial, and my memory of events are fuzzy. However, I do remember having the awareness of sneaking the pen that the bailiff gave me out of the courtroom. Possessing a pen in jail would have more than one useful function and inevitably come in handy. When the trial was over and the judge had exited, most everyone cleared the courtroom while Karla, Angelica and I were standing at the corner of the desk discussing the disappointing outcome of the trial. Karla was upset and completely caught off guard by the judge's unjust decision and insisted on filing for a new hearing right away regarding bail. While talking, I held the sheet of paper Karla gave me earlier and casually placed the pen in the same hand. I then positioned the paper at an angle to hide it from the guards' line of sight. I resisted the urge to hide the pen in my pocket to eliminate my blatant attempt at smuggling it out of the courtroom since getting caught would not be advantageous.

While exchanging goodbyes with the two women, Karla handed me the same type of business card Irvin gave me yesterday with her information on it. She said if I needed anything to give her a call. When I turned toward the door to leave, the bailiff caught my attention before I made a single step and made a hand gesture for the return of the pen. I displayed no signs of guilt and just acted as if I had forgotten about having it in my hand. No harm, no foul!

The courtroom guards escorted me back downstairs to the holding cell, where within a few minutes, the three-armed security officers showed up and handcuffed me. After picking up my two pillows (phone), blanket and manila envelope, they led me down the hallway back to the pickup truck. We pulled out of the parking garage and took a left turn heading back toward the jail, where I just spent the last three days. When we reached the jails parking entrance, they drove right past it, continuing straight down the street, leaving me clueless as to our destination. Still, it is safe to say it's not a Holiday Inn Express.

This anxious late-night road trip gave me a moment to ponder what awaited me at the end of our journey. Even though the drive was longer than the one to and from the jail and courthouse, it was still incredibly short. Only driving around the block where I soon gazed upon two heavily armed guards standing in front of my final ominous destination, the La Paz Prison!

Day 13 in Country

First day in prison

It was near two o'clock Monday morning when we drove through a large prison gate. As soon as the steel bars closed behind me, I began worrying about entering a Mexican prison and the extreme hardships that lie ahead. My heightened concerns were brought on by horror stories involving Mexican prisoners, which would scare a career criminal straight just to keep from doing time in one. I was preparing to enter a foreign prison, a 140-pound, clean-cut fifty-four-year-old white guy, no tattoos, wearing glasses, in shorts and flip-flops, with no grasp for the Spanish language. With that being said, I was about to be thrust into an unruly environment and lured into threatening altercations.

My first thought was how to survive among convicts. Would I need to get into a fight to earn a fraction of respect? How many ass-kicking's would I need to endure before being left alone? My lifelong physical confrontations with others had been few and far between. I consider myself non-aggressive yet have stood my ground many times during altercations refusing to take anybody's bullshit. Even if they were bigger than I. The most significant difficulty my enemy will have facing me is, I do not like to lose and will use unorthodox methods to win or get even. Hell, I even tried to run over a guy with my vehicle just to have the last aggressive act while defending a friend. Another altercation I had, was when I was very young having an angry confrontation with my sister Aja. She allowed me to retrieve a butcher knife in retaliation for her tossing me up to my bunkbed, whereas I threw the knife at her feet sticking it in the hardwood floor.

After exiting the truck, two security officers escorted me to a side door of the prison. They gave it a couple of knocks, initiating a prison guard to slide open a small viewing window to see who was at the door. This was followed by the sound of somebody unbolting the steel door. As the door opened, one of the officers handed a manila folder containing my personal information to a prison guard operating the door. Once inside, I could see the prison was as old as dirt and in great need of repair. The reception area or office was cluttered, disorganized, and a little dirty. There were about eight unarmed prison guards in the room, looking like they were just lounging around taking it easy; though what else were they to do at two thirty in the morning?

While a guard was thumbing through my file, he said something to me in Spanish, which led to my reply, "No Espanol." My response instantly amused the whole group and as I chuckled along, they displayed an enjoyment of disbelief while talking and laughing among themselves. This relieved some of my trepidation upon entering the prison, knowing I was amusing the guards and not agitating them. Also giving them a good first impression of their new arrival.

After one of the security officers removed my handcuffs, a prison guard performed a quick pat-down search. He surprisingly did not request a strip search, and only gestured with his hand that I remove my T-shirt. However, after taking off my shirt, I received the impression he only wanted me to raise my shirt up. They confiscated my two pillows, but let me keep the blanket, manila envelope that contained my case file information along with Irvin and Karla's business cards. Since I was given a receipt for the pillows, it motivated me to remove the phone from the pillowcase to receive a receipt for the phone. However, I didn't understand why pillows were not allowed. I guess the warden does not want inmates running around in their underwear, having pillow fights in his prison.

Office personal had me sit at a table across from them to fill out forms and answer questions on the paperwork they needed to complete. A simple task that quickly transformed into a problematic chore since all the forms were in Spanish as nobody in the office spoke English. With the staffs' failed attempts in trying to communi-

DIZNEY LAND by Way of Military Escort

cate with me, a guard standing in the doorway must have had enough of watching the comical frustration between the staff and stepped in to help translate. Even though he only spoke broken English, he still managed to move the process along to a certain degree.

He kindly asked, "Do you need anything?" I replied, "Yes, agua, thanks." He rinsed out a used twenty-ounce soda bottle, filled it with water—from what source I do not know—then handed it to me. This ended up being my only source of fluid for the next twenty-nine hours, calculating to .69 ounces or a little over a tablespoon of water per hour.

During our earlier struggle to fill out paperwork, one of the guards left the office, returning five minutes later with a prisoner who introduced himself as Frank (Sandoval), an American from California. Frank was an older looking man with a rough appearance, spoke fluent English, big build, tall, riddled with tattoos, and an aged face revealing many hard miles on it. All of this reflected an intimidating impression of someone I surely wouldn't what to tangle with.

So much for first impressions. Frank was friendly, soft-spoken, accommodating, and happy to see someone from the United States, plus he was more than willing to assist the staff with translating and filling out forms. I was truly relieved there was someone in the prison who could actually speak English and glad he was from the US, which meant I now had access to information. Information is knowledge and knowledge is power!

Office personnel had Frank read to me the prison rules from a printed-out sheet of paper, which consisted of no drugs, good behavior, keep your area clean, also respect and obey the guards etc. The list of rules was a little longer than that, but recalling what it all entailed eludes me, as my lack of attention was obscured by the fact that it was two in the morning in a Mexican prison with maximum sensory overload running through my brain. Besides, there were only two rules I needed to be concerned with (1) stay alive and (2) remember rule number 1. It's a short list and not easily forgotten! I honestly thought the guards reading from a list of rules was just a formality, and once I was inside among the prisoners, I would have to formulate my own set of survival rules.

After the captors of my freedom finished processing me, I realized they failed to indulge any prison procedures, scheduling, daily operations, or supply any helpful information. I was only handed a wool blanket just before Frank and two guards escorted me out of the office. I was led to the outside courtyard area by flashlight through a security gate to a short fifty-foot walk where we entered a door-less entryway to one of the cellblocks. Forty feet around a corner was a darkened prison cell that had metal bars spanning the width of the room and a door equipped with the same latch and bolt locking system as the cells in the jailhouse.

After one guard unlocked the padlock on the cell door, the other shinned what little light there was emitting from his weak flashlight into the room. As I slowly entered the cell, Frank told me the bathroom was at the back of the cell behind the hanging curtain and for me to find a place to sleep. When I peered into the darkened bathroom, all I could see was a five-gallon bucket on the floor raising concerns of its functionality. I turned around to look for a place to sleep and noticed there were no beds in the cell, so I found a vacant corner on the concrete floor to place my blankets. By the time my blankets hit the floor, the cell door was locked, and the two guards, along with Frank, were gone leaving me in darkness with no ability to see anything in great detail. I could barely see there were two other men in the cell sleeping on the floor who did not wake up during my intrusion.

I had to move their shoes, cups, and bowls out of the way to make enough room to layout my blankets, then folded them much as possible to add cushion between me and the hard-concrete floor. But by doing so, I gave up the length of my sleeping area for more comfort, forcing me to curl up on my blankets like a dog sleeping in a confined area. Lying down in a fetal position with a moment to myself, I quickly realize going to sleep was next to impossible, as my mind began processing how fucked up my situation truly was and how it all just became real!

The distressing thought of prolonged confinement in a prison cell raised major concerns that would be extremely problematic for my mental state of mind. The lack of proper nourishment from being a picky eater and the distaste I have for Mexican food. Also, the effects of sleeping on a concrete floor for an extended amount of time would create havoc on my body, not to mention the excessive amount of sleep deprivation. Eventually, my mind and body would slowly deteriorate, turning to mush while leaving me unable to defend or take care of myself properly. These and other worrisome problems continually plagued my mind, which had me thinking about escape scenarios from the prison and how to get out of the country throughout most of the night. In my distressed state of mind, I was thinking there was no way in *hell*, I would be able or willing to stay in prison for ten years, three years, or even thirty days until the next trial date. This was truly one of the darkest days of my life as I fell into the depths of despair!

While lying there on the blankets experiencing a feeling of hopelessness and dwelling over those five seconds of not hiding that damn gun, my mind began to slip deeper into desperation with thoughts on how to get injured badly enough to be admitted into the infirmary. Do I get in an altercation with an inmate or self-inflict an injury, and if so? What was the best logical way to get this done? My clouded judgment thought once inside the infirmary, there would be more opportunities for planning an escape, especially if they took me to a hospital, which would increase my options. The unrestrained darkness in my brain even conjured the forbidding thought of whether I would have to kill someone for the chance to be free. Of course, I could never answer that question until I actually faced such a desperate situation.

Once again, I found myself asking how many more times during my life will I have to say, "Nothing else matters but the present tragedy at hand!" I haven't a clue, though I'm sick and tired of repeating that gut-wrenching question! Will there come a time when I can "Break my rusty cage and run?"[12]

---

[12] A Johnny Cash song.

As my mind began to tire with relentless exhaustion overwhelming me, I was able to take short naps between rude awakenings which persisted throughout my slumber. For instance, the occasional potent odor of raw sewage floating in the air, the constant tossing and turning due to my lack of body fat to help cushion me from the concrete floor, and a strong urge to urinate that progressively transformed into a slight pain. I would have ventured to the bathroom but was not quite sure if the bucket was the toilet or a cover for a hole in the floor. It was too dark in the cell to make the distinction between the two, or maybe a third unknown option existed. So I decided to wait until daylight to utilize the correct procedure, which can't possibly be too far off in the distance.

As predicted, the morning came early. I was awakened by the sounds of the guards' activity in the cell block, so I took advantage of the morning light and went straight to the bathroom. Where I concluded the operational function was to use the drain hole in the floor as the toilet, pour water from the bucket down the hole, then cover it with the bucket to help contain the rancid smell from escaping. That concludes your lesson on how indoor plumbing works in a Mexican prison and explains the late-night aroma seeping into my nostrils. Hence, no lighting of a match as this shit is *literally* flammable.

With the glow from the morning light, I was able to see that the two young men in the cell were also sleeping on blankets. I was able to view what the cell was equipped with comparably to a Holiday Inn, of which absolutely nothing would be the answer. If it's possible to have less than nothing, this cell had it all—no beds, lights, sink, toilet, fixtures, electrical outlets, shelving, or a bathroom door. The 10'×10' cell was completely stripped of everything. The 4'×10' bathroom was only equipped with a shower spout cut off flush with the wall. Thereby making an interesting bathroom experience for someone who could shit, shower, and shave by using the same drain hole for all three functions. It can't get more efficient than that, though visualizing someone multi-tasking at this process is almost funny and a little disturbing.

After my interesting bathroom visit was complete, I laid down and went back to sleep. Only to be awakened slightly before seven o'clock by guards talking loudly while they were going around taking roll call throughout the cellblock. I assumed it was protocol to be awake and out of bed for roll call, so I folded my blankets into a more comfortable sitting arrangement and sat there waiting for the guards to arrive at my cell door. The guards approached each cell with a clipboard while calling out the prisoner's name from a corresponding list of occupants in the cell, expecting a verbal confirmation from each prisoner. When the guards walked over to my cell, one of them called out Miguel's name. A response came from the younger of the two. Yet when Paco's name was called out, there was no reply, provoking the guard to bang on the steel bars, and in a slightly elevated tone, repeated Paco's name. The sluggish Paco slowly rolled over and gave a faint response of his presence. The guard was not happy from the lackadaisical acknowledgment, and with little effort, reprimanded Paco just as he rolled over and fell back asleep.

With a puzzled stare, the guard looked at me, glanced back at his list of names, then back at me and, with a confused tone, asked for my nombre (name) as he checked his list once more. It was apparent there were only supposed to be two people in this cell. My name was nowhere to be found on the prison's list of occupants, revealing a flaw in their security procedures. Which could be the beginning of a good escape plan; come to think about it, I could have been hiding in the bathroom during role call and would never be missed by the guards!

After the ill-efficient roll call, a guard was going from cell to cell, unlocking the padlocks from everybody's cell door except for mine; I don't know why, as no explanation was given. Immediately after removal of the padlocks, an occupant of each cell would replace it with his own lock. From what I could see, this was done at every cell that had prison locks removed by the guard. I have never been in prison before, but this seemed bizarre to me and a little scary. Why were inmates locking themselves inside their own cells? Was this prison that dangerous which required extra safety, or was it for the protection of their personal items, or maybe a little of both?

While sitting on my blankets, watching Miguel perform his morning routine, he looked up and attempted to start a friendly conversation. It ended as quickly as it began as neither of us spoke the corresponding language and could only manage to exchange our names. It did not take long before I was overrun by the familiarity of complete boredom, persuading me to stand next to the cell door for a while, where I had nothing to do, but had all day to do it. I was getting fortunate breaks from the monotony by watching the occasional passer-by in doing so, I quickly learned this prison was multi-gender. Every now and then, a female guard walked past my cell, escorting female prisoners to and from an upstairs office, which I found to be quite interesting. Though not as intriguing to what I witnessed across the hall from my cell!

Last night during my extreme torment and deep depression, I assumed the living conditions of my cell were the norm throughout the prison. Yet from the looks of things across the hall, that might not have been a correct assumption. While observing activities coming from three cells across the twelve-foot wide hallway, I became shocked to learn I was living on the poor side of town! Made apparent by the cells packed full of personal items that were better equipped than a Holiday Inn. One cell I had a good line of sight into had every available square inch of space utilized, filled with storage tubs, boxes and items placed on shelving above their beds, plus a large variety of food products. The upscale cell to the right must have had even more stuff because to my bewilderment they had an overflow of items *outside* of their cell, consisting of a makeshift kitchen, table and four chairs, hot plates, coffee maker, and other small comforts of home. I *honestly* could not believe what I was looking at, was I stuck in purgatory or in a country club for convicts?

The two young men in the cell with me were much less fortunate than the inmates across the hall. Made evident by Paco's only possessions of two small bags, what appeared to be some clothes and toiletries, and Miguel had even less. I imagine from the looks of their bare necessities and the lack of a prison uniform they have not been in prison for very long.

After standing at the door for a while, I sat down on my minuscule comfort of blankets, not because of lost interest in the limited visual stimulation. But more directed to avoid a potential unfriendly

DIZNEY LAND by Way of Military Escort

confrontation with an inmate who walked past my cell a few times trying to eyeball me with a look of a bad attitude problem. He was a little taller and weighed about thirty pounds more than I, but his extra weight appeared to be body fat and not muscle tone. I was apprehensive about making eye contact with him, for it would have provoked me to address his attitude problem with a little bit of my own and aggressively ask, "What the fuck is your problem!" That would have no doubt created a problematic situation during the rest of my stay here. I have tried to be amiable and friendly toward everyone I have met during this whole ordeal. So for now, I avoided his rubbernecking stares and possible confrontation by sitting back down on my blankets. However, this ill-natured inmate should NOT mistake my kindness for weakness!

At eight o'clock in the morning, a guard showed up at our cell and after he unlocked the door, Miguel quickly stood up, grabbed two plastic bowls from the floor then left the cell. He soon returned with breakfast. After the guard locked the door behind him, Miguel handed me a bowl of stew along with two Kaiser rolls, awoke Paco to offer the other bowl to him, but he declined the meal and immediately went back to sleep, which apparently meant Miguel was willing to give up his breakfast to a complete stranger. I extended a much-appreciated gesture to Miguel, who's act of kindness was a pleasant surprise, especially now when I am a "Starven Marvin"[13] in need of some nourishment. Even though breakfast was slightly better than the jail's food, it wasn't saying much. Yet I was only able to eat ¾ of the stew due to my stomach being a little tight from not eating very much during the last three days.

After breakfast, I was still feeling the effects from the lack of sleep, so I laid down. But it was a losing battle at getting any kind of a long nap due to the noise, smell of cigarette smoke and unable to get comfortable. Not to mention the distressing thoughts of being locked in a Mexican prison!

Waking from my sporadic nap, I noticed Paco was still sleeping and continued sleeping until noon, making me a little envious, as my

---

[13] *South Park*, TV show.

body was sore from laying on the concrete floor. I could no longer tolerate the discomfort, so I stood by the door once more to try and alleviate some of the kinks from my body.

While I was standing at the door, an inmate approached and in broken English asked, "What are you in for?" Oh no! I did not want inmates to know I was in prison on a lame handgun charge. I wanted them to speculate on why I was in prison just in case I had to play the part of a crazy American, which might detour any aggressive inmates from approaching me. I definitely don't fit the description of a tough outlaw, so portraying crazy would probably be my best defense forcing their imaginations to run wild. Honestly, this strange logic ran through my mind within a fraction of a second upon meeting this inmate, so my reply to him was short and vague with "Possession of a handgun." His response was a familiar one "No problem, pay fine and go home." Excellent, the bird with limited vocabulary is back in its cage with me, offering comfort by way of an inmate whose words made me feel slightly more hopeful toward my predicament.

That was about the extent of our short conversation. He went back to his cell, but soon returned with an offering, a small package of wafer cookies. I responded, "No thanks," unsure of his intentions and wondered if I would have to owe him some sort of favor later. A careful thought process that came to me from watching too many prison movies. He extended his open hand to me in a more friendly gesture offering them once more, implying it was genuinely okay for me to accept the cookies. This time, I accepted and graciously thanked him. I figured repeating no might offend his gesture of kindness. Besides my stomach was screaming, "Hell yes, I'll accept some yummy cookies!"

As he walked back to his cell, I went over to my blankets, sat down, opened the package of cookies and offered some to Miguel, who removed one from the package. I extended my hand toward the sleeping Paco while gesturing to Miguel to offer him some. Miguel shook his head while waving his hand back and forth, and with a smirky grin said, "No, no," as if gesturing, "you snooze you lose." I responded with a nod of my head and a smile in agreement with his selfish gesture, more for us.

The extreme boredom painfully dragged on until noon when it was interrupted by the return of Miguel with today's lunch special of beans that looked and smelled unappetizing. I declined his kind offer, besides Paco was finally awake, and he only had two servings of food. I just ate a roll I saved from breakfast, two cookies and washed it down with the same bottle of water given to me upon entering the prison.

After lunch, Miguel and Paco took turns taking a shower. When they were finished, Paco gestured if I wanted to take one. "Si" (Yes). This is day 4 without a shower while still wearing the same clothes; surely, a good scrubbing of my ass is needed and very appreciated. He handed me a bottle of soap as I entered the bathroom. I noticed there was nowhere to hang my clothes to keep them off the wet bathroom floor; therefore, I started to get undressed outside of the bathroom. Paco quickly put that to an end as he frantically displayed a concern that I should be more discreet by pointing toward the curtain hanging in front of the bathroom. He obviously wanted me to get undressed behind the curtain, and I would have to agree, as I prefer getting naked in private. I thought that being discreet in prison was not a concern or even an issue. This was a wrong assumption on my part, especially after witnessing Paco's frantic facial expression while I removed my T-shirt. Yet I had totally forgotten about the occasional women passing by the cell, hard to believe I know!

I was not keen about putting my partially clean clothes on the same dirty floor that was used as a poop hole. I discreetly placed them on the other side of the curtain next to the wall but kept my flip-flops on for obvious reasons; they also needed to be washed.

After taking the bucket off the toilet drain, I turned on the shower only to receive room-temperature water. There were no hot and cold faucets, only one industrial type valve, and since the shower spout was cut off flush with the wall, there was no water pressure, it only poured out of the spout. Good thing I placed my clothes outside of the bathroom because the pouring water splashed aggressively more than shower spray, thoroughly drenching the entire 4'×10' floor. It felt good to take a shower even though it was an odd experience, especially after replacing the bucket over the poop hole, followed by using my T-shirt to dry off. I did have a long sleeve shirt to wear, so I did not have to display my half-naked body in a prison cell or attempt to win a wet T-shirt contest.

I should have realized the inmates here were discreet or uncomfortable with partial nudity. Their beds were incased with curtains, blankets, or towels, and I never saw anybody shirtless. Maybe it was some type of prison rule to keep them from revealing gang tattoos; also, one would have to consider the presence of females. Come to think of it, during the pat-down upon entry of the prison, the guards appeared uneasy when I took my shirt off and began to unzip my shorts; they quickly responded in an elevated tone with, "no, no!" I think they only wanted me to lift my shirt up to check for contraband instead of removing it, and they damn sure did not want me displaying my birthday suit.

When I finished getting dressed, I hung the wet T-shirt on their makeshift clothesline, then sat down on the blankets expecting the torturous boredom to quickly reappear. Sitting there, I was able to observe Paco performing an after-shower routine involving a lot of primping as if he were getting ready for the high school prom. He fussed with his hair applying jell, body lotion on face, hands, arms and feet, teeth brushed, deodorant on, clean civilian clothing that looked like they just came off the rack and new red tennis shoes. He truly resembled a young man ready to go on a hot date, although it was quite funny because our cell was in lockdown, so who was he getting all dolled up for, and where does he think he was going?

When nobody showed up to take Paco to the dance, he and Miguel started cleaning the cell. Being the older of the two, Paco took charge of this chore and had Miguel rearrange his bedding, so it was parallel with the sidewall to gain walking space between our sleeping areas. Paco then picked up a broom and started sweeping, while Miguel moved what few items there were from the floor out of the way, allowing the debris to be swept down the multi-purpose toilet drain. Next, he handed the broom and a bottle of all-purpose cleaner to Miguel with verbal instructions on what to clean next, Miguel's simple task was abruptly halted by an irritated Paco. Apparently, the adolescent man lacked the experience on how to correctly clean a bathroom floor, so Paco made it crystal clear to the inept youngster that he was doing it completely wrong.

Despite not understanding a single word Paco said to Miguel, I can recreate his instructional tutorial verbatim just by watching his body language, demeanor, facial expressions and the tones in his voice, also by my many years of personal cleaning experiences. Hell, I would have bet money on the accuracy of what Paco said! Here is what transpired:

"Miguel! Stop what you are doing that is not the proper way to clean a floor. Give me the *broom* and that (cleaning fluid). Now *listen*, you are supposed to start at the far end of the room (bathroom) and work your way back toward the drain. First, pour some of this over here then use the broom to scrub the floor like this with some muscle behind it! When you are done scrubbing the entire floor, fill this bucket with water and rinse the floor starting from the far end while sweeping all the water toward the drain, simple, got it?"

Miguel spoke not a word during his schooling, and the compliant expression on his face resembled a child learning something new who dared not interrupt his boisterous elder.

This unexpected break in the boredom was quite entertaining and put a slight smile on my face. I have been on both sides of that scenario and realized from the beginning Miguel was doing a "Horse shit job,"[14] due to my siblings, being raised old school by our parents, and knowing how to properly do household chores. So, I can truly relate to Paco's frustration with Miguel. "How do you not know how to clean a god damn floor?"

When all the interest had faded away from sitting on the blankets, I stood up and journeyed to my second favorite hangout place, the cell door. These short trips to and from the door and blanket are turning into a lackluster routine that is relieving the intense boredom by only a few seconds at a time, which is painfully hard to accept being stuck in this mind-numbing pattern for an indefinite amount of time; *pure insanity!*

---

[14] A familiar phrase from my father.

One reason why I prefer standing by the door was to put a greater distance between me and the cellmates who like to puff on their cancer sticks; the airflow in the hallway was a little more tolerable than breathing smoke from Paco and Miguel. Paco realized the cigarette smoke bothered me and tried to be accommodating by blowing his smoke in the opposite direction, unlike Miguel, who had not a clue. Paco made it clear to me with body gestures that Miguel was oblivious of my discomfort.

Within a short time of standing at the door, the inmate who gave me the cookies earlier offered me some chocolate-coated candy. The candy and the other bread roll were my dinner, plus the same bottle of water, which is just about gone. I'm worried about when the bottle is empty; who do I ask in order to get more, where do they get the water from and would it be safe to drink? If I'm forced to keep reusing the same plastic bottle, bacteria will eventually form, making the bathroom my new favorite hangout place hovering over the poop hole. It appears I have been thrown in this cage to fend for myself. There still has been absolutely no visitation by a guard, or staff member to explain any daily operations, or what to do about getting food and water.

Just before dinnertime, I observed four inmates across the hall in their makeshift kitchen, preparing a meal. They were working well together, making good use of their time and had the meal ready to eat in short order. Just as they were getting ready to sit down at the dinner table, the fourth inmate returned with a large stack of tortillas that I assume he retrieved them from the prison kitchen. The four men looked to be in their sixties, and from the clutter of their cell have been incarcerated here for a long time. Also evident was the respect from the guards and inmates as their out of cell kitchen setup was completely unprotected from thievery.

As I watched the four men sit down and started filling their plates, a guard showed up at our cell and unlocked the door allowing Paco to retrieve the evening dinner. I don't know what ingredients are in the prison's tortillas, but when Paco returned with a short stack of them and a side dish of fixings, the smell instantly deterred me from even trying to eat one. I remember attempting to nibble on a tortilla in the jailhouse, having no success in forcing it down my throat. I wasn't yet desperate enough to try again with these prison tortillas.

When the four men finished eating, one of them noticed me standing at the cell door. He walked over and, with pretty good English, asked, "Are you from the United States?"

"Yes, I am."

He continued, "What are you in for?"

I answered with my redundant response, "Possession of a handgun" (POH).

One guess on what his next response was. Yup, "no problem, pay fine" (NPPF).

His welcomed interruption from the dreariness continued with an inquiry of my name and what brought me to Mexico. I answered his questions with short replies and regrettably failed to keep our conversation going by not asking him any questions in return; the result, a missed opportunity to find out about getting some water.

Only after he walked back to his cell did I realize he too kept his distance, about six feet away, the same as the last inmate who spoke to me earlier. I wondered if it was prison policy that inmates are supposed to keep their distance from new arrivals?

No sooner did one stimulant end another arose. An inmate from across the hall pulled out a chair and guitar from his cell, sat next to his door and began softly playing like he was practicing a new song or a novice learning to play. Either way, it was nice listening to him play, receiving another break from the dullness; unfortunately, he stopped playing after a short amount of time, which ended my entertainment.

During the all-day observations of people walking past my cell, I noticed most of the activity was traffic to and from the cell left of mine, including the inmate who was trying to eyeball me, and a dainty inmate acting like he would be much more comfortable wearing a pretty dress and high heels instead of a prison uniform. At one point during the evening, Mr. Eyeball and another inmate who was short and slender stopped at our cell. The smaller inmate started talking to Paco, and when Mr. Eyeball turned his body to face the conversation, I noticed what looked to be fresh drool stains on his shirt just below his chin slightly to the right. Now it does not take a dentist to recognize who is coming to the party next door, especially when girls are not invited, or necessary in order to have a good time. I will be avoiding Mr. Eyeball and keep my distance from his merry friends! "There are a lot of strange men in cell block #10."[15]

At seven o'clock7:00, a guard was going around to all the cells having the prisoners remove their personal locks from the doors and replaced them with the prison locks. This ended the convicts twelve hours freedom from within their coop, and of course, my cell was omitted from this exclusive process. I would have to say being stuck in lockdown my first day in prison just might have been more beneficial for this white boy by keeping me safe from conflict with other inmates and protect me from harm.

There were three more hours of doing absolutely nothing before the cellblock went dark, forcing us less fortunate prisoners without the luxury of having lights in our cell to go directly to bed, which concluded my first day inside a Mexican prison.

I truly accepted, "I'm in a world of shit!" But it could be a lot worse. After all, it was the end of day 1 and I wasn't lying in the infirmary half-dead from a mass beating, and I still had a virgin ass! So it was time to place a handkerchief over my face, for a concrete floor and odors of raw sewage and cigarette smoke waited for my arrival. Also, the fear of having a bad dream about ten thousand nuns and orphans; you may ask, "What's so bad about ten thousand nuns and orphans?" "They were all eaten by *rats!*"[16]

---

[15] "The Wall" song by Johnny Cash.
[16] *Saturday Night Live* TV show with Jim Belushi and Jane Curtin.

Day 14 in Country

Second day in prison

My morning came early once more from the guard's commotion, but at least I was able to get more than two hours of sleep, unlike the horrific night before. During roll call, a guard acknowledged my presence in the cell though never called out my name; apparently, my name still hadn't made its way to his roll call list.

Soon after roll call, I was astounded by Frank's arrival at my cell door, the American who assisted in escorting me to this forbidding cell late Sunday night. Now that he could view my cell during the daylight hours, he noticed the living conditions of my cell was deplorable and displayed an expression of complete disgust on his face. The first words to come from his mouth were, "Is this your cell?" Not as a question but more of a statement with appalling disbelief and in an agitated tone, he instantly followed up with, "I will be right back" then briskly walked away.

I was clueless of what was to come from Frank's intensified disapproval at the condition of my cell, though I figured it probably would not matter anyway, as it's a Mexican prison, not Disney Land, or is it?

Frank returned moments later with a guard who unlocked my cell door, and with an authoritative command, said, "Get your stuff, I'm moving you to a better cell!" Awesome, my stuff consisted of a manila envelope, two blankets, toothbrush and paste, and a soda bottle containing one sip of water, so there was no need to involve a U-Haul with a bunch of boxes for my exodus. As quick as I was able to stand up, out the door I went, without even a wave or nod goodbye to my cellmates, which may have been rude, but all I could focus on was a speedy departure from this shithole containing a shithole, and when a guard opens your cell door you get the hell out without delay!

As Frank escorted me through various areas of the prison, I noticed the building was a baling wire and duct tape paradise and is what one might expect from a prison in a third world country. There was nothing new or modernized within the areas where the prisoners were housed, even the paint looked older than dirt, and the inside of the building appeared to be well over a hundred years old, though parts on the outside had modern renovations. The prison was an open-air facility, which meant no heating or air conditioning and no glass in the windows, only steel bars. The security doors were a sliding bolt latching system with padlocks, the same as the cells throughout the prison. "It took a ring of keys to move it."[17]

Frank immediately started talking as soon as I exited the cell and continued to do so with an elevated excitement all the way to our destination about 150 feet away. He spoke with a dialect as if he was raised in the inner streets of a big city, with most of his sentences containing the word "Man," though I cannot recall him ever using profanity. Frank spoke in a mild tone with respect, plus he appeared to have an excellent rapport with inmates and guards who exchanged friendly greetings as we walked throughout the prison.

Frank told me the captain (commandant) of the prison put him in charge of my welfare, safety, and had me placed on the safe side of the prison to avoid gang bangers and troublemakers where prisoners want to live in peace and safety. In a stern tone, Frank eagerly offered his personal protection, "If anybody gives you any trouble, let me know and I will take care of it; everyone here knows me and if they mess with you, they have to answer to me! Also, if you need anything, just ask!" I was in complete awe and spoke not a word while absorbing all of Frank's fantastic and unbelievable info, which was music to my ears, extending a *tremendous* amount of relief from my worried mind!

Frank came across as a gentle giant who you wouldn't want to provoke, but upon listening to him speak revealed his true nature,

---

[17] Greystone Chapel song by Johnny Cash.

therefore I partook in his kindness and asked for something to drink. He replied with, "No problem, I'll get it for you after we get to your new cell." Then asked, "What are you in for?" (WAYIF)

I responded, "POH" (Possession of a handgun). I think Frank had been an occupant of Mexico too long as his response of "NPPF" (No problem, pay fine) was identical to the residents of this land. Frank's exuberance continued while relaying the story of my early morning arrival when he became excited after being awakened by a guard who informed him of an American in the processing office needing help with translations. The news of an arrival a fellow countryman motivated Frank out of bed and eagerly looked forward to having a conversation with somebody who spoke English since there was only one other American in the entire prison of one thousand occupants.

During our walk, I continued to remain mostly silent. When we approached our destination, Frank's enthusiasm began to rise reassuring me the new cell was nicer, safe, no drugs, a good bunch of guys and he trusted the man (Emilio) in charge of the cell. When we arrived at the cell door, I had no idea there was going to be a Butterfly Effect, "The phenomenon whereby a minute localized in a complex system can have large effects elsewhere,"[18] that would drastically change which path this story was heading down and completely alter my destiny all because of the actions of one *man*!

While Frank was talking to Emilio, I stood in the doorway, getting a first impression of pure intimidation from the seven inmates in the overcrowded cell, which instantly put my mind in a state of uneasiness. Most of the men were substantially bulkier than me, and their blank stares gave a strong impression as to why is this white gringo at our cell door. This brought forth in me an overwhelming fear that my presence was going to be an intrusion in their already limited amount of personal space and worried I was not welcomed in their cell. Those first few seconds completely drew me back like a shy turtle into the safety of its shell incapable of making that first step across their threshold!

---

[18] Edward Lorenz quote.

Fortunately, all my fears and doubts were quickly put to rest, as I was able to breathe a great sigh of relief when Frank introduced me to Emilio and the rest of the men, who were very friendly and more than willing to be accommodating, especially from the two men in the cell who spoke English.

Just before Frank walked away, he once again extended reassurance I was in really good hands. He soon returned with a bottle of the same brand of orange drink I received in the jailhouse. After thanking him, he said he would periodically stop by to check up on me, and if I needed anything to let him know. No sooner than uttering those words, he referred to the blankets I was carrying and asked with a concerned tone, "Is that all you have to sleep on the floor with?"

My dispirited reply, "Yes," induced a look of total disbelief on Frank's face.

"I will be right back!" he replied with disgust and away he went, soon returning with a foam sleeping mat. *Holy shit*, Frank is truly a man of action and making me feel like it was Christmas morning, receiving the joy of knowing a hard-concrete floor was not going to be my mattress tonight!

Before I had a chance to thank Frank, he instantly asked with sincerity, "Is there anything else you need?"

At first, I said, "No thanks" while shaking his hand, but as he began to walk away, I remembered leaving my T-shirt in the shithole cell. Frank made a trip back to the cell and returned with the shirt in hand then repeated his kind gesture once more.

"Do you need anything else?" With Frank's eager kindness, I felt very humble and could not possibly ask him for anything else, even if my hair was on fire, I would be a little reluctant in asking for a glass of water.

Until now, I have been in the cell for about fifteen minutes, so I need to back up the story timeline to when I first entered the cell. It was a massive sensory overload, starting with the very first thing that caught my eye, a large blue painted word "CAFÉ" on the cells back wall and another word on the left wall that read "Restaurante." Compared to the shithole cell, this one was definitely an impressive upgrade, not a Holiday Inn quality, but more of a fancy Ritz standard. This cell had everything, and by prison standards, "everything" is a *huge* understatement! I literally felt like a kid in a candy store wanting to run around checking out all their amenities but had a strict parent forcefully holding my arm restricting my excitement.

The 10'×15' cell had three sets of bunkbeds incased with curtains and a 5'×5' bathroom in the back of the room. A short hallway led to their own 10'×10' outdoor kitchen area; YES, an outdoor kitchen! Most of the items I'm about to describe that the inmates had in this cell are not standard and are only allowed in prison by written permission signed by the captain of the prison. Items in the living area consisted of:

Microwave
Coffee maker
Urn-style coffee maker
Display flat top refrigerator/freezer chest
Display case cabinet full of food, i.e., candy, cup of soup, cereal, tea, microwavable popcorn, cookies, snacks, chips, etc.
Pastries in a cake display dish
Plus, there were a few items I will not reveal!

The bathroom was complete with a sink, shower, mirror, shelf, hooks, shower curtain and a toilet that may or may not require a Mexican owner's manual on how to operate. As a bonus, the bathroom door is a metal panel that can be locked from the inside.

Items in the kitchen area consisted of:

Sink with running water
Refrigerator with freezer
Chest freezer
Three hotplates
Steamer for hotdogs and buns
Table with one chair
Prep counter
Cooking and kitchen utensils, pots, pans, cups, plates and bowls etc.

It was quite obvious the men in this cell had their very own café/store business and from the amount of foot traffic showing up at their cell door, purchasing items in the limited amount of time I have been in here, it must be a lucrative cash machine.

Upon Frank's departure from the cell, I was instantly greeted with a smile and an outstretched hand from Emilio; the owner of the café, who eagerly shook my hand and with a friendly gesture spoke a few words in Spanish, "If you need anything just ask."

This was immediately translated by John Moreno, a fellow cellmate who reiterated the statement with his own enthusiastic greeting of, "There are some really good guys here and if you need anything, do not hesitate to ask!"

Emilio appeared to be thirty-five years old, had very short hair, six feet tall, 170 pounds and a stout build which gave a strong impression of intimidation, but while John was speaking to me, Emilio intently stared at us with sincerity of agreement in John's spoken words, which truly made me feel welcomed into their cell.

John appeared to be forty years old, 5'10" tall, 150 pounds, average build, soft-spoken, extremely mild-mannered, displayed an appearance and demeanor of a native American with long black hair and manicured beard, well-educated and spoke English more proficient than I.

During the meet and greet with a few of the men, John held a plastic rectangle shape milkcrate to put my blankets and manila envelope in, then placed it underneath a bed. There was no personal introduction between most of the men and myself, a result of my reserved demeanor and cramped quarters, which cautiously held me in one spot, only acknowledging them with a nod and a slight wave of the hand.

After John's cordial greeting, another cellmate (David Garrido) eagerly spoke up with assurance and said with inadequate English, "If you need anything, please ask, what is ours is yours, *really*." By the expression on his face and exuberant tone, I could tell he truly meant it and was not just spewing words from his mouth.

With the abundant amount of hospitality floating around the room, I was forced to emerge from the safety of my shell and once

DIZNEY LAND by Way of Military Escort

again answer the inevitable question of the day, "WAYIF?" (what are you in for).

With a slight grin, I gave them the standard answer, "POH."

John's quick reply was also a standard one, "NPPF and go home," and after his translation to the crew, a few of them also squawked, "No problem." Oh no, the parrot has followed me into this cell, now we have the bird flu in the café, which has infected my new cellmates with the "no problem" virus.

Everybody I have met has responded to my POH with the same statement NPPF, trying to convince me the crime committed was nothing to worry about and acted like it was a misdemeanor crime, which appeared to be quite common in Mexico. Yet they were missing a big piece of the puzzle, not realizing that having a 9mm handgun is a federal crime punishable by a ten-year prison sentence. Yet hearing NPPF repeatedly for five days straight has begun to ease my mind and started thinking just maybe everybody knows what they are talking about.

I have a saying, "There are three kinds of people who know the criminal justice system much better than you and me—judges, lawyers and convicts," and I just happen to have two out of the three in this cell with me right now! Come to find out, John is a well-established lawyer who is partnered with two others at a small law firm here in the town of La Paz. So when John utters the phrase NPPF, I received some comfort from his words, though they are only words and will only have true meaning and solace when I'm a free man outside of these prison walls giddy as a schoolgirl on prom night.

Our small talk conversation did not last long after the basic Q and A's were completed. The men all dispersed back into their morning routine, which oddly enough left me feeling all alone in this crowded cell. As Emilio and Adrian worked the café, Pablo and Jose went back into the kitchen, John sat on the edge of a bed reading a book, David and Roseudo returned to their beds and hid inside their cocoon shelters incased by curtains.

I haven't had anything to eat this morning, so while David was climbing up to his bunk to disappear, I asked to have one of the pastries they had for sale and would pay for it when I received money from Brenda. David looked to be forty years old, five feet, three inches, stocky, and a little overweight, short hair, mild-mannered, friendly, low-key and spoke English slowly with slight difficulty. David did not hesitate in his reply, "Yes, no problem, don't worry about paying, what is ours is yours, *no reeeally!*" Then partially repeated his response along with a strong emphasis on the word "really," which gave me slight uneasiness in asking for the pastry. He expected me to take it without asking, but there is no way in hell I'd take something without permission; proper etiquette is important to me, especially in today's world, which lacks it.

Space in the cell was minimal and finding a place to stand in order to stay clear of the men working the café would be inconveniently awkward, so I found the most logical place to put a milk crate to sit on by placing it against a wall next to the display cooler six feet from the cell door. Doing so, I sat down to eat my minuscule breakfast, washing it down with the orange drink.

Most of the morning consisted of just sitting there, keeping to myself watching my cellmates work the café. Even though I felt at ease being in this cell, I was not sure how to conduct myself or what to do. I'm more of an introvert and tend to keep a low profile until I'm more familiar with people and their surroundings. My seclusion was also aided in the fact that the only two people in the cell who spoke English were preoccupied, John was deeply immersed in reading a book, while David was incased in his cocoon (bed).

Despite not being involved in anybody's discussions or interactions, it was nice to have some visual stimulation from all the transactions between the café and their customers, which was *crazy*. There was a steady stream of customers showing up at the cell door. I must use the word "customers," not inmates, as this café's crew were not biased and had a wide variety of clientele. Besides the inmates, there were male and female prison guards, office personnel, and female secretaries. Was I in a Mexican prison, or the business end of a counter in a fast-food establishment?

Sales from the morning rush consisted of coffee, tea, pastries, omelets, and frosted flakes with milk and sliced banana, and inmates were responsible for most of the sales from cigarettes and two-liter bottles of water. The water sold at the café came from five-gallon jugs the cellmates purchased from an outside source and used that water to fill up old used two-liter plastic bottles then refrigerate them. I have not a clue what their profit margin was on water sales, though I do know they sold a shit load, almost as much as the cigarette sales, which were sold mainly two or three at a time, and never did I see anybody buy a whole pack of twenty.

The coffee sales came mainly from guards and office personal, so much that there were times when there was a line of customers at our cell door waiting for a cup of joe, and since I was sitting only six feet from the cell door, I noticed certain guards did not offer to pay and were not requested to so by Emilio. It was obvious Emilio had intricate connections with specific guards, but at what level is unclear. I did recognize it could be beneficial for me in one way or another.

Prolonged sitting on my Mexican style lounge chair made my boney ass a little sore, so I stood up and grabbed one of my blankets to soften the top of the milk crate, creating more cush for the tush while continuing with my visual stimulation of the cafes daily operations. From my vantage point, I was able to witness all the interactions between the cellmates and their customers, giving me a genuinely good feeling of the impressive camaraderie during many of their encounters. Most of their greetings started and ended with a homie handshake, fist bump, and a smile, though this form of friendship was not limited to only fellow inmates, it also extended to some of the guards and prison staff. Obviously, confirming this was the safe side of the prison, allowing me the option of not playing the part of a crazy American and could eliminate the façade from my repertoire.

While sitting there, I noticed most of the people who showed up at our cell door had an inquisitive stare toward the new face in the cafés cell, so I tried not to make any eye contact with them to avoid failed attempts at a conversation by revealing I was illiterate to their language. Brenda calls me the master of avoidance.

It seems a little strange to me that this cell is locked from within the cell with Emilio's own padlock, where the men have the option to leave their cell for twelve hours a day, yet few of them leave the cell at all. Personally, I was bored out of my freaking mind and wanted to get out of this cell and roam. Unfortunately, John told me it would be a few days before I was allowed by the prison to leave my cell; the rule had something to do with other inmates getting familiar with me being here.

Sometime after ten o'clock while standing at the cell door watching activity in the corridor just killing time, and giving my derriere a much-needed break, I noticed an influx of civilians entering the cell block through a solid metal door to my left. As these people walked past, I could see they were here to visit their loved ones. Each family member or group was accompanied by a delighted inmate. Most of the visitors were women and children though none were being escorted by a guard, and even though I had no idea where the visiting area was, it seemed bizarre to be trafficking families through a prison cell block.

During my amazement at the passersby, an inmate who looked to be thirty years old, branding many tattoos and wearing the standard prison-issue brown uniform, walked up to my cell door and asked, "How ya doing?"

My usual reply would typically be "pretty good" if I were in the US, but while in Mexico, I have been trying to keep my responses simple and easy for the listener to translate into Spanish. I don't know how "pretty good" would translate, and how can the word "good" be pretty? Is it just me, or do people think about what others hear before their words are spoken? Therefore, I need some sort of constant stimulus to keep my mind from an overload of overthinking.

Whatever my reply was to him at the time was irrelevant anyway, as he spoke adequate English and could converse with relative ease. There was no introduction between us, and I only found out his name by asking for it after our conversation was over as he started to walk away. Raúl who never revealed his last name, spoke in a soft tone with an inner-city slang dialect, was very calm, friendly, and conducted himself in a respectful manner. He did not speak like a well-educated man; his spoken sentences contained repetitive words like "man, shit, fucked up and crazy shit."

Our conversation started out by him, asking if I was from the States, then went straight into the standard question, answer and reply mode, "WAYIF, POH, NPPF" (WPN). I hope the structure of my unique sentence is understandable now that the three acronyms will be condensed down to one, as I'm getting tired of repeating myself over and over…and over.

As we continued with our friendly chat, Raúl said, "When you need a translator, just let me know, and I will help you."

I was suspicious of his motive and wondered to myself what his angle was and what did he want from me. Besides, I have Frank, John, and David, who can help me with translations, so I was not concerned about having another person involved in that process; however, the more I listened, the more sincere he sounded in offering to help. He also extended an offer to escort me to use the payphone in the courtyard and to the visitor's area when somebody came to visit me.

Raúl's gracious offer was valuable information; he was the only person to inform me of being allowed to leave my cell today if escorted by an inmate or guard. Everybody else has offered to get what I need, but I'm clueless of what I can and cannot have, or what I should be asking for, i.e., the use of a phone. I did not utilize Raúl's thoughtful gesture because I would have been extremely uncomfortable walking around a Mexican prison with a total stranger, along with reservations in trusting an unfamiliar inmate, and unsure of the validity at being allowed to leave my cell today. So after our informative conversation had ended, all I did was thank him for the offer, exchanged a fist bump, then watched him walk to his cell, which was across the corridor slightly off to the left from mine.

Before Raúl could enter back into his cell, he had to ask a guard to unlock the door. Apparently, his cell was in lockdown where its occupants did not have the luxury to come and go as they pleased, which could help explain why Raúl was so eager to help me. By doing so, he would have a justified reason for a guard to let him out of the cell, and if that was his motivation to gain a temporary escape from his cage, I'm all for it! As separate individuals, we had absolutely no resource and limited capability being confined in our cells, but if we worked together combining our efforts, his knowledge of prison rules and procedures would be his greatest asset to me, and I would be the freedom key to his forbidding confinement. Together we could capitalize on each other's unique attributes and spend more time roaming the larger cage and less time in the smaller one constricting our every movement.

I approached John and inquired about Raúl's character, whether he was a good or bad guy. John's only reply was, "He is okay." This was good to hear as now there is another ally, I could add to my arsenal to aid in combatting an easier stay in prison. I also asked if Brenda would be allowed to bring me some items, such as clothing, toiletries, and food. He said, "Oh yeah, no problem."

He went on to inform me that I was to have her put the items in a bag with my name on it and then give to a guard for inspection who would let me know when to retrieve the items. Good to know, as it's now day 5 wearing the same clothes which are getting overripe. Speaking of overripe, while having John's attention, I asked to borrow his soap and shampoo for taking a shower. He gladly said, "Yes, no problem," then pulled out a milkcrate from underneath a bed where he retrieved the items.

I took the items and ventured into the bathroom, where I would be able to enjoy a functional toilet and a real shower that came with the comforts of complete privacy. Yesterday's shower in the wonderful shithole cell failed to give me that fresh and clean smell, as I almost felt just as dirty coming out of the shower as entering, so hopefully today's shower experience will have a more beneficial outcome.

Before using any of the bathrooms amenities, I had a slight concern over the three five-gallon buckets of water in the corner of the shower floor and instantly assumed at least one of the three-bathroom functions were inoperable, requiring the assistance from the buckets of H_2O. I first turned on the sink faucet, yes it works, then flushed the toilet and made sure the tank refilled with water, yes, it too was okay. Oh no, did that mean I had to take a cold whore bath? I reluctantly turned the shower faucet to the left and discover it also was functional, plus I was fortunate to have warm water, so what are the buckets of water used for? I guess I'd find out later.

After getting fresh and clean, I returned John's soap and shampoo and sat down on my milkcrate, contemplating a plan of action for using a phone in order to have Brenda bring me some clean clothes. Earlier John did not offer to help me with that process, so I did not want to impose and tear him away from the book he was deeply absorbed in, besides I already have a willing participant from across the hall.

I kept glancing over to Raúl's cell in hopes of getting a glimpse of him standing at his cell door, and it wasn't long before he joined some of his cellmates at the door watching passersby. I went over to my door and made eye contact with him, partially raising my hand to wave for his attention.

"Do you need something?" he asked.

The hallway is about twelve feet wide, so to keep from raising my voice, I held my hand up to my ear as if I were using a phone and said, "Yes, I need to use a phone."

Raúl instantly grabbed the attention of a guard standing four feet away who oversaw a security door that separates our cellblock from the administration offices where visitors came through earlier, then began talking to him while pointing to me. It appeared Raúl was having difficulty convincing the guard to release him from the cell. Their discussion dragged on longer than one would expect, but eventually, the guard unhooked a keyring from his belt and unlocked Raúl's door.

After John unlocked our door, Raúl escorted me out of the cellblock and into the courtyard where the payphone was located. Since our cellblock only contains seven jail cells, it was a short walk of about thirty-five feet. It felt strange being outside the confines of my cage and made me slightly uncomfortable. I could feel that all eyes were focused on me by the inmates' inquisitive stares while walking past them, compelling me to walk with my head down, avoiding eye contact so as not to inadvertently agitate them.

As we entered the courtyard, I was relieved to see so few inmates standing around the area, reducing the number of staring eyes focusing on this white gringo wearing shorts and flip-flops. The courtyard was divided into two separate sections. The first area was the smaller of the two approximately 25'×15', with a tall fence, two eight-foot benches, sink, and a payphone. The larger section had considerably more room to wander around and equipped with many tables and chairs placed under an awning.

The unattended gate on the fence was left open, allowing prisoners the freedom to venture to the larger area, accounting for most of the human activity. When we arrived at the payphone, I took one look at it and instantly knew there was no way I could figure out how to use this contraption, being the type that did not allow the use of currency, and of course, all the instructions were in Spanish.

Without hesitation, I looked at Raúl with a puzzled expression and asked, "How do I use this?"

He replied, "You need to use a phonecard," then asked me if I had one.

Obviously, I did not have one. He pulled out a phone card from a lanyard pouch hanging from his neck and handed it to me, then proceeded to explain how to use the phone. I was unable to grasp his instructions and could not understand any of the prerecorded information coming through on the phone line and failed at my first few attempts at trying to contact Brenda.

Raúl could see I was having difficulties utilizing the prehistoric payphone and getting upset due to the importance of contacting Brenda. He relieved me from my continuous failed attempts and tried his luck at the contraption. He had a good understanding of how to use the payphone, but also, had trouble getting a connection outside of the country to Brenda's phone. The amount of numbers needed to complete a phone call from a Mexican prison to a US cellphone is crazy long, which requires two connections, one to get out of the prison and another from the country. Raúl displayed a lot of patience in helping me at this endeavor, and even though he suffered many failed attempts and not sure what the problem was, he was not willing or ready to quit trying.

Einstein once said that insanity is doing the same thing over and over expecting a different result. Therefore, I chose to put an end to this madness by telling Raúl not to worry about trying to place the call anymore, which left us no choice but to head back to our cells.

We were walking extremely slow to extend our temporary liberty, giving us more time to continue our conversation, which comprised the subject of Raúl's incarceration and my inquiry of how long he has been in prison. His response left me completely dumbfounded as all I could say was, "What the hell!"

Raúl has been imprisoned for *two* years while waiting to be sentenced for his crime by the court, and to my surprise, he was not complaining about being stuck in jail, just that he had no idea how long he was supposed to be in prison. His actual words were, "Man, that's some fucked up shit," though he expressed those words in a low-key manner and never raised his voice in anger, almost as if accepting his unfortunate demise, leading me to believe this is standard Mexican procedure, "SNAFU." (Situation normal all fucked up).

This latest bit of information was truly unsettling as Raúl's lawyer is a public defender, as is mine, and you can see how well that is working out for him. I wonder if two years ago, someone told him, "No problem?" Here is a thought, what if Raúl's crime is only punishable by an eighteen-month sentence? As we parted ways back into our separate cages, I could not but feel a trace of sorrow for Raúl's predicament and revisited my overwhelming urgency for acquiring a competent lawyer ASAP!

Once back inside the cell, I felt compelled to stroll over to what now appeared to be my personal space, the milkcrate with the chest cooler to my left, a wall at my back, a short stack of milk crates to my right and a half size shelf four-feet above my head; it felt like I was in my very own cocoon not ready, or comfortable enough to venture away from my pupa stage. I was sitting there for a prolonged period of time while successfully staying out of the cellmate's way, conscious of not disrupting their daily routine.

Frank showed up at my cell door, asking how I was doing and if the prison has allowed me to make my one obligatory phone call. I told him, "Okay," and "Not yet."

His response was quick, with a slight tone of disgust, "What?" He immediately turned to the same guard standing by the security door Raúl talked to earlier and spoke a few words to him with an authoritative explanation of his request, and within seconds I was once again out of my cage.

My observations of Frank and Raúl's approach to their interaction with the same guard is like night and day, and even though I don't know what was said in their separate encounters with the guard, I can tell you who had more authority and command over the guards. Raúl's cautious approach was made in a passive manner, taking much longer, convincing the guard to let me out of my cell than it did for Frank. Frank's style was slightly more aggressive, almost as if he were not asking for permission, but politely telling the guard what he wanted in an authoritative manner. I'm beginning to think Frank should be my number one cornermen in this prison bout!

Upon getting released from my boredom chamber again, Frank escorted be back to the same phone that halted my many attempts in reaching Brenda earlier. With this repeat trip, I felt much more at ease by walking into the courtyard with Frank, as his friendly familiarity with most of the guards and inmates resonated with a more relaxed atmosphere.

I don't think Frank had ever used the payphone, for he displayed a perplexed stare resembling the one I had earlier when first seeing the blue phone. I concluded the same outcome was about to unfold except for one minor detail. Frank instantly realized his limitations on the use of the phone and quickly enlisted the help of an inmate who was walking by.

The inmate had knowledge of the use of this blue boxed contraption, but he too failed at the task at hand, leading me to believe the phone card given to me by Raúl did not have enough minutes on it for allowing us to make a long-distance phone call. This left me standing there wondering what to do next, since I have just been defeated by an inanimate object, again. Blue box 2 Dennis 0.

After only a couple failed attempts, Frank made an executive decision to put an end to the torment and decided to take me to the captain's office to use the private landline phone. He did not mention anything about asking for permission in using the office phone, he just assumed that it would be allowed. I thought to myself, how could this even be possible and does Frank truly have that much leverage in this prison? I will believe it when I see it!

But first, Frank wanted to give me the grand tour of the courtyard. *Hell*, I thought I was in lockdown mode with limited access outside of my cell, but it appears Frank is my personal "Get out of jail free card,"[19] and all accomplished while I'm still in civilian clothing. It wasn't like a typical courtyard one would expect to see in a USA prison, it didn't have any weightlifting equipment, basketball court, or exercise area. All that stuff was on the bad, or what I would refer to as the unruly side of the prison, which could not be accessed by inmates from this side of the prison. This courtyard may have been lacking in one way, but the amenities it did have made it a much more advantageous place to be, especially without worry about dealing with unruly rough convicts.

The first structure Frank and I approached twenty feet away from the phone was a little store owned and operated by some inmates. The 10'×10' wooden shack was well supplied with a wide variety of food items, cold drinks, candy, chips, cookies, basic necessities and toiletries. This establishment resembled a 7-Eleven by having every square inch of space filled with products, included with a non-English speaking clerk behind the counter. Nevertheless, this small store had something a 7-Eleven did not, a working kitchen in the back that prepared made to order meals. My reaction in seeing this store in a Mexican prison should have given me more amazement, although after being in Emilio's café exposed to all their amenities, and watching other inmates cooking in a makeshift kitchen outside their cell, I'm beginning to think this is SOP on this side of the prison.

Across from the store was a large covered seating area that had a big screen TV mounted on the back wall, unfortunately, there were no subtitles at the bottom of the screen. This area was also used for family visitation, which explained why I was seeing children roaming around the courtyard among convicts completely void of guards, I shit you not!

---

[19] Monopoly game.

Frank continued his tour by walking around the corner of the store to the left, where two more shacks stood both offering made to order meals. The first shack was the larger of the two about 10'×16' and looked well organized, clean and a really nice kitchen set up. The crude smaller shack to the right was only 6'×8' and appeared limited on its functionality.

To the right, slightly behind the smaller shack was a large open area surrounded by a knee-high cinderblock wall, full of what appeared to be a hodgepodge of construction and maintenance materials with no organization in a messy area which did not seem to have any importance in the daily operations of the prison. Frank didn't point out this area, I just made an observation as we walked past it.

Next, he showed me a 20'×20' open-air woodshop to the right of the maintenance area that was surrounded by a tall chain-link fence containing a variety of hand tools, few power tools and a table saw. The back fence of the woodshop held an assortment of artwork made of wood hanging on it that looked cheap and tacky.

Our last stop on tour was a connection of buildings around the corner to the left next to the woodshop consisting of a church, prison kitchen, and bakery. Out of the three, the bakery is the only one I will be visiting during my extended vacation here in prison; for I have absolutely no interest venturing into the odorous kitchen and "I avoid church religiously."[20]

All I could say to myself is that this prison has more places to eat than the small town I live in back home, and when I receive some greenback from Brenda, I surely will not go hungry within these concrete walls.

Frank and I started to retrace our steps heading back toward my cellblock, but he stopped to face the visitor's area and conveyed an intense urgency to say to me, "Because of the extremely relaxed living conditions on this side of the prison and other perks it had to offer, convicts from other prisons across the country try very hard to get transferred here."

---

[20] *Mash*, TV show.

DIZNEY LAND by Way of Military Escort

Then with elevated excitement, he proceeded to explain in full detail a list of why our side of the prison was so unique and special. Some of the information has already been revealed earlier in this story, but it needs to be recapped to help justify Frank's enthusiasm, though these ten commandments are based on his testimony, which may not be 100 percent factual.

I. It was a unique prison in Mexico that allowed their prisoners to come and go freely from their cells twelve hours a day.
II. Visitation was from 10:00 a.m. to 4:00 p.m., seven days a week and visitors can stay in the courtyard with inmates for the entire duration, which was quite unique and unheard of in other prisons across the country. Six hours of visitation would explain why there were coolers with picnic-style lunches at some of the inmate's tables resembling a relaxed atmosphere in a theme pack picnic area.
III. Only prisoners willing to change their behavior and eliminate the lifestyle of a gangbanger could transfer from the bad side of the prison.
IV. This side of the prison was fenced off from the dangerous side, safe, friendly, and there was a good rapport between the guards and prisoners.
V. Access to a TV twelve hours a day.
VI. You can buy items from the store or order it if they fail to carry what you need.
VII. Farmers make routine trips to the prison, where you are allowed to buy fresh produce they sell near the visitor's area.
VIII. You can buy a variety of pastries from the bakery shop or have special orders made.
IX. Plenty of places to buy a made-to-order meal.
X. My own observation from noticing certain people at the visitor's area with a gender containing the two X chromosomes, also known as eye candy (women).

With elevated enthusiasm, Moses (Frank) said unto me before we left the courtyard, "This place is a joke, and everybody calls it Disney Land!"

His powerful statement became deeply etched in my mind! Maybe this place won't be so bad if people are comparing it to Disney Land, where all I must do in surviving behind these castle walls is to sit back, hold on and enjoy this terrifying ride!

Now that Frank's grand tour of the operational perks within this fortress was complete, he escorted me back through the cellblock to the door that led to the offices. The metal door had a bolting latch that was not locked, confirming the lackadaisical security on this side of the prison. With an authoritative tone, Frank spoke a few words to the guard handling the door, and without hesitation, the compliant guard let us through.

The 12'×25' corridor had three offices, two on the right and a smaller one on the left, with a narrow-recessed area containing three heavy gauge wire windows across the middle of an outside wall. This area was used for inmates who had visitors who did want to enter the prison. The far end of the corridor had a partition wall with the top half made of solid glass and a metal detector to the right, which wasn't handled by guards even though there was a lot of activity in this area.

Frank took me to the second office on the right and told me to stand next to the wall and wait while he went into the office. Standing there, I could see through the window of the partition wall and notice the influx of visitors in prison were coming from a large steel double-gated entrance that was on the left wall. Guest walked through the unmanned metal detector to meet their loved one (prisoner), then walk down the corridor past the offices and knock on the same door Frank and I came through. Followed by a guard sliding open a small metal viewing window to see who was at the door, then unlatched it and let them head toward the courtyard via my cellblock.

After a short wait outside the captain's office, Frank opened the door and told me to come inside. The office consisted of two small rooms, the first room only had enough space for two small office desks, the other was the captain's office with a single desk.

Once inside, Frank pointed to the phone on the desk closest to the door and said, "It's okay for you to use that phone." I asked what number needs to be dialed to get a connection out of the country, which quickly resulted in familiar Mexican mass confusion. There were five of us in this tiny office, so I could not avoid being the center of attention in another phone fiasco. As with the payphone, Frank didn't have a clue how to dial out of the country, so he asked the guards what numbers were needed. One guard didn't know, another one gave us a number that repeatedly failed, and the third tried to assist us in dialing the numbers after a few failed attempts from Frank and myself.

Realizing I was losing another phone battle and the score was about to be Alexander Gram Bell 3, Dennis 0, the thought came to me that maybe all the anxiety has interfered with my ability to remember Brenda's correct phone number, and most likely have inverted a set of numbers. I informed Frank of my unsureness of Brenda's phone number, to which he replied, "Do you have it wrote down somewhere?" I told him it was on my cellphone that was confiscated at the processing office on my first night here. He said, "That's no problem, let's go get it." And away we went.

We traversed back through the cellblock, stopped at my cell to retrieve the receipt for the phone, then went through the courtyard area and came upon a tall chain-link fence with an entry gate which was to the right of the outside visitor's area. This area was restricted from prisoners, and even though the gate was unlocked, it did have an unarmed guard staffing it who opened it right after Frank spoke a few convincing words to him. We walked ten feet to a doorway heading into the processing office, and within another ten feet, I was standing in front of the same desk where my pillows were confiscated. After handing my receipt to the clerk, Frank proceeded to work his magic with a short explanation of our request, which allowed the retrieval of my phone with relative ease.

I turned on the phone to find there was plenty of power remaining on the battery, so I was able to retrieve Brenda's phone number and write it down on the business card Karla gave to me at the trial. My prehistoric flip phone is only used for the occasional phone call as I adamantly refuse to answer it unless I know who is calling and sometimes not even then. I can go for days without touching the phone, having much better things to occupy my time than gluing my eyes to a little screen all day long; unlike the zombies who have their idiot (smart) phones surgically implanted to their hands compulsively staring at tiny pixels while scrolling their life away. What is so damn important? Excuse the rant, but my life-changing experience in Mexico has deeply altered my way of thinking and has elevated the extreme discomfort of how I already view this *insane* world.

When I finished confirming Brenda's phone number, I handed the phone back to the clerk and thanked her. Frank and I headed back to the captain's office to try our luck at defeating my phone nemesis. Once inside the office, Frank wasted little time enlisting the help of the guard who knew how to get a phone connection outside of the country, then proceeded to make the phone call as the guard relayed the set of numbers to him, and within ten seconds of placing the call, we were able to score one point for team Dennis. The arduous task of getting in touch with Brenda and finally hearing her sweet voice say hello, instantly relieved my anxiety and filled my heart with joy, which amplified my emotions making it difficult to conceal my excitement over the phone in a small room full of strangers.

Brenda sounded completely surprised to hear from me and asked with a concerned tone, "Are you okay?" Then she inquired on how I was able to call her. I told her I was okay and using a phone in the captain's office, which led to her exuberant reply, "*What?*" followed by questioning me for more details, but I interrupted her.

"I can't talk for very long." Because I felt extremely fortunate to be using the office phone at all and did not want to overstep my boundaries by yakking too long, I kept our conversation direct and short.

During the middle of our talk Frank spoke up informing me that Brenda would be able to visit me today if she wanted, which totally took me by surprise raising my excitement level to a tearful moment, and if I weren't in a room surrounded by strange men with peering eyes, I think I would have started sobbing like a big baby right then and there!

DIZNEY LAND by Way of Military Escort

Brenda was just as surprised as I was after hearing Franks wonderful news, and after telling her what items I needed such as clothing, food, toiletries, and money, she informed me that she had already gone to the store and was in the process of getting the items to the prison, via the rental car she rented for the week. Come to find out that retrieving the truck from the jails impound lot anytime soon was not going to be "no problem," as promised by office personal at the jailhouse, and sounded as if a bunch of legal documentation was needed to get possession of my truck; which ended up being a total nightmare from hell and still infuriates me to this day!

As our phone conversation drew near its end, Frank had me relay pertinent information to Brenda that she would not be allowed to enter the prison area which housed the prisoners and could only see me at the visiting area where the three wired windows were located across the corridor from the captains' office. Also, to give the bag of items, she brought for me to a guard for inspection who would see that I received the items in due time.

After Brenda and I voiced our love for each other and said our goodbyes, I hung up the phone and gave the guard who assisted us in the phone call an extra thanks of mucho gracias (much gratitude). Frank and I left the office and stood in the corridor for a while discussing what had just transpired, and Frank reiterated on what I should do and where to go when Brenda arrives. I was truly impressed by Frank's smooth ability to converse with the guards that assisted in our unshackled mobility throughout the prison, as well as his overwhelming eagerness to help in my time of need. My extreme gratitude toward Frank was overpowering, so much so that deep within my heart, I felt passionate about doing something special for him. I knew it would be totally unacceptable to only say, "thank you" to Frank for all he has done for me!

With that in mind, I expressed a sincerity, which I rarely reveal to others, to Frank and said, "I really appreciate all your help! What do you need or want, as I can have Brenda get it for you, no problem." Frank insisted he did not need anything and was just happy to help a fellow American. His words fell on deaf ears. I instantly rejected his polite response by putting my hand on the big man's shoulder and insistently said, "I really want to help, what do you *need?*" He reluctantly thought about it for a short moment and said, "If it's not too much of a problem, a multi-use radio would be nice to have." I instantly responded, "You got it, no problem!"

It was truly incredible! This large intimidating rough-looking convict was so humble and appreciative as if I were doing him a huge favor when, in reality, he was the one who supplied an unmeasurable service for me. In my emotional state of mind, acquiring a radio for Frank felt like a minuscule favor, for I was more than willing and able to accommodate his wish, which honestly felt rewarding to help a fellow inmate. An excellent example of inmates working in tandem for a beneficial outcome for both involved, just like with Raúl and myself.

Upon the completion of our emotional chat, Frank escorted me back to my cell. He told me that when Brenda arrives with the radio to have her put his name on the package, so a guard will know who it's for. He went on to say he must get written permission from the captain, allowing him to have the radio in prison and was going to take care of that right away. As a cellmate unlocked the cell door to let me in, I gratefully thanked Frank for all the help and firmly shook his hand. Once again, he asked me if I needed anything else and said he would come by later to check up on me. I said, "No thanks," then thanked him once more as he walked away.

Once back inside my cage, I walked over to the chest cooler, grabbed my orange drink, then went to the only place I felt comfortable enough to hang out, my personal cocoon the milkcrate. Before monotony had a chance to take hold, Frank had returned and oddly struck up a conversation consisting of trivial small talk. Soon after, the real reason for his arrival had become apparent as the big man's demeanor transformed into a somber mode while cautiously asking, "Would it be okay to get a TV instead of a radio?" He went on to explain the reason for the upgraded request though I was not concerned about the reason, as he said something about already having a small radio and it would be nice to have a TV. Television is a much larger request than a radio, but without hesitation, I quickly replied, "You got it Frank, no problem!" He was very appreciative and started going into detail about the type of TV he would like to have, nothing too big or fancy, just a plain flat-screen TV.

Frank already had the permission slip allowing him to receive a radio, so he had to make a trip back to the captain's office and get it revised, which most likely would be cross off "radio" and write in "TV" then have the captain sign off on it. If memory serves me right, I think this was the only time Frank did not ask if I needed anything just before walking away. It seemed as if our roles were instantly reversed, for he adamantly thanked me instead of the other way around.

It must have been getting close to lunchtime as the café has a steady stream of customers showing up at their cell door placing orders. Their operational function was impressive and was operated more smoothly than some of the fast-food joints I have visited in the states, especially their ability to give customers the *correct* change without the help of a computer screen.

Each cellmate shared in the responsibilities of the café's operations and daily chores. When a customer would place an order, one of the men would write it down on a napkin, walk it back to their outdoor kitchen and give it to Pablo, who did most of the cooking. He would hang the napkin up on one of the clothespins that were mounted on the wall in front of his work area, and when he finished preparing the order he placed the corresponding napkin with the meal, so there would be no confusion of which order was being sent out to the customer.

Some of the cafés lunch menus consisted of made to order hamburgers, hand-cut french-fries and frozen precut fries, hotdogs, instant cup-o-soup and a few Mexican dishes, though the Mexican meals the café served were few and far between. The café also had the option for customers to have a tab and pay their bill at the end of the week which consisted of customers names along with the tally wrote down on a small piece of cardboard the size of a playing card, which looked to be cut out from a cereal box. One thing I can say about the cafés cellmates is they were skillfully efficient and frugal, especially with items that typically get thrown in the trash and can be utilized for its unintended purpose. For instance, the cereal boxes, two-liter soda bottles used for their water sales, gallon milk jugs cut into makeshift dustpans, pull-top soup can lids for using as a functional cutting tool and the list goes on. They even went far as cutting the paper napkins in half to reduce their cost.

The café also had a unique attribute during mealtime by offering a delivery service of their meals to inmates who were in lockdown and did not have the luxury of getting all dolled up to go out to eat. Each man from the café alternated who was to be the delivery person (runner) each day. The runner would receive tips from their customers, so it was only fair to give each cellmate an opportunity to make extra money throughout the week. Pablo did the cooking, so he was never a runner, neither was John as he was a newbie and did not share in the café's earnings. The runner was responsible for taking orders, receiving money, and delivering food, cigarettes, water, and coffee etc. to those inmates stuck in lockdown.

When an inmate wanted to place an order, he would yell out, "*Emilio!*" Which was the owner's name of the café. When the runner heard the shout out and had a free moment, he would track down the appropriate cell and take the customer's order. This delivery service appeared to work out well for the café and most likely increased their profit margin. Not to mention the enormous benefit it gave the cooped-up inmate; for instance, visual stimulation, personal interaction with others and the joy of avoiding the less than desirable prison food. All three factors of which I can personally and genuinely relate to.

While sitting there on my milkcrate captivated with the visual stimulation, David walked past me, heading toward the door with a plate that had a cheeseburger and hand-cut french-fries on it. By now, witnessing a meal leaving our cell was SOP (standard operational procedure) and did not cause my eyebrows to rise, although the recipient of this made to order meal sure as hell did! One thing I noticed that was not SOP is the plate under the food was not made of Styrofoam and was being served on a real plate. I thought to myself, why was this kitchenware leaving our cell just for a customer, then I turned my head to follow the plates destination. Just like at breakfast time, I tried not to make eye contact with the café's customers and kept my line of sight at a lower altitude, however when the plate was

DIZNEY LAND by Way of Military Escort

handed to a "unique" customer, my eyebrows began to raise as I elevated my gaze. Standing there at our cell door was a pair of shiny red high heel shoes filled with smooth legs accompanied by a short dress, all held together by a pretty woman with long black hair. *Hell yes*, I'm still in a Mexican prison and this is clearly not a delusional daydream; you can't make this shit up!

The prison must have been keeping her hidden somewhere in a back office because she could have caused complete chaos at a blind man's convention. I have been yearning for some visual stimulation but admiring a Mexican Cinderella in prison had gone too far and may have overstimulated me. I wonder why the cellmates did not ask the princess if her order was for dine-in or carry out; hell, we did have a table and chair for one patron to sit in the outside kitchen area.

As the disrupter of a man's thought process walked away with her meal, I slowly scanned the room to see what kind of reaction the cellmates had from our exquisite visitor. To my surprise, there was no ogling, or sexual banter, almost as if the woman was one of the cellmate's sister, except for Adrian! I have no idea what few words were spoken from him, but the deviant stare on his face told the whole story.

Adrian was the youngest of the group, not quite thirty years old, five feet, ten inches tall, average weight, slender, prison-style haircut, spoke not a word of English excluding American profanity, jokester and displayed more amusing energy than the other men. I could tell by his body language his inner animal instinct has not yet been tamed by society's beliefs and rituals, and if that woman could have read his mind, she probably would have never stopped slapping his face as well as mine.

Due to the café's lunch rush slowing down to a trickle, I took advantage of the break in the action to ask David if I could have a cheeseburger and once again made the big mistake of offering to pay for it later. I wouldn't say he came unglued, but he sure was overzealous and insistent that I need not pay for the cheeseburger, then proceeded to rant in broken English trying his damnedest to convince me once more, "What is ours, is yours and if I need anything just ask, no problem, *no reeeally!*"

As you can tell by now, every one of David's sentences ended with either "no problem" or "no really." After politely getting scolded by David, he started to walk toward the kitchen, then stopped, turned around and just like at the "Golden Arches" (McDonald's) asked, "Do you want fries with that?"

I responded in an appreciative manner, "Yes, thanks so much!" Also, "please no mustard, or mayonnaise on the burger, thanks."

David said, "No problem," then went into the kitchen and began making my very first made to order Mexican prison meal. I was still a little uncomfortable excepting the fact they were treating me with such remarkable kindness and respect, even though they barely knew me.

To some, a cheeseburger and fries may appear to be just a meal and nothing more, however on the first day, while confined in the shithole cell, I had fears that my survival in a Mexican prison would be based on food consumption. Now here I am, having a meal prepared by a cellmate in an outdoor kitchen, soon to be eating my first real meal in five days of an American dish with hand-cut french-fries and a good chance of a candy bar for dessert, with great anticipation of a full stomach, how *cool* is that? By looking at my cellmates, it is apparent they haven't missed a meal in a long time, so I probably will not go to bed hungry anymore and most likely increase my TP usage, but not for the creation of little number ones and twos for Sudoku. So a meal is not just a meal; for me, it interprets into not only improving my basic survival but to a thriving one, and from now on I will be shitting in high cotton. All I can say is this day keeps getting progressively better by the hour!

While David was working his culinary magic for this Missouri convict, I decided to put an end at drinking that over-sweetened orange flavor drink I have been reluctantly sipping on all morning long and get a much-needed glass of water. By now, everyone had disappeared into their cocoons, or kitchen leaving me all alone, so I made my way toward the chest cooler where they stored the cold water and grabbed a large Styrofoam cup from the shelving above the coffee maker. Reorganizing water was one of the café's moneymakers, I searched for a water jug that had already been opened and was trying to expedite this process so as to avoid the "no problem" ritual between David and myself, or worse yet, trying to explain my activities to a cellmate who did not speak English inadvertently creating an uncomfortable setting all over a drink of water.

After filling the cup half full of water, I sat back down and waited in anticipation for the arrival of my lunch, which wasn't long after when David exited the kitchen with my feast on a real plate. I'm not going to say it was the best cheeseburger I ever had, but it damn sure was the best meal I have eaten in a week, including the last couple of meals at our condo's restaurant. Not to mention the restaurant we ate at in some small town in Mexico during our travels, where the cheeseburger I ordered was so bad and not made for human consumption, that I could not continue eating it after taking one bite. As a bonus kick in the groin, I miss-calculated the conversion rate of the peso and tipped the waiter way too much money.

It's a shame I had to visit Emilio's prison café in order to get a decent meal here in Mexico, though it lacked ambiance, seaside view, and the freedom to go home after finishing your meal. It was disheartening upon finishing my delicious meal recognizing the only thing that awaited me now was mind-numbing boredom sitting on an uncomfortable Mexican lounge chair, but at least I did so with a good meal in my belly and a little more time killed off the clock, "So I got that going for me!"[21]

At about two in the afternoon, I was sipping on some water when a guard came to our door and called out my name followed by a few words in Spanish, then in an elevated tone, John said, "Dennis, your wife is here!" *Cool,* what an awesome surprise! Though I didn't bother to tell them I wasn't married, avoiding a long drawn out explanation why we weren't married. I instantly stood up and headed toward the door to leave, but suddenly halted by John's statement that I needed to wear a prison uniform to where I was headed.

Then David spoke up, "Here you can wear my shirt." I inquired about wearing prison pants too. John said with an impatient tone, "Don't worry about it, just go!" So I hurriedly put on David's shirt

---

[21] *Caddy Shack* movie.

and headed out the door, though felt as if I were a small child wearing his father's clothing since David's large shirt was at least three sizes too big, which swallowed me up making me look ridicules.

I quickly walked across the hall to Raúl's cell and asked if he could go with me to act as my translator and assist me through the prison. Raúl was elated to help and eager to once again escape from his boredom chamber. This time the guard expedited Raúl's request of releasing him from the cell with less friction between them, unlike their previous encounter earlier this morning. I assume the guard realized I truly required a translator, especially if this white man were to be roaming the halls of a Mexican prison.

Raúl led me through the manned security door down the corridor to the visitor's area across from the captain's office, pointed to the three viewing windows and said, "That's where you will see her." I walked over to one of the three windows and waited for her arrival, but soon grew impatient as I knew from Frank's instructions this area only allowed five minutes of visitation, so I became a little concerned after standing there for a while without having a visitor.

The area only contained three windows, so it wasn't as if I were making an indecisive decision to "Monty Hall, from Let's Make a Deal, on which one to choose from. The windows were in an area that spanned only eight feet where all three could be viewed into from standing four feet away, so it was clear Brenda wasn't waiting for me behind window number 1, 2, or 3. I turned to look back at Raúl fifteen feet away, shrugged my shoulders and partially raised up my arms and hands, as to ask what's the *deal* and where is she?

Raúl's line of sight was in the direction of the processing area where Brenda would be entering through but failed to see her anywhere and questioned a guard of her whereabouts. Apparently, she was being delayed by a guard inspecting the bag of items she brought for me. Soon as the items were cleared for entry, Brenda was allowed to visit me at one of the caged windows, but which window would it be? Window #1 had a donkey pulling a cart full of manure, window #3 was a lifetime supply of tortillas, and the correct choice of window #2 is where I was able to view my fabulous prize, Brenda!

Seeing her standing there completely warmed my lonesome heart while feeling overcome with joy, knowing I now had a lifeline connection with someone from outside of these prison walls. Brenda was completely relieved to discover I was doing okay in prison and shared in our happiness to finally see each other. Since we were only allowed five minutes of visitation, we conducted the serious part of our conversation in a quick, efficient manner, then took care of the mushy intimacy stuff toward the end of our visitation.

Within seconds of our conversation, an inmate showed up at window number 3 and started talking loudly with his female visitor, so much so that we decided to move over to window number one so we could hear ourselves talk. The separation between the loud couple and us was only four feet, so we did not gain much at lowering the noise level; this area of the prison is busy with a lot of noisy activity. Luckily, the couple kept their conversation short and left the area within a minute, which helped lower the noise level giving Brenda an opportunity to whisper something to me without being overheard from a guard. She was unsure of what was allowed into the prison and concerned about some of the items she had given a guard to eventually give to me. One, in particular, was the money she hid in a soapbox with a bar of soap, so I needed to be careful when opening it, so the money doesn't fall out. It's surprising to see that Brenda was still in the smuggling business and outsmarting Mexican officials. I don't know how much money she hid in the soapbox, but her clever efforts were all for not, as the prison allows visitors to bring up to two hundred pesos ($11.00) a day to a prisoner.

We exchanged information pertaining to the items she brought and the items I wanted her to bring on her next visit, then verbally crossed off items she had already dropped off today. The list of items I had written down on a piece a paper could not be handed to her, due to the wire windows having ten inches of air space between the two screened panels; a difficult undertaking made apparent by many failed attempts of small pieces of paper trapped within the two panels. The list of items that I read to Brenda is still in my possession to this day. I found it amusing that toilet paper topped the list, followed by a towel, food, water, money, Zune and headphones, clothes, a deck of cards, toiletries, a water bottle, pillowcase, translation book, and a handkerchief. I found out later that having electrical devices in prison required written permission by the captain; also, decks of cards were not allowed, though that's not to say there weren't any cards in my cell! You may have questioned the twelfth item (pillowcase) on my list, even though pillows are not allowed, my plan was to stuff clothing inside the pillowcase to create my own pillow.

I was eager to inform Brenda about wanting to buy a TV for Frank, but before her look of total disbelief transformed into spoken words of, "A *what*, for *who*? Are you freaking crazy?" I quickly explained my justification for wanting her to purchase a TV for a prisoner. I enthusiastically told her of all the invaluable help Frank had provided during my time of need, and if not for him, our visitation would have never been possible. Also, that he was personally responsible for my exodus from the shithole cell, along with the amount of effort he put forth in securing our all-important phone call, was truly impressive. In my humble opinion, this remarkable man deserved a TV!

Somewhere in the middle of our speedy conversation, Brenda looked at me with a smile and an eagerness to inform me of some wonderful news. Family members were involved in our crisis and had acquired a real good lawyer from the United States who spoke English and Spanish, familiar with Mexican law, and was on his way to La Paz. This was an incredible communique instantly relieving the dread I have been agonizing over ever since my public defender failed to secure my bail. This lifted my spirits to hear the amazing support we were receiving from family members, and the fact of having a professional English-speaking lawyer defending me should be a huge game-changer, I hope!

It was time for Brenda and me to say our goodbyes when a guard showed up, spoke a few words in Spanish, pointed to his wristwatch, and walked away. We delayed his request a little longer before expressing our love for each other, then finally saying goodbye, as we were both forced to return to our strange worlds. As soon as Brenda turned and walked away, my heart instantly felt a deep-down sorrow, created by a fear that our recent encounter separated by a cage was going to become a routine. Regardless, all I can do is ride this emotional rollercoaster to the end and hope it does not completely derail my spirits along the way!

Raúl began to escort me back to my cell when I abruptly stopped and inquired about retrieving the items Brenda left for me. He said, "Oh yeah, let's go get them." I followed him around the corner of the partition wall through the unmanned metal detector to a caged wire window near the inspection area to the right of two large bared entry gates. These gates are the same that visitors pass through to enter the prison, and were manned by two guards, one on the inside of the prison and the other posted between the two gates with a shotgun strapped across his chest. From my vantage point, I can literally see traffic driving on the street that passes in front of the prison, revealing sweet freedom from this Micky Mouse house only one hundred feet away. *Remember*, knowledge is power, and now I have the advantage of knowing my cells' outdoor kitchen area is less than thirty-three yards away from the El Chapo freeway!

After receiving two bags of items from a guard, Raúl escorted me back to the cell where he received my extra thanks of gratitude, then he eagerly said, "If you need any more help come and get me." We exchanged a fist bump, I thanked him again, he walked over to his cell and had a guard unlocked his cell door that once again put an end to his short-lived freedom.

Once back in the cell, I took the bags of stuff and attempted to place the items in the milkcrate that held my blankets under Pablo's bed, only to realize there was not enough space in the crate for the extra items. So I grabbed one from a stack next to my boredom seat, placed the items inside then shoved the crate under Roseudo's bed.

John was curious regarding my visit with Brenda, enough so that he stopped reading his book, stood up to ask, "How did it go?"

I said with an elevated tone of excitement, "It was a nice visit with awesome news. A good lawyer was on his way from the States who spoke English and Spanish also is familiar with Mexican law."

John questioned me for more details of who, when, and what part of the States he is from etc. Unfortunately, that is all the information I knew and could not elaborate on his inquiry. Regardless, John noticed that Brenda's communique had lifted my spirits and appeared to be genuinely happy for me and said with a big smile, "This is good news!" This was coming from a man I just met this morning!

Our conversation was short, and as John sat back down, his eyes focused on his book, I took one step backward to sit on my milkcrate. It was ridiculous how the energy in the room went from a joyous excitement to a subdued feeling of solitude the instant I sat down. I honestly can't tolerate just sitting there doing nothing, and it didn't help that the activity in the cell was non-existent due to the lack of customers showing up at our door. All my time spent sitting there, consisted of watching the occasional passersby and receiving minuscule breaks from the boredom by the few customers showing up, sometimes requiring me to capture the attention of a cellmate to let them know someone was at the door.

This time of day must be the café's slow period for business activity, due to the cellmates spending most of the time hiding in their cocoons and did not seem to be concerned about manning the café. I almost felt obligated to be the café's hostess, for I was the only person customers could visually see when they came to our door; at least the hostess gig added a few seconds of visual stimulation into my day. I thought about making little toilet paper numbers, although the men might think I have gone completely insane and have me escorted to the psyche ward.

The boredom of sitting in my Mexican lounge chair for about an hour took control of my eyelids, forcing me to drift in and out of consciousness and even though the crate wasn't the most comfortable way of sleeping, the lack of sleep from the last four nights caught up with me and dozing off while sitting there came over me with relative ease.

While failing to reach the dream stage in my sporadic nap, Frank stopped by to inform me of his trip to the captain's office pertaining to the acquisition of his TV and was enthusiastically relaying the discussion he just had with the captain moments earlier. Because prison regulations forbid possession of a television, Frank had to incorporate deceit in acquiring a permission slip from the captain. He told the captain I wanted to purchase the television for the prison's clinic, to which the captain replied, "Why would he do that?"

Frank responded, "Because that's the kind of man he is!" He continued with some sort of bullshit story that I wanted to repay the prison with a charitable gesture, because of the exceptional treatment I have been receiving during my stay. Listening to Frank's cunning story gave me a grin from ear to ear, wondering what additional bold request we could get away with, as I'm sure they will continue!

Frank was very proud of his clever deception and anxious to receive an early birthday present. As Frank finalized our interaction and began to leave, he asked if I needed anything. I replied, "Yes, what do I need to do in getting Brenda inside the prison for visitation?"

Without hesitation, he responded with an energetic tone, "I will get right on it!"

I thanked him, and away he went. Frank was gone for a long time, making me think he had some difficulty with my request, which there was. Eventually he returned and explained there was a problem in getting permission for Brenda to enter the prison for visitation.

According to prison rules, people who come to visit prisoners inside the facility *must* be residents of Mexico for at least six months. *Damn*, that does not sound good! However, Frank is not an absent-minded politician; he actually gets shit done and did not give me a chance to dwell on this grim news, by quickly turning my frown upside down. Apparently, Mexican prison rules are flexible when Frank is involved, who told me not to worry about it and that he had already taken care of the situation by going to the captain and getting a signed handwritten permission slip allowing Brenda into the prison for visitation, and all that we had to do was go to the secretary's office to get a temporary visitors-pass for her. *How awesome is that?* What a great feeling of euphoria knowing my sweetie would soon be held in my arms!

I had to once again acquire a prison shirt obtained from John, who unlocked our door to set me free. Frank turned to the guard manning the entrance to the corridor, spoke a few words, showed him the permission slip, and once again with Franks commanding ability, we were able to enter the corridor without hindrance from the guard.

The 20'×20' secretary's office was adjacent to the captain's office containing four desks and one desk in a small inner office separated by a large plate-glass window. Frank sat me down in front of the desk of the same secretary who ordered lunch from the café earlier; by comparison, if she were Cinderella, the other secretaries looked to be the two stepsisters.

Frank explained my situation to the secretary. He handed her the permission slip signed by the captain, and a short disagreeable discussion ensued between them, which sounded like he was having difficulty convincing Cinderella that the story accompanying the permission slip wasn't a fairytale. I could see the doubt in her eyes as she stood up with permission slip in hand. She left the office abruptly apparently on her way to see the captain to confirm the legitimacy of Frank's odd request, obviously she was clueless of Frank's influential power in this prison. While she was out of the office, Frank told me not to worry and everything was okay, so I slid back into my chair and crossed my arms, chilling out in the extremely cold air-conditioned office. Upon returning, the secretary had Frank ask me pertinent information about the visitor in question, though all I remember giving her was Brenda's name; in my defense, this day has been a total sensory overload of information, whereas some small details are not etched into my memory.

In order to memorialize my experience, I started writing down notes within a few days upon my arrival in prison. Unfortunately, when I eventually made it back home to the States, a certain individual I knew had thrown my rough draft of forty pages into a fire! This utterly devastated me, bringing tears to my eyes, while fighting the strong urge to explode into a hateful rage. All induced by a chain of events beginning over a month before arriving into Mexico back in April. Though that is another story, I may or may not divulge it later as I have not yet decided whether to rip open another wound!

When all questions were answered and forms filled out, Frank told me Brenda's temporary pass would be ready for pick up tomorrow. We kindly thanked Cinderella and headed back into the corridor,

DIZNEY LAND by Way of Military Escort

where we stood and talked for a while, which was quickly becoming a routine. Once again, I found myself adamantly thanking Frank for all his help, and listening to his nonchalant reply, "No problem, glad I could help." His energy level slightly increased while informing me of the medical unit where his cell was located and wanted to show me around the area sometime later. After accepting his offer, he proceeded to escort me back to my cell, where we parted ways.

Now that I was back in the cage, it's time to stroll over to my comfort zone and continue secluded boredom amongst a crowded jail cell. Eventually, the monotony was interrupted more frequently by the activity from cellmates working the café; apparently, it was getting close to dinnertime due to the number of customers showing up placing orders. I decided to use this opportunity before the dinner rush kicked into full throttle and get myself something to eat and, by doing so, avoiding being in the cellmate's way during their busy time.

I retrieved the Ritz crackers, peanut butter, and some cookies for dessert from the bag of goodies Brenda brought me, grabbed my water and went into the cell's outdoor kitchen. The kitchen had a small plastic patio table with a chair and two five-gallon buckets placed around it, making the chair an easy choice on where to sit and to start spreading peanut butter on my crackers. This was my first lengthy venture into the kitchen area away from my comfort zone, so I was a little apprehensive and cautious intruding into Pablo's workspace. Pablo looked to be forty years old, six feet tall, average weight and build, spoke absolutely no English, low-keyed, mild-mannered, had a mustache and could play the part as a stereotypical Mexican character in a western movie.

Since he was the only person in the kitchen preparing food for the dinner rush, it helped ease my discomfort of being in somebody's way during the café's operational functions. Pablo started using an area of the tabletop for his prep work due to counter space being minimal; therefore, I gathered my food items and moved them closer to me in a more compact arrangement. Pablo instantly waved his hand back and forth while saying, "No, no," as if to say I wasn't in his way. Pablo was just as illiterate as I in speaking a foreign language, but I received his intent with perfect clarity and hoped to think he appreciated my gesture to keep clear of what little workspace he had.

While sitting there eating a poor man's meal and watching Pablo gathering items for his prep work, I noticed he retrieved a cutting board from underneath the counter and thought to myself, don't you need a knife to justify having a cutting board? Oh yeah, I forgot this is a Mexican prison! He then pulls out a *meat cleaver* and a fillet knife from his stash of kitchen utensils; honestly, how can anyone be expected to operate a prison kitchen without a *deadly weapon*? And yet the guards confiscated my pillows, which pains me trying to find any logic in this madness! One comforting note, the point on the fillet knife, was filed down, but I still think sharp knives might be a little more dangerous and deadly than my unacceptable, threatening pillows.

After eating the lackluster meal, I headed back to my comfort zone, the crate, and watched the men work the café's dinner operations. I noticed an increase in the café's activity and longer in duration than during a lunch rush; also, the cellmates seemed to be more involved with the evening operations. The number of customers showing up at our cell door was quite impressive, so much so, there were a few times when patrons had to patiently wait in line for service. It was still strange to witness that half of the café's customers were friendly prison guards, who walk up to our cell door, pull out their wallets and buy made to order meals cooked by inmates in prison. I get the strong impression the guards never had to say, "I would like my meal with no spit, please."

It only makes sense that the café is busier now because of the looming event of lockdown when everybody is preparing for their twelve hours of limited or no access to water, cigarettes, or food. I personally was looking forward to the seven o'clock lockdown, so there wouldn't be any more customers at our door making for a quiet evening, going to bed early to get some much-needed sleep on the mat Frank gave me. Just knowing a hard-naked concrete floor would not be my only companion tonight, gave hope of a more pleasurable slumber, but my fantasy of going to bed early with something soft under my weary body tonight maybe a little premature.

As seven o'clock drew near, the café's customers came to a halt followed by a guard coming to our cell door, having us remove Emilio's lock, then replaced it with a prison lock. *Yeah*, it's quitting time for Emilio's restaurant, hang up the "closed" sign, shut down the kitchen and turn off the hotplates, it's time to count today's take ($).

With the prison in lockdown, one would think the energy level in our cell would die down. *Wrong*, while sitting there waiting to see what activities took place in this cell after lockdown, a prisoner from across the cellblock yells out, "*Emilio!*" I thought to myself, is that not the same name as this establishment's owner? I listened for a loud verbal response from a man named Emilio or from within our cell yet heard nothing, leaving me puzzled on why the shout out was ignored. Moments later, an unescorted prisoner shows up at our door, *wait a minute*, I thought we were in complete lockdown. I looked up to focus my attention on the big man's face to realize it was Jose, one of my cellmates; what the hell is he doing out of his *cage*?

Jose spoke a few words to David, who then wrote down a food order on a napkin. *What?* Did someone take down the "closed" sign? I sure wish I had a transcript with subtitles to understand what the hell is going on around here! Come to find out, *yes*, the prison is in lockdown, and the only person other than the guards roaming the prison halls is Jose. Explaining this Mexican madness of Jose's reign of freedom amongst his fellow caged inmates is a bit bizarre. The café's runner (delivery person) for tonight just happens to be Jose, and when an inmate yells out "Emilio," it's the equivalent of someone calling Emilio's restaurant by phone placing an order for delivery, and the customers' address is tracked down by the shout out.

This barely explains anything at all, welcome to my world. There are many questions and few answers, though I do know there is no place for me to sleep while the café is still operational. I didn't ask anyone how, or why this late-night delivery service was possible, or even acceptable, all I could do was sit back, observe and speculate. There must have been some internal backscratching going on, or someone in this cell has connections with some very influential people to allow a convict free mobility throughout the cellblocks during the lockdown. If one were to think about it, the prison is taking a massive leap of faith as the convict could be delivering a wide variety of items to the men in lockdown other than food products.

Shout-outs of Emilio's name continued for two hours after lockdown and kept Jose busier than a one-legged man in an ass-kicking contest, but he was not the only person ringing the cash register, as a few of the guards continued purchasing items during the café's late-night service. When nine o'clock finally rolled around, a guard unlocked our door to let Jose back into the cell, officially ending his workday. I would have liked to say the café was officially closed for the evening; unfortunately, the guards kept showing up asking for items that didn't require cooking, such as cigarettes, coffee, and pastries delaying my date with a sleeping mat by an additional hour. I was forced to continue what I have been doing for the last one hundred eighty minutes, sitting here daydreaming about when I will be able to dream.

Finally, ten o'clock arrived, time for lights out and some needed shuteye. After completing my bathroom ritual, I retrieved my sleeping mat from underneath Pablo's bed, unfolded it to begin calculating the optimum placement for the mat in the room. My options were limited to only two choices: (1) Place the mat in front of the cell door. (2) Place it parallel with John's sleeping mat that would literally be close enough for us to share the same blanket. I sleep in my birthday suit, making that sleeping arrangement awkward for at least one of us; I think I will choose option number one!

While I was preparing for bed, David went over to the cell door with some clothespins in his hand and hung up a towel spanning a quarter of the lower half of the door. Not a word was spoken between us, so I don't know if he hung it up for my privacy from the cellblock or to shield me from the light coming through the door; either way, it had a positive outcome for both reasons.

As I laid down, some of the cellmates went into the kitchen where they had control of the lights allowing them to stay up as late as they wanted, which they did for a while smoking and joking, but not as long or loud as the rest of the cellblocks inmates. The noise and smoke made it difficult for me to fall asleep, also missing that mischievous pillow of mine didn't help, also let's not forget about the occasional cockroach's scampering by my face all night long.

Since the prison is an open-air facility, it created a draft through the doorway where I slept, making an efficient transport system for cigarette smoke, so I draped a handkerchief over my face to filter out some of the smoke and helped block the light coming from the corridor. I also laid on the right side of my body, placing my good ear against the mat drowning out some of the noise, by doing so, and the added fact I was completely exhausted helped me get some sleep throughout the night.

As this day came to an end, I can truly say it brought a huge wealth of information, moments of sensory overload that were welcomed interruptions from the mind-numbing boredom and the best part of all, I will not be sleeping in that retched smelling shithole cell on a cold hard concrete floor tonight! All made possible by the Butterfly Effect, which was dramatically altered by the actions of one thoughtful man, Frank!

Day 15 in Country

Third day in prison

Wednesday morning arrived way too early again by guards walking past our cell who didn't utilize their quiet time voices, though it didn't help that my head was only twelve inches from the door close to the source of the chatter. Repositioning my body to face the opposite direction would result in listening to the constant noise from the ill-efficient chest cooler, as well as the chance of getting my face burned by the overheated compressor, or freeze an appendage on the exposed copper-line that seemed to always have a thick layer of ice growing on it. Luckily, I was able to sleep much better than the two previous nights by sleeping on the comfortable mat avoiding the bare concrete floor, thanks to Frank.

Because my mat was partially blocking the cell's door, I knew there was no way lazing around a little longer in bed was a pliable option, unlike my mutated cellmates who stayed in their comfortable cocoons long as possible. John was an exception since the placement of his sleeping mat blocked the rooms' walking path, so we were the first out of bed, allowing for the onslaught of guards ordering their morning coffee. I folded my blankets and placed them back in the milk crate under Pablo's bed along with the mat, then after making a bathroom visit, ventured to my milk crate, contemplating on what to do next.

With the benefit of having cash burning a hole in my pocket, thanks to Brenda, I stood up and paid Emilio for a pastry, reluctantly grabbed my orange drink from the chest cooler and went into the kitchen, found a banana in the fridge and sat down in the patio to eat breakfast. For clarification, the kitchen and patio are a single entity, though doesn't it sound much better to say "patio" while in prison? I ate slowly as possible to prolong the enjoyment of my morning solitude in the outdoor air, producing a tranquil feeling of a cage-free animal.

While sitting at the table milking my breakfast, I overheard a guard calling out the names of my cellmates. It took a moment to realize it was morning roll call before I quickly stood up and walked over to the blanket hanging up in the doorway separating the patio from the cell. I poked my head through the curtain to announce my presence when the guard called out my name, but by the time I was able to get a visual of the guard, he had already walked away without calling my name. I hurriedly walked a few steps into the room looking toward the cell door with an inquisitive stare, when John waved his hand back and forth and said, "Don't worry about it." So that's what I did, by returning to the tranquility of the patio to finish my breakfast.

I thought about what had just transpired, for it's a bit of a conundrum. The guards had yet to call out my name during roll call for three mornings in a row, so if my name fails to appear on the prison's roll call list for this cell, where do they think I'm residing the shithole cell? And if so, where do they think I have gone upon discovery of my absence? If I'm nowhere, where should I be, if not here?

The prison's lack of ability to keep track of their convicts made me revisit the thought of escaping from this Micky Mouse prison. Would it not be easier escaping from here when the guards don't know I even exist or, if they did, they didn't know where I was.

My thought process was inspired by this outside patio area. I looked up to the only thing separating me from freedom, some rusty old rebar welded together in an eight-inch square pattern, which has not been securely maintained in a very long time. There are sections of the rebar that are no longer secured to the cinder block wall and is sagging down low enough to grab it by standing on a bucket. It definitely would not require much effort in taking flight by departing this coop vertically, plus the road right outside the prison wall is less than one hundred feet away from where I'm sitting and could be reached by traversing the rooftops of the prison confirmed by Google Earth.

I sat there enjoying the fresh cool morning air for long as possible contemplating an escape plan when Pablo and some cellmates began to wander in to start preparing their breakfast. The kitchen table only had three places to sit, yet there were seven more individuals in this cell, so I figured it was time to vacate the area and return to my designated seating area.

Not long after sitting on the crate, a guard showed up at our cell door and called out my name, then motioned for me to follow him. *Oh no*, they found me! Now my powers of invisibility had faded away dramatically, altering my plans of an escape. I thought I was in trouble at first, but John informed me when a new prisoner arrives here, they are stood in front of a formation of guards during a shift change to familiarize themselves with the new arrivals, which is carried out for each of the three shift changes.

Soon as John told me no uniform was needed, I left the cell where the guard led me and two other prisoners, one female and one male through the security door into the corridor where fifty guards were standing in formation and had us stand there facing them. A guard in charge of the shift change had each of us step forward as he called out our names while proceeding to read from the clipboard he held in his hand and what was said I haven't a clue.

I was extremely uncomfortable standing on display in front of fifty Mexican prison guards eyeballing me from head to toe. One thing was for certain, this was not intended to be a friendly meet and greet between the convicts and their arch-rivals, and there was no way in hell I was going to create an awkward moment ten times worse by making any eye contact with the male and female guards. Fortunately, my discomfort was short-lived by the guard, who didn't keep us standing there for very long. To be a US citizen put on exhibit in a Mexican prison has to be one of the strangest encounters I will never forget, which is odd to say because I have a difficult time remembering anything at all about going, or even when I went to the next two-shift change formations.

Within moments of being back in my cell, the herd of guards from the shift change migrated in front of our cell door and began ordering coffee, with a few of them grazing on a delicious pastry, which has become my personal favorite while being here in prison, minus the coffee and being corralled. Unlike Paul, my brother who prefers his coffee like his women, black and bitter. Since I was sitting only five feet away from our overcrowded cell door, it felt like being back on display from the number of guards standing there waiting to be served, making me feel a little uneasy from all their staring eyes. I had a powerful urge to stand up and walk away, but the logical side of my brain forced my derriere to stay glued to the seat. I deduced if the guards visually notice me in the café that supplies them with daily subsistence and their morning caffeine addiction, maybe it would help secure good relationships with the guards just by association with the café.

With an influx of customers, the café was overrun with activity involving most everyone in the cell. Emilio was working behind the chest cooler preparing coffee, tea, bowls of frosted flakes, operating the microwave and handling the cash box, though the cash was also managed by everyone in the cell when Emilio was elsewhere. Trust among the cellmates wasn't an issue, and there were times I accepted money from customers and put it in the cash box, which wasn't under lock and key, only an open face box with dividers. The more valuable items like cartons of cigarettes and stick matches were locked in a wooded box by a key hung around Emilio's neck, where at any given moment, there were only two packs of cigs out of the safe placed above the cash box with some matches. For some desperate inmates' money would be totally worthless to them if not for cigarettes.

David was taking orders and money at the door, plus handing the customers their items. Roseudo was the café's runner for the day. Adrian was relaying orders back to Pablo in the kitchen and on his return trip, delivering food to the customers at the door or handing them off to David. The big man, Jose, was in the kitchen doing whatever? John was reading a book and all I did was sit there and be unproductive.

When all the guards had been served and left the area to start their workday (poor bastards), the café slowed to a trickle, which was a prelude to my unwelcomed friend Mr. Boredom who put an end to all my visual stimulation. With nothing better to do while sitting there, I began to think about Frank, looking forward to his next visit as he always puts gaps between my boredom sessions by continuously benefiting from his presence in one way or another.

I would venture to say the café's slow time was between breakfast and lunch, based on the disappearance of the cellmates who digressed back into their cocoons or kitchen, except for John, who was a floor dweller as I and did not have the luxury of sleeping in a real bed. So he and I were left alone to man the café, but all I could do was grab his attention when a customer showed up at the door.

It was well over an hour of sitting there doing absolutely nothing, again. Frank showed up inquiring about how my sleep was in reference to the sleeping mat he gave me yesterday. I enthusiastically replied, "Much better!" And thanked him again, then mentioned being a little uncomfortable without a pillow.

He asked in an elevated tone, "*What*, you don't have a pillow?"

"No, the guards took it when I arrived here." He was slightly disgusted while looking at me; with disbelief, the prison would not allow me to have a pillow. Frank also asked if I received the permission slip for Brenda's visitation. His aggravation level rose a little more when I told him no. He then said, "I'll take care of it!" And away, he went.

I was expecting Frank to return a short time later with something in his hand, *come on*, it's Frank we're talking about! Has he ever come back to me empty-handed? *Well*, this time I was wrong. He returned with an item in *both* hands, a permission slip in one hand and a pillow in the other. Yes! I said pillow.

I didn't bother asking how he made that possible, I just thanked him with as much gratitude as my jaw finished hitting the floor with great awe. The acquisition of a pillow may seem trivial to some; however, this Mexican prison cell of mine has a freaking *meat cleaver* and not a single fluffy pillow to be found. Some of the men in this cell have been incarcerated here for years. I have been here for three days, and yet I'm the only one with a pillow. Trying to justify this convoluted logic would be completely insane!

Frank truly has become the "I got connections, man!" He hung around my door for a while, asking many questions such as, how were the guys in the cell treating me? Am I okay, is there anything

DIZNEY LAND by Way of Military Escort

I need, and have I gone outside to the courtyard area by myself yet? My answers were as follows, yes, yes, no and not yet, because I have not been issued a uniform allowing me to leave the cell unescorted. My last reply instantly triggered Frank's aggravation once again with an elevated response, "*What*, the prison didn't issue you a uniform? I will take care of it!" And away, he went. Classic Frank!

While Frank was away, I grabbed the milkcrate that held my other blanket and put the pillow along with it, then sat back down and patiently waited for Frank's return. My brain function must have been operating a little slow while sitting on my folded blanket, which has been partially protecting me from the milkcrate creating waffle patterns on my derriere. Wait a minute, did I just put away a soft pillow? Once the exchange for more comfort was complete, I no longer craved melted butter and maple syrup.

When "The gringo that always delivers"[22] returned, he was clutching a brand-new pair of brown prison pants with reflective stripes down both legs. While handing me the pants, Frank said, "It will be tomorrow before I can get you a shirt." After thanking him, I informed him that I needed a small size. Frank wasn't the type of person who had long drawn out goodbyes, and when our conversations were complete, he always asked in a hurried manner as if it were an automatic response, "Do you need anything else?" (DYNA) just before promptly walking away.

I felt slightly awkward each time Frank asked if I needed anything and a little reserved asking him for something, for I rarely ask anyone for anything, so Frank's continuous gestures of kindness are unique and foreign to me, which has awakened my humility from its unconscious state.

While putting my unfashionable pants into the crate with the items Brenda gave me, David drew back the curtain to exit the seclusion of his cocoon, then descended from the upper bunk bed and asked, "What do you need?"

---

[22] *American Made*, movie.

At that moment, I didn't need anything, but my stomach disagreed and instantly forced my voice box to speak in a soft tone, "Could I have a cheeseburger and fries?"

David's typical "No problem" response was followed by what is becoming his standard spiel, "If you need anything, just ask and whatever you want, I can get it for you, *reeeally!*"

When David returned from the kitchen after asking Pablo to make the burger for me, we struck up a conversation consisting of him speaking and me listening. David went on to say it was hard for him translating English into Spanish when spoken fast, so he wanted me to speak slowly in order for him to translate each word correctly. He used to be employed at a business that catered to English speaking tourists and is where he learned to speak English. His vocabulary exposure was limited to terminologies in that specific industry, so while speaking to him, I tried to dumb it down with short, simple sentences containing little detail void of problematic words; which works for me as I'm not a master of the English language by no means!

With a sincere facial expression, David was determined to assure me the men in this cell were a good bunch of guys and adamant there were no drugs in the cell, then said, "You do not have to worry about being safe in here, *no reeeally!*" When he stated, "in here," I assumed he was referring to this safe side of the prison due to his story that followed.

When David first arrived in prison, a good friend of his suggested giving him five-thousand pesos to personally protect him from harm while in this dangerous and unruly prison. David is a very kind man and comes across as the type of person who would never be involved in a physical confrontation, or survive in a hostile environment, so the thought of having protection in prison in exchange for money must have sounded extremely appealing to him. After giving his friend the money and being exposed to a convict's life on the safe side of the prison, void of any aggression, or threatening behavior toward him, he soon realized his friend's disquieting story was a total fabrication just to swindle him out of his money.

David was very perturbed with his so-called good friend and held a deep-seated grudge, also no longer spoke to him by completely severing their supposed friendship. Regardless of David's rudimentary broken English of his story, I was still able to grasp the magnitude of his high displeasure, especially when I raised the question, "How could a good friend do that!"

David's only response was of pure disgust ending our conversation with, "Fucking Mexicans!"

David never raised his voice in anger or with intense hatred during the entire conversation, or when responding to my question, it was as if he were stating a common factual occurrence of getting screwed over by a fellow countryman. His bold response didn't appear to be racially motivated as he is from Spanish descent and lives in Mexico, also displays more tolerance in humanity than I.

As David ascended back into his bunk, my cheeseburger and fries were ready, so I paid Emilio and sat down in the patio to eat my meal in the comforts of a real chair. When I finished making an effort to gain some weight loss and washed the plate, I vacated the area allowing the men in the patio the option to sit on a chair instead of a bucket, which led me to the only pillow in the room to prepare for Mr. Boredom to arrive. Its arrival delayed as a guard soon showed up and called out my name, followed by a few words in Spanish.

Then in an excited tone, John relayed, "Your lawyer is here!" What a pleasant surprise! I did not have a clue as to which lawyer was here to see me, wishing it was the USA lawyer, thought it might be Irvin my first appointed lawyer, and hoped it wasn't Karla who assisted in my newly unwanted mailing address. Either way, I was thrilled to have any lawyer show up at the prison to see me. I instantly stood up, grabbed my prison pants and slipped them over my shorts in a hasty manner, then headed out the door in a heated rush.

In the eagerness to see a lawyer, I ignored the fact my pants were entirely too big, failing to stay up around my waist and if I released my grasp of the waistband I would eventually find myself walking with pants down around my ankles looking like "The Jerk."[23] So I folded the waistband inward, tucking it into my shorts' waistband to

---

[23] *The Jerk*, movie starring Steve Martin.

help prevent my pants from falling down, which did the trick for the time being.

I walked over to Raúl's door to see if he could escort me; of course, he was more than willing to assist me once again and eager to be released from his cage that was still in lockdown. Raúl spoke a few words to a different guard posted at the security door, who must have realized the importance of Raúl's request and released him without hesitation. One could ask, "Why didn't you ask John or David to escort you?" I don't know. My first thought was to enlist the help of Raúl and free him from that depressing mind-numbing cage of his. Maybe I didn't want to burden my cellmates, or interrupt them, besides John and David have not left this cell since I have been here and show no interest in doing so; also, neither of them offered to help even though they were aware of my destination.

I had no idea where to go for meeting the lawyer, so it was a good thing Raúl accompanied me to lead the way. He took me down the corridor past the captain's office through the metal detector into the visitor's entrance area, then we walked twelve feet to a larger room. The female guard manning the entrance of the room didn't allow Raúl to enter and had him wait next to the glass panel wall by the doorway. The 20'×20' room had eight rows of long bench-style seats in front of a large table and ten viewing windows made of heavy gauge wire that were used to allow lawyers who didn't want to enter the prison to visit their clients.

There was only one person in the room smartly dressed as a lawyer; it wasn't Irvin, and the attire worn wasn't a pretty dress, which eliminates Karla. Assuming it had to be my lawyer from the States, I walked up to the man with hopeful anticipation and shook his hand, who then introduced himself as Edgar from the US consulates office. What no lawyer? My enthusiasm quickly left the room. It was disheartening my visitor wasn't a lawyer realizing I would still be in the dark about what was happening with my case.

Edgar is the same individual who spoke to Brenda and me on the phone from inside the jailhouse. He went on to explain that his trip from Mexico City was to check up on me, making sure I was being treated fairly and inform me he has been in touch with my sister (Maribeth) to bring her up to speed on my situation. Also, if I needed legal counsel, he had names and phone numbers of lawyers who lived in the La Paz area. Edgar rambled on with the standard spiel, "If you need anything, let me know etc. etc." It appeared his hands were tied in suppling any legal advice and limited at providing any tangible aid for me.

Don't get me wrong, I really appreciated Edgar's kind gestures and his presence at the prison, and I found it a little comforting to know the US consulate was involved in my safety and well-being, even though the US government had absolutely no real authoritative power here in a Mexico prison. Realistically I focused on the logical side of my incarceration and wasn't about to cry and whine to Edgar over expecting him to get me out of this prison. This hidden attitude of mine is what kept our visitation short. I held my replies to a minimum so as not to prolong false hope of a fairytale ending, realizing my freedom wasn't going to be provided by the US government. This is not a Hollywood movie that has a happy ending due to the efforts of my countries powers that be.

As we were saying our goodbyes, Edgar handed me a business card and said, "I will be back in thirty days to check up on you." Then parted ways. The thought of being stuck in this prison for thirty more days was a bit depressing, and I certainly hope when Edgar returns for our next visit, I'm sipping Mao-tai's on a beach somewhere, or better yet anesthetized in a dentist chair getting a root canal.

While heading back to our cells, Raúl inquired about the meeting with my lawyer, and after explaining all about the FUBAR encounter, he replied in his standard street lingo, "Man that's some fucked up shit." I would have to agree, but he seemed more bothered by my unproductive meeting than I.

When we reached Raúl's cell, I was troubled by the number of captivated faces pressed against the steel bars of his cell door, as there were absolutely no gaps between the condensed inmates, so much that I couldn't see the inside of their cell. Their heads were stacked tightly together resembling two totem poles with faces carved into it high and low, which would be funny if it weren't so damn pitiful.

I asked Raúl, "How many men does your cell hold?"

His answer was, "Eight."

My math skills are pretty good; however, when adding all the staring eyes, it wasn't calculating to sixteen. This observation had me rephrase my question to, "How many men are in your cell?"

He said, "Eleven." This explains the mathematical error and why the cell has men sleeping at the cell door at night. When I commented about Raúl's overcrowded cell, he responded with, "Yeah, that's some crazy shit, but two of them are getting moved out tomorrow."

After thanking Raúl for his help, we exchanged a fist bump, then he gave the standard reply, "If you need any more help, come and get me." He had the guard unlock the door, then proceeded to squeeze through the human logjam, as I returned to my boredom chamber to continue being busy doing nothing.

As time dragged on at a snail's pace, I spent the rest of the day idly sitting on my milk crate thinking, "This really sucks." Until I turned my head to the right and glanced at Raúl's cell to instantly realize my "*suckyness*" wasn't that bad compared to the demoralizing frozen faces from across the hall. The men were still huddled in a tight group against their cell door, searching for any source of stimulation, which instantly took me back to the shithole cell, a place where I can truly relate to those men! I said it once, and I will say it again, "No matter how bad you think you have it, it could always be worse!"

Since the café was between the lunch and dinner rush, most of the men were taking advantage of the break in the action to stand around and chat, fortunately supplying me with increased amounts of sight and sound stimulation. From what I have observed during many humdrum hours of sitting here, the men in this cell get along exceptionally well together and frequently joke around poking fun at each other. It was quite obvious recognizing when the men were mocking a fellow roommate because the recipient of the cellmates banter would be the only individual who had a reserved laugh while trying to respond in some sort of defensive manner, but was quickly interrupted by a fellow roommate with another comedic reply that instantly made everyone else laugh even harder. There was no reason for me to laugh alongside my roommate's antics, for I had no clue what was being said, although I'm all too familiar with their style of banter and consider myself an accomplished contender in the art of razzing. So I truly appreciated and understood their antics while sitting there watching them with a hidden smile, knowing there wasn't a shortage of jocularity amongst the men.

I never asked John or David what was so funny when they were all laughing unless one of them focused their attention in my direction, as the recipient of all their laughter, which became more prevalent as time went on. I clearly understood and accepted being the occasional butt of their jokes, also an easy target limited by a language barrier who couldn't respond sarcastically or defend against their targeted banter. *Hell*, I get it! If roles were reversed, I would be razzing them just as much; anything for a joke.

During the cellmate's bull session, inmates occasionally showed up, usually purchasing cigs or two-liter bottles of water, and since I was the first person they saw, some would greet me with a "What's up, how are you, hello etc." I assumed by now they knew I was the American gringo in cell #6 and were practicing what little English they knew on me. On one occasion, a customer at our cell door who spoke adequate English looked at me and said, "Hello," then initiated our standard Q&A spiel, "WAYIF, POH, NPPF," (WPN) which was the extent of our limited conversation. Even though exposer to the inmates was getting more familiar and comfortable, I still failed to have extended discussions with any of the customers.

With the excessive amount of wasted time plaguing my mind, I found myself lost in deep thought of what I needed while in prison, so I grabbed a small piece of paper from my manila envelope, found a pen next to the cash box and began to add more items to the next list of items I would be giving Brenda on her next visit. It may sound bizarre that the first thing I wanted and truly needed was not of food or water but of a Sudoku book. I kid you not! If I'm able to immerse my mind into the depths of a challenging Sudoku puzzle, I could escape this world and thrive in my underworld for many hours at a time without resurfacing for air.

From here, I must jump ahead in the story because, after numerous failed attempts in acquiring a Sudoku book, it appeared that no such book existed in La Paz or at least one that could challenge me. It bothered me not to have anything to keep my mind busy, although being denied a Sudoku book was the second most monumental Butterfly Effect, which completely altered how I spent my remaining days in this prison. If Brenda were able to obtain what I requested, my long list of unique experiences from here on out would have been drastically altered, whereas some would have never existed. The book would have undoubtedly engulfed my every waking hour ensnaring me in my own little world, while ignoring everything and everyone around me, finalizing my time in prison in solitude with solitude. But this is by no means the end of the Sudoku tale.

The banter between the cellmates began to dissipate as the café's activity increased with customers arriving at our door, revealing it was nearing dinnertime, prompting a repeat of my actions from yesterday heading into the kitchen before Pablo became overrun with orders. Upon entering, Pablo had already started cooking a meal for his fellow roomies; therefore, I ate a quick meal made for ex-champions of some junk food, then proceeded to exit the kitchen as some of the men entered to partake in Pablo's culinary creation.

Within two steps of reaching the curtain of the doorway, John offered me some dinner of which I declined, not because I just ate, but more of not being brave enough in trying their less than appetizing looking Mexican delight. Besides, I would have been extremely uncomfortable imposing on them, especially if I were to join them only to discover the meal wasn't compatible with my reserved palate, thus making a spectacle of myself by refusing their generous offer after already sitting down to join them. Oh, the burdens I must endure for being a picky eater.

As soon as that train wreck was averted, I continued my exodus from the patio, parked my caboose on the milkcrate and patiently waited *four hours* until the prison conductor announced, "Lights out!"

The only memorable interruption to spike my stimulation during those last few hours before bedtime, was an event I think completely changed how the cellmates viewed my conservative character.

DIZNEY LAND by Way of Military Escort

As the café was winding down for the night and the runner for the evening was let back into the cell, most of the men were congregated in the main area of the cell chatting, and when the sun disappeared, the moon came out along with the cockroaches. In all my time spent here, I have never witnessed an inmate kill a cockroach, not because there was a shortage of targets to squash, quite the opposite. Maybe the men thought, why bother killing one when ten more escape the wrath of their shoe?

While sitting there in my cocoon area being quiet and keeping to myself, a large cockroach tempted its fate by crawling within striking distance of my foot, not realizing that little bastard was trespassing into my sleeping area. I quickly extended my reach by partially standing up and, with my right foot, ending the encroacher's life with a loud *Stomp*! I swiftly brushed aside the corps under Roseudo's bed, which had David instantaneously cry out, "*Oh no!* You killed Lucy!"

For a fraction of second I feared, oh shit, did I just kill the cellmate's pet? A train of thought resulting from watching prison movies involving prisoners with a rat, mouse, or cockroach for a pet. However, this thought process was very short-lived as David and crew began laughing hysterically, followed by the men adding each of their own wisecracks to the mix extending the uncontrollable laughter throughout the cell even louder.

Emilio was highly entertained and displayed animated amusement from my sudden outburst toward the unsuspecting critter and kept laughing while trying to say something about Lucy La Cucaracha (the cockroach), inducing some of the men to start joyfully singing in an elevated tone, "♪♪La Cucaracha La Cucaracha na na na na, La Cucaracha La Cucaracha na na na na♪♪!"

It was comical entertainment watching the men acting like juveniles, even though I hadn't a clue what they were singing or talking about. During their animated theatrics, they were all laughing toward the actions they just witnessed from this quiet, conserved, shy American who has exploded out of his cocoon and ended the life of Lucy La Cucaracha. I wish I had a translated transcript of that memorable moment, though I was able to acquire one of many translated forms of the song the men were singing, derived from a Spanish folklore song linked to the 1910 Mexico Revolution that goes like this: "The cockroach, the cockroach can't walk anymore because it's lacking, because it doesn't have marijuana to smoke. The cockroach just died now they take her to be buried among four buzzards and a mouse as the sexton…" To this day, I can't look at a cockroach without smiling and singing, "♪♪La Cucaracha La Cucaracha na na na na, La Cucaracha La Cucaracha na na na na♪♪!"

Eventually, all the excitement dispersed along with the men as it neared bedtime, directing me to the bathroom and preparing for bed, followed by laying out the sleeping mat and hanging the towel on the cell door. When ten o'clock finally arrived, most of the prison lights were turned off; unfortunately, the noise level by some of the inmates in the cellblock was turned up.

The majority of the late-night chatter and loud laughter was emanating from Raúl's cell, most likely due to their cell being in lockdown all day long with little to no possessions to occupy or entertain them other than themselves, leaving them with nothing better to do during most of the day but sleep which keeps them restless at night. Raúl's inconsiderate cellmates obviously didn't give a damn about utilizing soft tones, as these morons continued their obnoxious behavior of smoking and joking well past midnight! Which was odd, because I never heard them having a good time during the day. Maybe the aroma of marijuana I have been smelling is responsible for their newfound laughter.

I was forced to repeat my sleeping arrangement from last night, by laying on my right side and placing a handkerchief over my face, although it obviously failed to rectify the problem, as I was conscious enough to be aware of the midnight hour.

Day 16 in Country

Fourth day in prison

This Thursday morning was pretty much a carbon copy of yesterdays, first one up, put my mat away, go to the bathroom, put a cinnamon roll in the microwave then made my way to the patio to eat a banana with the pastry, except there were two details that altered this morning's rerun from yesterdays. First, the trip to the microwave was an added luxury of having a warmed roll. Second, while trying to enjoy my breakfast in the outside air along with the peaceful blue sky, I heard a guard calling out names for roll call followed by John suddenly shouting out my name. I quickly stood up and poked my head through the curtain of the doorway and responded with, "Yo!" John instantly waved me on through so the guard could get visual verification of my presence, and not rely on just a voice for verification of my presence.

Now it's officially confirmed that I do exist in cell #6 and have been unfortunate to make it onto the prison's roll call list, taking a staggering four days to materialize. Hell, that would have been enough time to make it back home before I was even missed!

After roll call, most of my roomies migrated back into their cocoons, only reappearing when extra help was needed with the café's operations. I think they stayed up way too late last night and are trying to make up for lost sleep by going back to bed, lucky bastards. Sure wish I had that accommodating luxury. Damn, I would even trade that unlawful pillow of mine for an upgraded cocoon!

Since my breakfast was a little on the lite side, I poked around inside my bag of food items for something more to eat, though I can't remember what it was, I'm sure it wasn't very nutritious, yet good enough to make a turd. While sitting at the patio table nibbling on my snack, David finally crawled out of bed and made his way into the kitchen, where we struck up conversation involving my concerns over Brenda's no show yesterday. I wondered why she hadn't utilized the visitors pass Frank obtained for her and was worried something was wrong.

David displayed compassion listening to me and tried to help with my troubles by offering some advice, then with a sincere tone, said, "You should text her."

I responded with total confusion. "*What?*"

He spoke not a word, then suddenly left the patio returning with a cellphone in his hand. *Yes*, I said phone, though absolutely no information will be revealed on who's phone, or how it materialized in this cell! Let's just assume I can gain access to a cellphone and rely on your own imagination to answer a question for which I will not!

Since I refuse to conform with the rest of the zombies of the world by relinquishing my prehistoric flip phone, I'm unfamiliar with Spanish interface smartphones and those gadgets in general, so I had David send Brenda the text, "Are you okay?"

Her reply, "I'm waiting on our lawyer before I see you again." This was a great relief threefold, knowing she was okay, a lawyer was soon to arrive, and having the ability to communicate with her from within my cell! There was very little back and forth texting between us, which eludes my memory of what was said.

Later that morning, I took advantage of the forbidden device by having David send Brenda a message to bring my SD card on her next visitation, so I could play my music on David's crude music device. Brenda and I exchanged a few more texts pertaining to the late arrival of the lawyer. I relayed the messages to David in a short, simple fashion allowing him an easy understanding of what to type.

Unfortunately, my vagueness and David's interpretations raised Brenda's suspicion of who was actually sending her texts, so she eventually replied, "Who is this?" Her paranoia was completely understandable due to receiving messages in a foreign country from an unfamiliar phone number with no mention of the parties involved. These stumbling blocks motivating me to grab a small piece of paper and write down a message I wanted David to send her that contained her full name and address along with, "High candy pants, Dennis N. needs to hear from you."

No, "high" is not a typo. Even though it should have read "Hi," I realized the mistake moments before typing this phrase while confirming what I wrote down on the actual piece of paper I used in prison when the message was written. This was a clear indication of the massive amount of stress I was enduring; how is it possible to spell a two-letter word incorrectly?

Before David sent the text, he looked at me with a confused expression and said, "Are you sure?" I assumed he had difficulty with the translation of "candy pants" or thought the phrase was referring to myself raising concerns about my mental status on laundry day. In order to alleviate David's confusion, I informed him that this particular phrase was like a codeword that only Brenda would recognize because nobody has ever heard me address her as Candy Pants; therefore she would realize it was me trying to send the text and not some freak prowling the cyber world in search for edible underwear.

To my enjoyment, she immediately replied with, "Can I call you at this number?" I was in total amazement at the opportunity in talking to Brenda from within the patio, so I eagerly asked David if it was okay, and then had him send my response, "Yes!" Soon the vibrating phone alerted us of the incoming call. Obviously, the sound mode was turned off as David instantly handed me the phone. Brenda's first words were, "How the hell did you get a phone?" Even though I revealed the truth to her, it absolutely will not be publicized in print to protect the men still incarcerated! I must revert to my creed quoted by Marilyn Millian, "Say it-deny it, write it-regret it!"

What a great relief it was speaking to Brenda from within my cage, more so after receiving confirmation of the imminent arrival of my lawyer and the perfect opportunity in asking her for items to be added to the list of things I needed; also apprised her of the permission slip Frank acquired allowing her into the prison for visitation. Brenda reassured me she was going to visit me when the lawyer arrived in town, but then began divulging information pertaining to all the hardships she had been enduring while taking care of our affairs. She mentioned she had great difficulty managing by herself in a strange environment; all because of me. I found myself feeling ashamed and depressed that I couldn't be with her to offer comfort.

Our short phone call ended on the emotional side, and after exchanging our intimate goodbyes, I handed the phone back to David and extended a humbled appreciation. Then there, I sat in silence, dwelling over Brenda's undeserved difficulties.

My standard practice has been to always stay out of cellmates' way to avoid inconveniencing them, therefore when the kitchen area became busy with activity, I headed back to my uncomfortable lounge chair, minimalizing my exposure to the over-crowded cell. Soon after sitting down, I realized the waffling effect on my rump was soon to follow since I forgot to place the pillow on the crate. At about the same time I retrieved the pillow and placed it on the crate, David emerged from the kitchen witnessing my activity and displayed a highly inquisitive stare, then with a distressed tone asked, "How did you get a *pillow*?"

Sometimes I'm quick-witted with a funny/sarcastic answer to someone's question, and this was one of those occasions. My reply was short, truthful, and humorously vague (funny to me) with only three words. "I got connections!"

David instantly responded with a slightly aggravated tone, "*What?*"

After hearing his elevated voice, I recognized he wasn't pleased and did not care for my acquired luxury, thus refraining from further sarcasm while keeping a more somber tone with my response, "Frank got it for me."

David was annoyed at the ease in which I was able to obtain a pillow (contraband) and voiced his displeasure with, "*Reeeally?*" He then shook his head back and forth and said, "*Fucking Mexicans!*"

It doesn't take a therapist to figure out why David was so irritated, though it would involve a psychologist explaining the convoluted logic why I had a pillow after only four days after my arrival in prison, while David has been stuck in here for over eleven months with no such pleasure. To add insult to injury, my pillow has been atop the milkcrate most of yesterday in plain sight of the guards, yet nothing was mentioned to me about the broken rule.

Even with David's elevated blood pressure brought on by this gringo, he still held a soft spot in his heart after our conversation by offering me his familiar kind gesture, "If you need anything, just ask, and whatever you want I can get it for you, *reeeally!*" Because of David's sincere kindness, I felt a little uneasy receiving the pillow from Frank without first asking David if he could possibly get me one sensing that he wanted to be my, "I got connections" guy.

While continuously sitting in the boredom chamber for a couple hours slowly rotting my brain away, I figured it was time to be proactive and depart from this continuous inactivity. Since David was hiding in his cocoon, the only person I could ask questions pertaining to venturing out of the cell was John. I patiently watched and waited for him to look up from reading his book, knowing I would feel uncomfortable interrupting him while immersed in leisure activity. When I was finally able to grab John's attention, I asked him how much money was needed per day to get by in here, as well as leaving the cell to get something to eat. He said about two hundred pesos ($11.00) was needed, and I could leave the cell if I was wearing a prison-issue shirt or pants. It seemed bizarre to be receiving permission by a fellow inmate that I could leave my cell today and what to wear, and not from a prison guard or official. Who is running this dysfunctional theme park, the office fat cats, or the prison rats? Either way, John's latest bit of info had me quickly preparing for an exodus from the cell.

I retrieved some money from the soapbox, slipped on my oversized prison pants, but instead of folding the waistband into my shorts preventing them from sliding down, I overlapped the waistbands extra material into a fold clasped together by two clothespins, securing the pants much more effectively.

Even though my unfashionable wardrobe alterations were complete, I was still slightly apprehensive at leaving the privacy of my dressing room to stroll down the prisons runway and have all those staring eyes focused on me while walking around looking for a place to eat. So I walked over to Raúl's cell and enlisted his services to guide me through the prison and help with translations while ordering a meal. An extra bonus, it would help ease any anxiety that might arise by having him at my side.

Soon after the guard released Raúl from his cell, we walked outside to the courtyard area. It felt strange to be self-liberated from my cage, able to freely roam while blending in among the inmates; fortunately, Raúl's presence helped increase my comfort level. We walked over to the two food shacks around the corner from the store and looked to see what each establishment had to offer for lunch. The larger café with the appealing kitchen was my first choice on where to eat; unfortunately, nobody was staffing the restaurant, so I reluctantly decided to take four steps backward to see what the smaller shack had to offer. Raúl asked the young man (Hector) behind the counter what he had to offer for lunch. Raúl relayed the translated menu to me, but the options were minimal, whereas the only item that sounded appetizing was the cheeseburger and Frenchfries. Hector looked to be thirty years old, five feet, eight inches tall, average weight and build, had a reserved demeanor, and wore a full prison uniform that was a little dirty and well-worn.

While the meal was being prepared, we sat at one of the plastic patio tables outside next to the cafe, and struck up a conversation that mostly involved him talking and me listening, which is perfectly fine with me because as my brother Tom would say "You can't learn anything while you are talking." Unfortunately, Raúl is as closed mouth as I, and there were moments of uncomfortable silence between us, forcing me to break the silence by making a kind gesture of offering to purchase Raúl a meal. After he politely declined, I suggested something to drink and gave him enough money to purchase a drink from the store. That's when Raúl became insistent that I do not drink the prison water because it was stored in tanks on the roof that had dead mice in them contaminating the water. I clearly was not about to drink the prison's water anyway, though the thought of cooking meals with the tainted water is very unsettling.

It wasn't long into our sporadic conversation when Hector brought my meal to the table and asked, "Do you want something to drink?"

I was totally caught off guard by him speaking English and was slow to respond with, "Do you have lemonade?"

Hector's English was nowhere near fluent as Raúl's, but he was able to speak it well enough for me to understand him. He soon returned with a large homemade lemonade that tasted delicious as did the burger and fries, and all for forty-five pesos ($2.61). I would have to say that my first dining-out experience in a Mexican prison was exceptionally pleasurable.

While sitting there eating, I listened to Raúl talk about when he previously lived in the south-eastern part of the United States, had a real good job working for a lawn care business and oversaw his own crew, but couldn't return to the States due to a legality. I could tell Raúl was very proud of his past achievement in securing a job as foreman, made apparent when his reserved demeanor began to elevate while telling his story. Not to put the man down, but I work in the construction world of reality and can assume his position was probably secured do to the fact he was capable of speaking English more proficiently than his fellow workers, though still a dignified position for Raúl to have credited to his name.

My attention was diverted away from Raúl when I noticed an energetic inmate sweeping the courtyard area with a broken broom that was missing about ten inches off the handle. Normally this occurrence would not be noteworthy, yet watching this one-man cleanup crew in Mexican Dizney Land turned out to be quite the spectacle. The slender inmate had a defined muscle tone and an energy level that was completely off the charts, making me exhausted just watching him work. My first impression was either he was on drugs or a tad crazy. He swept the ground that contained little to no trash, adamantly sweeping every tiny pebble along with the loose dirt particles, and the small amount of trash in the area was just an added motivator justifying his enthusiastic madness. The bulk of the trash on the ground was scattered near a large trashcan, which appeared as if an animal had scavenged through the can searching for an easy meal, possibly by all the stray cats roaming around the prison.

The madness continued for almost an hour as the spirted inmate kept working at an elevated pace, and when finished sweeping all the loose dirt, he grabbed a water hose and began spraying the ground. When the hose no longer reached its target area, he filled up a five-gallon bucket and used a small tin can for scattering the water onto the dry areas. I can only conclude two reasons why this energetic inmate was dousing the courtyard with water, to either keep the dust down or cool off the area. But this is La Paz, Mexico, where the intense heat from the sun works almost as hard as the highly motivated inmate and would evaporate the moistened ground before the *project* was even completed, whatever it may have been?

In my wondering gaze, I also noticed about ten inmates' male and female in the courtyard seating area along with their visiting guests consisting mostly of women and children, leading me to address Raúl and inquire at the oddity of female prisoners socializing with their male counterparts. He told me there were about one-hundred female prisoners housed in the large cellblock behind the courtyards visiting area, who were only allowed to leave the safety of their cellblock unescorted while visiting a guest in the visitor's area. I still find it strange witnessing male and female prisoners among families with small children roaming the visitor's area without a single guard supervising, which might help explain the extremely relaxed atmosphere that occupies this playpen. On other occasions throughout my stay here, I witnessed about fifteen female inmates in full prison uniforms being escorted to the church by female guards, also to a section of the prison where they were allowed to do some knitting.

My visual stimulation remained constant while observing an inmate unlocking a cellblocks door from the inside, repeatedly allowing women and children to enter and exit without an escort from a guard. I was not about to speculate a scenario that could possibly explain what I had just witnessed; therefore, I once again looked to Raúl for justification of this illogical activity. I was told the small cellblock consisted of only four jail cells where the inmates residing there are fearful of violent retaliation from various gang members from within these prison walls who are still involved with the drug cartel organizations. Consequently, these targeted inmates our housed on the protected side of the prison and keep their cellblock door locked

DIZNEY LAND by Way of Military Escort

from the inside for twelve hours a day until a guard exchanges it for a prison lock at seven pm.

I don't know what other people would do in this same scenario, but when I'm in fear for my life in the confines of a Mexican prison, the first thing I would do is invite my wife and children into my threatening environment, so the whole family could be involved in the bloody carnage. "Now that's sarcasm!"

Shortly after eating lunch while sipping on my lemonade, an inmate walked over from the visitor's area and entered the larger café to the left of Hector's café` who was obviously the owner of the establishment. His name was Alexander. He had an aged face giving him the appearance that he was older than sixty (50?) 5'11" tall, 170 pounds, spoke English almost as proficient as Raúl, cordial, very mild-mannered and spoke with a reserved low tone.

I'd be guessing at how our friendly introduction began, but it quickly transformed from a meet and greet to a subject pertaining to Alexanders' menu items. He informed me of the long list of meals his cafe had to offer, also if I came back at dinnertime, he would cook whatever I wanted. *How cool is that?* Alexander went on to say he used to work as a cook at Denny's restaurant back in the States and was more than capable of preparing an American style breakfast for me in the morning. Alexander kept promoting his ability to make American dishes and displayed a slight eagerness for me to return to his café for a meal.

I certainly do not associate Denny's restaurant to fine dining or even a worthy place to eat, although I would rather eat a bad Denny's meal prepared by a Mexican prisoner than a good Mexican meal made by a white guy, *any day!* Therefore, I decided that a return trip to Alexander's café tonight for dinner would be favorable and sounded inviting, especially knowing I can communicate directly to the cook.

When Alexander finished recruiting a new customer, he walked back to the visitor's area and sat down next to a female prisoner who appeared to be more than just a friend seeing there was some touching and squeezing involved during their encounter. That's why nobody was manning the café when I arrived here, he was playing grab-ass in the playpen with his girlfriend. I found out later that she is Alexander's wife, which explains the type of affection the couple displayed toward each other, of a more reserved controlled behavior you might expect from an older couple that has been together for many years. I don't like to pry into the reason why someone is incarcerated, so I never did find out why the couple was stuck in prison; at least they had the luxury to lean-on each other when in need of some comfort.

Now that my delicious lemonade was consumed, it was time to give up the café's table and chairs to other potential customers, so I placed the plastic glass on Hector's countertop and thanked him with much gratitude. Raúl and I headed back to our boredom chambers, and like as before, our steps were short and slow. Why be in a hurry to arrive somewhere when there is absolutely nowhere else to go? As we entered the cellblock, I noticed that cell #7 had a raggedy curtain hanging in the doorway partially obscuring the cell from view, upon further inspection I discovered the cell had been destroyed by fire. I turned to Raúl, halting our leisurely stroll, then asked what the story was with the scorched jailcell. Raúl's explanation of the fire was a short one. I relay my interpretation of his story without all the colorful metaphors.

The prisoners who lived in the cell set the fire on purpose to destroy all the drugs in the room, so there would be no evidence to prove they were guilty of dealing drugs within the prison, which comes with a harsh penalty not to mention the exile from the pleasant side of the prison. Regardless, I imagine setting fire in Dizney Land comes with automatic lifetime banishment from the theme park, whether drugs where involved or not!

Raúl told me he used to live on the bad side of the prison that was so unruly that if you had any possessions when you went to sleep at night, by the time you woke up in the morning, everything was stolen. He finalized that statement in his standard low-key tone, "Man, that's some fucked up shit!"

We stopped short from reaching our cells, where we exchanged a fist bump, and I thanked him as he extended his standard sincere gesture of, "If you need any more help come get me." Knowing I now had

DIZNEY LAND by Way of Military Escort

the freedom to leave my jailcell whenever desired, diminished some of the dread while heading toward my cell door with a more optimistic stride, unlike Raúl's approach who slowly wandered over to his cage. Both of us entered our separate worlds, of which only one had the power to free the other from the clutches of his undesirable domain.

Once inside the cell, I had to bypass my cocoon because John had claimed my milkcrate along with the comforts of the pillow, which was fine by me, for it required me to stand among a few cellmates hanging around the area gabbing. After putting my prison pants away, the subject arose concerning my journey outside the cell. I shouldn't have revealed information about my trip to Hector's for lunch because, as soon as this disheartening news hit David's ears, it instantly brought out his aggressive kindness. Once again, he went straight into his customary rant with a slightly raised tone, "If you need anything just ask, *reeeally*, if you want something to eat, I can make it for you, *no, reeeally!*" I needed to start utilizing David's kind gestures soon before he eventually stops offering them to me.

Soon after my humility lesson from David was over, I heard Frank call out my name, prompting me to walk over to the door and greet my visitor. Of course, the gringo that always delivers had a brand-new prison-issue shirt, and as he handed it to me said, "I couldn't find small size, so I got you a medium." Followed by, "Have you seen Brenda yet?"

I replied, "No, maybe tomorrow." Frank must have been bored because he asked if I wanted to go with him to the courtyard and get something to drink. Hell yes, I'll go, anything to get out of this cage once more!

I quickly put the shirt under the bed, grabbed my pants, pinned them up with the clothespins then headed out the door. My wardrobe decision of wearing the baggy pants opposed to the newly acquired shirt was a temperature control issue due to the fact that the heat in the middle of the day has everyone hiding in the shadows, and wearing pants would be considerably cooler than wearing a shirt with thick material.

We went to the courtyard area next to Alexander's café, where I sat at a table, as Frank walked over to the store to get us a couple of drinks. We sat there and talked for about forty-five minutes, well I mostly just listened. He inquired about the treatment from my cellmates. I told him they have been very good to me and seem to be a good bunch of guys. Frank validated my statement with his own personal praise toward the men and added that I could trust them. He then abruptly changed the subject by asking if my pants were fitting okay. I stood up to reveal how loose the pants were without the clothespins attached. In the back of my mind, I emphatically knew that just by showing Frank the clothespins, that this poor man's belt was soon to be a thing of the past. I don't need to clarify his response, but I will. He eagerly said, "I will take care of it."

As our conversation progressed, we started talking about the details of my arrest. Frank was adamant that the charges against me were partially incorrect, and I should talk to my lawyer about correcting the case file, which in turn would lessen the severity of my crime. Apparently, he had been talking to a prison official who was processing this secondhand news then giving legal advice to Frank. Honestly, it didn't make any sense to me and sounded like a minor detail that probably wouldn't change a single thing, but I could be wrong.

When Frank finished focusing all the attention toward me, he began talking about his unfortunate incarceration that didn't start here in Dizney Land, but at a different prison in a much harsher environment ten years early. He never used profanity when speaking, or during his narrative, though the word "man" was used excessively and his limited vocabulary along with reserved demeanor made his interesting story sound a little mundane. Therefore, I will paraphrase his version of events to the best of my ability and recollection.

Frank, along with a good friend (Mike), were sitting in a police station's office somewhere in Mexico when a detective pulls out a photograph from his pocket and proceeds to point out the three smiling men posing in a friendly photo. The man on the left in the photo was Frank, the man on the right was Mike and the man in the middle was found shot dead. I should point out the man in the middle was alive at the time of the photo, smiling, bullet hole-free and clueless his days were numbered, but for how long is unclear. The unfortunate man taking a dirt nap was an associate of Mike's.

Frank did not know the man personally and had not a clue on how the deceased victim ended up on the wrong side of a gun. Frank was employed by Mike as a chauffeur and generally had no personal interaction with the mystery man.

During the lowkey interrogation, Mike stood up and had the detective follow him into an office room next door where Frank could see the two men through a glass wall, though he couldn't hear what they were saying. Mike was facing Frank while talking to the detective, so Frank was able to capture all the facial expressions on his friends' faces during their suspicious discussion. While the two men were talking, their body-language suggested a more relaxed vibe between them, as Mike placed his right hand on the detectives left shoulder and pointed to Frank, then the detective turned his head to peer over his right shoulder at Frank and nodded. Frank instantly realized what was about to transpire as the two men shook hands; he was getting stabbed in the back by a so-called good friend!

I don't think money exchanged hands during their interaction, but this is Mexico we are talking about, so it's highly likely someone ended up with a stack of cash in their hand! Frank was convicted of murder and sentenced to twenty years, even though there wasn't a murder weapon or motive. While telling his story, Frank paused for a moment to reflect on the man responsible for his imprisonment, then revealed Mike's full name in a stern tone and said, "I will *never* forget that name!" He displayed deep resentment while repeating the man's name a second time. Frank may not forget Mike's full name; unfortunately, I have, which slightly bothers me to this day. I truly believe Frank is an innocent man!

Frank's first bold action upon his arrival into a Mexican prison ten years earlier, was punching an inmate square in the face; consequently setting the tone of his unruly behavior which was met with prison punishments for the next several years and secured his position in the slammer as a real hard-ass. Frank wasn't a stranger to prison life, do to being in and out of California prisons most of his young adult life, so he knows how to effectively survive in prison. After many years of Frank's unruly and uncontrollable behavior, one day, a prison counselor had an insightful discussion with Frank concerning the destructive path he was heading down. A clear recollection of the counselor's motivational sermon Frank relayed to me is a little fuzzy, although I'm certain his spoken words to Frank were more profound and life-altering than I can possibly explain on paper. Because shortly after having the highly inspirational discussion with the counselor, Frank decided it was time to change his self-destructive behavior and realized the only person he was harming was himself!

With Frank's new and improved attitude adjustment, he soon became a model prisoner, ultimately allowing him to transfer here to Dizney Land. He continued to conduct himself in a proper manner here and began helping other inmates with their various problems, eventually taking care of the men in the clinic and psych ward, becoming a reliable asset to the prison. He also studied massage therapy diligently, becoming very knowledgeable in his accomplished skill. He had a clientele not limited to only inmates, but to customers entering the prison for therapy. *No, really!* It has been confirmed; I personally witnessed him performing massage therapy on an old lady who was visiting her son in the courtyard. Frank boasted about making pretty good money at this enterprise and was proud of his self-taught achievement, all of which was presented to me with strong contentment that he is truly comfortable with prison life!

As we continued to sip on our drinks, Frank transitioned from one story to the next, which I found to be just as interesting, if not more. His low-key excitement suddenly rose as he started talking about the good old days when he used to live in Las Vegas. What happens in Vegas stays in Vegas, unless Frank is telling the story, because he revealed some crazy shit that most people can only experience by watching it on a TV screen. I would have never expected this mild-mannered man used to live a lifestyle that can only be described as a free-wheeling party that had absolutely *no boundaries!*

Frank worked in Las Vegas as a driver (chauffeur), though nowhere in the definition of his job title did the word "chauffeur" ever arise, as a matter of fact, "driver" is a misleading description of Frank's field of work and could be better explained as the "gringo that always delivers!" Clients preferred hiring Frank as their driver because of his unique ability in acquiring *anything* they requested, such as liquor, women, drugs and guns, etc., with absolutely no questions asked! Frank was boastful of his special attribute and truly proud of the bond he held with clients who valued his silence concerning their outlandish requests and questionable activities.

Frank was able to reap the rewards from clients he drove to parties. He was frequently invited to outlandish gatherings and had access to all the booze, drugs, and women he could possibly want. He adamantly claimed those days were the best times of his life, because of all the extreme partying, freedom to do whatever he wanted and the many different women he enjoyed in the horizontal position.

Frank's successful ability at the adult style scavenger hunt in Vegas clearly followed him to this La Paz prison, or should I say his talent at acquiring what he wanted has led him here to Dizney Land! Either way, I now understand why Frank has been an exceptional "Connections man" for me, it's in his blood!

With few distractions in the courtyard during this time of day, I was able to retain most of what Frank said to me, which's surprises me as I tend to lose interest in what most people have to say unless it's important or interesting. It was beneficial that this environment lacked many diversions, allowing me to focus on most everything that happened and what was said during the entirety of my stay while in prison.

Frank informed me of some errands he had to take care of, so we concluded our visit, left the courtyard and walked to my cell, where he reminded me to give him the prison pants to get altered. As I handed the pants over and thanked him, he said, "Tomorrow, I will show you where I work and live," and away he went.

Before revisiting my pillow, I ventured into the patio for a quick snack to munch on. When I returned to the cell, David stopped me near the bathroom door next to Adrian's bed and struck up a conversation pertaining to his one-year anniversary, which just happened to be today. I would have congratulated him if I gave a shit, though I did show compassion for the man's worried expression written all over his face, as this anniversary date wasn't a milestone of celebration but more of a tragedy.

David said, "I have been in prison for one year today!"

In an optimistic tone, I asked, "How long do you have left in your prison sentence?"

He replied with an agitated tone, "I don't know, I haven't been sentenced yet!"

I was in total disbelief and cried out, "*What?* Are you freaking kidding me?"

He instantly replied, "*No*," then proceeded to explain why he was stuck behind these castle walls without a court's conviction or jail sentence.

I thought Raúl's predicament of being in here for two years with no sentence was distressing, until I listened to David's FUBAR story, then realized I had to revert to my adage, "It could always be worse!"

In order to help clarify David's unsettling story, first, I must disclose pertinent info of the discussion, a few of the cellmates had with me after talking with David. Since John was a well-established lawyer who was well versed in legal doctrine, he did a majority of the talking during our conversation while explaining Mexican law to me.

At the beginning of 2017, Mexico had a massive overhaul of its legal system, and one law in particular was related to human rights. Prior to 2017 anybody could go to the police station and accuse someone of a crime without any provocation, leading police to arrest the suspect and put them in jail, or prison without evidence, or proof that the accused committed a crime, thus forcing the accused to prove their innocence from within a jail.

Unlike the United States, where you are innocent until proven guilty, in Mexico, you were guilty until proven innocent. With the new law taking effect at the beginning of 2017, Mexico has taken a page from the US constitution, and now Mexico's citizens enjoy what we have taken for granted.

I can assume the new law will help keep innocent people out of jail, but not so much as to free them from their unjust imprisonment, as in David's case, who is a byproduct of the old system and is having difficulty benefiting from the new law. The only thing David's accuser needed to put him in prison was a convincing fabricated story, consequently creating a nightmare that quickly went from bad to worse.

The detective handling the case eventually received evidence that would prove David's innocence, yet no action was taken! David could not request that his lawyer pursue the critical evidence because after paying the lawyer a large sum of money, he was never heard from again. Now David can no longer afford another lawyer and worse yet can't trust one either, thus stranding him in this prison for a year without a sentence and clueless when he will be able to go home and see his wife. During David's depressing story, he never raised his voice in anger while finalizing his closing remark with a calm demeanor and said, "*Fucking Mexicans!*"

According to John, I was extremely fortunate *not* to be arrested in 2016 when human rights weren't a major concern of the Mexican government; also my legal matters should have a more favorable outcome now that it's 2017, but he added that the transition from the old to the new system has been a slow and problematic process.

With all this latest info supplied by John, I was able to finally understand why all the arresting procedures I had to endure were totally disorganized and confusing for everyone involved, as they were still in the learning process of all the new laws and have been implementing them for only five months. It probably didn't help that I was a unique international guinea pig who had committed a felony, which had officials running back and forth to the updated lawbook for info on how to correctly handle my situation and not to inadvertently violate my human rights. Lucky me!

The new laws could also explain why Karla was studying a lawbook during my pretrial, as she had to wait for the ink to dry on the new publication. Hell, I almost feel bad for ridiculing everybody orchestrating this dysfunctional judicial circus ever since being arrested by the military, although I personally couldn't do any better-performing as the ringleader in their amusing big top, because "It's not so easy to play the clown when you have to run the circus."[24]

Now that our discussion was over, a few of us returned to our daily routine. John sat on the edge of Rosuedo's bed to continue reading, David climbed into his cocoon and disappeared, my rump

---

[24] *Mash*, TV show.

had a date with a pillow as Mr. Boredom slowly crept in to occupy my time.

I see a pattern developing during this time of day with no activity in the café creating a void in my stimulation, but it was short-lived as I became startled by a loud banging noise from within our cell, followed by a shout out from a frightened Adrian who was in the bathroom taking a shower. I looked toward the source of the racket and saw Emilio walking past the bathroom door with a big grin on his face. Apparently, banging on the metal door is an ongoing quest to scare the shit out of a fellow roomie who is enjoying their peaceful solitude in the bathroom. Emilio's antics made me smile, but I'm not looking forward to when it's my turn to be the recipient of his unexpecting scare tactics.

I wondered why Adrian was taking a shower in the middle of the day, which oddly reminded me that my toiletry bag wasn't equipped with deodorant; therefore, I decided to take advantage of my new found freedom and go to the little store in the courtyard to buy some. I certainly wasn't about to take on this venture by myself, so I went over to my friendly neighbors' cell #1 to see if Raúl had any free time in his busy schedule to help me. Of course, his itinerary for the day was nonexistent; therefore, he was more than able and willing to escape his cell to assist me.

As Raúl asked the guard for permission to be released from the cell, I questioned him on how he gets drinking water while in lockdown since the prison water was undrinkable, and he was prevented from acquiring water outside of the cell. Raúl's lack of water consumption was twofold, the guards were supposed to supply drinking water to the inmates in lockdown, but rarely did so, and some guards did not like Raúl and never gave him any water. The second dilemma was his pockets were void of pesos, which was the main catalyst in acquiring drinking water in this prison. While slowly walking toward the courtyard, Raúl informed me of his unpleasant situation in a low tone and spoke as if were SOP in this prison to be denied the necessity of agua (water), then ended the sentence in his familiar reserved demeanor with, "Man that's some fucked up shit!"

DIZNEY LAND by Way of Military Escort

Upon arrival at the store, I had Raúl ask one of the inmates working there if they had any speed stick deodorant. They didn't have any, so I bought a spray-on for forty-five pesos and an orange drink for Raúl, then went around the corner and sat at a table. Shortly after concluding our small talk, Raúl broke the awkward silence by pointing out the cellblock left of the visitor's area that housed inmates who were in fear for their safety, then said, "That's where an inmate escaped from the prison." Then proceeded to tell the story of one mans "Great Escape,"[25] though never mentioned the fugitives name, so I will call him Steve McQueen. Also, because of Raúl's street dialect and continuous colorful metaphors, I will be paraphrasing most of what he said.

Raúl was previously housed in the same cell with Steve, where the escape took place; therefore, he was able to give accurate accounts of the day in question. His cellblock consisted of four individual jail cells butted against the wall of the woman's cellblock, and a 10'×40' common area void of a roof with one of the outer walls shorter than the others, which wasn't safeguarded at the top to prevent someone from traversing the wall.

Sometime in the evening before the guards came around to replace the cellmate's locks, Steve made his way to the shortest wall in the cellblock and enlisted Raúl's help to give a boost up to the top of the wall. From there, he scampered across until reaching a rooftop that led to the outer wall of the prison, all of which was only about one hundred feet before reaching his destination, where he climbed down to freedom.

Since the guards don't take roll call during the 7:00 p.m. lockdown they are clueless whether all or some of the prisoners are in their cells when the locks are replaced to the prison locks; therefore Steve would not be missed until the next day during the 7:00 a.m. roll call, giving him a huge head start on his run to freedom. When morning roll call arrived, a guard called out Steve's name, when no reply was heard, he once again cried out, "*Steve!*"

---

[25] *The Great Escape* movie.

Still no response. Instead of the guard unlocking the door to get a visual of Steve's presence, he yelled out, "Okay! If you do not answer me, I will leave the prison lock on your door until tomorrow so you can stay in lockdown all day!"

Obviously, there wasn't a disagreement from the absent prisoner, so the angry guard walked away arguing with himself. Other than Raúl, the inmates within the cellblock had no inkling that Steve was aggravating the guard from a much more enjoyable place other than his jail cell bed. Now instead of a twelve-hour head start, Steve will have the advantage of at least thirty-six hours to expand the distance from his dysfunctional captures.

When the next morning arrived, a more efficient guard in charge of roll call discovered Steve missing from his cell, prompting a few guards to grab Raúl and escort him to an undisclosed part of the prison to be interrogated. Prison official's aggressively questioned Raúl in the disappearance of Steve, who claimed to have no knowledge of the escape. When Raúl failed to supply any information to the prison officials, they commenced beating the living shit out of him for answers, but to no avail. I was able to identify that Raúl felt dignified for not ratting out his fellow comrade, especially paying a heavy price for his silence with a battered body.

Prison officials searched for the guard responsible for Steve's disappearance, by looking through previous work schedules to see who was operating that areas guard tower at the time of the escape. When the guard who was at fault was identified, he received a harsh punishment, but Raúl wasn't made aware of this information until three days later when he had an up-close and personal conversation with the guard in question, who said he had been sleeping in the tower during the escape. Their little run-in together wasn't by accident, the unwilling accomplice (guard) was placed in the cellblock not to watch Raúl, but to join him and stay locked up until the fugitive was caught and returned to the prison. This meant that the troubled guard would be enjoying his siestas in the shadows of the same tower he was sleeping in, while a fellow armed comrade reluctantly kept him in the crosshairs for the next *three months!*

Raúl's story explains why the prison no longer allows just verbalization of a prisoner's presence and must include visual verification by the guard taking roll call. When Raúl finished his orange drink, we returned to our cells and exchanged our usual departing spiel. As the steel cage closed behind Raúl, a thought crossed my mind; maybe his involvement in the great escape is why the guards hold resentment toward Raúl and refuse to supply water to him while in lockdown.

Upon entering the cell, Emilio noticed the can of deodorant in my hand, then extended his hand out as if he wanted to look at my purchase. After displaying the can to Emilio, he acted shocked with an expression of disbelief, said something in Spanish then looked to John for a translation into English. "Expensive" is all he said. I would think $2.61 for deodorant inside a Mexican prison is well worth the markup price for the convenience of shopping within my own neighborhood.

Before having a chance to put away my deodorant, John grabbed my attention and pointed to the two bags of items and two one-gallon jugs of water that were next to Roseudo's bed and said, "Those bags of stuff are yours, and we put the cold items in the fridge." I was pleasantly surprised receiving Brenda's care package of food, water, clothing, and sweet treats, though concerned about her whereabouts. I questioned John if she was here. He said, "No, a guard dropped off the items." Soon as I found out Brenda had been at the prison and hadn't come inside to see me, I instantly became a little saddened wondering why I wasn't informed she was here, but soon realized there was nothing I could do about it, except inform Frank of my absentee visitor the next time I see him, who could hopefully rectify the problem.

I condensed my food items into one bag and went into the kitchen where storage space was limited, requiring me to make room for the items on a small shelf above the deep-freeze. The little shelf was cluttered with a variety of items that sparked my curiosity; one strange item, in particular, was a little wooden pink chair covered in pastels. It was strange to see this feminine object amongst burly convicts in a jail cell, raising the thought maybe it's a step stool, but why is it pink, petite, and pretty? My question was soon answered when I noticed a small plastic bucket filled with little toys, thus concluding one of the men must have a daughter and the objects are for when the small child is here to visit her daddy.

Two hours were consumed while sitting on the crate, observing the guys working the café and occasionally having the pleasure of enjoying their antics and elevated humor. More time was taken off the clock by retrieving the notes I have been writing down during my extended vacation here in prison, and due to the wealth of information I have acquired today, it was paramount to add the highlights of the day thus far. Writing paper was in short supply, so all my notes were condensed onto two sheets of paper, and since I was long on ink and short on paper, a note pad had made the list of items for Brenda to bring me.

When the monotony of my motionless body and idle mind began to sedate me, I decided it was time to grab my prison-issue shirt and head to Alexander's café for an early dinner. I had trepidations toward embarking on this first solo trip, knowing there wouldn't be a translator by my side. Upon the exodus, I wanted to appear confidant but not cocky among the prisoners, therefore keeping a calm and relaxed demeanor was paramount, but internally I was a nervous wreck with uncertainty. One thing that helped lower my anxiety was knowing my destination had a familiar English-speaking inmate, putting a purposeful stride in my step while walking through the courtyard.

When arriving at Alexander's food shack, an uneasiness suddenly came over me do to the absence of Alexander, reluctantly requiring me to attempt communicating with a non-English speaking staff member. No sooner than confirming the café worker spoke only Spanish, Alexander arrived from across the courtyard and unknowingly eased my anxiety with his friendly greeting, "How are you?" He rambled off a long list of menu items he had to offer and reiterated he could also prepare an American dish for me, then suggested a cordon-bleu type of meal with mashed potatoes. I told him that sounded good, then ordered a lemonade and sat down at a table to wait for my dinner.

A few minutes later, Alexander handed me the lemonade and struck up a conversation while his assistant prepared my meal. We started off our conversation with the familiar spiel, "WPN" (WAYIF, POH, NPPF). Alexander wasn't much of a conversationalist, though his presence gave me a feeling of solace as if I were just one of the guys sitting around chatting. I get the impression Alexander has been stuck in this prison for an extended amount of time because he complained about the overwhelming boredom and everyday monotony; which appeared to affect his reserved attitude and who has given up trying to make his time in prison a little more enjoyable or at least tolerable. His grievances sounded like what I have been experiencing with the extreme boredom, but I will do my damnedest not to end up going down the same path as him by refusing to deny myself of any stimulation that may arise, keeping my mind sharp and body busy while incarcerated.

During our lengthy moments of silence, I thought to myself, if Alexander doesn't modify his humdrum existence in prison, who will? I would have thought by having his wife incarcerated alongside him should help ease some of the depression he displays. But sometimes even a strong-willed man with a positive attitude can only suck so much shit through a straw for so long, before he says, "I've had *enough!*" Sooner or later, one proceeds to just give up, finding himself in a bell tower with a high-powered rifle, trying to rid his body of all the *vile* from within by taking out his frustrations on innocent bystanders below. *Everybody* has their own breaking point!

When the cook had finished preparing my meal, Alexander brought it to my table, then headed back to the courtyards visiting area to sit next to his wife, who was also wearing a prison-issue uniform. I peacefully sat there alone, eating dinner while observing what little activity there was in the courtyard, oddly feeling more comfortable than one would expect while being in a Mexican prison. My cordon-bleu and mashed potatoes came with two slices of cantaloupe, making for a delicious dessert and complemented the enjoyable dinner, all for under five dollars. I felt fortunate receiving four enjoyable meals in three days from inside this prison and could have never anticipated from those first two dreadful nights here that I would find myself being served a home-cooked meal prepared by a former Denny's restaurant cook!

Because of the limited amount of food consumption in the last six days, my tight stomach didn't allow me to finish the meal; therefore, I saved the tasty leftovers for tomorrow's lunch. When I stood up and went to the café's counter to get a to-go box and pay my bill, Alexander walked back over to the café to receive my money. After I thanked him and the cook, he eagerly began promoting his American style breakfast and wanted me to return in the morning to give it a try. I said, "Okay," and graciously thanked him once more before walking away. I usually don't eat a big breakfast and seriously doubt I will return tomorrow morning, though it's really nice to know there is another option at where to eat.

Upon returning to the cell, there was no mention to David of my dining experience, in order to avoid his persistent kindness in offering to cook a meal for me once he discovered I had dined elsewhere. I was able to slip past him unnoticed with the Styrofoam box in my hand while making my way to the kitchen, where I had to rearrange the jam-packed fridge, making room for my leftovers.

I made my way back through the cell to the crate and resumed observations of the café's activity, where the phrase "it could always be worse" reappeared in my thought process while watching inmates at our door. From the countless hours of sitting in this broken lounge chair, I've noticed a select few of inmates show up at the café's door wearing dirty and worn prison uniforms who appear to be impoverished. With little to no money in their pockets, they rarely purchased food products from the café and bought mostly cigarettes or two-liter bottles of water. Sometimes the penniless customer was a peso or two short from purchasing his cigarettes and would plead to Emilio for an acceptable price, he was willing to agree upon.

I witnessed one desperate inmate who bartered with Emilio, offering three pesos and a used empty two-liter plastic bottle in exchange for two cigs. I think Emilio was selling the cigarettes two for 5 pesos. The impoverished inmate pleaded with him and was able to finalize the deal, walking away with his cancer sticks once again, ensnared by a habit for which he could not financially support. Side note: US brand name cigarettes on average cost 150 percent more than Mexico's due to the extra taxation, *smoke on that!*

On the flip side of the coin, not only did I witness impoverished inmates at our cell door, there were some who usually wore civilian clothing along with a prison issue shirt or pants, which were tater free and clean. Those cash positive inmates seemed more apt in exchanging a more friendly greeting with Emilio and the guys, also hung around the door a little longer while engaging in sociable interaction. Another correlation between the have and have nots revealed by what the inmate wore, was if they had access to somebody from outside of these prison walls. For example, Frank and Raúl who always wore a full prison uniform, unlike some of my cellmates who usually wore some sort of civilian clothing, whereas I *never* wore prison clothing while in my jailcell.

The café's runner for the evening was busy running around making house calls, which meant the prison was in its 7:00 p.m. lockdown mode while I continued with unneeded and unwanted relaxation in purgatory. It was some time after seven when a guard showed up at our door and called out my name, then after saying something in Spanish, John responded in a raised voice, "Your lawyer is here!" Deja vu! Let's hope it's an actual lawyer here to see me this time. For some strange reason, I was optimistic a lawyer was truly awaiting my arrival, unlike yesterday's letdown; therefore, I politely interrupted John from his book and eagerly enlisted his help to accompany me in this late-night visit from a mystery lawyer.

Because we were headed to the area of the prison where a complete uniform was required, I hurriedly put on my prison-issue shirt while inquiring about borrowing someone's pants; however, John had quickly halted my search and impatiently said, "Don't worry about it, *let's go!*" I received the impression from his energetic reaction that time was of the essence, by not wanting me to dawdle. I was at a loss at the broken rule of John's wardrobe decision, but I didn't question his command; neither did the guard who allowed us entry into the corridor without delay.

We traversed down the corridor through the metal detector and headed toward the same visitor's room where I previously met

Edgar. When we entered the room, I was surprised to see Karla, my court-appointed lawyer standing there along with Angelica, the court-appointed translator. It was comforting to see that Karla had brought a translator with her and was more prepared to communicate with me than she was during my pretrial. However, the decision to bring my own interpreter, who is a very knowledgeable lawyer, is by no means an accident and having him by my side to clarify legal issues that will not be lost in translation, has trumped her helpful sidekicks' presence.

After the meet and greet and familiarizing them with John, the four of us stood alone in the large room and began discussing matters concerning my case. Karla and John did the majority of the talking while communicating back and forth in a professional and friendly manner. Angelica mostly stood there, nodding her head in agreement with the duo's discussion while I patiently waited for any tangible information which would answer my many questions.

During their discussion, Karla divulged pertinent information for John to relay to me, but he displayed an incredible amount of trepidation, refraining from hastily relaying *any* information to me without first questioning Karla for further details and clarification. At times, John took charge of their discussion and never looked confused or at a loss for words impressing the hell out of me! Karla must have been astonished, or completely taken back by a prisoner who possessed the knowledge and understanding of the judicial system, appearing to be equal to, or surpass her own ability. Either way, she displayed an impressive amount of patience and listened just as much as she spoke! I didn't know what the duo was saying, but I could tell progress was surely being made!

John's explanation of what was happening with my case and what was to be expected later was precise, informative, and easy to understand. As a matter of fact, this is the most knowledge I have acquired since getting arrested and no longer felt in the dark about what's developing in my case. Ah! The advantage of having an interpreter who is fluent in law! I truly believe John pushed for more answers from Karla than she was willing to reveal and came away with a much better understanding of my situation! If I had to choose

DIZNEY LAND by Way of Military Escort

between the two lawyers who I wanted by my side in a courtroom, it would definitely be the one with the most confidence, authoritative demeanor, communication skills and impressive knowledge of the judicial system, and truly the smartest person in the room, *John!*

There was a lot of information being exchanged during our extensive discussion, so there was no way I could possibly remember verbatim what was explained to me, although I do possess the two most important facts of our meeting. First: The judge had no legal right to deny my bail based on a prejudiced decision that I'm an American citizen with money. *Damn,* that's exactly what I said to myself the night of my pretrial!

Second: Karla had already submitted the paperwork to file a motion to grant my bail, which would be about two weeks before having a decision from the court. Karla concluded that it should be "No problem" *awk,* to get bail. Now the last time I heard from that boisterous bird was when Alexander squawked out "No problem" while I was drinking lemonade during dinnertime. But this time the parrot migrated into the room landing on John's shoulder and the squawks were heard in triplicate, as Karla, Angelica, and John were all in agreement that my bail was inevitable and tried convincing me with their repetitive phrase of, "*Awk,* No problem, *awk!*" Maybe it's time to start listening to the imaginary bird with the limited vocabulary and trust my stay in this fortified mouse house will be a short one.

This cheerful news was almost too good to be true, and John was adamantly convinced my case was heading down the right path and excited for me with a grin from ear to ear. As he finalized our discussion with Karla, I gave the two women a grateful thanks for their help plus an extra sincere appreciation to Karla for her diligent work. I certainly did not expect her to be the supplier of good news regarding my bail; nevertheless, it has been made apparent that her skills as a lawyer are much more qualified outside of the courtroom than from within.

A calm feeling of euphoria began to emerge while walking away with John from the informative visitation; unfortunately, it was short-lived as there was a power struggle in my mind between acceptance and doubt, when the "I'll believe it when I see it" logic took control of my thought process, containing my excitement to a minimum while letting John play the part of a joyful recipient of the encouraging news.

When we returned to our cell, John continued to be thrilled about my fortunate news, eagerly reiterating that getting bail was only a matter of time, and all I had to do is patiently wait while the judicial system completed its slow, laborious process. As our low-keyed excitement quickly died down, John resumed reading his book, while I returned to my pillow and began processing data from our recent encounter. Time spent on the milkcrate was brief as I decided to grab some clean clothes from my crate and make good use of my time by going to the bathroom for a shower.

Upon entering, I turned on the water to let it warm up, removed my nasty clothing, only to find myself standing there naked for a long time, followed by the realization of why my cellmates have been taking their showers early in the day. The prison water heater is not located in a very convenient area in which to adjust the water temperature, and for some reason, the pilot light always goes out late in the evening. Therefore, it was a logistical nightmare for the maintenance man to relight it, especially traversing 93,000,000 miles in which to do so. Well, that might be an exaggeration, for there is no maintenance man, pilot light, or water heater.

Since the prison stores its water in storage tanks on the roof, they rely on the free energy of the sun to heat the water. As water consumption during the day drains the hot water from the tanks, cold water entering doesn't have enough time to get warm while keeping up with demand, thus forcing inmates to take their showers early in the day if they want warm, or marginally hot water leaving uninformed individuals like myself stuck taking a cold shower and shrinkage of my extremity, "Like a frightened turtle."[26]

The water was so cold that I altogether avoided standing under the showerhead and limited my shower to a two-step process, getting lathered up all at once, then quickly rinsing off. I kept my chilling shower very short, as I'm a wimp when it comes to cold water,

---

[26] *Seinfeld*, TV show.

making me more appreciative of the rooms' warm air as it began to reemerge my tortoise. I finally had the pleasure of putting on *clean* clothes; one more day of wearing those same dirty clothes would have made one week.

After concealing the filthy clothing in a small shopping bag and placing it the crate under Roseudo's bed, I returned to my cocoon and waited for ten o'clock to arrive. Two hours later, I carried out my nighttime ritual, placing the sleeping mat by the door, hung up the towel on the door, put the handkerchief over my face then impatiently tried to ignore the smoke and noise, which lasted another hour and a half before I fell asleep.

Day 17 in Country

Fifth day in prison

Once again, I was awakened way too early by that annoying loud alarm clock of boisterous guards walking past our cell door, who unknowingly alerted me that there was about an hour before I physically had to get out of bed. Therefore, I pulled the covers over my head, attempting to prolong my slumber, even though I knew it would be periodically interrupted by guards wanting their morning coffee. What added sleep I was able to receive damn sure wasn't enough, plus waking up with a sore neck interfered with extending my siesta.

Just a little before roll call, I reluctantly dragged myself out of bed, put the mat away, then went into the patio for some cereal and a banana. While sitting there eating and contemplating over the twelve hours of freedom we were allowed each day from our boredom chamber, I decided it was time to take full advantage of it by going for a walk in the courtyard and get some *much needed* exercise; unlike some of my roomies who seem to be content spending most of their day in confinement. After finishing a light breakfast, I put on my prison shirt then had John unlock our cell door, allowing me to roam freely.

My casual walk around the courtyard area soon turned into the equivalent of a dog pacing back and forth in a caged enclosure, making me feel a little uncomfortable from the inquisitive stares from the inmates. The courtyard wasn't designed to be exercise-friendly and was limited at providing an area extensive enough for jogging, or a long course for walking. The only place in the compound capable of getting my heart rate elevated ran parallel with the east outer prison wall cross from the woodshop, only extending about one hundred feet. So my brisk walk would be interrupted every fifty feet by completing an about-face in order to continue with my blood pumping exercise.

I noticed a couple of inmates utilizing the area for their morning exercise who were walking at an elevated pace within the limited course, so I also decided to take advantage of this area for walking and work out some of the kinks my motionless body has accumulated throughout the week; unfortunately, I was only wearing ill-equipped flip-flops limiting my trek to a slower pace.

It took a while for me to realize that the two inmates exercising weren't wearing any prison-issued clothing, making me question their actions of violating the prison rule. Come to find out, anybody who was exercising in the courtyard during the morning was not required to wear a uniform, though I chose to wear a prison shirt as the extra layer helped keep me warm. The mornings in La Paz during the month of May are *cold*, especially while walking in the shadows of the prison walls, forcing me to keep clear from the chilly shaded air and traverse a path closer to the buildings in the warmth of the sun.

Cold is a relative word. When it's fifty-five degrees outside, my sister who lives in Florida would be wearing a heavy jacket, my other sister in Michigan would be wearing shorts, and I, hailing from Missouri would need a long sleeve shirt. However, the guards walking around here during the cold mornings were wearing insulated jackets, gloves, winter hats, and some even had balaclavas (ski mask) on. No joke! I have seen less winter gear worn by snow skiers in Michigan than in this tropical prison, and that's a *fact!*

Since the prison is surrounded by twenty-foot tall concrete walls, it traps the cool nighttime air within the courtyard, also blocks the late morning warm air from entering, effectively forcing the guards to dress like Eskimo's. Until midday, when the noontime sun starts heating the walls massive surface area creating Thermal Mass (the ability of a material to absorb and store heat energy) eventually resulting in elevated temperatures in the courtyard. The wide range of temperatures could be best described as a refrigerator in the early morning and an oven during the day. This lesson in thermal dynamics had me avoiding the morning shade as if it were an infectious disease and pursuing it during the extreme heat of the day as if it had the cure.

Because of my early arrival into the courtyard, I discovered where the dirt cleaning guy starts his obsessive cleaning ritual. Toward the far end of the west wall was an old shipping container the prison utilized for their trash, that someone had left the large double-hung door wide open, allowing the birds and stray cats to scatter the garbage. Some of the trash had found its way to the stretch of ground where I was walking, containing a section that had fresh groove marks from a rake, along with small piles of trash off to the side. This is when I found out the Dirt Cleaner guy possessed a rake in his arsenal of cleaning implements.

Soon after starting my walk, he emerged from a nearby building and vigorously resumed the project he obviously started earlier in the morning. The thought of having someone shut the shipping container doors at night would have been a simple solution in keeping the area clean; unfortunately, that would effectively put an end to the energetic inmate's daily routine and create a huge gap of idle time. My idle time spent in prison has me believing that it is much more important staying busy most of the day accomplishing little than it is to accomplish something productive for a fraction of the day!

My early morning walk also allowed the opportunity to observe the kitchen's prison staff through the open door of their building, busy making those nasty smelling tortillas using an ancient and crude machine that was pumping out flat round disc at an impressive rate. While standing there for a moment watching the inmates working alongside the loud machine, the aroma of the tortillas instantly brought me back to that miserable stay in the shithole cell, forcibly ending my visual amazement and quickly walked away to escape the unpleasant odor.

Even though I only walked for about twenty minutes before heading back to my cell, my stroll had a beneficial outcome other than some exercise. Since I cannot be totally expectant on bail, and unsure of the length of my stay here in Dizney Land, I have been nonchalantly scanning for weakness in the prison's security during my walk. I did notice a couple of places within the courtyard that could be scaled by a competent climber, such as myself, to gain access to the roof of the cellblock, then traverse it toward the outer wall of the prison. A plausible tactic assisted by the nonexistent roll call at night, whereas someone could hide amongst the construction materials behind Hector's café, then use the cover of darkness to aid in their ascent. According to John, my bail was imminent, so taking advantage of the flaws in the prison design may never come to play, though it never hurts to have options.

Upon returning to the cell, I paid Emilio for a Danish then sat on the crate and began filling the void in my stomach the small breakfast had left behind. Not long after eating, the gringo that always delivers showed up at our cell door asking how I was doing and if I had seen Brenda yet. After informing Frank that I haven't seen her, he displayed a concerned interest while questioning me for answers. All I could tell him was she dropped off some items for me yesterday, and there must have been a problem because it's highly unlikely she showed up at the prison and not come inside to visit me. Frank's worried expression revealed he was bothered by her no show, but I had no doubt he would be able to rectify the problem, as he instantly responded, "I will take care of it!" And away, he went. FRANK, the man of action, who clearly takes care of any problematic issues immediately!

About thirty minutes later, Frank returned with the reason for Brenda's no show, making it known there were two major problems with Brenda's visitation issue. First, her visitors' pass was only good for three days starting from Tuesday and expired yesterday. Second, she was to renew the pass while in prison, which obviously did not happen. Therefore, Frank by-passed going to the captain's office for assistance and went straight to the warden's office in order to expedite the setback. While there, he had to perform his Vegas magic by procuring a ten-day pass for Brenda, even though it was in violation of the prison rule: no visits allowed for nonresidents of Mexico. I never questioned the reason why the pass was only valid for ten days or thought about the implications it would have toward me after it had expired.

Soon after Frank left, I retrieved the word seek booklet from the bag of items Brenda dropped off yesterday, though I found it a little disappointing that it wasn't a Sudoku book, but any diversions from boredom are more desirable than no distractions at all. I attempted to keep my mind preoccupied as long as possible by searching for those hidden words amongst jumbled characters within the pages, but after sitting in my cocoon for a short period circling meaningless hidden text, I lost what little enthusiasm there was in the mindless activity and decided to call it quits to go outside to the courtyard.

Upon arriving into the yard, I was pleasantly surprised to see a familiar face among the inmates sitting on one of the benches. Without hesitation, I walked over to the bench and sat down next to Raúl and asked, "How did you get out of your cage?"

Raúl's explanation of his newly found freedom sounded a little vague, insisting if a guard likes you, he will let you out of your cell, and if not, you stay locked in and rot. I may be paraphrasing his actual words a bit; nevertheless, his soft-spoken standard phrase arose at the end of his sentence, "Man, that's some fucked up shit!"

During my encounters with Raúl, while he was helping me with the task at hand, I felt the need to repay his kindness and would occasionally ask, "What do you need?"

His first response was always spoken with a reserved graciousness, "Nothing." But I truly knew his list of needs had to be a long one, and he was just being polite declining my offer. When I pressed him a second or third time with an offer, only then would he accept, or ask for something to drink, giving me some solace knowing I was able to supply him with a necessity of which is so readily denied.

However, today's interaction with Raúl was out of the ordinary. His demeanor and body language had changed during our conversation into a more somber mood as he cautiously approached the subject concerning his grandma, who was supposed to visit him. The last time he communicated with her, she was going to enlist the help of a family member for a ride to the prison. When grandma never showed up, Raúl attempted to contact her many times, but to no avail, raising concerns about her whereabouts.

In Raúl's familiar soft-spoken tone, he politely reminded me of my previous offer of "What do you need?" and asked, "Could you buy me a phone card so I can call my grandma to see if she is okay?"

Now that I had money in my pocket to assist in Raúl's request, I stood right up and said, "*No problem*, where do we get one?" He pointed to the little store twenty feet away, then led us to the shack where he chose a phonecard that was the least expensive of thirty-five pesos, only costing me about two bucks. Raúl was very appreciative while continuing to voice strong concerns toward his grandma, a common reaction after receiving a favor from someone.

As Raúl continued expressing the justification for the phonecard, we walked around the corner of the store, where I noticed two inmates playing a game of chess, instantly sparking my interest and led to an inquiry of Raúl's ability at playing chess. I haven't sat down to play a good game of chess in over twenty years, so I eagerly jumped at the opportunity to play a game of strategic wit and challenged Raúl to a match. He willingly excepted and inquired if I had a chess set. It just so happens there was one in my cell on the shelf along with the little pink chair that I could probably borrow from the owner. Raúl advised me, while I retrieved the chess set, he was going to try and call his grandma, then we could meet back at a table when he finished with the phone call.

After returning with the game, I sat at a table that butted against Alexander's café and waited for Raúl's arrival. A short time later, he returned with a disheartening look on his face and said he couldn't contact grandma and would try again later to call her. When he sat down, we began setting up the chess pieces on the board when I noticed the black king was missing, and the only object remaining in the box was a small wooded toy turtle. I assumed it was the replacement piece for the absent king, which is only fitting as they are both encumbered in their ability to *swiftly* evade an enemy attack.

Even though I haven't played a game of chess in over two decades, I still have retained much of my accomplished skill throughout the years. While preparing to play against Raúl, who is an unfamiliar opponent, I felt a little anxious at his skill level, wondering if I will be humiliated by advanced gameplay. If my opponent is an average player, I tend to play more relaxed and at a faster pace, not worrying about losing, if they possess an advanced skill, I always play extremely slower while deeply immersed in thought refusing to lose. Nevertheless, I quickly realized Raúl's skill level was slightly less than average, and it would only be a matter of time before I ended up winning the game.

My thought of pre-victory wasn't of arrogance or cockiness but based on hundreds of years from grandmasters playing chess who have calculated the most effective and advantageous strategy for their plan of attack while securing a fortified defense. In my twenties, I studied chess books to improve gameplay and frequently played against computers that were set at a high skill level, eventually becoming proficient at figuring out what the computers' next moves were going to be. Having that knowledge in the game of chess is a huge advantage and has assisted me in many victories in defeating the computer.

With all my past experience at playing chess and the ability to capitalize on an opponent's single mistake, I knew from Raúl's opening moves it would be hard for him to defend against my attack. He also played too fast and didn't consider that aggressive offense should include a strong defense. Raúl's lack of experience led me to capture his helpless turtle with relative ease and defeat him two games to none.

While Raúl and I were in deep thought during our first game, I became perplexed from the arrival of Adrian at our table who has not had much personal interaction with me as a cellmate, but I quickly discovered his unexpected appearance wasn't to make a social call on my account. Adrian went straight to Raúl with an assertive approach leaned over and firmly gripped his shoulder, then with a dominant behavior whispered into his ear. I would have to be completely blind not to realize Raúl was getting reprimanded by a fellow inmate, but for *what?* Raúl responded to Adrian's presence in a calm and respectful manner who didn't agitate Adrian any more than he already was. After Adrian finished his short assertive chat with Raúl, he abruptly walked away without saying a single word to me or even acknowledging my presence.

I wasn't about to pry into Raúl's personal business and ask what just transpired; therefore, all I said to him was, "Man, that didn't look good!" He responded with a subdued tone, "Yeah," followed by a short, vague explanation of Adrian's unpleasant encounter. Apparently, somebody has been observing my activities while in prison and informed Adrian I bought a phone card for Raúl. This incited concern he was exploiting my generosity do to the fact I had money, which may be true, but *hell*, we are in Mexico where the almighty dollar is what drives most people's motivation in their daily decisions, and besides, I'm the one who initiated Raúl's request by continuing to ask him what he needed.

I was completely caught off guard from Adrian's bold action and deeply honored by his concern for my welfare, especially from a man I only met four days ago! Raúl may have felt a little threatened, or discomfort from Adrian's confrontation, though I felt a hell of a lot safer and extremely more at ease with my surroundings now than I did before Raúl's disquieting visitor showed up.

During our second game, Hector walked over from his food shack to our table and showed interest in our game, watching us play. Most people who watch others play chess are usually familiar with the game and are intrigued by the progress of each players' positioned pieces on the board; case in point, Hector, who challenged me to a game after Raúl and I finished playing.

From Hector's second move, I knew this was going to be a fast-paced game as he played like Raúl, involving his queen too early in gameplay and wasted valuable time with aggressive unproductive moves. With his queen now unprotected, I was able to eventually capitalize on his bad decision, game over! So now I was 3 and 0.

The news of the arrival of fresh meat must have been released among the prisoners, as another inmate approached our table, challenging me to a game, wanting to play for fifty pesos. My first response was to decline the offer, but Raúl convinced me to accept the challenge. The thought of playing for money worried me a little, not because of the less than three-dollar bet, but more of a concern in playing someone who is willing and confident enough to gamble money playing chess, creating a fear of losing, and I hate to *lose* at chess!

I found out later from Raúl that my opponent's name was Chewie. I have no idea how he spelled his name. No, he wasn't a furry Star Wars character (Chewbacca). Chewie looked to be sixty years old, clean-cut, short stature always wore a full prison uniform, had a calm demeanor, spoke almost no English, who conducted himself with the maturity of an older gentleman.

Chewie took one look at the turtle on the chessboard and decided to retrieve his chess game. While he was doing that, Raúl rearranged the pieces on our board and began playing a game with Hector. After Chewie returned with his small chess set, we began playing our game void of any small talk, due to his limited vocabulary of the English language. Such is the same as an old married couple—no exchange of words needs to be spoken during our interaction.

Chewie was an exceptionally good chess player who played fast, with confidence revealing many years of experience through his gameplay. He inadvertently forced me to play extremely cautious and at a slow pace, but by doing so, I severely aggravated my impatient opponent who tried to rush me along during gameplay. I refused to submit to his irritated pressure, since I would rather play slow and win than play fast and loose. If anybody doesn't understand that, they can go play checkers with the children! I have *never* rushed my opponent during a game of chess and never will. Doing so would only place undue pressure on them to make a faulty move, and much as I don't like to lose, I have less tolerance for winning when the game is in haste! I don't understand the urgency by my opponents to play fast; where else do they need to be that's more important? They are stuck in prison!

Chewie kept his fast pace during most of the match until I made an outstanding move taking him by complete surprise, forcing him to hesitate and rethink his next move. Unfortunately for him, it was already too late—it was the beginning of the end; even Raúl realized Chewie's dilemma as he looked at me with a smirk. His hasty aggressive attack had turned into a frantic retreat. He struggled to assist his threatened king and tried to camouflage his distress from my startling move by attempting to continue with his fast pace. Though the continuous hesitation displayed from his retreating hand while reaching for a chess piece during the next few moves revealed, he was in a world of *shit!*

I knew he would be in trouble a few moves prior, by luring him into a misleading attack that was designed to assist in my assault on his king. The ultimate attack is the one your opponent doesn't see coming until it's too late, giving me my greatest joy at playing chess; god damn, I truly love that feeling! Chewie assumed that my slow playing was a sign of weakness, as overconfidence was his, allowing me to stuff fifty pesos into my pocket and improve my record to 4 and 0.

After the game, there was a discussion between Raúl and Hector as to who was going to play the next game against me. I wanted to appease both challengers, so I offered to play them both at the same time. They looked slightly confused and were not sure on how to respond and declined my offer in a manner suggesting it would be unfair to myself playing them at the same time, also didn't want to impose on my generosity in order to entertain both of their requests. I'm quite proficient at multitasking and confident the unfairness would only be against Raúl and Hector, so I convinced them I was more than willing to play against them both.

I borrowed Chewie's chess set in order to allow for a dual match, but Raúl and Hector still appeared to be a little reluctant while setting up the chess pieces; that soon dissipated once we started playing. I have no recollection of our gameplay during the dual match, except that both opponents failed to capitalize on the one mistake I made in each game, resulting in a record of 6 and 0.

When the carnage was over, and the conquered kings were laid to rest in a cardboard box, my growling stomach made it known it was well past lunchtime, prompting a trip back to my cell for the leftover meal I had from Alexander's café yesterday. As soon as I entered with the chess set in hand, Emilio looked at me, raised his right hand up to his forehead, making the "L" sign with his fingers, then with a big grin uttered, "Loser?"

With arms raised in victory, I replied, "No, no, winner!" I immediately received an elated thumbs up from Emilio. Our interaction may have been brief, but it felt good to receive an uplifting greeting from a cellmate upon entering the cell. I'm starting to be more relaxed in here and not feel like an outsider, even though I am, yet my cellmates certainly don't treat me that way.

Since John and Adrian were also in the room with Emilio, I figured it would be a good time to take advantage of their presence and defuse the situation that happened earlier today between Raúl and Adrian, inadvertently caused by me. I asked for John's assistance in translating to Adrian my concerns of Raúl's questionable actions. I made it clear to Adrian that I didn't believe Raúl was hustling me and I was very grateful to Raúl for all his help and willingly offered to get him what he needed, only then did Raúl ask for the phonecard. John must have articulated the translation to perfection, as there was no rebuttal or disagreement from Adrian; therefore, I assumed everything would be okay between the two combatants.

My stomach was still waiting to be fed, so I grabbed the leftovers from the fridge, zapped it in the microwave then sat in the patio to enjoy my lunch. While eating, I heard a slight commotion from across the cell and heard my name being mentioned. I proceeded to leave the kitchen and inquire about why I was the subject of someone's discussion. Within a few steps upon entering the room, I met David and asked, "What's going on?"

He informed me there was an inmate at our cell door, wanting money from me for the use of the table and chairs during my recent visit to the courtyard while playing chess.

I responded with disgust, "What?" I was at a loss for words and wondered what the hell David was talking about. Apparently, the inmate at the door was the owner of all the table and chairs in the courtyard, charges a rental fee for the use of said property, and wanted me to pay him five pesos. I wasn't concerned about the minuscule five pesos (27¢) though I was slightly aggravated that out of the four of us who used the patio furniture, I'm the only person who was tracked down to pay the rental fee. Even though David quickly eased my discomfort by telling me not to worry about paying, because the inmate owed him a favor, I continued with my rant to David about being singled out, just before walking back into the patio. Though I did find out later that rental fees are exempt when utilized by a customer from the store or the two-outside café's, which explains why my occupation of the tables yesterday was gratis.

After eating my late lunch, I went over to the café's counter and stood next to Emilio, who was in the room, along with a few roommates involved in a discussion. Through David's and John's partial translations, I was able to get the gist of what they were talking about, mainly consisting of legal battles and incarceration stories. Emilio made a remark about jail time in reference to Pablo's twenty-year prison sentence, prompting me to ask John how many years Emilio had left in his sentence, he replied, "Thirteen years."

I took advantage of the rooms' carefree mood by placing my right hand on Emilio's shoulder and jokingly said. "You poor bastard." David had to translate my wisecrack to him, inducing a chuckle from everybody in the room. Emilio's facial expression told the whole story of his unfortunate amount of time left in prison, as he tried to partially disguise his discomfort with a saddened smile and a shrug of his shoulders.

While we were on the subject of imprisonment, I questioned John on the length of his prison sentence, expecting his answer to be much less severe than his fellow cellmates. I made this assumption based on his status as a lawyer and that he had an intellect much superior to my own and most likely to everyone else inside this prison. But my hypothesis was completely wrong! From this point on, I held a deep respect for John, as his unbelievable story ensnared my attention with utter disbelief.

John and I had something in common, we had yet to be sentenced, arrested on the same day and processed in the same jailhouse, yet our paths never crossed while inside a building with only three jail cells. This certainly exposed a judicial system that expedited John's incarceration from the jailhouse straight to prison on the same day, which is bizarre as hell for anybody who is familiar with legal doctrine. John's fast track to prison was due to the court having evidence he violated a court order from a previous trial while representing a client. Even though he could prove beyond a shadow of a doubt he was never in court during the day in question, the court had signed documents by John and government officials to the contrary proving his guilt. The catalyst that drove the chain of events forcing corrupt government officials to imprison John was based on a substantial financial windfall for all who were involved. We're talking about the kind of money that makes problems and people disappear, the "two point five billion" kind!

Somebody went through an extreme amount of trouble to put this highly publicized lawyer behind bars; consequently, the headline news considers him to be a radical prisoner of the state. *Shit*, I thought I had problems, *not!* Even though John had trepidation in venturing out of his prison cell, fearing for his safety, who by no means was going to allow this injustice to prevail. He diligently studied his court case files daily, reading law books, working on his summarization and keeping in contact with his fellow attorneys at the law firm, which must have been the books I had witnessed him reading all week. Not only was John dealing with his own troublesome legal matters, but he also was helping other inmates with their legal problems. John's integrity is truly remarkable! Even for a well-versed lawyer such as John, the overwhelming number of forged documents would prove to be an uphill battle during his entire stay in prison. The correlation between John and the 2.5 billion dollars will be revealed later when the information became available to me.

After listening to John's FUBAR story, I sat down on my crate and continued to be partially involved among the men's conversation that quickly transformed into friendly banter. Most of their interactions were void of translation until David, or John directed their attention to me with various questions, or when I was the recipient of someone's wisecrack. While patiently waiting to be involved in their ongoing jocularity, I grabbed the word seek booklet to help occupy some of my time.

Nothing noteworthy happened for the next couple of hours, just sitting around bullshitting and joking with the guys, occasionally accepting money and handing customers their purchases. Even though I had the freedom to leave the cell, it felt more important

DIZNEY LAND by Way of Military Escort

at that moment to hang out with fellow cellmates improving and expanding my connection with them, especially while we were all together in the same room immersed with amusing banter.

Sometime later, Frank stopped by to confirm that all the paperwork had been completed for Brenda's visitors' pass, which would be waiting for her at the visitor's check-in area upon her arrival. He also informed me that the captain wanted to see me in his office. Before having a chance to be concerned about the peculiar request, Frank told me not to worry about it, as it was only a formality.

Once inside the captain's office, we sat at his desk while Frank translated our conversation. The captain was sharply dressed in a suit and tie, clean-shaven, amiable and spoke with a calm, authoritative tone, which created a relaxed atmosphere. He voiced concerns for me to obey prison rules, such as no drugs, stay out of trouble and yada yada yada; essentially a short version of the prison regulations that were relayed to me upon my first night's arrival. Our informal meeting was concise and quick, and as we stood up to leave, I found myself amazed by the concern and interest the captain showed in my acquisition of Brenda's visitors' pass. He also inquired if everything was taken care of, "Yes." Thanks to Frank. Just before we left the office, I expressed my personal gratitude toward the hospitable captain and headed back to my cell.

Even after Frank completed the task of acquiring Brenda's unsanctioned ten-day pass, he still had the fortitude in asking if I needed anything else just before walking away from my cell door.

I decided to take advantage of the unoccupied bathroom and take a shower, figuring it being in the middle of the day, my chances of having warm water were in my favor, in addition, I wanted to make up for the short ineffective cold shower I experienced yesterday.

Upon completion of a successful warm shower, I headed outside with a glass of water and wandered around the courtyard for a while. My outside stroll was cut short as soon as I noticed Hector standing by his food shack. He didn't look like he was busy, so I used the opportunity to walk over and order an early dinner to make up for the leftover lunch that wasn't filling. I politely asked Hector if he could make a double cheeseburger and fries, but he looked at me with a confused expression while he repeated my request.

I had to rephrase my order to "A cheeseburger with two pieces of meat" to clarify what I wanted. At that moment, I didn't think about the translation of "double cheeseburger," as it doesn't imply anything about having two pieces of meat, which explains Hector's perplexed stare.

Soon after eating my delicious burger, Hector walked over to my table and struck up a conversation, mainly consisting of the standard spiel of WPN, then he asked if I wanted to play a game of dominos. I gladly accepted and informed him I had only played dominos as a child and was never taught the official rules of the game. He quickly gave me instructions and supplied some key components of basic gameplay during our game. I consider dominos a game that requires more luck than skill, but Hector proved to be more skillful winning at dominos than my desperate attempt at being lucky, by repeatedly winning game after game. Though he never gloated or displayed much emotion from his victories, the nuance of his body language suggested being quite gratified at defeating the individual who eradicated his king earlier in the day.

I don't mind losing at games in which I haven't much experience playing or games relying on the luck of the draw; therefore, I continued playing dominos for long as he was willing to keep his winning streak alive. At least both of us were enjoying cheap entertainment; regrettably, only fifty percent of us would be going to our cell with the big "L" in front of our forehead. We were starting our fifth game when an inmate approached us and began talking to Hector, then directed his attention toward me, and asked if it was okay for a third person to join us. I thought to myself, sure why not, this newcomer will not help my odds at winning, however, it would hinder Hector's chances in continually humiliating me.

After agreeing, the inmate spoke to me in English with a sincere tone, asking, "Are you sure?"

I responded, "Yes, no problem," then gestured for him to take a seat to join us.

His name was Carlos. He spoke adequate English, looked to be thirty-five years old, five feet, eleven inches tall, average build and weight, candid, well-groomed, and no visible tattoos. The energetic behavior Carlos displayed was totally opposite of Hector's reserved demeanor and could be best described as a friendly extrovert with a slight authoritative mindset.

Carlos eagerly recommended playing dominos for five pesos per game, though he had some resistance from Hector as to the amount of money per game, who wanted to play for only three pesos. I personally didn't give a shit, for I was willing to play Dominos for whatever price the two could agree upon; *hell*, we are only talking about 16¢ or 27¢ per game. We had less than two hours until lockdown, giving us enough time to play about twelve games at most, so playing for five pesos per game the most I could possibly lose is three bucks if losing every game. Carlos reluctantly agreed with Hector's minuscule amount of three pesos, which worked out well for us, as most of the winnings went into Carlos's pocket.

The three of us were still playing dominos near the seven o'clock lockdown when a guard showed up and pressed us to finish our game. Sadly, Hector and Carlos relieved me of my spare change of about $1.80. I failed to win a single game and was beaten like a bad stepchild but was able to learn some beneficial strategy, which led me to a few close victories by only a few points. After we scooped up our change from the table and exchanged our gratitude for playing, we quickly headed back to our cells to avoid being reprimanded by the guard, since we were the last inmates to leave the courtyard.

Upon entering the cell, I was greeted by Emilio with the big "L" in front of his forehead while looking at me with an inquisitive gesture. With a dejected frown, I grudgingly raised my hand and mirrored his action admitting my defeat. He then imitated my facial expression with a sad frown while shrugging his shoulders. After we finished our unspoken chat, I made my way into the kitchen for a snack and some water to prepare for the next three dreaded hours waiting for bedtime.

Once again, I found myself sitting on the crate, killing time, thumbing through the word seek pages searching for an escape. The book was equipped with a few various word puzzles that were slightly more interesting than the boring word search, but those puzzles were far from challenging enough to keep me from completing them at a fast rate. Which meant the puzzles of interest would soon be extinct, leaving me with only the brain-dead activity of circling words, therefore I had to pace myself to extend what little stimulation the booklet was offering.

While sitting there staring at the jumbled letters, David made a rare appearance emerging from his cocoon and took an interest in my activity, then asked, "Do you like doing word search?"

I said, "Not at all! I would rather be working on a Sudoku puzzle, but Brenda couldn't find one challenging enough for me."

David informed me he preferred doing word search instead of Sudoku because he had trouble staying focused for a long period of time, making it extremely hard for him to complete a Sudoku puzzle. I like to describe David's attention disorder as, *oh look*, little shiny red ball, syndrome. He also told me he owned a Sudoku book and was willing to give it to me as soon as he could retrieve it from an inmate who borrowed the book.

I was in awe and appreciative of his fine gesture, and looked forward to a more worthy mind challenge; therefore, I offered to trade my word seek booklet in exchange for his Sudoku book as soon as he was able to retrieve it from the inmate. David was elated toward the impending trade acting like I was doing him a huge favor, while responding with a concerned tone, "*Reeeally*, are you sure?" In my mind, I was getting a much better deal and tried to downplay his excitement, by reassuring him I was more than okay with the trade and happy to rid myself of the word search book.

The stimulating day was approaching its end, time to retrieve my notes to write down the highlights of the day. Then a bathroom ritual followed by a couple of hours of tossing and turning on my sleeping mat, struggling to ignore the noise and smoke. The six or less, hours of sleep I'm getting at night is turning into a problematic sleep pattern and starting to discourage my pleasant anticipation of going to bed; I guess I can always make up for lost sleep when I'm dead and pushing up daisies!

Day 18 in Country

Sixth day in prison

Like clockwork, my Saturday morning slumber was interrupted early, accompanied by my sore neck that has been progressively getting worse each morning. I tried extending my horizontal hiatus, but just as yesterday's, it was made impossible by the guard's morning coffee addiction. I was slightly more brazen this morning by staying in bed a little longer, just because I could. Eventually, the commotion at our door motivated me to put the sleeping mat away and head to the patio for a quick breakfast. By the time I finished eating a light breakfast, the guards had already completed roll call, so I headed out the door to the courtyard for a morning walk.

My back and forth stroll took place in the same area as yesterday. There I was able to witness the Dirt Cleaning guy working feverishly at his never-ending madness, yet the trash debris scattered by the animals in the area hadn't been raked up by the high-strung inmate. My observation was also made apparent by walking past a black cat who was hiding under a large wooden wagon that the kitchen staff used for transporting meals to the encaged area of the courtyard. The motionless cat was in a hunting posture, stalking an unaware bird who was enjoying its morning breakfast on the scattered trash. The clueless bird didn't seem to mind that I was continuously walking past it during my trek, nor did the determined feline. The two were focusing intently on their choice of meal and not on the ogling prisoner amused of the impending battle that never materialized. The cat was unsuccessful in its hunt and would have to wait until tomorrow morning. Maybe it could catch a free meal before the Dirt Cleaner guy removed the bird's reason for lingering in the kill zone.

About five minutes into my morning exercise while walking past the kitchen area, I spotted Chewie walking from the kitchen to an adjoining building that appeared to be a small office. Since we had made eye contact, I felt obligated to exchange a morning greeting as I walked past by extending a wave hello to the man who put fifty pesos into my pocket yesterday due to his defeat at chess. A few minutes later, while passing by the office again, Chewie was exiting and looked at me with slight concern while gesturing a crippling limp walking slowly, then pointed to me as if he were making fun of my slow pace. I nodded my head, yes, to confirm my sluggish movement and pointed to my left knee as if in pain.

Years ago, I injured my knee playing ice hockey and every so often, it bothers me with some minor pain. I use a Copper Fit knee brace to alleviate most of the discomfort, but of course, I don't have it in my possession here in prison; oh well, guess I'll rub some dirt on it.

On my next pass by the office, Chewie was standing in the doorway and raised his hand, motioning for me to walk over to him. When I approached, he invited me into the building. There was a small office cluttered with many items making the room only traversable through a narrow path. All the perimeter walls had large fifty-pound sacks of flour stacked six-feet high. The middle of the room had one chair and a small table with a TV placed in the center surrounded by clutter covering the surface of the table. The wall on the right had a refrigerator, a small area with shelving, food items, and various large cooking implements on the floor.

I hadn't a clue why Chewie wanted to see me, other than maybe socialize a bit, but his limited ability to speak English made our attempted conversation incredibly difficult. Our language barrier also made me feel uncomfortable struggling to keep our discussion alive, which kept me thinking about escaping from the office and end the fruitless interaction. Escape was futile as Chewie tried his damnedest to keep our awkward silence to a minimum, ensnaring me deeper into his unique world with pleasantry. Most of his sentences were short and incomplete, as mine were mainly responses to him of yes or no. If memory serves me right, Chewie was the only inmate I have met who hasn't asked me WAYIF, though someone could have already relayed my circumstances to him, eliminating our WPN spiel.

Chewie retrieved a Spanish-to-English translation book and told me his wife was teaching him English. He searched through the book for a word in order to complete his next sentence; of what, I don't recall. Then he picked up the chess set and looked at me with an inquisitive stare. It was too early in the morning for chess, so I shook my head and said, "No."

Next, he went over to the shelving and pointed to a basketball player who was on the front of a cereal box and asked, "Do you like…?"

I assumed he was referring to the player, or the basketball team, as the last word in his phrase was unclear. I politely responded, "Not really," and refrained from giving him my preferred response of "hell no!"

Then Chewie pointed to another box that displayed a big frog on the front. *Oh shit*, now I get it. He wasn't asking if I liked the game of basketball or a big frog that was wearing clothing but offering breakfast with the choice of Frosted Flakes or Sugar Smacks. I also declined his second offer of the frog on the box but accepted his kind offer of breakfast moments later when he repeated the gesture after I realized he was referring to cereal and not toward a basketball reference. Chewie must have thought I was a peculiar American at my decision to eat the Frosted Flakes after I had already told him I didn't like them.

Chewie cleared a small area from the cluttered table for a bowl and the box of cereal, offered me a seat, adding a banana and some milk to my unexpected breakfast. The thought of sitting in a kitchen office within a Mexican prison eating cereal offered by this generous inmate who I just met yesterday was well beyond belief! Typically, I would express the legality of my story by saying, "You can't make this shit up," although that statement would be slightly premature.

Chewie extended my amazement by pointing to a stack of DVDs to the right of the table and gestured for me to pick out a movie to watch. *Movie?* Is this date night with a meal and a movie in the morning, or am I trapped in a strange episode of the Twilight Zone? I'm beginning to think that prison rules of no TVs are just a suggestion for the chosen few, or for more who have the right connections.

After Chewie displayed the various DVDs that were in English, I searched through the small selection and chose a movie I haven't seen before that looks appealing to watch. The title of the film escaped my memory until days before I wrote this paragraph while scrolling through Netflix titles where I noticed the familiar film preview, The Mine, truly a conveniently odd coincidence.

Just before Chewie left the room, I extended my humbled appreciation toward his generosity, then sat there baffled at how I ended up in this unique setting, not sure if I should feel grateful or ashamed that so few inmates fail to have this luxury.

After starting the movie, I put some cereal and sliced banana into my bowl, only to realize that watching the movie all the way through was not going to be an option, as the acting, writing, and storyline was atrocious. The film's setting was in a middle eastern desert with two US military snipers on a mission. Early in the movie, their mission went horribly wrong when one of the soldiers was killed, and the surviving man ended up stepping on a landmine, where the unexploded ordnance held him hostage. Most of the movie that I painfully sat through, consisted of the soldier stuck there in one spot trying to figure out a way to get off the landmine without getting blown to pieces. I kept waiting for the movie to get better, but the brain-dead film just progressively became worse, so after finishing my second bowl of cereal, I impatiently watched the awful movie for about another thirty minutes, just to be polite toward Chewie's kind gesture.

The thought of Brenda's probable arrival to the prison during the ten o'clock visitation had crossed my mind and since I hadn't a clue of the present time, compounded with the fact that nobody knew I had disappeared into the kitchens office, gave me a restless, uneasy feeling of missing a visitation with her. Therefore, I used that dilemma as a valid excuse for my urgency in leaving prematurely from Chewie's morning matinee. As I extended my gratitude toward

DIZNEY LAND by Way of Military Escort

Chewie's generosity, he suggested playing a game of chess sometime soon, to which I gladly agreed upon then headed back to my cell.

While sitting on my crate minding my own business, a boisterous guard with a bushy handlebar mustache arrived at our cell door, looked at me with a big grin then shouted out in a friendly greeting, "*Hey Harry Potter!*" Everybody within earshot started laughing, as I was once again the recipient of the group's laughter.

Unsure of the guard's ability to understand English or the degree of his sense of humor, I refrained from a smart-ass response free from vulgarity, or personal attack, leaving me with a lame juvenile comeback of, "If I had my stick I'd turn you into a frog!"

It's painful admitting that I even said that phrase, what am I seven years old? Come to find out the guard couldn't understand a single word I said, so next time we have an encounter, my interaction will be more of an R rated side of Shawshank Redemption, and not a G rating of a Disney film. The only possible similarities I had with Harry Potter, which could have motivated the guards' weak attempt at being funny was being a white male, short hair, and wearing glasses. "Other than that,"[27] there are absolutely no familiar attributes between us. At least it was comforting to know my presence was amusing a guard and not provoking animosity.

It was about two hours of trying to stay preoccupied with Word Seek and eyeballing the clock with hopeful anticipation of Brenda's arrival when I started getting depressed by surmising her visitation may not materialize. Consequently, I decided that sitting in a prison cell moping around wasn't how I wanted to spend my day, so I informed John that I could be found in the courtyard if, or when Brenda arrived, then slipped on my prison pants and headed out the door.

While approaching the area where the two benches were located, I noticed Raúl was once again free from his cage and sitting among gathered inmates. Since there was no room for me to sit, I stood near him while engaging in a discussion concerning his grandmother. He appeared to be relieved at finally being able to contact her via the

---

[27] My dad's familiar phrase passed down to my sister Maribeth.

phone and found out why she didn't come to visit him. Apparently, her driver had ended up going to the hospital for a serious medical problem, and it was unclear when she would be able to visit Raúl. That was about the extent of our short interaction. He exited the area immediately after, leaving me standing there among strangers.

As soon as Raúl walked away, my anxiety level began to rise, feeling awkward standing there all by myself. Luckily shortly after, an inmate walked over to me and struck up a conversation, quickly easing my comfort level. Even though he spoke a little broken English, we were still able to communicate the "WPN" spiel, prompting me to keep our conversation alive by asking how long he had left in his prison sentence. His answer gave me absolutely no reassurance; his prison sentence had been completed three months prior, yet for some crazy-ass reason, he was still held captive behind these walls.

From the disheartening stories I have heard from inside this Micky Mouse house, maybe the prison slogan of "Where dreams come true," should be changed to "You can check out any time you like, but you can never leave!"[28] My cellmate John may not find the irony of that statement very amusing, for he lives in the area of Todos Santos, Mexico, which is the same town where the original Hotel California is located.

When our short encounter ended and the discouraged inmate walked away, another one showed up to take his place. This inmate who approached me was slightly more adequate in speaking English, and after completing our "WPN" spiel, he tried to ensnare my interest with his sad sob story on how rough it was to function in prison because of his lack of money. He went to explain that he could not make enough money cleaning prisoners' uniforms, as there were not enough inmates who could afford his services. I received a strong impression this desperate inmate was trying to pressure me in utilizing his laundry service by means of sympathy.

I ended my brief encounter with the Laundry Guy by saying, "Thanks, but no thanks," and walked away. I have no problem with washing my own clothes by hand. I think the word must be out that

---

[28] "Hotel California," song by the Eagles.

DIZNEY LAND by Way of Military Escort

this American has money, therefore from this point on, I need to be more aware of the Baja Sharks circling my wallet waiting for the chum to spill out.

After escaping the bloody waters, I meandered over to Alexander's café for lunch and ordered the cordon-bleu, assuming the meal would be just as good from the one I had on Thursday. Unfortunately, I was sorely disappointed; it lacked any flavor. Maybe Denny's manager was deported back to the United States due to the lack of quality control.

While sitting there trying to force down my lunch, I observed the Dirt Cleaning guy continuing his daily routine by frantically watering the courtyard area, attempting to stay ahead of the evaporating moisture. I have to say he is one extremely determined inmate, who will be addressed from now as the Energizer Bunny on speed.

Soon after finishing my less than desirable lunch, Hector walked over to my table and asked if I wanted to play Dominos, then added if it was okay to play for three pesos a game. I was well aware that he knew playing for money was a huge advantage for him, but its only chump-change we're talking about, so I replied, "Sure, why not!" I never give money to charity, though I'm sure Hector could benefit from some extra cash more than myself. So I proceeded to transfer funds from my pocket to his, as he once again won every game, but his reign of victory will soon end, as I have been steadily improving my gameplay with each passing moment. I may not need money from a poor man's defeat, but I damn sure will accept it in victory!

During my humiliation at Dominos, I was pleasantly surprised by an inmate who showed up at our table selling an assortment of freshly baked pastries, *awesome!* Frank never informed me this theme park was equipped with street vendors. The thought of an enjoyable after lunch dessert sounded good, so I bought two lemon cream-filled pastries for ten pesos (56¢), then proceeded to devour one of the "sweet treats"[29] and saved the other one for later.

Hector must have been tired of winning and taking my money because only after a few games of playing Dominos, he asked if I

---

[29] My sister Debbie's familiar saying.

was willing to play checkers for a while. I reluctantly agreed to play a child's game with him, as it was slightly more constructive than staring at fortified concrete walls all day.

We were about four moves into our first game when a cellmate arrived in the courtyard at one o'clock, informing me that I had a visitor. I instantly stood up to abandon the checker game and told Hector I had to leave. I quickly made my way back to the cell, where I found out from John that Brenda was here to see me. I quickly grabbed my prison shirt and headed back out the door. This fantastic news put an energetic stride in my step while walking over to Raúl's cell to enlist his help to accompany me to the reception area. When we arrived at the metal detector, Brenda was nowhere in sight. Raúl walked over to the entry gate where a guard was standing who operated the intercom system used for notifying visitors it was their turn to enter the prison and asked him Brenda's whereabouts.

A couple of minutes later, a guard unlatched the gate, allowing Brenda to enter the prison. She walked through the metal detector, where we were able to greet each other with a passionate hug. I instantly felt a bunch of mixed emotions coursing through my veins during our embrace. It was very surreal having Brenda next to me inside a Mexican prison, putting me at a loss on how to conduct myself in her presence. It was also evident Brenda was extremely uncomfortable within this strange environment, she displayed elevated apprehension at being on the wrong side of steel bars, once again!

As I introduced Brenda to Raúl, he started to lead us to the courtyard area, but Brenda halted our forward progress by refusing to venture any further into the prison and was adamant toward sitting on a bench in the corridor that was across from the captain's office. I wasn't sure if we were allowed to visit each other in this area of the prison, but I knew for a *fact* if the guards had pressed the issue of us moving into the courtyard she would have instantly come unglued, spoke a few colorful metaphors, then walked out the door she came through leaving the prison in a heated rush. Therefore, I only asked her one time, "Are you sure you don't want to go outside to the courtyard," then tentatively agreed for us to sit on the bench.

As we sat close together, keeping our public display of affection to a minimum, I ignored the prying stares of passersby while focusing my full attention on Brenda. After she mentioned being thirsty, I gave Raúl some money to purchase a Pepsi from the store, plus whatever he wanted to drink. While he was away, Brenda took advantage of our affectionate conjoined bodies by inconspicuously slipping me some cash, even though she understood it was okay for me to receive money, she didn't want to make it known publicly.

The thought of accessibility to a prison store triggered an exuberant clarification to Brenda of my time spent here in Dizney Land, regarding the amenities of the café, relaxed atmosphere and friendly encounters with inmates and guards, "Et cetera, et cetera, et cetera."[30] I could hardly contain my excitement while sharing detailed information about Frank and all that he has done for me, including that John was an English speaking lawyer who is in the same cell as mine and is extremely knowledgeable of the legal system. From Brenda's body language and the look of doubt in her eyes, common sense would dictate my overzealous remarks concerning attributes of fellow inmates, had her questioning my perception of their character by not carefully evaluating them, which could be possible but not probable!

After Brenda listened to my less than hardship story, she began revealing all the perils of her very stressful encounters, and the long list of difficult hurdles she faced during the entire week. The most recent daunting task was gaining access to the prison. The language barrier between her and the prison staff had dramatically hindered the check-in process and had been frustrating her ever since nine o'clock this morning, a reminder it's one o'clock now! She was denied entry three times today for various reasons, the type and color of clothing she was wearing, items she had brought for me, and items on her person. Brenda's mission to visit me ended up turning into a *four-hour* struggle, and of course, each problem wasn't addressed at the same time, forcing her to return to the rental car repeatedly to abandon items not allowed in prison.

---

[30] *The King and I*, movie.

Since it was Saturday, the prison had many visitors, making parking a vehicle in proximity to the prison virtually impossible, forcing Brenda to make long treks back and forth to the car; resulting in the ominous feeling of walking through the prisons main gate a total of seven times. *Hell*, if I were Brenda, I would have said, "Said screw that dumb bastard I'm going home for the day!"

Also, adding to Brenda's intensified stress was the denial to retrieve our truck from the jails impound lot yesterday. She was told she needed proper legal documents in order to do so, which completely contradicted what they said on the day of her release from jail, "No problem, you just have to sign a form." From the sounds of it, I think a lawyer's involvement might be required!

While we were sitting there talking, I heard a shoutout of "*Harry Potter*." I looked over and saw a familiar grin on a prison guards' face as he walked by.

With an extended wave of my hand, I gave a jovial shout out, "Hey Frog-Man!" From an outsider's point of view, this peculiar encounter must have appeared strange and surely needed an explanation to Brenda as to why I was greeting the guard with a nickname.

During a break in our conversation, Brenda addressed Raúl and involved him in a friendly Q&A discussion. Raúl kept his usual lowkey demeanor while respectfully answering Brenda's inquisitive questions and didn't appear to mind sharing personal information with her. After a short period of time of them talking and getting better acquainted, Brenda's kind heart began showing concern in Raúl's unfortunate predicament of being held captive for two years without being sentenced, by offering to help with his legal matters and inquired about his case number. Raúl was completely caught off guard at her overzealous gesture, though contained his emotional excitement, which was most likely a posture of "I will believe it when I see it." He displayed modest interest from Brenda's offer, though sadly couldn't remember his case number, but said he could find out what it was by going to the secretary's office later.

Brenda and Raúl were still involved in discussion when Frank walked by and noticed us sitting there. He walked over and joined us in the discussion. As I introduced Brenda to Frank, he displayed a

DIZNEY LAND by Way of Military Escort

genuine concern for her well-being by asking with a sincere gesture, "Is there anything I can get you?"

Of course, her answer was "No." After an exchange of pleasantries, Frank graciously thanked us for the soon to be delivered TV and gave us detailed information in getting the TV inside the prison.

With slight concern, Frank asked Brenda if she had the permission slip. I relieved his worried mind and said, "Yes, I gave it to her when she arrived here."

I believe Frank's next statement was a gesture of gratitude toward his impending gift, which staggered my imagination and invoked a hopeful outcome for myself, as Frank addressed us with sincerity and said, "I can get you two a conjugal visit." I instantly looked at Brenda for a flirtatious response, unfortunately, I was quickly disappointed like a teenage boy on prom night, as she adamantly refused his peculiar offer.

Frank's extraordinary proposal did not end there, as he pleaded, "Are you sure? I can reserve a room for you guys tonight."

Brenda didn't alter from her first response, which in turn forced my reluctant reply to Frank, "No, thanks."

Damn! A horizontal bop in a foreign prison may not have been on my bucket list, although I'm sure a story of a seductive rendezvous with Brenda in a Mexican prison would have been more captivating than someone's tale in the mile-high club.

As soon as Frank gave up trying to book our room in Hotel California, he began to leave the corridor, mentioning he still wanted to take me on a tour of the area where he worked and would be back later to do so after running a few errands.

As our visitation was drawing near its end, we clarified over the list of items I needed, and she reminded me that the bags of items she brought were at the inspection area. One of the last spoken words to come from Brenda as were saying our sadden goodbyes was addressed to Raúl with a sincere gesture, "I promise you; I will help with your case!"

I thought to myself, what a bold statement to make!" How can such a pivotal pledge be made without knowing all the intricate details involved with the case, plus dealing with a dysfunctional judicial system hampering your every move? Hopefully, Raúl wouldn't be severely disappointed if the promise fails to materialize.

It was disheartening to watch Brenda walk away as she exited the prison, and even though my spirits were dampened, I felt considerably grateful for Raúl's help and had a strong urge to repay his kindness. I knew he would decline my offer for acquiring something for him, as he has done in the past; therefore, I passionately insisted he accept a gift from me. Just as I thought! His first lowkey response was, "No thanks." But I once again pressed the offer, which he eventually humbly gave in to my persistence than with a soft appreciative tone said, "A portable radio."

Raúl's description of what he wanted was similar to a low budget Walkman, a device I was familiar with by noticing a few inmates wearing the gadget hung around their necks. After retrieving my bags of items from the inspection area, we returned to our cellblock, where I expressed my gratitude and exchanged a fist bump and then parted ways.

Upon making my way into the kitchen to put my bags of goodies away, I was relieved to find the all-important translation handbook in one of the bags and a lot of food products within both, though deeply confused by a few items at the bottom of one bag. There were three small thin plastic bags filled with a thick liquid substance, which had been sealed with a tied knot at the top of each bag. It looked like a gory science project gone horribly wrong that I dare not open the substandard containers in fear of making a mess. It took me a while to decipher the bags of the mystery goo Brenda had given me. One was obviously apple sauce, and only upon further examination of the other items within the bags, where I found spaghetti and pancake mix, was I able to conclude one bag contained pasta sauce and the other syrup. Therefore, I can now quote Peter Sellers from his Pink Panther movie "Case solvid."

Come to find out, a glass of any kind is not permitted inside the prison, so Brenda, with no prior knowledge of the said rule, had to be creative with limited resources by emptying all the food products from the glass containers into plastic bags, ultimately added to her long delay upon entering the prison.

DIZNEY LAND by Way of Military Escort

At about the time I finished putting away the groceries, Frank showed up and asked if I was ready to take the tour of his work area. I thought to myself, *cool*, more time spent outside of my cage. "Yes, let's go!"

We proceeded to walk through the same corridor in which I visited Brenda moments earlier, went down a hallway to the right of the captain's office, and exited the building through a back door where we ventured into a section of the prison that was unfamiliar to me. Once outside, we walked down a concrete ramp leading to a long sidewalk that ran parallel to a tall chain-link fence, which separated the good side of the prison from the nonconformist and riffraff side, housing most of the prison's population. That area contained a large courtyard with a basketball court and an exercise building, along with some sizeable three-story housing units and other small various buildings.

The smaller area that we were in held two buildings; one contained the medical unit and the other a psych ward housing the mentally unstable. This section of the prison surprisingly had a few trees and patches of grass, giving me a slight feeling of pleasure as we walked onward.

During the tour, while heading to our destination, Frank continuously spoke with an energetic eagerness while describing his job description of daily duties performed in the clinic and psych ward, an accomplishment he was truly proud of revealing to me.

Frank repeated to me the story from when he first arrived at this prison many years earlier when he abandoned his negative behavior and begun taking care of inmates who stayed in the clinic and psych wards. He elaborated on the subject by revealing the deplorable living conditions of the psych ward and the nonexistent care given to the men while locked in solitary confinement. Frank wasn't asked by the prison staff to take care of the mistreated prisoners, or their appalling living conditions; he just took it upon himself to take charge and rectify the wretched problem.

The men in the psych ward had untrimmed fingernails that were curling into spirals, long dirty hair that was matted with their bodies and jailcell covered in human feces. It required Frank a massive amount of time and energy in transforming the inmate's wild animal appearance from years of neglect, restoring them back into presentable humans, which he continues to take care of the men and incorporates it into his daily routine. However, that meticulous ordeal was only half the battle, as Frank endured the painstaking chore of and cleaning scrapping years of caked-on human excrement from each jail cell. The amount of compassion this American held for these men is truly remarkable, and his rebellious history is absolutely no reflection of the great man he is today!

After a short trek of forty feet from the concrete ramp, we ended up at the doorway of the medical building where a guard was sitting at a desk controlling who had access to the clinic. Frank barely broke stride as he spoke a few words to the guard on duty, then pointed to me as we walked on by. It's becoming a common occurrence for me to roam freely amongst these castle walls, providing Frank is by my side unlocking barriers with his verbal commands.

As we entered through the left side of the building where the unstable prisoners were housed, I instantly was able to confirm some validity of Frank's story, as the overpowering stench in the air was reminiscent of entering a zoos enclosure that housed wild animals. The surrounding area and twelve jail cells had a cleanliness appearance, but the wretched smell revealed the hidden secrets of past neglect. I was relieved that Frank kept his tour of the psych ward at a steady pace and not linger amongst the unpleasant odor.

While walking through the ward I avoided looking at the three inmates held in separate jail cells, by doing so, I could detach myself from their unfortunate desolation, but my wandering eye caught a quick glance of a dejected prisoner in one of the cells, instantly feeling the overwhelming hopelessness emanating from this deprived man. It may be bizarre for me to admit while being captive in a Mexican prison that this very distressing experience in the psych ward made me more aware of my own predicament, realizing I was truly fortunate. Once again, finding myself saying, *"It could always be worse!"*

As we began to exit the ward, one of the inmates asked Frank for some agua. I assume Frank responded with, "I'll be right back with your water," because after entering the clinic side of the building, Frank had me sit on a bench and wait for him to run a few errands.

The clinic housed three jail cells. Two were unoccupied as the third had a piece of plywood placed in the middle of the floor covered by a partially completed puzzle. On the right side of the hallway was the doctor's office and an examination office, on the left side was a dentist office and a modernized medical treatment room that contained three examination tables. The area was quiet, with minimal human activity. The doctor was in the examination office with a patient, while another inmate waited in the hallway. No commotion coming from the dentist's office, it was closed for the day. Even though the entire area was clean and orderly, the faint odor of feces seeping in from the adjacent psych ward could raise concerns about the air quality within the clinic.

Frank soon returned and continued the tour by showing me around the clinic area, then we went down the hallway and took a left turn where we entered a secluded miniature outdoor courtyard situated within the confines of the clinic walls. *Awesome!* This little oasis was only a 12'×12' area, but was very quaint, private, quiet and equipped with a homemade BBQ grill, all accompanied with a tall palm tree and a view of the beautiful blue sky that could be viewed without the unpleasant reminder of guard towers providing your shade.

The only downside that might arise in this hidden paradise would be if the dentist had a patient in his office during somebody's escape to the quiet oasis. The correlation between the dentist and oasis is the crude gas-powered generator mounted in the corner of the courtyard, which is required in operating the dental equipment; consequently, disturbing somebody's tranquility lounging in the mini courtyard.

Frank said a new generator was supposed to be purchased and installed by a sub-contractor who received a budget from the prison to do so, yet the shady character installed an old used generator while pocketing the extra money. This left the dentist stuck with an unreliable piece of equipment that gives him frequent problems, forcing him to adjust the daily hours of operation due to a temperamental generator, resulting with a closed sign on his door that reads, "Closed, due to a failed attitude adjustment."

As the tour continued through the oasis, Frank led me down a short hallway where he presented his living quarters. The corridor consisted of four jail cells, two of which were very small and not compatible with any kind of long-term captivity, assuming the ill-equipped cells were in relation to clinic patients. The larger cells were three times the size and only housed one bed in each, allowing for a more comfortable living space.

Frank was completely void of disturbing neighbors and abundant in tranquility, which might explain why he eagerly invited me to live in the cell next door to his. It was a tempting offer that instantly compelled me to weigh my options, which delayed my yes-or-no response to Frank by giving him an indecisive answer. There is a fine line between an abundance of human interaction and excessive tranquility, although if I had my choice, it would certainly be the latter, as the thought of a peaceful night's sleep was extremely alluring.

The next day I declined Frank's offer, mostly because I wasn't thrilled about staying caged in seclusion in an empty cell that had aromas drifting in from the psych ward smelling like an animal enclosure. The second determining factor, I wasn't willing to give up the massive number of amenities the café had to offer. I prevented Frank from getting offended by not giving him an explanation of my unwillingness to change my mailing address, again.

Frank walked over to his cell, unlocked the padlock from the door, then invited me in with an almost childlike eagerness, then began pointing out all the amenities in his cell. His cell clearly had a lived-in look that had been occupied for a long time; not that it was cluttered with a bunch of junk, it just possessed items that can be associated in a typical household—for instance, a throw rug next to the bed, radio in the corner, shelving with personal items and food products, also a patio table partly covered with papers and small objects in a cluttered stack, just like my house.

Frank cleared off the items from one of the patio chairs and offered me a seat at the table, then, with an earnest tone, offered me something to drink. After I declined, he cleared a spot on the table then asked if I wanted something to eat. "No, thanks." Next, he rearranged the cash that was laid out on the table and asked, "Do you need some money?"

My typical smart-ass response when someone asks me that question is, "Yeah, 2.5 million," but Frank's unexpected sincere offer completely caught me off guard, keeping my quick-witted reply to a "No." Even if I needed money, I would-be hard-pressed to accept it from him.

From an outsider's perspective, Frank's motives may appear a little strange or questionable. Normally I would have totally agreed, although his demeanor strongly suggested he was just ecstatic to have a visitor in his home who spoke English, also someone to relate with and tell stories of his accomplishments from within these prison walls. Case in point, after Frank offered me some cash, he proudly said, "I'm doing okay!" Then passionately elaborated on his statement. Frank boasted that he stayed busy most of the day, where his mornings mainly consisted of taking care of the psych and clinic wards, followed up with small odd and end paying jobs during the day.

As I have stated before, Frank's most gratifying achievement was hitting the books hard and learning a self-taught trade as massage therapy, creating a modest income for a better standard of living inside Dizney Land. This could explain the cash strewn upon the table, though the big stack of pesos might have added up to twenty-five dollars if that! And let's not forget about Frank's civilian clientele receiving specialized therapy, furthering his bankroll.

Frank's elevated exuberance continued onto another subject, as he began deliberating on a suitable placement for his new TV that was on backorder from Brenda dot com. He was a bit unsatisfied with his second choice on where to mount the TV, as his options were limited due to the lack of well-placed electrical outlets. I thought to myself, I'll just order an extension cord from Amazon Woman dot com. Then I asked Frank, "How long of a cord do you need in order to place the TV where you want it?"

He pointed to the back wall at the far end of the cell and let me calculate what length was needed. He was thrilled and appreciated that I added an extension cord into the checkout cart, allowing for optimal placement of the TV for a comfortable viewing area for several guests to watch movies.

When Frank finished envisioning his first movie night with friends, I somehow managed to incorporate his table and chairs into our next discussion. I think I said something like, "It must be nice having a real chair to sit in, while eating a meal at your table." Considering that my cell had eight men sharing only one chair, therefore mealtime around the table involves a lot of five-gallon buckets, with one lucky person allowed to sit in comfort while eating. I also informed Frank that most of my relaxation is done on a milk crate. I wasn't trying to play the sympathy card and score a chair for my derriere, but that's exactly what happened!

Frank instantly replied to my statement, "I'll bring one over to your cell later." How cool is that! Now I can go back to my cell and inform the guys of the good news, that their odds of winning at Musical Chair has just doubled.

Now that Frank's grand tour of his living quarters and work area was concluded, we began to make our way toward the exit, when we came across an inmate in a wheelchair gingerly maneuvering himself through the hallway. The extremely feeble inmate looked about thirty years old, had a colostomy bag attached to his side and appeared to be on death's door. Frank said the man is a patient who stays in one of the jail cells in the clinic and had been recently shot *six* times, regrettably, that is the only information he relayed to me. DAMN, the holy man's misfortune, would have made for an interesting story. I assume the slugs dug out of his body were of small caliber because the only people who can survive being shot six times in their torso by a large caliber weapon are zombies. I wonder if the frail young man ever thought, "it could always be worse," especially if the slugs in his tattered body were from an illegal 9mm, he would find himself be six feet underground feeding the worms.

When Frank and I exited the building, we took a left turn and walked fifteen feet toward the unruly side of the prison, where we stood on a patch of grass under an ineffective shade tree. For some unexplainable reason, while we stood on the soft green grass, I unconsciously blocked out Frank's voice as a calming sense of freedom came over me while gazing through the chain-link barrier toward the less fortunate of others trapped within their own inescapable snares!

Frank pointed out a few buildings that were on the opposite side of the fence and revealed their functionality, though some of his detailed information escapes my memory. The buildings were accessible from our side of the fence by entering through a small gate operated by a guard. The building nearest the fence was a restaurant where Frank purchased most of his meals, the other building next to it was a rec center. With this latest information, the running tally of places to order a cooked meal is five, excluding the undesirable choice of the poor man's prison cuisine.

While Frank was on the subject of his dining preference, he enthusiastically mentioned taking me over to the restaurant and buying lunch sometime in the next few days. The thought of entering the risky side of the prison wasn't on my vacation's itinerary, and if the moment of an invite for lunch materialized, I undoubtedly would have declined Frank's kind offer. *However*, while writing that last paragraph thinking about that moment in time and not exploring outside of my comfort zone, brought forth a strong sorrowful feeling pondering over the thought of undoubtedly missing out on an interesting experience and sadly have the realization of a unique memory that will never come to be! *Damn it* why am I so emotionally upset?

Now that the exclusive tour had concluded, Frank escorted me back to cell #6, where just before he walked away, spoke those familiar words, "DYNA?" (Do you need anything).

Once inside my cell, I grabbed a quick snack, hung around for a short while then headed back out the door. I walked over to Hector's café in search of playing some sort of game, but to my disappointment, neither Hector or anyone else was in sight; therefore, I passed on by and continued onward for a casual walk. While approaching the woodshop, I decided to take a closer look at the artwork displayed on the back fence, to see if there was anything interesting that I could get for Brenda. There were only four or five items to view, but none of them sparked my interest, except for a gaudy looking wooden painted butterfly, which had me wondering if the shopkeeper would be capable of creating a more appealing butterfly than the one on display. I thought it would be special to have something handmade for Brenda, especially a butterfly, for she has an affection for the delicate creatures.

If the task was too difficult for the shopkeeper, I could simplify my request by having him fabricate a replacement piece for the turtle used in the chess set in order to reinstate a king to its throne. Either way, I would have to delay my request until I was accompanied by someone who can help translate my instructions to the craftsman. This shouldn't be a problem in completing that endeavor because thus far, I have met eleven people here in prison who speak English and oddly enough, one of my biggest fears upon entering a Mexican prison was not being able to communicate with inmates or my captors. Huh, go, figure!

Oh no, I have lingered too long in the area, an inquisitive inmate has caught my attention and waved me on over to the church window where he was standing. The inmate wasn't clothed in theology garb, so I assumed it was safe to walk over to the young man to see what he wanted besides, don't think I will burst into flames by standing outside of a temple. Well, I assumed wrong! It clearly was not safe. The preacher man jumped right into his sermon, attempting to solicit my demented soul into his brainwashing chapel. During our short encounter, most of my responses consisted of a nod of the head and the occasional verbal, "okay." I was respectful to the polite young man while listening to his sales pitch, although it pained me standing there waiting for him to finish talking, looking for that window of opportunity to end our one-sided conversation. After escaping from his recruitment reflecting on what had just transpired, a memory from a quoted line in a Jack Nicholson movie As Good As It Gets made me chuckle, "Don't try to sell me crazy, we're all full up." Oh, by the way, the recruiting disciple was the "twelfth" man within these stone walls who spoke to me in English.

Making my way back through the courtyard, I noticed Alexander sitting next to Hector's food shack, so I pulled a chair over next to his, sat down, and asked how he was doing. Alexander responded in his familiar negative demeanor, once again pointing out the obvious

DIZNEY LAND by Way of Military Escort

gloomy attributes of the prison and repeated verbatim from our last conversation yesterday. Prompting me to immediately think it was a mistake sitting here joining him in discussion and started planning an exit strategy from this man with depressing behavior.

Alexander truly needs to schedule a tour to the psych ward to experience pure desperation of the unfortunate wretched prisoners, who would probably kill to have Alexander's luxuries of a home-cooked meal while dining with their wife basking in the warmth of the sun.

After a long pause of uncomfortable silence, while staring at the courtyard's activity, Alexander spoke up to confirm my occupancy in the café's cell #6, then said he used to work in there some time ago and was very displeased with the filthy conditions of the kitchen. I wholeheartedly agreed with his assessment of the unsanitary café; however, I'm sure the hoard of cockroaches residing there are quite satisfied with the cleaning crew's lack of ability to properly clean a kitchen. One could say the roach problem was out of control, but that would be a false statement as the bold cockroaches were in *complete control*.

Thankfully, my visit with Alexander was cut short, altering my early exit plan, when Raúl showed up asking if I wanted to play a game of chess. I quickly responded with an eager acceptance, elated to be free from Alexander's lackluster interaction, and immediately went to my cell to retrieve the chess set.

Since I was familiar with Raúl's ability to play chess, my concern was focused more on teaching him effective strategies during gameplay and less on winning the game. Toward the end of our game, Hector walked over from his food shack and witnessed my record improve to 7 and 0. I was somewhat hopeful Hector wanted to play the next game of chess with me; unfortunately, he must have thought his chances at winning were better served at Dominos.

Before having an opportunity to set up the Dominos, Carlos had arrived and asked to join us, who strongly suggested we play for five pesos per game instead of three; obviously, I accepted and surprisingly there was no resistance from Hector, so we moved to a bigger table and set up the game to begin playing. We were halfway into our first game when a fellow inmate showed up, wanting to convert our three-way into a four-way by getting involved at relieving this rookie of my money, so without hesitation, we stopped playing, reshuffled the tiles, and the four of us began a new game.

It didn't take long to realize Carlos and the newcomer were good friends and very competitive in trying to torment each other during gameplay. The two focused most of their defense strategy and energy toward their opponent, giving them great satisfaction when the other suffered a demoralizing defeat. Their energetic antics during gameplay made it entertaining and made for an interesting diversion from the woes of incarceration for the next two hours. It was also amusing when I received a competitor's praise for placing a tile that blocked an opponent from playing his tiles, giving them the great pleasure that I was hindering their adversary's gameplay. With the men concentrating their ruthless aggression toward each other, it diverted their attention away from me, consequently allowing me to actually win a few games, though sadly, when we finished our last game for the evening, my peso tally ended up being a little in the red.

As I stood up to walk back to the cell, I reflected on the unique interaction that had just transpired, of playing Dominos in a Mexican prison with four people sitting at a table of which three spoke English. Hell, it would be hard-pressed to find those kinds of odds at a border town in Texas!

Shortly after arriving in my cell, I went to the kitchen to start preparing a spaghetti dinner, thanks to my sweetheart, Brenda. Pablo was already working in the kitchen when I entered the patio, giving me an uneasy feeling for invading his workspace, especially not being able to communicate with him the reason for my intrusion. Therefore, I performed an about-face leaving the room to talk with David and find out if it was okay for me to cook my dinner in the kitchen while Pablo was in there.

Immediately after "no problem" rolled off David's tongue, he energetically followed up with, "What do you need?" He proceeded to accompany me back into the kitchen and eagerly accommodated me with items required in preparing my meal. David continually tried to assist in the task at hand, but it was more help than I needed or wanted; therefore, I had to be persistent convincing him I could manage cooking the meal without his help; only then did he leave the kitchen allowing me to proceed uninterrupted.

Cooking my first homemade meal in this foreign environment proved to be quite taxing; nevertheless, I was successful at preparing a fine tasting spaghetti dinner, while minimizing my presence and avoid disrupting Pablo's culinary activity. It was gratifying to accomplish this significant task and becoming one step closer at being self-reliant in this very strange Dizney Land.

Since nobody was sitting at the table, I had the luxury of choosing to sit in a chair, or on a bucket, however, today my options now include which side of the table to sit at while enjoying my dining experience because there were two patio chairs in which to choose from. The extra chair had an engraving on the front of the backrest that read Frank Jules Sandoval. How cool is that, Frank had made good on his delivery promise while I was away in the courtyard. There was no mention from my cellmates about our extra piece of dining room furniture. Surely Frank informed them the reason for the special delivery.

Now that dinner was over, I put the leftovers in the fridge and prepared to wash the dishes, but soon realized the tap water from the kitchen sink was lukewarm at best. Attempting to wash spaghetti sauce from a pan and plastic plate without the luxury of hot water would be arduous, so I used a hotplate to boil some water to expedite my chore with efficiency, leaving the kitchen the way I found it—well, actually a little cleaner than I found it. Oddly, I have yet to witness anybody boil water in this cell for any type of cleaning activity.

At about the time I finished washing dishes, a cellmate called out my name from the other room, prompting me to do a quick peek through the curtain's doorway to see the Table Rental guy was once again at our cell door wanting money. Since the common denominator involved in utilizing a total of six chairs and two tables earlier, was yours truly, I gladly forked over the minuscule five pesos.

Since it was getting close to the seven o'clock lockdown, escaping from my cell again today wasn't an option, so after eating a low budget dessert of a few cookies, I grabbed my notes to jot down the day's events and made my way to the lonely milk crate that I have successfully avoided for most of the day. Followed by retrieving the Word Seek from the shelf above my head, thumbing through the pages in search for a puzzle that would spark my interest, knowing damn good and well one didn't exist, nevertheless, like a crazy person I continued with the madness.

The only unprescribed therapy I was able to receive from the boring insanity was from the occasional activity brought on by the evening's café runner placing orders at our cell door and once in a while lucky enough to get involved accepting money and handing him food items. However, it was just a slight diversion from the unavoidable problem that was inevitably going to arrive, "ten o'clock, lights out," indicating at least another two hours of delayed sleep brought on by unruly neighbors. That was the main reason why I seriously contemplated moving into Frank's quiet neighborhood—to get an uninterrupted good night's sleep!

When ten o'clock finally arrived, I performed my routine starting with the bathroom, followed by the sleeping mat, curtain, pillow, and handkerchief, then finalizing with hopefulness for a more peaceful night's rest.

Day 19 in Country

Seventh day in prison

The only variance between yesterday morning and this early Sunday interruption of my slumber is the pain in my neck has increased, also I had been held captive within these walls for one week. Every morning before any of us crawled out of bed, Emilio would wake up early to make the morning coffee, then climb back into his bunk and go back to sleep. Even though I was always the first person awake in our cell, I would lay in bed until John woke up and put his sleeping mat away to clear a walking path. My sore neck prevented me from lying in bed any longer, therefore as soon as John tucked his mat under Pablo's bed, I went to the kitchen for a light breakfast and waited for the seven o'clock roll call before going outside for my morning walk.

Upon approaching the exercise area, I noticed Carlos was there walking at an elevated pace during his morning walk and was dressed in civilian clothing, who instantly spotted my arrival and waved me over to join him. I was slightly tentative to approach him, as I prefer my mornings peaceful, quiet, and do not like to engage with a conversation so early in the day, also reluctant to walk at his fast pace due to my ill-equipped flip-flops. Nevertheless, I exchanged a friendly smile with a wave hello, then went over and joined him in a brisk walk in the chilly morning air. Not only did the lower temperature prompt me to walk in the warmth of the sun as I did on Friday morning, but it also motivated the guards who were working outside to wear their winter garb, which I still found amusing.

Carlos and I were not the only two people wearing civilian clothing on their morning walk. There were two other inmates who repeatedly passed by us during their back and forth route. One of the men was Roseudo, a cellmate who slept in the bunk bed below Emilio, and because of Roseudo's short stature, it made him the recipient of a more aggressive workout than his taller counterpart, who had to feverishly keep pace with the long stride of the lengthy inmate. Two other creatures in the area immersed in their morning routine, consisted of the unsuccessful black cat eyeballing a clueless bird, who was indulging in the trash that the Energizer Bunny had not yet picked up this morning.

During our fast pace stroll, while heading in the direction of the shipping container used for trash disposal, I noticed two inmates rummaging through the pile of trash, which I can only assume were in search of items to recycle or reclaim; an occurrence I frequently witnessed during my walks.

Carlos is more of an extrovert than I, and even though he periodically had difficulty pronouncing English words, he ambitiously kept our conversation alive and wasted little time with the familiar Q&A spiel WPN. He immediately proceeded to voice his frustration toward the Mexican judicial system, which had unjustly imprisoned him, while searching for answers on how this could happen. Carlos never raised his voice in anger while revealing his story; he only became more disgusted during the explanation of the unsubstantiated evidence that led to the chain of events that brought him here.

He was tried and convicted of theft, even though he personally had irrefutable evidence of being in a different town during the same time the crime was being committed. Carlos was almost finished with his infuriating rant when he answered his own question of "*how?*" with almost the same response David gives during one of his rants against Mexicans, but without the expletive.

Carlos only had three months remaining in his prison sentence and had completely given up trying to fight the broken system, so now he impatiently waits while counting the days until his release. The displeasure Carlos displayed was more directed toward the Mexican government and not the people, although what the hell is the difference between the two? If one were to truly calculate the common denominator of all the world's problems, the answer would be the infestation of *humans!*

I informed Carlos of a conversation I recently had with a fellow inmate who actually did the crime and had done time, plus an additional three months and counting. He confidently assured me, "That wasn't going to happen with him!" Sure hope I'm not stuck in this feline-infested mouse house long enough to witness if he is correct!

My sore feet just about had enough torture from exercising in unconventional footwear, so I told Carlos it was time for me to head back to my cell and get some breakfast. With mild enthusiasm, he asked if we could get together after breakfast and play some chess. I gladly agreed to the challenge and said, "Come to my cell and get me after you finish eating."

While walking back to my cell, an older looking inmate stopped me along the way, then with slightly adequate English attempted to strike up a conversation, by inducing the WPN spiel. However, we were interrupted by a young inmate who acted like he was extremely proud to be gay, who pranced over to the old man and with a flirtatious smile whispered into his ear. I may have displeasure with most humans in this dysfunctional world; *however*, I'm cordial to all until I have had enough of their insanity, then I just walk away! And that's what I did after questioning what was said to the old man. He jokingly relayed the flamboyant young man's remark to me even though the translation was partially fragmented and in reverse order, I was able to get the gist of the obnoxious offer, though it will be written in the format as it was told to me. You may want to cover your eyes before reading. "Job blow, I like to give him." I instantly walked away while saying, "No thanks, I already have a girlfriend, besides, I haven't been here that long!" By fate or design, that was my last encounter with a prisoner who had questionable motives! Knowing what I know now, I truly believe it was by *pure* design!

After eating a quick breakfast, I began wondering how long I would be sitting here waiting for Carlos to arrive, possessing me to grab the chess set and head out the door in a heated rush. I had not a clue which cell Carlos was residing in, though I figured if he wasn't present in the courtyard when I arrived, surely someone else would be interested in losing at a game of chess. Yeah, I know, cocky, or confident, pick one. Upon exiting the cell, I saw Raúl with a broom energetically sweeping the cellblock area, inducing a reflection of previous thought, it's more important to stay busy than the importance of the activity.

With my chess game in hand, I made my way into the courtyard. Sadly, nobody was present who I was familiar with, generating an uncomfortable feeling on where to go and what to do next. Luckily Raúl wasn't far behind, who arrived to engage me in conversation and inadvertently relieved my looming anxiety. In Raúl's typical low-key excitement, he updated me with good news concerning his case file, which can be best described as "Raúl's conundrum wrapped in a paradox." He went to the secretary's office and found out that the less severe of the two charges filed against him was dropped, leaving him with only a stolen vehicle offense that would inevitably shorten his prison sentence, but how does one reduce a man's prison sentence which has yet to be determined by the court system? What I fail to understand is why it took Raúl two years of imprisonment before taking action to acquire this vital information and was proactive only after Brenda's recent inquiry of his case file number.

During a long pause in our conversation, my focus was diverted by the activity in the courtyards visitor's area, where I spotted Chewie holding a small child while talking with a young woman at least half his age who was also dressed in a prison uniform. My puzzled stare must have sparked Raúl's need to reveal Chewie's personal story to me.

Chewie was in prison for kidnapping, with only two months remaining on his ten-year sentence. The young woman was his wife and mother of the one-year-old child he was cradling. She was tried and convicted for possession of a handgun and sentenced to five years in prison. Wait a minute! What happened to the "no problem" bird? *Oh*, it gets worse! She also was from the United States and apparently has been incarcerated here for a while, raising concerns of a long stay for us American gun owners in a Mexican prison. I don't know how her dire situation differed from my own, only that John was involved in helping with her legal matters, making me wonder should there be a concern for my future and continue searching for an exit strategy from this un-amusement park!

DIZNEY LAND by Way of Military Escort

Before having a chance to dwell at Chewie's inner workings of a prison family, Carlos arrived eagerly ready to play chess. Raúl hung around for a while watching us play at our slow, methodical progress, though some may ask why, but what else was he to do, push a broom all day.

Carlos played in the same fashion as his fellow counterparts and posed no threat, but took more time contemplating his next moves than my previous opponents. As we continued to play more games, I also began teaching him the basic do's and don'ts of chess. Carlos was more than willing and determined to learn a more efficient and productive way of playing chess, and even though he lost every match, his urge to continue playing was inspiring. He displayed gratitude for my beneficial guidance, but I, too, was grateful for the friendly interaction while improving my untarnished record to 10 and 0.

Within about seven moves into our fourth game, Raúl had returned to the courtyard and briskly walked toward our table and said, "Brenda is here!" Awesome! I instantly stood up and asked Hector if he wanted to finish playing the game and informed Carlos to please return the chess set to my cell when finished with it because it wasn't mine to lend out.

I immediately headed toward the visitor's entrance area following Raúl, who had a sense of urgency in his stride and concern in his voice telling me there was a problem involving Brenda! My first thought was she had complications gaining access into the prison, though before reaching our destination, Raúl suddenly stopped in front of the captain's office and knocked on the door.

As soon as we were allowed entry into the small office, I became utterly surprised to gaze upon Brenda and Frank sitting at a desk with an officer staring at a substantial amount of cash laid out over the desktop. *Holy shit!* This shocking scene looked like a drug bust in which cops were counting cash on top of the hood of a car. The desktop displayed the loot in two orderly rows of small stacks in order of their denomination value, one row consisted of US currency of two one hundred dollar bills, while the other contained over twelve hundred pesos; and with the exchange rate almost equaling eighteen to one, the number of Mexican bills displayed was quite substantial.

Brenda's failed attempt at smuggling cash hidden inside her shoes into a Mexican prison, roughly totaled five-thousand pesos, dwarfing the allowable amount of two hundred pesos per day. What the hell was that woman thinking! During the entirety of Frank's attempt to calmly defuse the severity of this massive infraction, Brenda continued to be upset and very flustered, frantically repeating herself that she didn't know there was a limit on how much money could be brought into the prison; which was a complete lie.

By the time I arrived in the office, most of the concerns toward the infraction must have already been addressed between Raúl, Frank and the officer because there was little rebuttal by the officer who was recounting the cash. After Brenda was allowed to retain two hundred pesos, the officer bagged and tagged the rest of the loot and safely kept it in the office, until Brenda finished with her visitation then receive it back on her departure from the prison. When the inquisition was finalized, we profusely apologized and thanked the officer for not escalating the ordeal as we headed out the door. I personally thanked Frank for his ability to smooth over a potential disaster.

As the four of us stood in the corridor, I addressed Frank and sincerely apologized for Brenda's actions by putting him in an uncomfortable situation and once again thanked him for helping us. The somber mood in the room quickly transformed into jovial anticipation as soon as Brenda told Frank his television was at the inspection area, instantly clearing our retention toward Brenda's infraction. After Frank assisted me at retrieving the bags of items from the inspection area that Brenda brought, we converged back in the corridor where Brenda and I headed toward the courtyard, while Frank ambitiously went to retrieve a television made by Polaroid and Raúl's unknown destination can only be one of two places, yard or cell.

My slight unyielding tone suggesting we go in the courtyard was met with only modest discomfort from Brenda, so we continued onward through the security door and dropped off the bags of goodies at my cell, then headed to the outside visitor's area. Our trek through the prison would be Brenda's first journey deeper into my strange reality. Later she revealed that her first impression of the courtyard reminded her of walking into a Mexican back alley open-

DIZNEY LAND by Way of Military Escort

air market with vendors. Then I added, "Yeah, without worrying about getting ripped off!"

Upon obtaining a table next to the food shacks, Brenda wasted little time covertly handing me the two hundred pesos, plus a pocket full of change, easily adding up to seventy-five pesos. I had to laugh! Brenda was just reprimanded ten minutes ago, now here she is achieving her original mission of giving me extra money; just when I thought her smuggling days were over—or were they? As she repeatedly defied authority by filling my pockets with loose change every time that she visited me, I usually ended up doubling the allowable amount.

One of our first topics of discussion was the amount of energy emerging from Mr. Bunny, who was deeply engaged in soil conservation. Brenda was thoroughly impressed by his unbridled dedication and ability at continuously working at such an accelerated pace.

Our personal time spent together was cut short by Frank's arrival, who sat down to join us in conversation, and as usual, the gringo didn't come empty-handed, bringing the altered prison pants that I gave him days ago. Even though Frank never revealed the seamstress who made the alterations, I could tell the quality of work was performed by a proficient individual, due to the quality of the stitchwork and pants that fit like a glove no longer requiring clothespins functioning as a belt.

Frank took the lead in our discussion by exchanging pleasantries with Brenda, also asked with sincerity if she needed anything, followed by confirming her, "No thanks" response with, "Are you sure?" Then continued to proudly address her, by describing his daily responsibilities and inspiring personal achievements during his incarceration.

Brenda intently listened to Frank, but I was already familiar with his narrative, so my attention was directed more toward the courtyard's activity, where I noticed the volume of visitors had dramatically increased from previous days due to it being Sunday. The bustling scene resembled a summer day at the park during lunchtime, with coolers placed next to every picnic table, women serving food to their children and couples involved in public displays of affection.

The crowded courtyard answered my inquiry of the little pink chair in my cell; due to table vacancy being non-existent it forced Emilio and visiting wife to grab a small table across from ours. It was then I saw Emilio carrying a small child wearing a pretty dress, also explaining the mystery owner of the toys in the bucket on the kitchen shelf. I dare not intrude on a man's precious family time, so I spoke not a word and only gave Emilio a glancing smile.

As Frank's friendly chat continued, Raúl was walking through the courtyard and caught Brenda's and my acknowledgment of his presence, consequently capturing Frank's attention of our interest in Raúl. This led Frank to reveal all Raúl's personal tribulations during his last two years spent in prison.

When Raúl first entered the prison, he had the moral and financial support from his grandmother, also consistent personal guidance and help from Frank. Despite that, Raúl's ability to acquire money from grandma was the perfect opportunity in purchasing drugs; drugs in a Mexican prison who would have thought? Soon Raúl's habit completely controlled his need to always get high, consequently damaging his relationship with Frank, who terminated his repeated willingness to help the troubled young man.

His addiction also destroyed his relationship with grandma, who stopped coming to visit and closed her purse strings in a desperate attempt to end his addiction. At one point in time, Raúl could no longer financially support his escape from reality and was fortunate enough to be allowed residency in the safe side of the prison, unfortunately by then his close ties with grandma were severed as she hasn't been back since, ending all hope of Raúl's outside assistance. This newly acquired information clarifies why it took Raúl two years to be proactive in his own legal matters, also the urgency he displayed in contacting his grandma. Only time will tell if he is truly a changed man.

Soon after Frank's history report of Raúl was complete, he stood up and said, "I'm going to leave you two alone." It was nice he wasn't willing to wear out his welcome, and just before walking away, he asked, "DYNA?"

I was a little hesitant taking advantage of Frank's connections with the captain, once again, *yet*, it has already been a few minutes since I last benefited from Frank's services, so I responded, "Yes, a permission slip for a chess game." Moments later, he returned with a permission slip with the captain's signature. Was there ever any *doubt?*

Brenda's first impression of Frank yesterday had her questioning his character and motives; however, after today's congenial social visit, I believe she now realizes he is truly genuine, kind, and a beneficial asset for my personal welfare.

Now that we were alone, Brenda began to voice stressful conflicts involving prison staff, when she was again denied entry four times for various reasons, one of which was for wearing a black shirt, resulting in multiple trips back and forth to the car. Not only was today's parking more hopeless than Saturdays, but she also had to traverse through a large crowd of protesters just outside of the main gate. Brenda was clueless as to why the boisterous huddled masses were so upset, although she did say it was a peaceful demonstration with at least twelve military vehicles on site cordoning off the area.

Brenda's dejected spirits were also exacerbated by her lack of sleep, stress, physically sick and paranoid thoughts that affected her ability and desire to consume any sustainable meals during the week. After learning of her minimal daily food consumption, I suggested ordering a cheeseburger with french-fries and a homemade lemonade from Hector's café. Her reluctancy required me to convince her that Hector's burgers were delicious, and only after I said, "I'm going to get one whether or not you do," she agreed to have lunch with me.

After we finished eating, I slid my chair close to hers, resuming my touchy-feely delight, conferring over the new list of items I needed, including the purchasing of an inexpensive plastic chess set. Moments later, the street vendor was making his rounds and stopped at our table, displaying the assortment of pastries. Brenda declined his gestured offer, though I bought two, one for dessert and the other for tomorrow's addition to breakfast, which is quickly becoming a routine of mine.

During our entire visitation, Brenda displayed signs of extreme fatigue, eventually morphing our discussion concerning her exhaustion and overwhelming desire to go back to her hotel room for some much-needed sleep. I was in total agreement for her leaving early and make it priority one that she takes care of herself. I escorted her back to the security door leading to the corridor, where we exchanged goodbyes with a hug and a kiss; also, there may have been a squeeze or pat on her ass just before parting ways.

I returned to my cell and went into the kitchen to wrap an extra napkin around my pastry before placing it in the overcrowded fridge. While exiting the patio, I noticed the chess set on the corner shelf, that obviously had been returned by Carlos in my absence. My elevated gaze also caught the attention of the dominos game, instantly motivating me to retrieve it and study the tiles in search of patterns in the color and numerical sequences, in order to advance my gameplay to a higher level and eventually become a worthy contender able to relinquish dinero (money) from my opponents. Since most of the men were molting in their cocoons, the kitchen was void of human activity, consequently creating a peaceful environment allowing me to analyze the domino tiles undisturbed. I analyzed the tiles and quickly recognized the pattern within each group of sequenced colored patterns and the exact numerical combinations in each group of tiles. Familiarizing myself with the dominos tiles will surely assist in my opponents' defeat.

Speaking of opponents, Carlos showed up at the cell door, wanting to enlist me in a game of dominos, along with two others waiting in the courtyard ready to take my money; we will see! There were only two of us at the table who spoke English, so I was less involved in their chatter and more focused in deep thought toward winning. With my improved knowledge of the game, I was able to apply more strategy in gameplay, permitting me to break even for the evenings' peso tally and aided in some very close scoring games denying my victories by only a few points. I don't recall how many games we played, though the four of us continued to play dominos until a couple of hours before lockdown. I walked away from the

DIZNEY LAND by Way of Military Escort

table thinking, it's only a matter of time before my pockets weigh more after playing dominos.

Back in the cell, I warmed up my leftover spaghetti in the microwave, sat in Frank's patio chair and enjoyed my dinner with a few cookies for dessert, while watching Pablo preparing meals for the café's patrons and the runners delivery service. Upon completion of the delicious meal, I rinsed out my bowl with some warm tap water and soap and placed it in the sink along with the other dirty dishes, then headed to my milkcrate.

While perched upon my pillow, writing a lengthy description of today's events due to Brenda's delivery of a note pad, I noticed that for some unexplainable reason, the evening atmosphere in the cell was more energetic and animated than previous nights. The elevated banter amongst the men created amusing entertainment and once again continued to periodically razz me, especially from Emilio, who appeared to receive great joy in doing so.

Moments later, while Emilio was taking a shower, Adrian was walking by the bathroom and turned off the light while repeatedly banging on the door, which was met with a loud holler from the startled Emilio who was today's recipient of the ongoing gag. With the light switch mounted on the outside of the bathroom, it adds a shock factor to the unexpecting victim, inciting laughter from bystanders. When Emilio exited the bathroom, not a word was spoken of who was responsible for his alarming interruption and displayed an energetic enjoyment as he wasn't bothered by the escapade.

A few minutes later, while in the patio, I heard laughter coming from the other room. Adrian entered with a big smile and began showing everyone a disturbing porno video from a cellphone. He was intent in sharing the shocking footage of a grossly overweight woman participating in an anal sexual activity, which can best be politely described as no traction, "Like throwing a hotdog down a hallway."[31] The actions of this repugnant woman were so deranged that it made everybody in the cell laugh toward the reactions of others watching the unsettling video.

---

[31] *Family Guy*, TV show.

Emilio's recent high spirits weren't brought on by this nasty plump woman. Quite the contrary, his focused energy was purely toward packing a large clear plastic bag with essentials for an overnight slumber with a more delightful lady, his lovely wife, lucky bastard! Obviously, a byproduct of the big grin pasted on his face for the last fifteen minutes.

Soon after finding out about Emilio's late-night rendezvous, I felt joy for the man, a little envious and slightly mischievous, compelling me to be the contributor of a practical joke instead of a receiver of one. Therefore, I nonchalantly sauntered over to the chest cooler where the key was kept for unlocking the cell door, then placed it in my pocket, thinking this was going to be freaking hilarious, a prisoners date night delayed because of a misplaced key! *However*, I quickly processed the thought of an unpleasant outcome, of Emilio who could snap me in half like a twig when finding out I was responsible for hindering playtime with his senorita.

So I casually removed the key from my pocket and partially hid it amongst the items on the cabinet shelving that laid upon the cooler, then meandered four feet away from the impending crime scene. Now I can be totally honest when I look Emilio in the eyes and with sincerity say, "I don't have the key," while preserving an unbroken torso. Everybody was clueless of the misplaced key and of the approaching accusations; let the follies commence!

Emilio was standing close to the door, all packed up eagerly ready to leave the cell, then looked at David and gestured for him to retrieve the key for his departure. Without looking, David reached around the corner of the shelf to grab the key, only to realize he couldn't feel it, so he took one step backward to get a visual of the area to grasp the key but to no avail. David instantly performed a more thorough search of the area, then, with an inquisitive gesture, looked up toward Emilio and others for the whereabouts of the missing key. During this moment of panic, I had to suppress the urge to grin, when Emilio's concerns began to rise as heads were turning toward each other for answers while pockets were being checked. It didn't take long for Emilio's smirk to be inverted and start searching the area in panic mode, questioning everybody if they had the key.

Then his smirky grin reappeared while focusing his attention toward me and extended his hand outward.

Of course, I calmly told him the truth, "I don't have the key," while shaking my head no. After a more thorough search, Emilio soon found the elusive key and set himself free.

When Emilio exited the cell, I revealed to my roommates of the entertaining prank I just provided for them, who were undoubtedly impressed with my antics, giving them quite a laugh, so much so that Roseudo and Adrian cheerfully exchanged high fives with me, while grinning from ear to ear. Their enthusiastic gestures toward my actions also put a smile on my face and secured a feeling that I was truly accepted as just one of the guys.

Soon after the laughter died down, I decided to try my luck at obtaining a warm shower since it was late in the evening, I considered leaving my clothes on until confirmation of hot water was present. My hopeful anticipation was suddenly thwarted as the only thing coming from the showerhead was a solved mystery of the three five-gallon buckets full of water in the corner of the shower. For now, I will have to remain unbathed and use the reserved H2O for brushing my teeth and filling the toilet tank to give it a proper flush. If it wasn't crystal clear before, it is now! I undoubtedly need to keep my scheduled showers earlier in the day if I want to increase my odds of avoiding a cold whore bath from a bucket.

Now that another disappointing bathroom ordeal was over, all I had to do was impatiently wait for a couple of hours before beginning my bedtime ritual. When ten o'clock arrived, a guard came to our door and altered my routine by telling me hanging up a curtain on the cell door wasn't allowed; well, that's my interpretation when he pointed to the curtain hung on the door and shook his head side to side while saying, "No no!"

After removing the curtain, I voiced my displeasure to John of the guard's enforcement of a failed prison violation that has been ignored for the last five nights. He explained that the importance of enforcing prison rules fluctuates from each guard and differs toward inmates according to who they were, or what connections they had. I would have to agree with John's assessment, as Frank and Raúl make a fine example of the guard's sporadic transgression.

I wasn't going to allow a disagreeable guard deny me some form of shielding from the hallways light shining in my eyes, so I stacked a couple of milk crates together next to the door and draped a towel over the top, allowing me to achieve the same goal with a modified setup. Upon completion of erecting the defiant structure, I laid down and inserted the earplugs Brenda gave me in hopes of muffling out the noisy neighbors while attempting to acquire more sleep than previous nights. For now, an optimistic goodnight!

Day 20 in Country

Eighth day in prison

The first person in our cell to be rudely awakened in the morning, and the last one to fall asleep at night, has certainly shortened the amount of Z's required to be a happy camper or at least a functional participant. The lack of sleep is undoubtedly wearisome and makes me envious of the roommate's luxury in having the option of taking daily naps, or sleeping-in after roll call extending their metamorphosis inside their cocoons only to emerge as well-rested humans.

As soon as I made David aware of my tiresome eyes and weary yawns, he instantly offered his earbuds and music to use during bedtime to help drown out the noise from our boisterous neighbors. *Hell yeah!* I eagerly excepted his very kind gesture, looking forward to a temporary escape from the reality of incarceration via the joy of peaceful music.

A few minutes before the seven o'clock roll call, Emilio had returned from his all-night playdate, then after a guard unlocked our cell door allowing Emilio to enter, him and the exhausted smile on his face went straight to bed.

Upon completion of a pre-breakfast, I went to the courtyard for a morning walk, where I met up with Carlos, who arrived moments later and struck up a conversation relating to our job titles. Before Carlos was thrown into prison, he worked in the construction field building houses and boasted his abilities in performing many of the different aspects involved in building a house. When he finished revealing his aspirations of working after getting out of prison, he questioned me for my occupation. My experience in Mexico had altered my usual response, "I hang and finish drywall for a living."

Every time I have mentioned the words sheetrock, drywall, or gypsum to somebody here in Mexico, a look of utter confusion always appears on their face. Therefore, to avoid a long drawn out descriptive explanation of which never ends in any kind of comprehension from the listener, I only responded with, "I do construction," which Carlos clearly understood. My simple reply was all for not because he pressed me for a descriptive explanation of the type of work in my trade, so I no longer could hide behind a vague reply and ended up uttering a long spiel about drywall, accomplishing absolutely nothing. Apparently, drywall is not widely used in certain parts of Mexico, or lost in translation, as Carlos hadn't a clue what I was talking about.

When we finished with our walk and talk, I had Carlos go with me to the woodshop to help translate an order I wanted to place with the shopkeeper. I thought it would be a nice gesture to the owner of the chess set to have a king crafted to replace the wooden tortoise. After giving detailed instructions to Carlos of what I wanted, he relayed the information to the shopkeeper, who seemed to grasp the request while agreeing to make the chess piece, though there wasn't confirmation when it would be completed, or a price.

Once back inside the cell, I completed the second phase of my breakfast with some cantaloupe and cereal, thanks to Brenda. Then I conducted an exploratory trip to the bathroom to discovered there will be no early morning shower, as I had to use the agua from a bucket to flush my recycled meals down the sewer drain.

It was about an hour of observing the café's morning activities when I thought of bailing myself out of this jail cell to take a stroll in the courtyard, but when I stood up to grab the freedom key, a customer's companion caught my attention with a familiar malevolent stare. It was Mr. Eyeball from my days spent in the shithole cell, so I instantly avoided my acknowledgment of his presence by looking the other way toward John, while asking him, "I should stay away from him, right?" An adamant "Yes," was John's only response inducing a decision to put my exodus on hold for a while. Remember, I'm the master of avoidance.

Moments later, while exiting the cell, Frank showed up to see how I was doing and as we walked toward the courtyard, I let it be known to him that I was a little tired due to a sore neck interfering with my sleep. He was quick to respond with a compassionate tone, "I can take care of that!" (massage therapy). I politely declined his concerned offer with, "I'll be alright." Our discussion was quickly diverted when an inmate passed by us and exchanged a head nod with Frank, compelling Frank to tell me a harsh story.

In 2016 the power struggles between the drug cartels in Baja California Sur were completely out of control, increasing the murder rate to all-time highs with many murders taking place in front of this prison, which explains the heavily armed military and police presence here in La Paz. Frank's actual words were, "In 2016, there were *daily* murders in front of this prison!" This may have been a slight exaggeration, although the embellishment of the grim facts makes absolutely no difference to families of the slain victims. It may sound strange, but Frank is the second person to tell me I was lucky to have been arrested in 2017 as opposed to 2016.

The *inmate* who just walked past us was one of four former captains of this prison, whereas the other three were brutally murdered within a short period of time by members of drug cartels. Which interprets to; corrupt captains who get caught collaborating with a drug cartel receive imprisonment, while others who refuse to get involved end up taking a permanent dirt nap. I wonder which side of the fence our current captain is on and how long before he ends up like one of his unfortunate predecessors, or maybe he is struggling to be impartial by straddling the gate which separates the prison yard from the graveyard.

Upon entering the courtyard, Frank revisited our discussion concerning the pain in my neck and informed me he was waiting for the arrival of a client from outside of the prison, so he had some spare time to work the knots out of my neck free of charge. Because of Frank's unyielding interest in relieving my pain and the discomfort that repeatedly bothered my slumber, I eventually accepted his gracious offer.

Frank had me sit in a patio chair in front of the small shack that rented out the table and chairs adjoining the woodshop. I was skeptical at his ability in relieving my pain and very uneasy sitting there on display in a prison's courtyard receiving massage therapy from a fellow inmate. *Who wouldn't?* The strangeness was elevated when he introduced the use of lotion, although I must admit Frank was a pure professional and truly knew how to manipulate the kinks out of my neck and shoulders. From that day forward, I no longer had issues with my neck during my stay in Frank's Dizney Land!

After thanking Frank for my successful pain reliever, he enthusiastically suggested getting breakfast tomorrow morning at his usual place of dining, which was on the other side of the prison. I declined his nice offer, for I was apprehensive at venturing into the unruly area of the prison, so I altered our destination by inviting him to my cell instead, for pancakes and bacon. He was thrilled at the invite expressing an eagerness to eat an American style breakfast and looked forward to tomorrow with great anticipation.

I was getting ready to go back to the cell when Frank uttered his standard question, "DYNA?" I was hesitant to reply, with fear that my odd request would be pushing the boundaries of favoritism, and even though Frank may not have needed an explanation of my strange request, I supplied him with one anyway. To help alleviate the lack of exercise and monotony of prison boredom, I asked for a permission slip to allow me the possession of a Frisbee, yes, I said Frisbee! Though the thought of the only gringo publicizing pleasurable recreation with the only Frisbee in prison could cause resentment amongst fellow inmates, therefore I added four more to the cart hoping the order could be delivered by Amazon Woman.com, allowing me to give the extra flying disc away to interested parties. An unforeseen dilemma crossed my mind, why would prison staff allow an object that can be used to transport items back and forth over a twenty-foot wall? Just think of the implications! Either way, later that day, Frank dropped off the captain's signed permission slip allowing my possession of *five* Frisbees. To once again quote Raúl, "Man, that's some crazy shit!"

I thanked Frank once more as he prepared for a paying customer, then attempted to head back to my cell, when Chewie caught my attention and challenged me to a game of chess for fifty pesos. "Sure, why not," may have been my response, as I don't recall then sat down and waited for him to return with his chess set.

During our match, Chewie had completely altered his style of play from the last time we played and simplified his thought process by exchanging pieces of equal value every time I challenged him with a perplexing move, in effect leaving us with very few pieces to play a well thought out interesting game. This lack of thought process had bothered me so much that it interfered with my concentration, leading to my first defeat caused by a lazy oversight by me and not from a well-played out game from Chewie. This match tarnished my record to 10 and 1, though I was by no means done playing against Chewie in the near future!

After relinquishing fifty pesos with an elevated aggravation, I went back to the cell for some lunch, where I stood in front of the fridge with the door open contemplating what to eat, John shouted, "Dennis, your lawyer is here!"

To hear those uplifting words always makes me hopeful of good news, although I have reservations of the actual mystery guest here to see me. I quickly made my way to the cell door to find Raúl standing there, apparently the one who relayed the message to John. Raúl's demeanor suggested he was already willing to escort me to see the lawyer, so few words were spoken as we promptly headed toward the meeting room, via the security door with no resistance from the guard.

Once inside the room, I found it void of people, so with a curious stare, I looked back toward the guard who was standing at the doorway, who then pointed to the row of caged windows on the left wall; where I was able to see Brenda standing on the other side of a window with two casually dressed men. One of them looked to be of oriental descent, while the other could pass as El Chapo's brother. Brenda introduced them as Gilbert and Roberto, the lawyers Maribeth (my sister) hired. I was very relieved at the arrival of my English-speaking US support team and honestly thought questions would get answered, while the progress of my case would quickly be expedited in a more efficient manner.

Regrettably, that all turned to shit as soon as Roberto opened his mouth! He leaned in real close to the caged window, glanced over his left shoulder behind him, then spoke his first words with a whispered tone, "You trust me, I trust you, okay?"

Are you fucking kidding me! What kind of introduction was that? Let me guess, another lawyer who took ten years to graduate college and five years to pass the bar exam, only to walk away with the knowledge of quoting gibberish from the same lawbook as Mr. Puppet Man, the prosecuting attorney.

First of all, the two men were not from the United States, they resided in the Mexico City area, and their ability to speak English was atrocious. Even though Gilbert's English was slightly more capable than Roberto's, he relied on his partner to do all the talking, which was unintelligible. Oddly the thirteen men I spoke to in this prison thus far speak more fluently than these two lawyers sent here for my liberation!

It pained me to listen to Roberto's broken English as I found it hard to understand, so much that I disregarded most of what he said to me, especially after his "trust me" opening line. While he babbled on, I began devising a new plan of action which didn't involve him, realizing this shady character wasn't going to be the key to my freedom. The agonizing one-sided discussion couldn't *end* soon enough for me, and of course, I sped up our interaction by not asking Roberto a single question! Hard to believe, I know! How does a US citizen incarcerated in a Mexican prison express absolutely no interest pertaining to information leading to their release? It's not because of a strong belief in Karla's ability in securing my bail, but more of a major concern of Roberto's questionable character!

My suspicions toward Roberto's lack of integrity was validated when Brenda informed me of his intention of extracting more money from us. I also found out Maribeth wired money to Roberto with instructions for him to get me released from prison by any means possible, also, no additional funds would be sent until he did so. Roberto was persistent with Brenda that 88,500. pesos ($5,000) would not be enough money for the lengthy amount of time required for him to stay in La Paz.

Let me get this straight! This leech had been in town for only one day and was already attempting to suck us dry. *Not* going to happen with this gringo! I was well aware of getting shafted by others from listening to inmates' stories that trust should be used with extreme caution while in Mexico! Brenda and I were only allowed a few words together before she unwillingly had to chauffeur the demanding duo to their next destination.

Upon entering my cell, John displayed interest pertaining to my visit with the lawyer and asked, "How did it go?"

I instantly responded with an agitated tone, "Not good at all!" My level of frustration began to boil over while voicing my extreme displeasure toward Roberto's questionable motives and suspicious character.

John was shocked to hear of the five-thousand-dollar retainer for the shady lawyer and expressed his concerns by saying, "That amount of money for your type of case in Mexico is *entirely* too much!"

My aggravation was also exacerbated by the fact that Roberto didn't want to replace Karla as my attorney and tried convincing me the process of changing lawyers at this juncture would be very difficult to achieve; though John strongly disagreed, as him and I questioned why was Roberto getting paid 5k if he wasn't willing to act as my legal counsel also why was this blood sucking worm asking for more money? I had yet to figure that out!

During our discussion, John spoke in a comforting tone, keeping a calm composure and carefully chose his words to keep the subject focused in an analytical direction and not toward angry frustration. His awareness of my dramatically altered mood prompted him to extend a sincere offer in contacting a lawyer he personally knew and completely trusted and could arrange for us to meet. I humbly accepted and extended heartfelt gratitude toward his thoughtful gesture, which instantly eased my disgusted frustration and replaced it with hopeful anticipation of a more competent lawyer.

My stomach was telling me it was well past lunchtime and too impatient in waiting for me to prepare a meal; therefore, I grabbed the chess game in anticipation of meeting Carlos, then went to Hector's café, who could expedite a lunch quicker than I and silence my growling belly. While enjoying my cheeseburger, the vendor guy walked over to my table, displaying his tray of handmade low budget jewelry. My first reaction was to wave him away, but a quick glance of his tray revealed a set of butterfly earrings, how convenient is that? A much better-quality butterfly than the one on display at the woodshop, plus a simpler resolve in my search for Brenda's gift while in prison.

Brenda's birthday was soon to arrive on June 3, but this by no means was going to be her present, for there is no way in *hell* I would imply to her that it was! I realized our journey wouldn't lead us home in time for me to give her the birthday present I had planned back in April. Therefore, I had to improvise a "thinking of you gift." What else was I to do? My hands were literally tied!

Our relationship is unique. We have been together since April 2009 by a product of eHarmony. If we get married, she will be denied her late husbands' monthly pension and medical insurance; besides, we both agree a marriage license is just a piece of paper generated by government, religion, and society.

Brenda has an on-going razzing spiel of, "You never bought me a ring."

I routinely jokingly reply, "Let's get married."

Her response is always, "Okay, when we are ninety-nine years old."

With all that in mind, I purchased a ring back in April and planned on giving it to Brenda upon the return from our Mexico vacation. However, I adamantly refused to bestow the ring in the stereotypical display of theatrics one would expect. Therefore, I placed the ring in an envelope along with nine others in two stacks of five. One stack of envelopes each held a worthless nonsensical gift, i.e., a button, piece of hard candy, taillight bulb, etc. The other four contained various amounts of one-hundred-dollar bills ranging from 100 to 500 dollars.

The gag was for me to place one stack of envelopes in my left back pocket and the other in the right, then tell Brenda her birthday present was in one of my pockets and for her to choose left or right. No matter which pocket she selected, I would hand her an envelope containing a gag gift and asked if she wanted to trade it for an envelope from the opposing pocket that might hold a more favorable gift. Of course, she would opt for the latter, who wouldn't! Her chosen envelope would contain a one-hundred-dollar bill, then asked to trade it for the chance of an upgraded gift or a downgraded gift. It might take some convincing to keep Brenda buying gag envelopes, but the lure of increasing dollar amounts in the alternating envelopes would incite greed and entice her to keep playing my version of "Let's Make a Deal." The finale would be Brenda holding the remaining envelope containing the ring, "Game over, she wins!"

To make a long story even longer, when we eventually made it back home, Brenda discovered the ring was manufactured in Mexico and didn't want to have daily reminders of our tortuous trip to hell, making her adamant toward returning the ring to the store for a substantial upgrade. Consequently, officially we are now unofficially married!

Shortly after eating my late lunch, Carlos arrived eagerly ready to play some chess with anticipation of gaining helpful knowledge to improve his gameplay through my tutoring. As with his fellow counterparts, Carlos needed to be schooled on what he was doing wrong and eliminate his bad habits before I could teach him better chess skills. We only played two games before Chewie showed up and challenged me to a game for one hundred pesos, then stared at me for a few seconds while I displayed reluctancy whether to accept his wager. Raúl was standing close by and overheard Chewie's bold challenge, then turned to me and said, "You can take him." Since Raúl has witnessed both matches between Chewie and myself as an objective bystander and able to analyze our gameplay from a different point of view, I trusted his input and excepted Chewie's duel to the death between our kings.

My recent loss to Chewie had increased my understanding of his type of gameplay and weakness, assisting me in dishonorably laying his king to rest and adding one hundred pesos to my bankroll, improving my record to 11 and 1.

Raúl displayed a smirky grin after I defeated Chewie's overconfidence, and as we walked away from the table, he suggested receiving a cut of the winnings because he was responsible for convincing me to play for one hundred pesos. After gladly handing him twenty pesos ($1.16), I questioned him about reports of him being a hustler, which he denied by saying, "All that is in the past." Either way, I wanted Raúl to know that I was aware of the possibility and not to be viewed as an easy mark.

Earlier that day before playing chess with anybody, Raúl had approached me in the courtyard with a smile on his face and happily shared information about his recent visitation with his grandma. This was good news to hear as it revealed Raúl's sensitivity concerning his grandma and his appreciation toward the purchase of the phone card, which brought forth his reunion. By Raúl sharing that bit of mindful information with me, I felt at ease with his true character, which is why I was comfortable in handing him the twenty pesos!

The word must have been out about the chess match between Chewie and me, because as soon as I approached my cell door while giving a friendly shout out, "Open the door," I was received with a spirited reception by a few of the men, who displayed grins along with the big "L" placed in front of their foreheads. I told them, "*No no*," then joyfully announced my victory over Chewie boasting about taking his money. My elevated energy was reciprocated with big smiles and fist bumps of congratulatory achievement from Arian and Emilio. Apparently, Chewie is "was" the best chess player in prison, as expressed by my cellmate's excitement in having one of their roomies dethrone the Chess Master.

The amusing banter continued to flourish, so I took a seat on my pillow covered milk crate to watch and wait for the opportune moment to chime in or be drawn into their jocularity. It wasn't long after when my observation focused on the amusing discussion a few were having with Roseudo. Though they spoke not a word of English to each other, I was still able to grasp their storyline by hearing one unique word, along with the exchange and timing of the participant's laughter. The men were relentlessly razzing Roseudo for his stature, which was well under five feet, though it was made clear by his easy-going attitude he didn't mind that all the wisecracks were directed toward himself, who happily joined in their humorous banter.

I deduced the men were searching for a suitable comical nickname for their height impaired friend. The familiar word "Oompa Loompa" from the Willy Wonka movie was repeatedly exchanged between the men, followed by someone imitating a waddling midget that brought on a room full of elevated laughter. With Oompa Loompa being the keyword that tied their entire discussion together, it gave me the perfect opportunity to involve myself in their teasing of a fellow roomie with a witty remark.

I politely interjected with, "No, you should call him Mini-Me!"

In reference to "The Spy who Shagged me" movie.

The whole room exploded in uncontrollable laughter, while some of the men added their own banter by mocking Roseudo in a jokingly manner and pointing at him, saying, "Yeah, yeah, Mini-Me!"

With a big smile, Roseudo repeated their teasing phrase and agreed it was the perfect nickname, so much so that after some translation, Roseudo made it be known that he didn't like his given name and preferred Mini-Me. So for the entirety of my stay in prison, I addressed him as Mini-Me, which was *always* received with a big smile on his face!

A disturbing side note: Frank offered to reveal the reason behind Mini-Me's imprisonment, yet he cautioned me against wanting to know. So I elected to be oblivious of knowledge, which could cause resentment and end a comfortable relationship.

As the laughter began to die down, David altered the mood in the room by revisiting the subject of chess by informing me that Adrian was good at playing the game. I fail to recall what my discussion was with David in reference to Adrian's ability to play chess, though the inquisitive gaze of intrigue between Adrian and myself from across the room was quite memorable. Neither of us spoke a communicative word as we studied each other's facial expressions, displaying a raised brow as to ask a question followed by a hand gesture holding an invisible chess piece. We exchanged a nod of the head to silently agree to the challenge of a chess match, then without delay, made our way into the patio to begin playing.

Adrian's skill level was below Chewie's, though more experienced than my previous opponents, as he displayed a natural grasp for the game. During our match, Emilio showed interest in the progression of our game, demonstrating great enjoyment every time I captured one of Adrian's pieces. The entertainment level was dramatically raised upon finishing our game, when Mini-Me received immense pleasure persistently razzing Adrian for the humiliating loss he suffered due to my commanding victory, consequently encouraging everyone else to join the laughter from his humorous outburst. Then he added to Adrian's shame by placing the big "L" at his forehead and exchanged a congratulatory fist bump with me.

The only thing I did during this display of amusing harassment toward Adrian, was to remain sitting there with a smug expression trying not to laugh, inviting the next victim (David) to sit down and prepare to partake in a piece of humble pie.

For some odd reason, after David's quick defeat, it lacked the fanfare toward his crushed spirits compared to the level of hype Adrian received from his loss. It appeared the men had more enjoyment from the defeat of a quality player, or maybe they were aware of his attention disorder, which makes it extremely arduous for David to be proficient at chess when he is busy chasing that little red ball around the room.

The next participant who engaged me in a battle of wit had suddenly raised my concerns toward my possible second defeat in prison, as the man who I recognized with the most intellectual brainpower in this prison has just sat down across from me. Nevertheless, my anxiety was short-lived as John revealed within a few moves that he was by no means proficient as I. He soon walked away from the table, leaving behind his vanquished king. The animated comments from the peanut gallery (guys) were very lowkey, most likely due to the respect the men held toward him.

During the battles between the kings, Adrian observed keen interest in learning more about my style of gameplay and was willing to play another game with me, inspiring me to help teach him a more proficient way to play and enlisted John's help to translate my instructions to Adrian.

The first lesson of important guidelines I invoked to Adrian were the following: (1) Slow down! Play to win, why be in a hurry to go nowhere? (2) Don't involve your queen too early in gameplay; otherwise, you will waste valuable time retreating your queen in order to protect it from capture. (3) Gain control of the center of the board. It will give you more options, mobility, and control over your opponent. (4) Don't move the same piece repeatedly. For each wasted move you make your opponent can release a power piece into gameplay. Think of playing chess as if it were a war; the more forces that are involved on the battlefield, the more options you have for attack and defense.

Adrian was attentive while listening to John relaying my instructions and a good student of the game as he quickly applied his newly found knowledge in our second game. During the next few days, I supplied Adrian with more detailed tactics after playing each game. Like a sponge, his young mind quickly soaked up vital knowledge, rapidly transforming into a viable opponent, *truly* giving me great pleasure in mentoring him during my stay in prison.

Not long after completing Adrian's daily lesson, Frank arrived at our cell door and wanted me to go with him to the office that oversaw taking fingerprints of the prisoners. I was slightly confused because this process had already been performed at the jailhouse though the trip to get my fingers blotted in ink was just an easier explanation by Frank as to the main reason why my visit to the office was required.

We entered a small office that was across the hall from the captain's office, where Frank introduced me to the staff member in charge who then prepared to take my fingerprints. Shortly after our arrival, Frank told me he had to leave and take care of some errands and would send Raúl to the office to assist in translating further instructions.

Since this wasn't my first or second rodeo, I was familiar with this process and was able to follow the staffer's visual instructions with ease. Within a couple of minutes in my adult-supervised finger-painting session, Raúl arrived with a trace of negative attitude toward the ordeal I was being subjected to, not caused by having ink colored fingers, but more directed toward an event which was about to transpire.

Raúl relayed the staffer's instructions that I was to sit in the chair in the adjacent room and speak into the microphone that was mounted on a small desk.

"Do what now?" I was at a complete loss of what was expected of me and looked to Raúl for clarification.

He spoke with a dejected tone, "Yeah man, I know, this is some crazy shit," then explained I was to give personal info to the staffer like name, address, etc. via the microphone.

"*Oh*, now I get it!" The staffer could care less about what kind of information I relayed to him, as long as he receives voice recognition in order to connect me to present and, or future crimes committed in Mexico.

The length of my spiel was entirely too short, made apparent by Raúl, who informed me to keep talking into the microphone for another two minutes. I extended my broadcast with the subject of my relationship with Brenda and our adventurous compatibility, though I stopped speaking after what I thought was two minutes, only to be spurred on by Raúl to continue my chatter. I don't know who was more uncomfortable in the confined room, me for continuously talking to myself, or Raúl for being forced to stand there and witness this nonsensical torment.

As we exited the office heading back to our cells, Raúl reiterated our awkward ordeal with, "Man, that's some fucked up shit!" At least I now have the added insight of knowing, not only will I be wearing gloves on my next crime spree in Mexico, but I'll also be performing it as a lawbreaking mime.

Upon entering the cell, I observed a familiar stranger receiving money from Emilio, who was holding freshly cleaned clothing on hangers, exchanging gratitude of thanks toward each other. The laundry Guy was the same individual who was bellyaching to me days ago in the courtyard about his insignificant cashflow. I wasn't aware of who else from our cell utilized his laundry service, though I can eliminate four frugal roomies from his clientele list. I witnessed

David, Pablo, Jose, and Mini-Me hand washing their clothes in the kitchen sink, then placing the garments on hangers and used a long stick to prop the hanger on the elevated rebar that straddled the patio ceiling. I also partook in the use of the poor man's washing machine to clean my prison uniform, while sending my personal clothing out with Brenda to be washed.

I slid past the duo standing in the middle of the room, who were finalizing their commerce transaction, then headed into the kitchen to prepare a chicken and rice dinner. I also took the time to make the pancake batter for tomorrow's breakfast I planned to have with Frank. Preparation of my dinner was uneventful and was completed with relative ease. Sadly, the meal was less than desirable. I under-seasoned the chicken and overcooked it, whereas the rice was a strange brand of Mexican wild rice, proving to be quite taxing on my palate, forcing me to avoid the foreign substance leaving me with only the chicken as my meal.

Now that my leftovers were tucked inside the fridge waiting to be thrown away in the trash at a later date, I gathered up all the ingredients required for making pancakes; unfortunately, the kitchen was only stocked with three eggs. Since I refuse to leave my cellmates with only one egg, I grabbed my translation book and clarified the pronunciation of "egg" with John, then headed out the door to purchase some embryos encased by a delicate shell. This would be my first unescorted visit to the store, giving me a slight feeling of proud accomplishment, especially after engaging with the two inmates who worked the store.

They displayed amazement and appreciation at my attempt to communicate with them in Spanish, even though I only spoke three words to them: "Huevo" (egg) "Ocho," while holding up eight fingers and "Gracias" (thanks).

As I headed back to my cell with the eggs in a thin paper bag, a humorous, nonsensical thought occurred to me. Some people say one should never put all their eggs in one basket, however, would one not appear ridiculous carrying eight individual baskets with only one object in each?

The bag of pancake mix instructions was obviously in Spanish, so I enlisted David's help to translate the ingredients needed to accomplish my task. Upon completion of making the pancake mix, I searched for a container to store the mix in, but none could be found that was big enough, so I had to use a two-liter soda bottle, crude but very effective.

While exiting the kitchen, I came upon the men standing around having a bull session, where David turned toward me and asked, "DYNA?"

I instantly replied with sarcasm, "Yeah, some strippers!"

He acted surprised to hear those words coming from me, then displayed an obscured smile and said, "Okay, no problem, but you probably wouldn't want the strippers that are here, as they have a big surprise for you when they remove their clothing."

I had to agree with David and should have been gender-specific with my request, so I said, "No thanks!"

A few more laughs and humorous remarks were added to the mix from the men as David translated our discussion, which also triggered perverted theatrics from Adrian.

The group's attention was diverted back to their original discussion, which must have been related to current political events, as I distinctively heard a politician's name mentioned that dramatically altered the behavior of the room. I immediately thought about turning around and quickly returning to the patio, unfortunately, before my brain waves reached their nerve endings to accelerate my exodus from the gathered men, David suddenly turned to me and instantly ensnared me in their heated debate by asking, "What do you think of Trump?" *Holy shit*, are we about to have a discussion on US politics in a Mexican prison cell?

In all my years, I've learned to carefully voice my opinion on the subject of religion and politics, for no matter what my point of view is on either topic, fifty percent of my listeners will disagree, or have a negative reaction toward my way of thinking. Even though historically, the information supplied to the public of events are at best, versions of distorted opinions! I'm a true believer of, "Do not believe anything you read and only half the things you see!" Which has me completely avoiding TV news, or internet bullshit, as it insults my intelligence and just aggravates me to no end.

I wanted to keep my response to David short and vague, and as I hesitated, Emilio shouted out, "Yeah, crazy Trump!" Prompting me to follow suit with a safe verbal agreement, "Yes, he is crazy." But I only added fuel to the fire, by instigating a few of the men to display cheerful discontentment while chanting, "Crazy Trump, crazy Trump…!"

Regrettably, David was in an inquisitive mood and kept me involved in their heated discussion, who looked at me with a dispirited frown and said, "Trump hates Mexicans!" Which I found to be exceedingly ironic coming from David's mouth, who constantly utters those similar words. I felt compelled to respond to his misguided perceptions, even though I knew for a fact it would be a complete waste of my breath, "Trump doesn't hate Mexicans," followed by a short statement of conjecture, "He just wants to secure the border." That was the extent of my discussion with David on the subject, even though I had an overwhelming urge to extend my rant!

I may be treading on a delicate subject and piss off many people; nevertheless, it is purely printed in black and white, "8 US code 1325 Improper entry by an alien." To clarify the translation of the code for uninformed individuals, it's a *crime* to improperly enter the United States! Simple as that! Some may argue, scream, throw rocks, and spit in my face; still, there is absolutely no gray area in the law! It appears to me that people's interest and angry protesters were nonexistent when the law was enacted many years ago and has only become chaotic mayhem when Trump wanted to enforce the *law!* I fully recognize the United States was founded by emigration and many of us are descendants of emigrants.

My grandpa came over to the US on a boat from Poland, spoke not a word of English, and went through the complete legal process of becoming a US citizen. Though if one were to truly question wrongful immigration, the only inhabitants who justly belong in this country are Native American Indians! Here is something to ponder over concerning the subject of border security. Why do we lock our vehicles, install security systems, erect a fence around our property, build a wall protecting our home, lock ourselves in at night and for some carry a 9mm? It is clearly not a question of hating your neighbors! Fear already has us cowering behind the protection of an enormous wall, which impacts our daily lives at a *much* grander scale!

The energy level in the room showed no sign of diminishing after Trump once again inadvertently entertained me, as the craziness began to spiral completely out of control for the duration of the evening! The spirited men continued to involve me in their rambunctious behavior. Adrian, Emilio, and Mini-Me questioned me through an interpreter for cuss words in order to add humorous vernacular to their repertoire, who all found it quite entertaining shouting out nonsensical vulgarity across the cellblock.

While translations were being tossed around as cheap entertainment, Emilio received one for "son of a bitch," which quickly became one of his favorite shout outs while confronting me after I pulled a prank or made him a recipient of a joke. It was funny to hear him speak those words with his broken English accent, which came across as "Sonnof beech." Not only did it make me smile, it completely solidified our friendship by allowing us to be comfortable enough at exchanging comical insults toward each other without repercussions.

The greatest battles of comical sarcasm between Emilio and I were achieved when either of us would cross the fine line of acceptable satire to objectionable wisecracks, or when our radical remarks were adamantly refused to be translated by David or John. They were too reserved at partaking in the loud, obnoxious behavior that a few of their fellow roommate's exhibited, although they did have a good sense of humor and joined in with their lowkey style of banter.

My quick-witted sarcasm was slightly more aggressive than Emilio's, which I assume prompted him to enlist the help of David and John for his search of a more profound translated remark other than "Sonnof beech" (SOB). After Emilio acquired the translation of what he wanted to say to me in English, he directed his newly acquired retaliatory remark, "My lady, I love you" in an attempt to razz me. Even though it wasn't that funny or aggressive, it was undoubtedly effective in limiting my options of a clever comeback.

DIZNEY LAND by Way of Military Escort

So without hesitation, the gloves came off to hit Emilio below the belt. I looked at him with a big smirky grin and said, "When I get out of here, I'm going to make a friendly visit to your pretty wife!" I figured that visual would engrain a disturbing image in his mind, of "Now who is *loving* whom?"

With an inquisitive smile, Emilio looked to David for a translation but was denied any response from David, who faced me then cowardly shook his head no and said, "I'm not repeating that to him!" Damn an undelivered knockout blow! All I could do was pick up my gloves off the ice and skate away, avoiding a bloody nose and a trip to the sin bin (penalty box).

From this day forward, the increasing rate of jocularity became more prevalent between the cellmates and myself; also, my involvement of pranks, poking fun at each other, joking around and translations of vulgarity were being performed daily. Who would have thought this Mexican Dizney Land could be so amusing? Tonight is the first time of waiting for "lights out" during my stay in prison that hadn't appeared to slowly drag on forever, as ten o'clock snuck up on me without any warning!

While preparing for bed, I caught David's attention before he disappeared into his cocoon and politely reminded him of the offer he extended to me this morning. David gladly handed me earbuds with a crude looking MP3 player containing his music. I extended a gracious appreciation, followed by, "You are the man!"

The small plastic contraption was difficult to figure out how to use, and only after repeatedly pushing the few buttons there were, I was finally able to hear some music. I was fortunate enough that David wasn't a big fan of Latin music and had the luxury of listening to a variety of songs that were tolerable to the ears. I was now equipped with a pleasant escape from the nighttime noise during my slumber, though my face still needed to be covered by a handkerchief in order to help filter out the marijuana smoke finding its way into our cell. While the prison was in lockdown mode, guards were seldomly seen, encouraging the jokers and tokers to partake in their enjoyable diversion from incarcerated reality.

Day 21 in Country

Ninth day in prison

Ah! Another early morning dream killer brought on by the keepers of convicts; tried to sleep in, but how did that work out for me? Even though Adrian kindly offered his bed to extend my morning shut-eye after roll call, I sadly had to refuse his compassionate gesture. Noisy activity in the cell would deny me the pleasure, compounded with an uncomfortable feeling of encroaching on another man's personal sanctuary.

No prebreakfast this morning, I wanted to go for an early walk allowing enough time to prepare breakfast for my invited guest, Frank. My hasty approach to unlock the cell door was halted by John, who said, "*Wait*, the guards haven't finished with roll call." Oops! Guess I will wait a few more minutes listening to guards call off names before exiting.

Upon removal of the prison lock, I headed out the door along with the word seek to immerse my focus during the morning walk, accepting that the prison scenery hadn't changed from yesterday, so what was I to gaze upon that would spark my interest, surely not the Energizer Bunny, again! However, my assumption had proven inaccurate within seconds of my trek, when my peripheral vision had rerouted my attention to a bloody carnage activity taking place alongside the prison wall. I surmised that an oblivious bird was deeply engrossed searching through the scattered trash for a feast and failed to realize its own juicy innards were about to be the delicious meal; also, the ability of flight was useless to the slain prey as it was being devoured by the black feline.

Within ten minutes of walking, Carlos joined me and soon began extracting more helpful info concerning chess and once again wanted to hook up later for a lesson. Another ten minutes later, when I broke stride from Carlos and headed back to the cell to prepare breakfast, an unfamiliar guard was in pace with my gait encroaching alongside our path of travel, inducing eye contact and an exchange of a mutual, "How are you?" I said, "Good." His subdued reply, "Not so good." For some strange reason, I was compelled to do something that would be completely unacceptable in a US prison, I actually made physical contact with the guard by placing my left hand on the guard's right shoulder and said, "At least you are not stuck in here." It didn't dawn on me at that moment of the possible repercussions from my bold action; nevertheless, the friendly guard showed absolutely no reaction from the personal contact, who agreed with my statement with a reserved tone while continuing to walk away with a humbled grin.

Back in the cell, I anticipated Frank's arrival; regrettably, preparation of breakfast quickly turned into a fiasco as the hotplate only had two settings high and off, which made cooking the paper-thin bacon in a sticky pan a stressful ordeal I wasn't prepared for. Very much so, that my aggravation level was boiling over with a frustrated attitude of "*fuck it*" and just threw the entire package of bacon in the pan cooking it like scrambled eggs, resulting in a mangled mess looking like extra crispy curly fries on a plate.

The second phase of my torment was worse than the first, by the gluten-free pancakes that tasted awful and quickly found its way into the trashcan along with the two-liter bottle that contained the gooey swill. It never dawned on me there might have been a slight miscommunication of David's translated pancake mix instructions, or I could have inadvertently left out a key ingredient. Nevertheless, it all wasn't a complete disaster. Frank failed to show up for breakfast, which was fortunate for both of us avoiding disappointment. Also, John enjoyed helping me in devouring the tangled array of bacon while I concluded my breakfast with cereal, banana, and a Danish.

This valuable lesson has taught me to minimize my attempts to cook meals in this unfamiliar environment, especially if I want to keep my composure and quit inadvertently supplying the cats with feather-covered meals.

Now that my belly was full and the negative frustration had dissipated, I grabbed the chess set and headed out to the courtyard, soon returning to the cell as Carlos was nowhere in sight. Maybe I should have found out where his cell was located, though by doing so, I would lose my status as an introvert.

While in the cell, I played a game of chess with Adrian along with some more tutoring, but that was limited to only one game as Carlos tracked me down, wanting to play chess in the courtyard. We sat at a table next to Hector's café, where we began to set up the chessboard when I felt a radiant heat upon my back emanating from the plywood structure that was ten inches from my chair. While running my hand across the surface of the plywood searching for the area emitting the warm temperature, I suddenly had to remove my hand as the intensity of the heat would have severely burned my hand within a second of leaving it placed there.

Not only was my amazement toward the extreme temperature of the plywood, but also that Hector's wooden food shack hadn't already burned down to the ground! I stood up and poked my head into the service window area investigating the source of heat, where I viewed Hector's cooking area had hotplates damn near butted up against the plywood wall. I'm truly astonished Hector isn't a discouraged owner of a pile of ashes. It was that hot! Forcing me to abruptly retreat from our current sitting arrangement to a different table.

During our chess match, Carlos demonstrated an undertone of excitement while saying, "I'm getting good enough to maybe beat you this game!" Making him appear like an adolescent hopeful of defeating his father at a child's game.

I spoke not a word as my reply of the truth, "You don't have a chance in hell of winning," would have crushed his optimistic enthusiasm. Unlike Adrian, Carlos didn't apply all his newly acquired knowledge to the game as instructed, diverting most of my focus away from the lackluster game as I frequently stood up, taking a few steps into the warmth of the sun, while he pondered over his next move.

During our second game, Frank unexpectantly showed up in the courtyard, to my astonishment, arrived with a cute girl by his side, who was wearing blue shorts that doubled as a skirt (skort), revealing quite a bit of skin. Oh yeah! I recognize those legs anywhere, they belong to Brenda! I failed to question them on their joined arrival into the courtyard, though I found out later how it transpired. Brenda was at my cell door dropping off bags of essentials and getting ready to inquire of my whereabouts when Frank just happened to be walking by and noticed the familiar senorita standing there all by *herself* which seems totally weird to me, then he rectified Brenda's dilemma by escorting her to the courtyard in search of me.

Visitation is obviously the most significant event within a prison second to staying alive, so no explanation was given to Carlos for my hasty departure from our game. Frank didn't sit down to join Brenda and me, though after saying, "Don't worry about paying for the table, he (rental guy) owes me," he placed some objects on the table and asked if we could watch them until he returned later. In about half my encounters with Frank, I have witnessed him carrying a massage therapy book, two small plastic jars, one of lotion the other oil, hand towel and some cash, all of which he entrusted in our care.

Before Frank walked away, we informed him of our intention of getting a burger from Hector's café and eagerly offered to buy him one as well. He was totally unaware that Hector even served cheeseburgers and looked forward to trying one, who gladly accepted our invitation for lunch then added, "Go ahead and order me one now and I'll be right back."

While we were alone, Brenda covertly slipped me my allowable two hundred pesos plus a bunch of spare change. After ordering lunch, I gave Brenda the butterfly earrings, which seemed to be received in a less than joyful manner, although what else could be expected under these adverse circumstances.

One of the first statements Brenda conveyed during our visit was voiced with a harsh recommendation of, "You need to *listen* to John!" Brenda diligently researched him online and became truly impressed by the uncompromised conviction he held toward helping his native countrymen. I was already aware of John's compassionate character and informed her of the fact, also of his willingness to help me by contacting another lawyer, who was competent and trustworthy.

Our conversation shifted to a more concerning matter as Brenda informed me of a homemade tool that was lying outside of her hotel room window and deduced from the design of the crude instrument it most likely was used for unlatching windows to gain access into hotel rooms. It was late-night when she discovered the malicious item, inducing a fearful sense of uneasiness and drastically interfered in her ability in going to sleep. Even though she found a mop handle to prop in the window track to prevent someone from opening the window, her security measure failed to relieve her anxiety enough to get a good night's sleep. The next morning Brenda went straight to the hotel office in a heated rush and displayed the B&E (breaking and entering) devise to the clerk, demanding a different room which didn't have easy access to a window by an uninvited guest! The clerk wanted possession of the B&E tool; however, Brenda adamantly refused to hand it over, and to this day, she still has the device for show and tell.

In a dispirited tone, Brenda once again voiced her hardships of being tired, sick, and overstressed. Her stressed-out behavior had been intensified from the humiliating strip search she had to endure by a female guard who was quite thorough with her leering visual inspection of Brenda's partially naked body. The news of Brenda's demoralizing ordeal made me question the guards' motivation for the intensive strip search for contraband, thus informing Brenda I was allowed to enter the prison with my dignity intact by leaving my lower extremity and white ass a mystery to the homophobic guards, who quickly halted my action in attempting to drop my shorts.

I found out later from the scuttlebutt going around the prison that all the female guards were gay, though not sure if the gossip was true, or even the motivation behind the guard's quest to sneak a peek of a naked American woman. That type of trivial info only makes perverted minds like mine go "huh."

I honestly believe the reason behind Brenda's strip search was brought on by her attempt at smuggling the massive amount of cash into the prison on her last visitation. Either way, the discomfort emanating from Brenda while sitting next to me was truly heartfelt, making me feel like the sympathy I should extend to her had overpowered the sympathy one would expect for myself being stuck in prison. This is certainly understandable, but no matter how distressing it was for Brenda, there is no way in hell she would ever trade places with me!

By the time Frank returned to our table for lunch, Brenda and I were just finishing up with our meal, though only split a burger and fries between us, so we were quick in doing so. Once again, Frank seemed to be more comfortable leading our discussion than listening, prolonging his indulgence in the cold meal while speaking his mind pertaining to his incarceration and personal matters. Most of Frank's focus was directed to Brenda, as I was already familiar with what he had to say, although there were two bits of new info I heard, of which tugged on Brenda's heartstrings. First, Frank was saddened by the assumption his mother hadn't a clue of his whereabouts and presumed he was dead, as it has been well over ten years of absolutely no contact between them. Second, he was hopeful of the outcome from the upcoming parole hearing, but the discouraging expression on his face revealed a more extended stay in prison was imminent.

Since Brenda is inflicted with a tender heart, she couldn't help but be very concerned for the fifty-seven-year-old man while asking, "Frank, what can I get for you?"

With an elevated sincerity, he referred to our generosity for the TV and that he didn't need anything else. After repeating her offer and insisting Frank oblige, he humbly accepted and said, "I could use some more oil and lotion." To the kindhearted goes rewards from the kindhearted!

Just before Frank departed from our company, his standard query of DYNA arose, triggering a thought of a conversation I had with Raúl earlier in the day. When I asked Raúl what type of shaving devices was allowed in prison and what kind did he use; he was unable to offer any information and just looked at me with a grin while rubbing his smooth face and said, "I don't need (never) to shave." Raúl's useless response inspired me to answer Frank's question with, "Yes, approval for an electric razor." And away he went, soon returning with permission slip in hand.

I handed the small piece of paper to Brenda along with a list of items I wanted, also the permission slip for the five Frisbees, requiring a specific explanation of my strange request, though no more outlandish than a TV. Brenda's weary body had prompted a decision that it was time to go back to the hotel for a nap; besides, our conversation had dwindled into long pauses of silence and observing the Energizer Bunny exert a strain on his battery had lost all interest.

We made our way back to my cell where we said our goodbyes and went our separate ways, she toward the exit and I to the cage. While I grabbed the cell door with a forceful shake preparing to shout out "open the door," Mini-Me instantly cried out before I had a chance to utter a single word, with "Open the window!" His grasp for the English language is nonexistent, so the thought of him trying to be humorous by saying the window instead of the door was probably more a translation error and not by choice. Either way, every time I arrived at our door from this day forward, Mini-Me would acknowledge my presence with that jovial greeting of "open the window," inducing Emilio, David, or Adrian to shout out my name upon entry, as if they were glad to see me.

My fellow roomies made me feel just like "Norm Peterson," a TV character on *Cheers*, as he too was always greeted with a loud recognition of *Norm!* Although unlike him, I failed to respond with a witty remark and usually voiced a simple, emphatic reply of, "*What's up*," as a quick-witted response was hard to muster with enthusiasm while entering a prison cell, especially one requiring translation.

While entering the cell, David made an appearance by emerging from his cocoon, which I have noticed becoming more of a common occurrence since my first days in this cell. As his feet touched the floor, he immediately turned toward me, and with a discouraged frown said he was unable to retrieve the Sudoku book that he lent to a fellow inmate, who no longer had it in his possession. Then David handed me two sheets of paper and said, "I had my wife print these out for you." To my astonishment, there were two Sudoku puzzles in my hand! The logistics involved in the acquisition of a thoughtful gift for this foreign stranger has truly humbled me once more, especially after finding out David's wife had to hop on a bus in order to make the inner-city trip to the prison.

After adamantly reminding David, "You are the man!" I went to the chest cooler and poured some cold water from my gallon jug into the Nalgene bottle Brenda gave me; that displays the phrase "Never give up," how appropriate. I went to the patio and took a seat in Frank's chair, turned on some music with the luxury of upgraded headphones provided by David and began to deeply immerse myself in Sudoku. My temporary escape from reality was thwarted by my own ability to complete the puzzle in an expedient fashion since the difficulty level was less than challenging. David and a few of the crew were impressed by my quick work, almost at disbelief, as David studied the sheet of paper verifying a correct completion.

While listening to music and calculating number placements on the second puzzle, a Johnny Cash song from David's playlist evoked a memory of my music collection that also contained the same artist. One tune in particular, "The Long Black Veil," recorded live at Folsom Prison in California 1968. Upon completion of the song, a prison official comes over the PA system and addresses the assembled convicts, "I have an announcement here, Sandoval 88419 is wanted in reception."

To ensure my memory of the engraving on the backrest of my chair, I leaned forward, looked over my left shoulder and read the name, "Frank Jules Sandoval." My first thought was, "What a small world after all," followed by "what are the odds?" Then after a quick cipher of Frank's age, I deduced the inmate mentioned in the song could not be Frank as he would have been only eight years old in 1968, and unlike Mexican prisons, you won't find children in lockup amongst thugs and thieves in a California prison.

Though I was intrigued at the prospect of Frank's father, or uncle being in Folsom prison during that same time period and wondered if a possible dull story could be transformed into a probable interesting one. When Frank stopped by my cell moments later, I questioned if his dad had been incarcerated at Folsom. Unfortunately, Frank wasn't here for a social call; he was to escort me to see my lawyer.

Therefore, our discussion was hastily performed while walking to the visitor's room, only allowing me to gather partial info that his father was no stranger to prison life and had been incarcerated in multiple prisons for many years. Frank was unclear of exact places and dates, which is completely understandable as a fatherless child how would he know or want to care.

When I informed Frank the reason behind my inquiry, he replied with, "Oh yeah, I got to see Cash when I was in a California prison many years ago." The validity of his response seemed questionable, but plausible, as Johnny Cash did preform many prison concerts during the seventies, also Frank followed in his fathers' footsteps in the revolving door of prison life as a young man during that time period.

My expectation of seeing a lawyer was once again met with disappointment. We entered the room to find Oscar standing there, the court-appointed liaison who offered to acquire a couple of hotdogs for me before my infamous trial on Sunday. Oscar was graciously checking up on me, making sure I was being treated properly and wanted to know if I had any concerns, or if I needed anything. Even though Oscar was very friendly and truly willing to help, I expect his ability to aid me in any legal capacity was limited in the same fashion as Edger's from the US consulate, and couldn't assist with further needs that I don't already have secured through my contacts. However, Oscar did have knowledge pertaining to Karla's progress in appealing the judge's decision of denying my bail and displayed optimism that she would soon obtain bail. Very reassuring news to hear from court officials!

Since Oscar was on the topic of legal issues, Frank joined in with his speculative input of a minor technicality pertaining to my arrest, which Frank and I have already discussed days earlier, that I dismissed as irrelevant and not worth pursuing. Frank failed to recognize, even if Oscar valued his input concerning my case, there was nothing he could do about it anyway. I didn't get involved in their mini discussion, for I knew Frank was just wasting Oscars time, though deep down, I admired Frank's concerns, knowing he was only trying to help. That's what defines Frank's true character!

After expressing much gratitude to Oscar, Frank and I went back to my cell, where he uttered the usual question DYNA, just before walking away. Once inside the cell and my smile faded away from the effect of Mini-Me's shout out, "Open the window," I went straight to the kitchen, rummaging through my bag of goodies for something to satisfy my munch attack. During my search of the bag, a familiar Cheetah caught my eye sparking interest, so I grabbed a glass of water and sat at the table with anticipation of turning my fingers yellow from my choice of snack.

After opening the bag, I grabbed one Cheeto to bring forth a tasty crunch; "sonnof beech!" Another food product destined for the trash! Or not? I sealed the bag closed with a clothespin and placed it on the shelf behind me, to save the Cheetos for a Latinos palate more suitable to enjoy a savory kick.

This spicy torment to my taste buds wasn't the first time it happened while in Mexico nor my last. I assumed popular US brand name snacks that didn't display any info pertaining to hot or spicy flavor would be safe for me to eat. Clearly, I was wrong, Doritos, beer nuts, and now Cheetos are on my list of food items never to buy while in Mexico. Even though beer nuts would never be on my shopping list, I had the unpleasant misfortune of tasting them from a bag labeled "Mild," which was translated to me by fellow cellmates. Them dumb bastards wanted me to try a hand full, but "stupid" is not tattooed on my forehead, so I only took one bite of a single nut which had me instantly spitting the insanely hot fragmented pieces into my cupped hand. My exacerbated reaction prompted the whole room to erupt with uncontrollable laughter, who tried convincing me the nuts were mildly flavored. I instantly disagreed and responded to their incitement by saying, "Bullshit!" If there was a slim chance, I wasn't the recipient of a prank, then my roomies must be missing their taste buds and are not affected by the blistering heat brought on by the spicy peanuts.

While eating my second choice of snack, David, Mini-Me and Pablo entered the kitchen and sat down at the table, compelling me to stop eating, reach behind me for the bag of spicy Cheetos than offered it to David and crew. He graciously accepted, then after clutching a small handful, he attempted to return the bag to me, but I refused to accept it while saying, "No, the whole bag is for you guys."

David's demeanor suddenly morphed into one of great humility, acting like I just handed him a bag of money, inducing his familiar response, "*Reeeally?*" Are you sure, how much?"

I replied, "Yes, the Cheetos are too spicy for me," and, "I don't want your money." My gesture elevated David's gratitude even more, who continued enjoying the crunchy snack all to himself, making me wonder why he hadn't shared any with Mini-Me and Pablo.

Since Mini-Me and Pablo were incapable of understanding what had transpired between David and me due to their limited grasp for the English language, it made for the perfect opportunity to torment the unexpecting duo. Even though the initial provocation wasn't brought on by my design, I was able to assist David in his sly attempt at hoarding the Cheetos for himself. Because there were absolutely no translations between the four of us during our comical banter and only spoken lies from David who relayed what I seemingly said to him, I'm forced once again to use deductive reasoning by observing facial expressions, tone, mannerism and body language to recreate our humorous interaction. Consequently, a few quoted statements will be perceived as close to factual that coincide with my interpretation of the amusing dispute.

As Mini-Me casually reached for the bag of Cheetos to share amongst Pablo and himself, David quickly pulled the bag close to his chest with a slight discouraging smirk and said, "*No*, Dennis gave them to me!" Mini-Me assumed David was full of shit as he instantly shook his head no while scanning his pointed finger to each of them with a distrustful grin while saying, "No no, Dennis gave them to all of us!" Then aggressively extended his hand out as to say, "Give us some Cheetos you lying bastard!"

Pablo did not get involved with David's and Mini-Me's rebuttal, whose laidback demeanor appeared to show no concern over who to believe while quietly sitting there observing the duo's theatrics; most likely thinking David was being stingy by not sharing the crunchy snack, or perhaps I was the culprit behind David's hoarding.

DIZNEY LAND by Way of Military Escort

David emphatically denied Mini-Me's request for the Cheetos a second time, while looking to me for an agreement of his deception. At that moment, I decided to play devil's advocate toward both men involved, by responding with a nonverbal gesture to David with a nod of my head yes, a raised brow and evil grin confirming our ruse. Then with a duplicated mannerism looked into Mini-Me's eyes while shaking my head no, slightly adjusting facial expression with a lowered brow and frown validating his earlier statement of, "The Cheetos are for everybody." I repeated this process one more time toward both men, not to legitimize their stance in the matter, but to put extreme doubt in their minds of who was justifiably correct and whose side I was truly on. It was quite entertaining pitting the duo against each other while addressing their adversary in plain sight of each other.

To keep the amusing banter alive, I wanted Mini-Me to think that I was generous and that his assumption was correct that yellow fingers were to be shared by all. Therefore, I looked to David with a sincere smile pointing to the bag of Cheetos, then pointed my finger toward Pablo and Mini-Me and said, "You should give them only one Cheeto each," knowing they were incapable of translating my true gesture.

David usually displays politeness and appears to be slightly religious; however, the tiny devil on his shoulder (me) convinced him to carry out the cruel deed. After repeating my hand gesture while telling David, "Go ahead and do it!" He reached into the bag, pulled out two Cheetos, then handed one to each of the men, accompanied with a big sadistic grin. Don't think Mini-Me and Pablo thought it was hilarious, but it was! So much, that I couldn't make eye contact with the disappointed recipients so as not to start laughing out loud, revealing my true involvement of David's humorous action. Which made me feel a little bad at suggesting the cruelty, though well worth the amusement.

Mini-Me never lost that distinctive smile of his during the razzing and was eventually rewarded with a handful of the spicy snack when David released the Cheetah from his captivity. I wonder who was perceived as the evil instigator when it was all said and done,

David or Goliath? (me). As the jocularity came to an end, David continued enjoying the crunchy snack while looking at me with inquisitive confusion, as to wonder why I gave the Cheetos away that didn't taste spicy at all.

I failed to fully recollect what had transpired next. My original notes were written with only a few words toward each subject matter to spark my memory and didn't require writing a whole sentence to remind me what transpired in that moment of time. For example, the entire Cheeto ordeal was completely recalled by only writing down five words, "Cheetos story, Mini-Me, David, Cook (Pablo)." Unfortunately, the next set of words that started a new subject was "Played dominos in cell."

Typically, those words would be more than enough info to reconstruct the event and timeline, though playing dominos a week ago in prison was an event of great importance, today it has just become another common occurrence which failed to have any memorable impact. Also, I hadn't recently mentioned anything about being bored, for I have been busy as a bee with little time to ponder over playing dominos. Though I can honestly say I must have lost, otherwise, a victory would have registered a noteworthy event; also, quite confident, my opponents were Adrian or Emilio, who received great joy defeating me.

My time may be altered a bit from the actual duration spent playing dominos, though I do know my next task involved making a trip to the bathroom to confirm whether a shower was on my agenda. I was pleased to discover soon after entering that a whore bath wouldn't be required, being early enough in the day to have two luxuries—warm water and a functional toilet. Within moments of stinking up the air quality, I was suddenly frightened by loud banging on the bathroom door! "*Damn it!*" I forgot all about that ongoing gag, which has just startled the hell out of me! I certainly did not want to acknowledge my distress to the obnoxious culprit, for it would only incite their motivation to continuously use me as an easy target for a good laugh.

To downplay the fright and release my initial shock, I instantly shouted, "I just shit myself!" I failed to hear any clever response, or laughter from my roomies, allowing me to finish my business in peace and quiet before enjoying a warm shower.

While exiting the bathroom, David walked up behind me without signifying an impending conversation by asking, "Are we the 'Wal-Martians'?" Strangely enough, I knew exactly what he was referring to, as it related to the delivery of some clean clothes I received from Brenda. One article of clothing, in particular, was a T-shirt that I had custom made with a phrase printed on the back, the same shirt I just put on after taking a shower, that read "I'm surrounded by Wal-Martians."

David's tone seemed to suggest that I adorned the shirt to display a bold statement referring to my cellmates. Though that was furthest from the truth as my motive was purely focused on wearing a clean shirt and nothing more. My response was swift and straight to the point, wanting to quickly prevent any misconceptions toward my actions in displaying the humorous shirt, "No, it's not directed toward you guys! It's for all the freaks who roam the aisles of Walmart stores." Followed by eagerly telling him to "Google it," for it would explain the meaning of the phrase and expose everybody in the cell to a wide variety of strange characters who will make you laugh while cringing with disgust. My suggestion had immediately evoked a cell-phone frenzy of a Google search, soon erupting the room with laughter as the men viewed the distasteful images of bizarre humans in Walmart stores.

Years ago, I had the shirt made to wear while shopping in Walmart, to silently voice my disgust for people who have absolutely no shame in proudly displaying themselves as if every day is Halloween; in a land where I would have to dress up as a dysfunctional adult just to be inconspicuous! Unlike a permanent tattoo, I can alter my message or belief for the day by simply wearing a different shirt, with the option of throwing it in the trash years later when it becomes unrecognizable from its original form.

After successfully averting a potential incident with my roomies, I inadvertently created another one during their bull session by mentioning something to John about me being an American. I don't recall my actual statement, only what John relayed to me after I voiced it.

John spoke with a soft respectful tone informing me Mexicans get offended when somebody from the United States refers themselves as an American to differentiate them from people of Mexican heritage. This is completely understandable as Mexico is also part of the North American Continent, though it never occurred to me as being offensive. John's objective wasn't to berate me in front of our cellmates, but to make me aware of the statement so as not to mistakenly utter it again, in turn, would preserve my good rapport with the men.

I wanted to eat before the café's dinner rush kicked into full gear, so I headed into the kitchen contemplating eating the leftover chicken and rice, but the thought of eating the nasty rice was well worth the inconvenience of cooking a different meal. Nevertheless, I decided to compromise by making some mashed potatoes to go with the chicken and throw the rice in the trashcan. Since the café had the option of making store-bought frozen French-fries or fresh hand-cut ones, I figured changing a menu item for dinner wouldn't be a problem, wrong again! After a complete search of the kitchen for some potatoes, a dilemma quickly arose as none could be found. Though I wasn't about to be denied, I grabbed the translation book and went to John for the correct pronunciation of "Patata" (potato), which was simple enough.

While getting ready to leave the cell, John was compelled to delay my trip by eagerly wanting to teach me some basic Spanish before I headed to the corner store. He immediately retrieved a sheet of paper and began writing down frequently used Spanish words along with their translated counterpart, in an attempt to help with my vocabulary while in prison. As John was going over the word's pronunciation with me, somebody blurted out, "Bitch," prompting him to write down "Parra."

Then Emilio joined in the mix with "Sick." Which was one of his responses to me during our banter bouts that consisted of him shaking his head no while saying, "Sick sick sick!" So "Enfermo" was added to the list of words, along with "Good=Bueno, Bad=Malo, Chess=Ajedrez."

John pointed out a word on the list that required a rolling R sound to articulate the word, and even though he diligently aided

DIZNEY LAND by Way of Military Escort

me in the pronunciation, I had extreme difficulty rolling my R, so much that it discouraged me from continuing any further. This arduous task quickly became overwhelming to absorb all at once, giving me an attitude of "Who cares!" Besides, I'm surrounded by English speaking individuals, and even though I will eventually learn some Spanish, the longer I'm stuck in here, for now, it will just have to wait!

With my discouraged frame of mind hidden from view, I folded the sheet of paper and placed it between the pages of the translation book then headed out the door to resume my quest for some spuds. The oddity of a casual stroll to the Mexican prison grocery store holds no comparison to the controversial purchase I was about to make. Come to find out, Brenda was previously denied entries into the prison by attempting to bring me a bag of potatoes; apparently, inmates are forbidden from having them in their possession, to prevent them from making homemade moonshine.

Strangely enough, I was allowed to buy the prohibited spuds from the storekeeper with no questions asked, so what would discourage a convict from brewing his own hooch while on the safe side of the prison? His own motivation? The only thing the guard accomplished by confiscating Brenda's bag of earthly vegetables was to alter the spuds' delivery system to my possession, also revealing Brenda's kindness by donating the bag of potatoes to a female guard.

With cuatro (four) spuds in hand, I went back to my cell, where I was greeted by Mini-Me's shout out, "Open the window!" I proceeded into the kitchen to prepare my contraband into mashed potatoes to compliment the chicken dinner. Other than not having a potato masher, I was quite pleased with how easy the preparation of the meal was, also satisfied with the flavor of the mashed potatoes. After offering some to David due to his keen interest in trying them, he confirmed they were delicious by asking for a second helping raising concerns if there would be enough for a second serving for myself. I was pleasantly surprised by David's enjoyment of my creation, particularly knowing his Hispanic palate could deem the potatoes under-seasoned; though discovered he preferred not to have his meals over spiced, so he could taste the actual flavor of the food.

Upon finishing my meal and cleaning what little mess was made in the kitchen, I converged with the men in the other room where David turned toward me and, with a concerned tone asked an imprudent question, "Do you hate Mexicans?"

I fought off the strong urge to respond with an aggressive reaction of, "What the hell are you talking about!" I was bothered by the implication, which had absolutely no merit! Other than people, or humans in general, I haven't displayed harsh actions, or voiced animosity toward inmates or Mexicans during my stay in this cell, also been diligent at carefully conducting my behavior so as not to offend anybody; excluding friendly needling among each other.

I can only assume David's inquiry was a continuation of the Wal-Martian T-shirt, but why would he ask such a sensitive question that only had one obvious answer. What the hell did he expect my response to be? "Yes, I'm a racist and intolerant of being the only cracker in this bowl full of beaners?" During my incarceration, I tried to avoid unlocking the personal inner workings of my mind, unless forced by others to hand over the key, which David has done, again! Was I to tell him the truth, or what he wanted to hear? A simple response of "No," would be expected and probably dismissed as a safe answer, however, simple and safe are no longer a route I'm willing to traverse.

My comfort level with the men within this cell has increased along with my willingness to untie the knot from my tongue. My truthful response to David was spoken with prompt conviction, which has been a standard reply of mine over many years, "I'm not a racist, I hate everybody equally until I get to know them, then I can hate them for who they are."

The perplexed expression on David's face revealed he had great difficulty processing my hurried response, who only replied with, "What?" I repeated my statement in a slower articulated manner with John assisting the interpretation.

My harsh statement may be an exaggeration and used more like a rebellious, sarcastic response to society's enforcement of tolerance toward lazy, or stupid humans. Although, we all have some degree of stupidity, or laziness embedded into our core, though some levels are exceedingly higher than others, which is what I preach to the choir.

Society says one should be tolerant of others, so society must be tolerant of my intolerance. Also, can I be perceived as prejudice against the same species as I? Remember, Emilio, says I'm "Sick sick sick!"

I'm unsure on how much of my statement David was able to accurately comprehend, though he did adopt a line from it, occasionally incorrectly quoting, "I hate everyone," as he too voiced displeasure toward humanity, which might have some correlation to his one-year prison stay with no sentence. I can't imagine what that would do to my already distorted attitude, though we will wait and see.

I had the misfortune of not knowing what was being translated to the rest of the men via David and John in relation to what I said, or why the obnoxious banter in the room began to spiral completely out of control. Nevertheless, most of the outlandish behavior came from the three extroverts in the cell, Adrian, Mini-Me, and Emilio, who incited my unruly conduct as a participant in the madness. I think the spark that ignited all the animated enthusiasm in the room started with Adrian because after he listened to the clarification of my "Hate everybody equally" statement, he spoke up with a raised voice and said, "Yeah, fucking Mexicans!"

This totally mystified me, failing to recognize the correlation between our animosity toward others, but there wasn't time to try and make sense of his outburst, as Mini-Me quickly joined in with, "Yeah, fucking Mexicans!" Inciting Emilio to shout out, "Sonnof beech!"

The scene quickly escalated into a room full of parrots with Tourette's syndrome, who were repeatedly shouting English swear words amongst the four of us.

Adrian was the loudest and most aggressive with his profanity, who kept shouting "Fucking niggers," which had no repercussions as there were no black inmates in this prison.

Emilio, Mini-Me and I were spurred on by Adrian's energy, instigating their repeated shout outs, and I of "Fuck Americans!"

My outburst was brought forth by being ashamed that I was linked to a spoiled, dysfunctional society that has countless people who lack self-responsibility, logic, or common sense, though that could also be said about most of the planet!

In all the ridiculous chaos, I totally forgot about the reprimand John made to me earlier related to the "American" reference, which means my recent outburst wasn't just degrading people from the US but included everybody from North America. During my overzealous rant, John approached me and once again politely reminded me of the offensive remark, inadvertently causing me to reclaim my introvert status by sitting down on the milk crate while keeping my mouth shut for a while.

When the antics in the cell rapidly came to an end, three of the men disappeared into their cocoons, two worked the café in tandem with the runner who was diligently working the late-night delivery service, while John immersed himself in a book as I sat there wondering who flipped the switch that killed all the laughter.

As the day drew near its end, I was exiting the bathroom after completing a nighttime routine when I heard beating drums nearby. It sounded like a few harmonious inmates were involved in a musical pow-wow. I wondered who and why they were involved in a jam session so late in the evening and hoped they were respectful enough to silence their racket soon, allowing me the opportunity for a tolerable night's sleep.

While patiently sitting on my crate waiting for lights out, Emilio climbed up to his bunk and from behind his curtain, cried out with a spirited tone, "My lady, I love you!" He made some type of promiscuous remark about joining him, and even though I immediately responded with an elevated tone, "I'm going to visit your wife when I get out of here," it lacked entertainment value, as nobody was in the room to translate my statement to Emilio. For a second, I thought about climbing up to his bunk, peek behind his curtain accompanied by a big grin and a twinkle in my eye, but that might be taking it a little too far just to accomplish a good laugh.

After nullifying three of my senses from light, sound, and smell of wacky tobacky, I laid in bed listening to David's music through the new earbuds Brenda brought me. Even though I have no problem falling asleep while listening to music, I can't stay asleep with earbuds in my ears as they bother me too much. After removing them, I was forced to deal with the noisy cellblock that seemed to drag on longer

DIZNEY LAND by Way of Military Escort

and louder than previous nights. I voiced my displeasure to John, who acknowledged that the unruly men in the cellblock were louder than usual, altering my aggravation into pure disgust by shouting out, "Shut the hell up!" There wasn't any response, or change in the cellblock's decibel level, most likely due to the void of translation and the mid-range of my outburst.

Two in the morning, a full bladder motivated my trip to the bathroom, whereupon raising the toilet seat cover, I was suddenly startled by a frightened mouse attempting to jump out of the toilet bowl by scurrying atop the rim. I quickly knocked the mouse off the rim back into the water in hopes of getting its paws wet, limiting its traction and ability to climb out to freedom, but to no avail. The little critter didn't seem to be affected by the late-night swim continuing to jump for the rim. Therefore, I immediately grabbed the plunger in order to contain the tenacious mouse within the water to assess its proficiency at freediving. When Mickey failed the swimming lesson and the H_2O transformed him from a jumper to a floater, I was able to send the limp corpse to its final destination with a single flush. If I have inadvertently upset folks at PETA origination, please call me at 1-800-768-6372 ext. 63 (POUND SAND up your ass).

My recent encounter confirms John's concern over leaving the soap, or toilet paper in the bathroom, for it invites the mice to chew on. All I can say is that's one animated mouse who won't escape from these castle walls alive; Poor Minnie will worry that Micky didn't return home from his all-night drinking binge.

Day 22 in Country

Tenth day in prison

COCKADOODLEDOO! It can't possibly be time to wake up, I'm still tired! "I had a dream last night that I was asleep, and I dreamt it while I was awake!"[32] Something needs to dramatically change or I will soon mutate into a dysfunctional zombie; maybe it's time to accept a roommate's offer of their bed for a mid-day nap.

After breakfast, I went for my routine morning walk, which consisted of a few deviations from yesterday's, a tower guard saying hello to me, the absence of Carlos and the hungry cat on its prowl. Since my focus was toward the Word Seek book, I was unaware of the tower guard observing me while walking by and was pleasantly surprised by his friendly shout out. I failed to recognize the familiar stranger as I only did a quick glance behind me to extend a smile and a wave hello.

Upon approaching my cell, there wasn't a shout out of "open the window" from Mini-Me, who was in the kitchen taking care of some chores. Which had me thinking after sitting on my crate for a few seconds, that this would be a good opportunity to help earn my keep around here by going into the kitchen and help him. When I enter the kitchen, Mini-Me was in the process of washing out two-liter plastic soda bottles the café used for selling their water and appeared to have just begun the task, because there were three large milk crates containing empty bottles the inmates return to the café for trade or money.

Without gesturing to Mini-Me if he needed any help, I instantly proceeded to assist him by removing the screw caps and the plastic

---

[32] *Mash*, TV show.

labels from the bottles, then exchanged the dirty bottles for the clean ones with him while replacing them in the crates. Oddly, there wasn't a single exchange of communicative interaction between us while completing our task, realizing with nobody in the room to translate, nothing could be said anyway.

There is an error in stating "Washing the bottles" and should be corrected to "Rinsing the bottles," because there wasn't any hot water or soap used to sanitize the dirty jugs which seems strange to rinse out used bottles with contaminated water that must be boiled before it's safe for human consumption. To paraphrase David, "Anything consumed by Mexicans must be bad in order to be good for them." Which interprets to strengthen one's immune system by exposing it with harmful substances, though not a foreign journey I'm willing to explore, or will I?

While Mini-Me began the slow, tedious process of filling the bottles with water from five-gallon jugs without the use of a funnel, I returned to my crate and performed my three basic tasks, write down notes, Word Seek and occasionally assist customers at the door. I no longer felt uncomfortable sitting so close to the cell door, as the strange stares from customers disappeared while friendly greetings increased from guards and inmates alike. Though still no acknowledgment of my presence from female patrons, who were masters of avoidance and eye contact.

A little after ten o'clock, I was pleasantly surprised to see Brenda approaching my cell with a bag full of goodies and just as astonished to see her roaming the prison unescorted. After quickly handing off the bag to a roomie and hugging Brenda, we went to the courtyard, took a seat next to Alexander's café and ordered lemonade and a Pepsi. By purchasing something from the café, I wouldn't be hunted down later to pay the rental fee for the use of our table and chairs. While sipping on our drinks and observing the Energizer Bunny frantically moistening the parched dirt, Brenda mentioned that he should water the thirsty plants that were near our table. I personally had no concerns for the struggling shrubbery, though Brenda did; and after Mr. Bunny dropped the garden hose and walked away, she went over and picked it up to carry out a task of a sane person, by watering something that actually grows and not for the sole purpose of making mud.

Frank arrived at our table soon after Brenda's green thumb activity was complete, though he only stayed long enough to reveal a story about a religious experience he had many years ago, that motivated him to believe there was a god. Frank's story was brief; however, I will convey an even shorter one, as most of my attentiveness faded during his narrative regarding religion. From what I retained, Frank was in an altered state of mind, from what substance is unclear, when he suffered a painful shoulder injury, how is also unclear. Then somehow, he ended up in a church praying for relief, proceeded to pass out, for how long unclear, and when he awoke, the pain had miraculously disappeared.

Some say humans only use ten percent of their brain capacity, which could explain when unexplainable events occur one tends to adamantly insist it's because of God (Angels) or a higher power (Extraterrestrials). Referring to the Old Testament and doctrine from other religions, was there not mention of epic battles in the skies (heavens) thousands of years ago? So by definition, theory and logic could angels and aliens be one and the same?

As Frank displayed a slight energetic passion toward his belief of said miracle, he inquired about our interest pertaining to religion, though our response may have provoked his early departure from our company. We informed Frank of babies being born with tails while suggesting proof of Darwin's theory of evolution. In order to not dampen his spirits, we trod lightly on the subject by omitting certain facts of our statements. For instance, all mammals have a tail at some point in their development, and human embryos have a tail twelve centimeters long within four to five weeks from conception known as "Human Vestigial." Also, according to medical documentation, there have been twenty-three humans around the world born with a tail.

Frank's baffled expression revealed he was clueless about Darwinism, only responding with, "I didn't know that, it gives me something to think about." Followed by walking away, after asking me, "DYNA?" My simple request of Q-tips was brought on by allergic reaction from consuming gluten during the past thirteen days, that induces a runny nose and constant discomfort in my ears, filling up with a substance that feels like I have been swimming underwater all day and have to spend the rest of my time trying to drain the fluid. Sadly, the Q-tips only alleviated some discomfort for a short period of time; maybe I should rub some dirt on it.

Brenda's exodus wasn't far behinds Frank's, for she still exhibited signs of pure exhaustion, lacked the ability to concentrate and struggled through another embarrassing strip search. She was very determined to leave early from our visitation and get some sleep, with explicit instructions for me not to tell anybody where she was going. Brenda was downright irritated with Roberto's objectionable behavior and his demanding personality, who had her constantly performing as his personal chauffeur. Brenda's overwhelming desperation to get uninterrupted sleep and avoid being bothered by Roberto, possessed her to check out early from the motel and ignore his phone calls, to refrain from revealing her plans of disappearing to a new location.

Just before we parted ways, Brenda informed me the name of the motel she planned on staying at, regrettably, I forgot it soon after entering my cell, disregarding the info as immaterial, though at the time didn't realize my lack of retention would create a fearful state of panic in the near future!

While sitting in the cell watching Mini-Me tear apart a twelve-inch oscillating fan attempting to fix it, Frank showed up with a small plastic sandwich bag containing some Q-tips, then proceeded to reveal the challenging undertaking required to procure them. When Frank had completely exhausted all his resources scouring the prison in search of the cotton-top sticks, he deduced when the guards clean their weapons they most likely use Q-tips to reach the tiny crevices within the mechanisms, so as a last resort started going to each of the guard towers asking the guards if they had any. Frank was still coming up empty-handed until his last stop at tower #4, where a guard placed some Q-tips in a bag then dropped it down to him. The Gringo that always delivers truly impressive!

If that wasn't enough, Frank then asked, "Did you get your Frisbees?" Come to find out they were in the captain's office for some odd reason, though I had no idea Brenda even brought them today as she made no mention of it.

While Frank was away retrieving the Frisbees, David questioned me on the contents of the mystery bag clutched in my hand, then with an elevated concerned tone followed up with. "Where did you get them?"

I responded, "I got connections."

He proceeded to politely lecture me, "Why didn't you come to me, I have Q-tips and all you had to do was ask, *reeeally*, whatever you want, just ask, no really!" My bad, it didn't dawn on me in asking someone in my cell for some Q-tips. David was compassionate with his persistent offer in supporting my needs and once again seemed a little put off by me getting help from outside of this cell.

When David's blood pressure began to lower, I soon received possession of five brand new Frisbees, and even sooner, the shit was about to hit the fan! I reluctantly turned around with the stack of flying discs in my hand, to see David standing there with utter disbelief written all over his face who attempted to speak, but pure disgust hampered his ability to verbalize a complete sentence, shortening his perturbed comment to, "A *Frisbee, reeeally?*" I instantly erased the grin from my face and quickly put the Frisbees under Mini-Me's bed out of sight to help defuse the impending detonation.

Luckily for David, there wasn't anybody else in the room witnessing his distress, evoking needling among his roommates furthering his torment. It was inevitable that David's next question was, "How did you get the Frisbee?"

No, I wasn't about to reply with "I got connections," even though I had a strong urge to do so; however, I couldn't but help correct his assumption from having one Frisbee to five, which instantly caused him to come unglued, then started ranting with an elevated tone, "*No reeeally, five frisbees*, really, why five, REEEALLY?" I found David's elevated anguish to be quite amusing but kept my enjoyment hidden from view, for he didn't need any more help increasing his blood pressure.

My explanation of sharing the Frisbees with the other inmates failed to appease or lower David's aggravation level and only incited more disgust toward his captors. He went on to explain that it took three long months of arduous dealings with prison staff before getting permission to obtain a radio, whereas it only took ten days for the possession of my five Frisbees. Just before retreating into his cocoon, David ended his justifiable rant with his trademark line, "Fucking Mexicans!" Though as usual, it wasn't voiced in anger, only pure disgust.

To help ease David's disgust, I ended up giving him a Frisbee moments later, to which he responded with pure elation, "*Reeeally*, for me, how much?" I reassured him it was a gift that no money was needed.

Idle time spent in my cell had been steadily decreasing each day, and today was no exception, by once again heading outside in search of stimulus. Soon upon entering the courtyard, I met up with Frank involved in a conversation with the captain, who, through Frank's translation, asked if I was okay and being treated fairly; then, to my surprise, he wondered if I had received my Frisbees. Unbelievable! The captain's concern toward my possession of a toy was truly unexpected!

After replying with a very appreciative, "Yes," I graciously thanked him. Is it inconceivable to believe that a captain inquiring about a white man having five Frisbees in a Mexican prison has *never* transpired before? To put it into perspective, there is a much greater chance one will *not* see anybody tossing around a Frisbee inside Disney Land.

Next, the captain kindly brought it to my attention that I was out of uniform and needed to wear prison-issue pants or a shirt while out of my cell. Oh shit! I totally forgot! So now I find myself standing next to the captain in the courtyard wearing civilian clothing feeling awkward trying to convey a sympathetic apology while explaining I was well aware of the rule, but it totally slipped my mind. It was peculiar that my attire went completely unnoticed by the guards and required the captain of the prison to be aware that I was out of uniform. Am I under the watchful eyes of a platoon full of sergeant Schultz's from "Hogan's Heroes'" uttering, "I see *nothing!*"

As the captain walked away, I told Frank I would be right back, then scampered back to the cell for a quick wardrobe change. Now that I will no longer be mistaken as a visitor roaming the prison, I enlisted Frank's help to accompany me to the woodshop to check on the status of the chess piece I ordered. Our trip ended with disappointment as there was some confusion by the shopkeeper of my earlier request. Frank was willing to rectify the problem, though I was not and told him, "Just forget about it," while slowly walking away. So for now, the wooden tortoise would stay in power over his kingdom for the time being.

Since the bakery was in the adjacent building four doors down, I decided to take advantage of my personal translating gringo and pick up a couple of lemon pudding filled pastries and eliminate the middleman's upcharge delivery service. Frank's presence would eliminate concerns of getting overcharged, placing the correct order and relieve my anxiety during another unique experience amongst a room of foreign strangers.

The 15'x25' spacious bakery was slightly modernized with stainless steel workbenches and some degree of organization and cleanliness. The staff members were friendly and eager to please when Frank relayed my order to them. The simple task of handing out two pastries from a tray seemed to gravitate toward a more important undertaking when Frank conveyed specific instructions to the personnel. When one of the men walked over to retrieve the pastries, he was redirected by a co-worker to go where the freshly cooked pastries were at, then over to the other side of the kitchen to fill them with lemon cream. Before he handed me the two pastries, I gave another staff member the money; even though the cost eludes me, I do remember they were very inexpensive and wished I had bought more while we were exiting the bakery.

During our stroll back to the common area of the courtyard, Frank stopped at a table where four older inmates were playing dominos and asked one of the men if he could make a chess piece. After Frank relayed detailed instructions to the man of my request, I was told the king would be completed manana (tomorrow). Because of Frank's brief discussion with the inmate and my avoidance of personal interaction with the four men, I failed to absorb any detailed attributes of the men. Plus, the fact I respectfully kept my distance from their table, limiting my intrusion of the group's gameplay and avoided eye contact while standing slightly behind and to the left of Frank. After thanking the inmate and Frank, I walked away with the reassurance that Frank would expedite the process of reuniting the Queens Mate.

There were no cellmates in my line of sight upon my arrival at the cell, so to get somebody's attention to unlock the door, I cried out my customary "Open the door!" and was met with "Open the window" from Mini-Me, who was in the confines of his cocoon, most likely watching the idiot box (TV). After John unlocked the door, I went straight to the kitchen to put my pastries in the refrigerator, though as usual, only one made it to the fridge as the other quickly found its way into my belly.

Once again, time spent in the cell was short-lived, as Adrian and I headed out to the courtyard along with my new chess set in hand. Even though we ended up sitting at a table in the visitor's area, there was no mention of paying a rental fee, or any visual exchange of money between Adrian and the owner of said property.

Within a few moves into our game, I noticed an improvement in Adrian's gameplay, though not enough for me to be concerned about losing. During our match, a few curious inmates, along with Raúl, began gathering around the table watching us play, sparking interest from a spectator who challenged me to a game after I defeated Adrian, to which I gladly excepted.

I quickly discovered that my new opponent mirrored the previous contender's gameplay by playing fast and exposing his queen too early in the game, prompting my thought, "I'm going to punish him for getting his queen out too early!" But failed to adjust my defense accordingly and accompanied with overconfidence, I soon realized my Knight (horse) was in a precarious situation. At least I was able to foresee the impending doom of losing a Knight within our next few exchanges of pieces, giving me the opportunity to stop and cogitate a way out of my predicament. After much deliberation over possible outcomes, I determined there was no chance in avoiding the loss of my Knight, therefore, if I cannot protect the piece, or retreat it to safety, my only plan of action is to devise a strategy of attack.

Unfortunately, my opponent became agitated due to the lengthy duration of inactivity while I was contemplating my next move and began revealing his impatience by voicing his displeasure to fellow observers.

I looked to Raúl and asked, "What did he say?"

He replied, "You are playing too slow."

This instantly gave me a defensive attitude inciting my gesture to leave the table, then had Raúl relay my grievance to the impatient opponent, "We can stop playing if he wants, I don't care!"

After Raúl confirmed that I was to keep playing, I continued my perturbed rant with an elevated tone, "I play to win, not to be in a hurry to go nowhere..." though the latter was all for not, as it went untranslated. I wasn't about to be swayed by my opponent's passive-aggressive behavior to play faster or alter my style of play just to appease him!

Since I knew what my opponent's next two moves were going to be in capturing my Knight, I used that knowledge to my advantage and methodically designed a plan of attack that would completely take him by surprise! My next nonthreatening move of a Bishop had absolutely no effect at protecting my Knight, giving the appearance I wasn't aware of the Knights plight or didn't care; however, two moves later it was the catalyst that drove his queen to retreat and put his king in jeopardy at the same time.

It gave me *great* satisfaction to reverse roles and watch my challenger play slow, contemplating the world of shit he was in, though at that moment, he acted like I was incapable of winning the game. My impatient opponent suddenly went from a dominant aggressor to a subdued defender in only three moves, due to his lack of defense brought on by the aggressive attack toward my Knight and overconfidence quickly leading him to a humiliating defeat. Followed by me standing up hovering over the table with a smirk on my face, then pointed to the chessboard and spoke in a raised tone with proud conviction, "That's why I play slow!" Then I packed up my game and walked away with a record of 18 and 1.

Upon entering the cell, Adrian instantly looked at me with an inquisitive stare and gestured as to ask a question. I responded with a smile and two thumbs up, evoking Adrian's big smile, a nod of his head with a congratulatory fist bump. David witnessed the exchange of our silent exuberance, sparking his interest to start questioning me for details concerning the chess match. I was more than willing to share my victorious experience with him and enjoyed he could also translate my story to Adrian while I had their undivided attention. My excitement level rose while attempting to describe the brilliant stealthy attack against my adversary, though I found it difficult explaining what transpired without a visual to do it justice. Therefore, I requested David and Adrian to follow me into the kitchen, where I set up the chessboard and began placing the chess pieces in the same configuration of the game I just finished playing, in order to visually assist them with my play by play reenactment.

While doing so, David had a look of utter confusion written all over his face while asking, "What are you doing?"

After I responded, he continued with, "How can you remember all that?"

I thought to myself, how could I not? It was only ten minutes ago. Hell, I can still visualize most of the layout from that game to this day. Adrian displayed more interest in the layout than David, who intently studied the board in search of alternate moves my opponent could have played to defend against my attack.

Despite the chessboard being laid out on the table, Adrian and I ended up playing a couple games of dominos, which I failed to win, then extended my losing streak with the help of Emilio, my next opponent. My luck at winning a game of chance had dramatically improved when we put the dominos away and started playing a game requiring a roll of the dice. The same game I witnessed a few inmates playing in the courtyard days earlier, where Raúl informed me the game was called "Make me angry." Upon further investigation, I realized it was identical to the game I played as a child called "Aggravation," a fine example of another board game of many that will soon be extinct from our human existence!

The game board Emilio and I were using was crudely made from a piece of plywood with drilled divots and hand-painted to resemble the original Parker Brothers game. Playing against Emilio elevated the entertainment factor with his antics and humorous competitive drive to win, mimicking my own, constantly keeping us disrupting each other's gameplay by forcing marbles back to their starting position, with great pleasure in doing so. The expressions on Emilio's face was quite amusing every time I dislodged one of his marbles to send it back home like he was being unjustly punished for doing something wrong. It didn't help that his fellow roomies, mainly Mini-Me, continuously razzed him during those setbacks, usually inducing him to say "Sonnof Beech" directed toward me.

Our first game went by fast due to the fact that inmates play "Make me angry" in the same fashion as Chess, with impatience by using three dice instead of two in order to speed up the game, leaving them more time to do nothing later. Emilio's smirky grin displayed great pleasure defeating me, though it was only victorious by a small margin as I had less than ten spaces from placing my fifth marble into the finale divot.

With anticipation at redeeming myself from the loss, I began resetting the marbles in their starting position for a rematch with Emilio, when a new set of colored marbles where added to the board in preparation of Mini-Me joining us. His cheerful attitude quickly brought forth increased entertainment during gameplay; also, the three of us now had alternating allies in which to provoke each other's adversary in choosing whose marble to send back to its starting position.

I frequently relied on using my body language to divert their urge in dislodging my marbles, opposed to sending someone else's back to start, the majority of our game was void of translation though not required to keep us from having fun! Every time I chose which opponents' marble to pounce on and send it back where it started from, it received amusing pleasure from the opposing player along with some facetious needling to increase the recipients' torment of their unfortunate setback. Though it was just as funny to others when I was forced to retrieve my marble as it rolled uncontrollably across the board due to a swift bump by an opponent's aggressive sphere. It was comical on how much pleasure we truly received at inflicting aggravation toward each other!

As the game progressed, two of Mini-Me's marbles were positioned halfway around the board, and due to his short stature of four-foot nothing, it required some effort in reaching across the table to move his marbles. Therefore, to be accommodating and not get noticed of my gesture, I nonchalantly placed my right hand on the edge of the table and slowly extended my fingers outward to slide the board a few inches closer to him. This instantly prompted Emilio's outburst of uncontrollable laughter, followed by mimicking my movement of adjusting the board while relaying some sort of wisecrack to Mini-Me, then escalated his own laughter by impersonating a T-rex's limited arm length. From what I surmised, Emilio thought the intent of my stealthy gesture was to tease Mini-Me's ability at reaching the distant marbles, and even though it wasn't my intention to be humorous, it was made hilarious by Emilio's theatrical animations. Once again, the recipient of all the rooms laughter, Mini-Me didn't mind that the wisecracks were directed toward him while joining in the banter.

I realized from the start of the game, I would have a slight advantage during the beginning part of the game, due to their starting positions were in proximity of each other's onslaught on the opposite side of the board from mine, allowing me the freedom to roam unmolested. Unbeknownst to them, that was why I chose the blue marbles, to be furthest from the duo's battlefield. Even though it was beneficial as I jumped to an early lead in the game, the latter part created havoc when my adversaries approached my area of the board and relentlessly kept knocking my blue balls from their divots just before reaching the entrance to safety. I swear, it felt like I was the lightning rod of hatred, as my dislodged marbles spent more time capriciously rolling around the board than in their track, allowing for a very close race to the finish between T-rex (Emilio) and me. Luckily, the dice fell from my unclutched hand more favorably, allowing me to boast a victory over the disappointing duo!

After all the marbles were gathered up and placed inside a plastic bag. I started heading toward the other room, where I met up with Adrian, who was exiting the bathroom after taking a shower. He was wearing a short-sleeve shirt revealing scars on his left arm that looked all too familiar. I also have similar disfigurement on my right arm due to the tragic house fire, so I stood alongside Adrian and raised my arm next to his while exposing my scare in comparison to his, gesturing we have both suffered a severe pain of being burned. He looked at me with a sorrowful frown and a nod of his head to acknowledge our pain of the past. I don't know if it was compassion or camaraderie that compelled me to say, "We are like brothers," as it had no relevance, or of a relayed translation.

When I entered the room, it was full of friendly chatter among the cellmates and busy with activity from customers placing orders. David immediately inquired about the outcome of the games I played. While revealing the winners and losers, a big smile appeared on Mini-Me's face and made a remark pertaining to our game, then held up the big L in front of his forehead while laughing. Followed by Adrian joining the mix with his jocularity of some sort of witty remark about my dominos defeat; so, I responded with a quick outreached hand in front of his face and said, "Talk to the hand!"

Adrian hadn't a clue of what the hell I was doing, nor did David, who both stared at me with intrigued confusion. I explained the nonsensical gesture was a retaliatory action of refusing to listen to somebody's remark, which David found to be quite amusing, so much so, that he received great enjoyment using the US culture sarcasm on me the next day.

David and I were still involved in discussion when a familiar voice shouted out, "*Harry Potter*," followed by a humorous statement that induced laughter from the gathered customers and cellmates.

I took one step to the right, leaned over to get a visual of the boisterous guard standing at our door, then gave him a loud greeting of, "Hey Frogman," with a wave hello, then withdrew from his view. His elevated energy seemed to feed off the laughter from the entertained spectators, which enticed him to continue poking fun at me.

DIZNEY LAND by Way of Military Escort

Therefore, I wanted to redirect the laughter toward the guard by putting my mild manner demeanor aside and go on the offensive with, "Watch it, Frogman, or I will stab you!"

Since I knew his grasp for the English language was nonexistent, my bold remark was directed toward those who understood English as I expected nobody would be brave enough to translate my threatening comment to the guard.

Mini-Me noticed I was willing to exchange banter with the obnoxious guard then, with a smirky grin, began intently rambling on as if I understood what he was saying. I quickly concluded he wanted me to razz Frogman, by calling him something he had been repeating to me in a whispered tone, so as not to be overheard from the guard. Once again, I wasn't about to be duped into repeating a Spanish word of which I haven't a clue of its meaning, especially when Mini-Me adamantly refused my gestured request to repeat the mystery word to the guard.

Even though the amusing Frogman soon left with his purchase and I was no longer being used as an easy target, the banter showed no signs of slowing down while the men continued razzing each other, filling the room with laughter. While no longer involved in their jocularity, I retrieved the translation book that I usually carry while venturing outside, then headed to the corner store in search for some orange juice, where none could be found. The trip to the courtyard wasn't a complete waste of time, because I met up with Carlos and crew where we played dominos for a while, consequently walking away from the table with little to no variation of pesos in my pocket, though the jingle of loose change was less distinguishable as some coins were exchanged for a MilkyWay candy bar to the wandering vendor.

Here is a thought to ponder over, we were in the courtyard playing dominos while gambling with a small pile of money on the table in full view of the guards, and yet possessing a deck of cards is against prison rules to prevent inmates from gambling. Yes, you can bet a deck of cards found its way into this mouse house unbeknownst to prison staff or depending on an inmate's connections, maybe the guards are the catalyst behind the smuggling ring. An assumption made evident during Brenda's second visitation when we were sitting on the bench across from the captain's office, where she witnessed a guard and inmate standing shoulder to shoulder in front of the secretaries office nonchalantly exchanging a bag of white powder for cash; I don't think the inmate was buying sugar!

It was nearing lockdown upon entering the cell when I saw an unfamiliar guest and John sitting on the edge of Mini-Me's bed with a few legal documents placed in their laps; apparently, John was helping the troubled inmate with his legal matters by writing a deposition for him. I walked past the involved duo and put my candy bar into the chest cooler, then went to the kitchen for an uneventful dinner, followed an uneventful evening that mainly consisted of some small chitchat, occasionally observing the café's runner and waiting for lights out.

Leisure time spent on the milkcrate allowed me a moment to dwell on the approaching irritation of lying in bed, knowing it would be at least two tortuous hours until dreams consumed my unconscious mind. The longer I stewed over the impending annoyance, the more determined I became to alter my sleeping arrangement, yet my only option was outside in the dirty, cockroach-infested kitchen with limited space for a sleeping mat. Considering where I lay my head now, sleeping in a patio-like atmosphere would be paradise!

The staggered rebar spanning the patio supported old sheets of tin roofing covering ¾ of the area, leaving the rest exposed to the elements, though rain wasn't much of a concern due to the average rainfall in La Paz is only 2.6 inches a year and 0 percent during the whole month of May.

While informing David of my plans to sleep in the kitchen, he looked at me as if I were quite insane then responded with an elevated tone, "*Reeeally?*" Then thoughtfully pressed me for assurance of my decision, I told him my mind was made up and that I needed more than five hours of sleep a night, which could be achieved by distancing myself from our noisy neighbors. David's familiar compassion instantly kicked-in as he once again offered his headphones to assist me in a more pleasurable night's sleep. My migration was put on hold for an hour after lights out, due to a few roomies in the patio who were most likely communicating with their loved ones via a Scottish-born scientist's invention (telephone).

When able to relocate to the kitchen, I had to rearrange the table, chairs, and buckets in order to make enough space next to the deep freeze for the mat. By placing the mat between the table and the freezer, it cleared most of the walking path. With my head butted against the west wall, I had the luxury of lying there looking up at the stars in the clear nighttime sky and enjoying the fresh air while listening to music. In adding to the serenity, I had the pleasure of observing a gecko on the wall two feet away, as it patiently waited for its next meal to appear. This peaceful evening experience was truly a wonderful moment of pure Zen!

Day 23 in Country

Eleventh day in prison

Unbelievable! I had the gratification of sleeping-in all the way to roll call and receiving the best nights rest in thirteen days. My late morning alarm clock was the sound of fluttering wings from a small bird transporting food scraps from our trashcan then, as I laid in bed waiting for its return, a second visitor caught my attention as a butterfly quietly glided into the patio. My tranquility was soon interrupted by a guard calling out my name, after poking my head through the curtain to give a visual and verbal "Yoh," I laid back down and waited for the morning activity from my roomies entering the kitchen before forcing myself out of the comforts of my bed. If felt awesome to be in partial control of the pace at which I was willing to start my day! Why didn't I think about abandoning my previous sleeping arrangement days earlier?

The morning air was a little on the chilly side, so I decided to wear the prison pants for extra warmth during my walk, however, upon entering the courtyard, I was informed by a guard that I needed to wear the entire uniform. I didn't question why another prison rule was altered, which seemed to be on my behalf, I just went back to the cell to don a prison shirt and appease his authoritative power, then soon returned to begin my sunrise stroll.

My morning walks and daily trips into the courtyard increased my familiarity with the inmates and guards, producing recurring friendly greetings of hello and a wave of the hand. While circling scrambled letters in the Word Search book during my walk, frequent interruptions forced my hand from the page to relieve an itch on the back of my neck just below the hairline, though the gratification of scratching transformed into an irritation. I felt a few small lesions comparative to have been recently shanked in the neck with a toothpick, it dawned on me, the only recent encounter I had with an adversary was the hoard of nighttime scavengers scurrying throughout the infested kitchen; apparently, the early bird wasn't the only creature enjoying a free meal, as the cockroaches also partook in the all-night diner with my "neck" on the menu.

Once back in the cell, I ate breakfast, sat on my pillowed covered crate patiently waiting for ten o'clock in hopeful anticipation of Brenda's arrival. A little past ten, my interest was sparked by a guard approaching our cell who spoke those four words a prisoner loves to hear, "Your lawyer is here." I quickly enlisted John's help, and within seconds, we were out the door heading down the corridor at a steady pace. My eagerness to see a lawyer upon entering the meeting room was instantly put on hold, as Karla was deeply involved with seven female inmates, so John and I took a seat and patiently waited for them to finalize their interaction.

The young women gathered in front of Karla spoke not a word while they intently listened to her explain details pertaining to the legalities of their case; they displayed a very somber demeanor as Karla was trying to ease their worried minds. I questioned John for particulars concerning the sad women, though the distressing information only increased the sorrow I felt for these women and a strong disgust of what led them to prison.

The women were indigenous to Mexico, comparable to Native Americans in the USA, who were all mothers making their living by handcrafting merchandise and selling it to the public. Since their children were also partaking in the creation and selling of said items, the seven women were consequently accused of breaking the "Child labor law," then charged for the crime and sent to prison. Consequently, these native mothers who were trying to eke out an existence and support their families are treated as criminals among convicts and have been separated from their children for three months.

Sitting there gazing at their dejected body language was all too familiar. I truly felt their desperation emanating from within, forcing me to look down toward the floor with a heavy heart to keep my emotions under control as I began to tear up. I can't imagine what Karla could possibly say to relieve the embedded pain the women possessed as she hugged each one of them goodbye; no matter, for it wasn't enough solace to keep their dispirited smiles from quickly disappearing as they slowly meandered back toward their cages. When tears fail to relieve your harsh pain, remember *it could always be worse!*

Witnessing the depressing by-product of the Mexican judicial system in action dampened my optimism in meeting with Karla, yet I was totally shocked when she looked at me with a big smile and, through John's translation, said, "Your appeal for bail was granted!" Are you freaking kidding me? I was completely speechless, and to keep from babbling, I tried to process what questions to ask Karla, but before I was able to address them to John, he had already taken charge of the discussion and began asking questions and confirming all the facts with Karla.

John's intellectual ability at processing information was so damn thorough and precise, that when he finally addressed me, he was able to answer all the questions I had for Karla. The most pertinent information I gathered from John was that Karla had to wait for the judge to sign the order for bail, which could take about a week, or sooner, depending on if she could get his signature before the weekend. The only untranslated words to come from Karla concerning bail was "No problem." Since bail was a certainty, the only question I had was, "when" and not of how much it would cost. My first concern was get released from prison and worry about bail money second!

The last bit of information they relayed to me was the most dreadful news that worried the hell out of me. Karla and the prosecuting attorney were working on an agreement to cut my possible ten-year prison sentence in half to five. John and Karla relayed this dire news to me with a smile as if it were good news that would make me happy. As Raúl would say, "Man, that's some crazy shit!" Ten years, five years—what the fuck is the difference? Either one translates to the exact same definition, "*Escape!*"

As soon as I heard them utter a five-year sentence, elevated anxiety completely seized my thought process, focusing on jumping bail and telling the prosecuting attorney to shove those five years up his ass!

Before my negative emotions took total control of my brain function and totally block out what John was saying, he captured my attention when I heard the word "probation," as the smile on his face began to coincide with his explanation of what a shortened sentence meant for me. John revealed that anybody with a five-year or less sentence is allowed by law to apply for what is known as an "Abbreviated Process," which interprets to receiving two-year probation with no jail time and paying a small fine. Hell yeah! I would even agree to pay a large fine, anything to get the hell out of here!

In order to make sure Brenda and I would be financially prepared when it came time to pay the fine to the court, I asked John and Karla if they had any idea how much it would be. Their casual response brought disbelief as I questioned the accuracy of their estimation. How is it possible that I was caught committing a federal crime and put through the trouble of being sent to jail facing a ten-year prison sentence all for only $250? It's almost laughable! Is it conceivable that everybody was correct in their notion of "No problem, pay fine and go home?" We would have to wait and see!

Before finalizing our discussion, I asked Karla if she could help find out about getting my truck released from the impound lot and if she had been contacted by Roberto, or had any involvement with him pertaining to my case. My curiosity was due to what Roberto said during our previous encounter, that he had been in contact with my public defender and reassured me he was diligently working for my release in tandem with Karla's office. When I mentioned Roberto's name to Karla, she reacted with a perplexed response and was adamant that nobody contacted or notified her of any involvement by a third party concerning my case. I don't know who Roberto claimed he talked to at the public defender's office, but I had a bad feeling the five-grand is not being utilized correctly!

I found out later from John that Karla was quite perturbed and offended I hired Roberto to assist in my legal battle since she had already completed most of the leg work securing my bail before he even arrived in La Paz. After learning of this, I was upset and felt completely ashamed for being perceived as someone who put their faith in a shady character who I didn't know while devaluing Karla's self-worth. What else was I to do? Put my faith in the hands of the Mexican judicial system and be patient for months or years just like some of the poor bastards stuck in this prison and hope everything works out for the best; I think not!

After John finalized our discussion, I humbly extended sincere appreciation to Karla for all her help, though due to our language barrier, it felt like my thankfulness lacked the sincerity I truly wanted to express to her.

While heading back to our cell, John's elevated excitement once again over-shadowed mine, as he cheerfully spoke with a big grin, "You are getting out of here soon!" In the back of my mind, the unconfirmed "Abbreviated Process" had me thinking about that five—to ten-year prison sentence and jumping bail if plans don't go as anticipated. John was genuinely happy for me while continuing his enthusiasm within our cell, summarizing what Karla had talked about and reiterated that he was very optimistic toward the Abbreviated Process.

Time spent in the cell with John, and I was short-lived because, within an hour, we journeyed back to the meeting room in search of my next visiting lawyer. For some odd reason, Roberto once again didn't venture inside the prison, minimalizing my importance by meeting me at one of the caged windows.

As I approached Roberto, he failed to exhibit any concern toward my wellbeing, or relay a friendly greeting, and only directed his insistent response to my presence by first asking, "Where is Brenda?"

If I wasn't on the wrong side of the wire window, I would have told him, "None of your damn business!" First of all, Roberto needs to learn proper etiquette on how to start a conversation, second, why would he expect me to know where Brenda was; I'm in a freaking prison!

Yes, Brenda told me where she was going in order to avoid the overbearing narcissist, but he didn't know that, or that I forgot the name of the hotel.

I acted ignorantly and politely said, "I don't know, yesterday she said she wasn't feeling well and was going to get some rest at her hotel."

Roberto responded with a dejected tone, "She is no longer there," then waited for me to disclose her whereabouts. I didn't say a word.

Before dwelling any further on the subject, Roberto caught a glimpse of John standing nearby, instantly demonstrating a look of paranoia while repositioning his line of sight by leaning forward to peer at John, then with a distrustful manner asked, "Who is that?"

I quickly suppressed his suspicion by responding with an authoritative tone, "He's my translator!" I was expecting some resistant drama from Roberto in trusting a stranger from within a prison, but John wasted little time utilizing his communicative skills and quickly withdrew Roberto's trepidation.

I was quite relieved when John worked his interpretive magic by taking control of their ten minutes discussion, allowing me to stand off to the side, eliminating my need to interact with Roberto. It was apparent John informed Roberto about my impending bail because before we parted ways, Roberto said he would let me know when it came time for my release, which he never did! Then he extended an obvious piece of advice, "Listen to your public defender and do what they say." No shit! At least Roberto ended our discussion the same way he started it, by wasting my not so precious time!

John clarified the purpose of Roberto's visit, which I thought at the time had important relevance to my case. I was to contact Brenda and have her give Roberto specific documents and info to assist him in securing a fictitious place of residence in La Paz for Brenda and myself, giving us the appearance of being frequent visitors to the country. Roberto was attempting to conjure up a perception of my character to the court that I was not criminally motivated, yet Karla's legal approach toward my criminal case seemed to be faring much better than Roberto's shady attempt at deception!

It was well past lunch when my hopeful arrival for Brenda began to diminish, so I retrieved a Frisbee from my crate of personal items, looked to Adrian with a raised brow, a nod of the head and with a Frisbee in hand gestured a flick of the wrist. Before venturing outside, I grabbed another Frisbee and gave it to Raúl, realizing it might be traded, or sold later, especially if he wasn't in favor of tossing around a plastic disc; nevertheless, my primary intention was to eventually disperse the Frisbees throughout the prison.

While playing Frisbee in the same area as my morning walks, I felt strange tossing it around next to a prison wall, expecting an inquisitive guard to question the legality of our activity; oddly enough, nothing was ever mentioned. Even though I had a good time with Adrian, my enjoyment was slightly diminished, due to the lightweight and cheap design of the Frisbee, making flight somewhat erratic and hard to control its accuracy. We were able to entertain ourselves and a tower guard by chasing around the sporadic disc for about thirty minutes before returning to our cell.

Upon entering the cell, David addressed Adrian and me inquiring about our leisure activity in the courtyard, prompting me to hand him the Frisbee. After David held it for a few seconds, he suddenly became uneasy, discovering the slightly dirty Frisbee had been in contact with the ground, then eked out a squeamish "*Yuk*" while abruptly handing it back to me as if it were contaminated.

This was when David revealed to all of us that his Kryptonite was being a germophobe, which instantly brought out the Lex Luther in Adrian and me. We started tormenting him by trying to hand him the Frisbee that Adrian cleaned by wiping it under his armpit and to elevate David's discomfort, I cleaned it further by using my crotch. With a dramatic cowardly reaction, David totally refused to touch the green mineral again or even come in close contact with it. The more he resisted, the more entertained we became, spurring us to wave the Kryptonite in front of his face. Rule number one in the art of comedic banter, never reveal your phobias, or weakness to your comrades, as it will supply them with a lifetime of humor at your own expense.

Harassing David led to other moments of out of control banter among the men, as we began feeding off each other's overzealous energy. It even motivated me to terrorize an unsuspecting victim minding his own business, by rapidly banging on the bathroom door with a heavy hand. After hearing Mini-Me's startled shout out from behind the door, I proceeded to respond to him by talking with a Mexican street lingo, "No man, Dave's not here," which gave John a big grin.

With a total look of confusion on David's face, he questioned me with, "What?"

I said, "You know, Cheech and Chong!" I attempted to explain myself with a familiar line from one of their songs by singing in Cheech's Mexican accent, "Mexican Americans don't like to just get into gang fights, they like flowers and music and white girls named Debbie too!"

Even though it produced a laugh from John, it only created a perplexed stare from David, so John took charge of the conversation and helped clarify who the famous duo was by speaking Spanish to David. From there, I was out of the loop, soon to realize that John and I were truly the only two people in the room amused.

My obnoxious behavior continued by telling a customer standing at our door to speak English when placing an order (I don't know why); also when Emilio walked over to the patron, I grabbed a sixteen-ounce soda bottle from the counter that he just placed there and gave it a vigorous shake for a few seconds.

When Emilio finished taking care of the customer, he returned to the counter, picked up the bottle, and began to twist off the cap. David witnessed my antics and casually took three steps backward, which immediately caught Emilio's attention and looked at him with a very suspicious grin, then quickly moved closer to David while acting like he was going to open the bottle and give him a merciless spray. David frantically cried out, *"No, no, it wasn't me,"* placing his hands in front of his face, attempting to retreat even though there was nowhere he could go. Emilio quickly scanned the room for the guilty party, then eyeballed me, pointed his finger then said with an evil grin, "My Lady?" I played it cool and calm by just sitting there with the confidence of being presumed innocent and said, "It wasn't me." Emilio spared us a soda shower by leaving the bottle cap on for a little while longer.

I could say Emilio joined in our banter, but it was just a continuation of his all-day razzing toward me, along with his wisecrack of "My lady, I love you," which escalated into a battle of nonsensical sarcasm between us.

I may have claimed victory over my nemeses by performing an animated sexual gesture with an evil grin while saying, "When I get out of here, I'm going to visit your pretty wife!" With David's acceptance to translate for me, I was finally able to get Emilio to comprehend the severity of my obnoxious intent.

He instantly expressed a look of shock with eyes wide open and shook his head side to side while saying, "No, no, no!"

With a nod and a sadistic smirk, I said, "Yes, yes, yes!" Even though I was able to suppress a witty response from Emilio, his silence only lasted for a short time.

The amusing distractions in the cell continued as Adrian conducted himself as a sexual deviant by performing a sexual gesture while observing a pretty female wearing a short dress, who was standing in the hallway talking to a group of people. When the lady began to leave, Adrian quickly went over to the door to watch her walk away, clutching the steel bars and drooling like a caged animal. While all eyes were focused on Adrian's antics, I swiftly snuck up behind him, anchored both hands on the bars to use my body to wedge him firmly against the door while dry humping him like a wild dog. Since Adrian was tightly pinned against the door, his reaction options were limited to be a good sport and only displayed slight resistance, which instantly engulfed the room with hysterical laughter followed by comedic comments from the peanut gallery.

The guys' wisecracks were void of translation, though it must have been sidesplitting because David was forced to sit down on my crate in severe pain from the uncontrollable laughter. He sat there slightly bent over, holding the left side of his gut, as his smile and laughter suddenly vanished only to be replaced with pure anguish.

After voicing my concern, "Are you alright?" David partially raised his shirt to reveal a large surgical scar from an operation he had years ago, prompting me to ask if he had any medicine for the pain, unfortunately, he was all out of the pills. I questioned him for the type of medicine he used to relieve the pain, not because I was knowledgeable about pharmaceuticals, far from it, as I can't even remember the last time taking a pain reliever. My motive was purely directed toward acquiring the drug through my connections guy, though not a word was revealed to David of my intent. All I needed was a plan of action!

Our midday entertainment somewhat came to a halt after David flashed his tiny titties to a room full of convicts; luckily for me, Frank soon arrived, allowing me to set the wheels in motion for the acquisition of David's meds! Frank stopped by to deliver the black wooden king, even though the cost of the chess piece eludes my memory, I recall that it was a little expensive.

After Frank inquired about my wellbeing, I responded with a somber tone, "I'm not feeling too good." Without hesitation, he offered to immediately take me to the clinic while eagerly reassuring me the doctor was a real good guy; I should hope so!

During our walk to the clinic, Frank informed me of a failed prison break that occurred late last night by individuals from outside of the prison involving some sort of explosives. He failed to share any details, leaving me clueless about an interesting story. I wonder if that's why I was told by the guard this morning to wear a complete uniform?

Upon entering the clinic, we noticed the doctor was busy with an inmate, so I sat on the bench outside the office, acting as a patient in pain. In order to ease the procurement of the specific medicine, I felt the need to disclose my sly plan to Frank, which surprisingly was accomplished effortlessly as the doc only performed a verbal assessment of my medical condition. The only dilemma I didn't foresee was wearing prison pants void of pockets, leaving me unable to pay for the medicine that I assumed I wouldn't have to pay for anyway. Luckily, Frank pulled out some money from the lanyard pouch hanging from his neck and offered to pay the 180-peso bill ($10.44).

It took me a week to realize that the pouches hanging around many of the inmate's necks were due to nonexistent pockets on their uniforms and were needed to hold small items such as cash. Most of the pouches were slightly bigger than a deck of cards and uniquely fashioned to differentiate them from others, notably Frank's, which was decorated with multicolored beads.

I found it difficult containing my exuberance while entering my cell in anticipation of David's surprise, but I downplayed our interaction by nonchalantly handing him the medicine as if it were an insignificant object. I couldn't figure out whether his facial expression was utter disbelief, or total amazement, which also mirrored his verbal response of "*Reeeally*, for me! How much?"

With an unyielding tone, I reassured him that his money was not needed. Which induced another exuberant "*Reeeally?*"

David's next obvious question was soon to follow, though I don't know why he would upset himself by asking a question in which he already knows my standard reply is going to be "I got connections."

Out of courtesy, I voiced it in a low tone just before walking away, leaving him without an accurate understanding of what was involved in procuring his pain killers.

David's final appreciative words spoke to me from across the room "You are the man," gave me a great sense of pride accomplishing a selfless act for a friend.

Moments later, while in the kitchen conversing with Emilio about the thirteen years left on his prison sentence, I displayed slight disgust while stating, "If it were me, there would be no way in hell this flawed prison security could possibly keep me here for that long!" While eagerly proceeding to divulge a generalized plan on how to escape, Emilio stared at me with intrigue while focusing on David's every translated word.

Since Emilio had plenty of time to execute an escape, I explained a good plan of action to minimize his risk of getting caught, would be to hire someone he trusted to rent, or acquire a building across the street from the prison, preferably a property in need of repairs to mask the actual work of dig-

LaPaz prison arial view

ging a tunnel. Seeing as the array of buildings across the street are less than two-hundred feet from our cell and with the help of Google Earth, GPS, and a compass, one could dig straight to our cell with relative ease. The patio area would be the perfect place for an escape tunnel; it has no visible line of sight from the guard towers or view from guards standing at our cell door.

Due to my elevated enthusiasm, Emilio must have established the impression that I was very knowledgeable in the art of prison escape since he intently gazed at me with conviction and said, "How much?" then offered to pay me 100,000 pesos. After a quick calculation of the conversion rate, common sense, and telling him it wouldn't be enough to cover the cost of that type of operation, he upped the ante to 200,000 pesos. Some people can be bought for just about anything if the price is right, but the monetary value is certainly not worth the risk of getting thrown in jail, especially for only eleven-grand, maybe if it were 200,000 US dollars. Even though I have squirmed through countless holes underground and dug out a few to find caverns of grandeur, I had to politely decline his offer; while not disclosing the real reason behind my refusal, of "Not my monkey, not my circus."

Emilio didn't dwell over his failed attempt in employing a mole man to create a burrow for his freedom, instead focused his moment of grandeur toward the seven o'clock lockdown, when his release from this locked cage would be traded for a private locked room with his waiting wife, *again!*

At about the time Emilio was taking a shower, Adrian had returned to the cell after playing soccer in the courtyard, allowing him to witness and partake in the antics that were about to commence. My provocation to pull a prank on Emilio was brought on earlier in the day when I went to the chest cooler to retrieve my candy bar and discovered it was gone.

I tried not to display concern while looking for the missing treat, as I thought maybe a fellow roomie claimed it for themself, or I misplaced it; either way, I soon gave up the search with disappointment. Unbeknownst to me (translated later), I was being observed by Emilio during my search for the elusive MilkyWay, who was waiting to see how long he could contain his laughter before revealing to me he had eaten the candy bar; rubbing his belly while making an "mmm" sound. The joke was on me, so was all the rooms laughter and giggling, which didn't bother me at all, because of reflecting on what was said to me day 1 of my arrival into this cell, "What's ours is yours," and in retrospect, it's also, "What's mine is theirs." Although what's good for the Spanish goose is good for the English gander, thus elevating my foul play against Emilio by involving others in the prank to help alleviate some of the blame.

Emilio had already packed a trash bag full of items for his overnight conjugal visit with my future ex-wife and was taking his time primping in the bathroom. Giving me enough time to retrieve a cucumber from the fridge, then handed it to David and said, "Put this in Emilio's bag."

Of course, he looked at me as if I were crazy, trying to hand the cucumber back to me which suddenly focused my gesture to volunteer Mini-Me with the prank, but he quickly responded with a big smile, a wave of the hand and an unyielding, "*No, no!*"

The guys kept insisting that I should be the one who puts the green vegetable into Emilio's bag, though I was unsure of the repercussions from Emilio due to the reaction from his wife, so I too joined in their refusal. Adrian's zealous behavior, on the other hand, forced him to grab the cold vegetable and stuff it deep into the bag. I felt there needed to be a love note along with his big surprise, so I found a small piece of paper and wrote, "Thanks for the good time, Love Debbie," then placed it next to the hidden cucumber.

As Emilio exited the bathroom, a hush fell upon the room, replaced with concealed grins, silent chuckles and nervous concerns over the premature discovery of the hidden items. Emilio continued to add more items to the bag and, at one point, searched through the bag to confirm a packed item, which had us nervously looking at each other while getting ready to start pointing fingers at the culprit.

As Emilio headed out the door with the bag across his shoulder, I don't know who displayed the biggest shit-eating grin on their face, him or us? The thought of visualizing the dismayed expression on Emilio's face while trying to explain to his wife why he chose to pack an eight-inch cucumber and who the hell Debbie was—freaking hilarious!

It was a shame we had to wait until tomorrow morning before we could razz Emilio regarding his bag of trick or treats. As luck would have it, there was an unforeseeable chain of events leading to a much earlier comical outcome. Emilio soon returned to retrieve a forgotten item and immediately directed all of his attention toward me, then with a boastful smile and (through David's translation) said, "The guard found the hidden vegetable while inspecting the bag," also with a suggestive mischievous grin said, "The wife says thanks for the cucumber!" His implied visual of the pretty woman's statement left me completely speechless; *damn*, Emilio, had left the cell by having the last word. Well played!

I may have been tongued tied upon Emilio's exit, but my mind quickly thought of a retaliatory action that would surely score one point for team worm. I suggested to David that when Emilio has his next conjugal visit, we should put a pair of woman's panties in his bag. His reaction was total disbelief of such a risqué prank, prompting him to ask, "Where are you going to get them?"

Where else? "Brenda."

David's shocked response of "No really, how would you get her to do that?" once again proved he was much more proper than I in the art of comedic satire. I told him, all I would have to do is just ask her, though it might take a lot of persuading. I don't foresee David partaking in an activity requiring him to handle another person's underwear, hell, he can't even touch a dusty Frisbee. Either way, I think it would be funnier completing the mission in stealth mode and easier to claim deniability if nobody knows the culprit. Executing such a prank would be well worth the effort just to see Emilio's animated reaction, whatever it takes for a good laugh and the win!

As the evening's energy in the cell began to dissipate, David and I were in the patio having an in-depth discussion relating to Brenda's no show today, including concerns at the failed attempts trying to reach her by phone. David could see I was distraught, as he ambitiously tried rectifying my dilemma and was more than willing to contact her by calling the hotel she was staying at. Oh shit! I realized right then and there, the importance I held for remembering Brenda's hotel is now coming back to bite me in the ass!

David had connections with people who worked in the hotel industry and began contacting them to help search for Brenda, but the absence of pertinent information was proving too problematic; therefore, he enlisted Adrian's help, who had connections with people in the rental car business. The duo diligently worked in tandem texting and making phone calls for about fifteen minutes, refusing to give up while trying their damnedest to track down Brenda. They might have had better results finding her, if I would have remembered she registered into the new hotel under an alias, also claimed to be Mary Smith when purchasing a second phone from the La Paz mobile store. No wonder we couldn't track her down!

I thought of a new plan of action and asked David if he had a Facebook account, he did, but there was a slight challenge, for he and I belong to the same anti-social club. The only person on his Facebook was his wife, which would be problematic for David while searching for an unfamiliar woman named Brenda, knowing his wife would be the first person to see it on their Facebook page. David was uncomfortable in continuing with his search, so to avoid paying for a divorce lawyer, his first task was to inform his wife of the impending search for a girl named Brenda. His search went by smoothly and was able to send a friend request, but Brenda's understandable paranoia denied the strangers' request. When all options where exhausted, I graciously thanked David and Adrian for their dedicated persistence. The failed mission left me with a great fear of the unknown, as all I could do was hope that Brenda was okay!

It was nearing bedtime when I found myself once again waiting for the occupants of the patio to vacate before finalizing my night by laying underneath the stars. I need not leave the milkcrate and venture into the patio to figure out how the guys were getting entertained; it was made obvious by the loud cheers and joyous outcries in unison throughout our cellblock and our patio. Clearly, many of the inmates were listening or watching a soccer game on their electronic gadgets, and when a goal was scored, it revealed that all the loud inmates were rooting for the same team. It must have been a low scoring game, made evident by only two outbursts of enjoyment from the men in the cellblock and our cell. Not all individuals in the surrounding area showed interest in the soccer game, mainly the men without gadgets and the ones who were once again beating on their rhythmic drums.

It was after eleven o'clock when my body was finally able to get horizontal and prepare for the approaching feeding frenzy by forming a blanket berm around the bed to partially protect myself. I slid the mat a little further away from the wall to eliminate the advantage of elevation from the roach's attack toward their cranial buffet. Time to say goodnight and don't let the bed bugs bite, too much.

Day 24 in Country

Twelfth day in prison

The joy of sleeping in again sure does have its reward and no fresh lesions on the back of my neck, although that does not mean those scurrying little bastards didn't tap into the existing wounds. Reluctancy to crawl out of bed delayed my early morning walk, negating my encounter with Carlos in the courtyard, though it did reveal a rare appearance from Emilio who was heading back toward our cell. Emilio interrupted my Word Seek by relaying a message from the tower guard who voiced a loud command that I was to be aware of the boundary line, which prevented us from veering close to the unruly side of the prison. I was able to identify what Emilio was trying to communicate by his animated gesture, though I was already well aware of the regulation due to observing other inmates during their morning walk. Days earlier Carlos pointed out the official placement of the imaginary line drawn in the sand to me as well, which was conveniently indicated by a concrete step next to a fence dividing the prison. It can't get more unofficial than that!

After breakfast, I performed a rarity of late by hanging out at my cell door, taking a short gander into the hallway, when the doctor just happened to be walking by and gestured if I was feeling better by displaying a raised brow, a nod of the head and a thumbs up; he received a duplicated response from me.

I don't recall the exact moment of my epiphany to give the kitchen an extreme cleaning, maybe last night when the lights were out, as countless, brazen creatures were scurrying throughout my unsanitary bedroom. I questioned John for permission and for the best time to carry out my task, as not to interfere with the café's daily operations in utilizing their kitchen. He said, "From now till about eleven." Now with John's consent and no time to waste, I immediately headed straight to the kitchen with an elevated motivation that drove my step.

I was confident that the galley would be significantly cleaner upon my completion, as I have stated before, I'm no stranger to household chores, thanks to my parents who embedded a strong work ethic and knowledge on how to correctly clean a home; maybe that's why I despise clutter and filth to this day.

At first glance, cleaning the 10'×10' kitchen should be easy; there were no cabinets, limited open shelving, a small countertop next to a makeshift worktable and a five-foot plank supporting three hotplates. After gathering cleaning supplies and boiling a big pot of water to aid in the removal of the grime, I began removing items from the shelf above the deep freeze to wipe down the surface, only to suddenly realize it was time to rethink my plan of attack!

There is a correct systematic approach to cleaning a kitchen, but that way of thinking will surely not work today because when I removed the first item off the shelf, a few cockroaches scattered, and the more items I displaced, the more bugs there were. It doesn't take a competent Orkin man to recognize when the shelf is wiped down with cleanser, and the items are returned, the little vermin will quickly migrate back there when disturbed from their new hiding place.

My new plan of action was to cordon off a 5'×5' section area and use the patio table as the base of operations for temporarily storing items on, then give the area an extensive cleaning while not permitting any roaches to escape my deadly wrath. The first section A, involved the stomping of nearly fifty cockroaches, followed by scrubbing the floor using a broom with a mixture of hot water and a cleaning solution. The next section B, proved to be exceedingly challenging, as escapees were allowed to scatter into the uncleaned section, but they were absolutely not permitted to venture into section A. I slid the table to the center of the room, to make sure my stomping ground was wide enough to give plenty of time and space to squash hundreds of the advancing hoard toward the clean section A.

During the first wave of attack, I was successful at killing the fleeing bugs by stomping them in a moderate pace while using both feet preventing any escapees. While lifting up the small worktable to clean behind it, juvenile size roaches immediately started dropping out from the hollow legs like water from a faucet, so I quickly set the table back down and feverishly began stomping the infested area; a few escaped, but none to section A. Once again, a revised plan of action was surely needed, therefore, instead of lifting the whole table up, I dragged it closer to the stomping ground and raised one corner slightly off the floor, only allowing a manageable number of bugs out to be extinguished. During my continuous foot-stomping dance, Crunch, Crunch, Crunch of the scattering roaches, I found it quite entertaining that I could not stop singing "♪♪La cockaroacha La cockaroacha na na na na na♪♪" in my head; but the enjoyment quickly turned into a workout from my legs in hyper-speed keeping section A bug free.

By now, a small audience had gathered at the doorway of the kitchen to witness this madman wreaking havoc on the thousands of dead Lucy's that littered the floor, along with a layer of guts caked to the bottom of my flip-flops. The men spoke not a word while gazing at the spectacle or showed signs of wanting to laugh until I started singing to them the La Cockaroacha song, which had to be freaking funny as hell to watch!

When I thought the table leg was mostly cleared of bugs, I gave it a hard tap against the concrete floor, *Oh crap*, that was a big mistake as more of them fell out than previously, revealing the leg had been *completely* packed full of roaches! Consequently, I was forced to amend the revised plan by gently tapping the leg against the floor to further control the outflow of victims to be squashed. It required at least six taps of each leg to finally clear out all the occupants from their exceedingly cramped quarters, and to say there were thousands of cockroaches is undeniably *not* an overstatement and was distressing enough to inflict nightmares for most people! Oh yeah, I almost forgot. During my nighttime slumber, the bug-filled table legs were only four feet from my face; dream about that tonight when you lay your head on a pillow!

Wait, it's not over; section C&D still awaited my arrival. Section C was less intense yet more disturbing. While removing the Formica countertop from its base, that was used for preparing meals, mature size roaches began creeping out of the cracks from the rotted particleboard. When I suddenly set it down on the floor to prevent them from crawling all over me, hundreds were forced out from the impact, requiring a massive amount of stomping; also, many forceful taps of the Formica to the floor was required to eradicate the dwellers wedged deep within the crevices. Some items on the shelf below the Formica had to be thrown away, a byproduct of years of pure neglect. Section D was the least infested; it only contained the hotplates and the fridge, although I didn't tilt the full-size fridge sideways to explore underneath it, so who knows how many of Lucy's' cousins were hiding beneath nesting within the components.

My unaltered determination was proven to be quite successful. There are no visible signs of Lucy's' dead or alive, so now I can proudly exit the kitchen, permitting Pablo to enter and start preparing for the lunch rush in his less disgusting environment. My next mission was to take my flip-flops into the shower and wash off the layers of caked-on guts and butts, consequently revealing my sore feet from all the repetitive stomping.

Sometime after one o'clock, when Frank stopped by, I relayed the sob story of my failed attempt in contacting Brenda and revealed concerns about her whereabouts. Next thing I know, we're heading down the corridor immediately after Frank said, "I know a guy in the clinic who has a cellphone." My optimism for a successful outcome was almost nonexistent, as the use of a different phone wouldn't rectify my predicament, but it couldn't hurt to try. To appease Frank and raise false hope for myself, we went to the clinic and used a cellphone from the inmate who had the six bullet holes in him. As expected, another failed mission, but Frank tried to make the best of the situation by suggesting we chill out in the clinic's mini courtyard for a while. The weakened inmate rolled his wheelchair into the open area, while Frank retrieved two chairs and some water for me. The three of us sat under the lone palm tree while enjoying a peaceful escape from the rest of the prison. Unfortunately, our fifteen-minute chitchat wasn't very interesting and seemed a little awkward by trying to keep the conversation alive with nothing to say, therefore I decided to head back to my cell.

While we were leaving, our path led us past the dentist's office, where Frank offered to schedule me an appointment. That idea never did materialize because the generator that ran the dental equipment broke down, creating a backlog of patients, leaving the dentist no time to see me and probably a good thing not to have my teeth poked at by a prison dentist in Mexico!

Upon arrival to the cellblock, I saw two female nurses setting up a table and chairs next to my cell; apparently, they were here for Aids testing, according to John. Fortunately, I haven't been involved in any questionable activities during my incarceration that would require such an apprehensive examination, so for now, I avoided being poked by a needle in a Mexican prison. Unlike Adrian, who was one of the first participants to volunteer in relinquishing a vial of blood to a pretty nurse, I believe he was the only man from our cell to get his vein tapped. That's one scary test to fail!

Soon after Adrian returned from getting poked in the arm, he and I set up the chessboard in the patio and began playing. A few minutes into our game, David showed me a screenshot from a cellphone revealing a news story of Brenda and myself getting arrested, stating we were apprehended by the military attempting to smuggle guns into the country. The article was quite comical, for it contained more false statements than truths, hell, even a photo of our arrest was of other people who better resembled criminals. It appears the US is not the only news media who exaggerates a cover story to enhance their ratings by altering the appearance of facts. Nevertheless, it did give David and the guys a good laugh that Brenda and I were portrayed as dangerous gun smugglers, particularly after being witness to my true character.

Next, David handed me the phone with some negative text messages on it from Brenda, stating her concerns regarding trust issues with Roberto and Gilbert, while aggressively demanding I rectify a crisis she deemed important. Normally I would have to agree with her assessment of the situation to prevent our disagreement from escalating into an argument, but I altered my response after recalling what John said to me after our meeting with Roberto. John revealed that Roberto's plan was to acquire a place of residency for Brenda and me before going back to trial and that I should trust Roberto in doing so, as it could help with my defense strategy. Based on that information, I responded to Brenda's text with a slight disagreement that she should listen to Roberto, only to be met by her strong resistance pertaining to Roberto's questionable character.

My aggravation brought on by the back and forth text messages were distracting me from the chess game with Adrian, so much that David and John pointed out that I had faltered during gameplay, giving Adrian a big advantage, possibly resulting in my first loss from him. At that point, Adrian suggested we stop playing, realizing I was upset with Brenda's inflexibility and had trouble concentrating on the game. I immediately refused his concerning gesture, by insisting we continue playing; for I no longer paid attention to a god damn phone while disregarding a subject matter I had little control over! Fearing a loss, I diligently devised a plan of attack to divert Adrian's focus toward his stronghold on my positioned pieces, which led him to make one mistake and consequently giving me the victory.

My humbled celebration was short-lived by the vibrating phone from Brenda's incoming call; oh shit, here we go! At the time of our stressful conversation, I failed to realize how toxic her relationship was with Roberto and Gilbert and had yet to bear witness to all the discouraging stories of the mistrusting duo. With that being said, in my emotional state of mind, I adamantly tried forcing her to accept and work with them in preventing me from returning to prison after the upcoming trial; regrettably, that was a huge mistake!

My remarks were instantly met with hostility and unjust resentment as she aggressively said, "Do it my way, or I'm going to fucking leave you!" After hearing those harsh words that completely ripped a gashing hole through my heart, I…, I painfully and slowly turned my body away from the gathered onlookers, hanging my head down in utter disbelief, instantaneously losing all fear of being entombed in prison, only to be replaced with pure dread from the thought of losing the one that I truly love.

Brenda didn't distinguish whether she was leaving me to go home, or leaving me permanently; either way, the ramifications resembled a distressing problem we endured back in April when I discovered our relationship might have been nearing its end! Brenda accused me of having an affair and responded to my denial in pure disbelief with eyes engulfed in sheer hatred; a facial expression that I'm all too familiar with when Helen (ex-wife) made the same accusation during our marriage. On both occasions, I was completely defenseless when logic, common sense, and truth didn't find its way into our one-sided argument! I have never been the same man since that dreadful day back in April, an event that still weighs heavy on my heart; consequently, the phone conversation with Brenda dramatically added to the fear of losing another battle, having absolutely nothing to do with being stuck in prison. How can a relationship survive when indisputable trust has been vanquished by tainted speculation and cancerous paranoia? If this is all it takes to unravel a strong relationship, why continue when it's all held together by a tattered string.

I never had any doubt that my first marriage of twenty-six years would end until it did; now, I find myself staring down a shotgun barrel waiting for someone to pull the trigger, forcing me to once again start a new life! *Be mindful,* my deep-seated rant may explain my future actions, during July and August, but damn sure don't justify them!

My hesitant response to Brenda's harsh statement, "Okay," was spoken under duress, as I completely lost all ability to communicate anything else. While continuing to listen to her speak, I leaned my forehead against the cinderblock wall and fought a losing battle to keep the tears from rolling down my face!

"The ones who really love you walk up and down outside the wall. And when they given you their all, some stagger and fall. After all, it's not easy banging your heart against some mad buggers wall." (by Pink Floyd)

When our phone call ended, I voiced my heightened fears to John concerning Brenda's extreme stress, health issues, and paranoia. He suggested I send her home to Missouri as soon as possible, as her involvement could be detrimental to my legal proceedings and inadvertently divert my focus from legal matters in caring for her. I whole heartily agreed with John's assessment and relayed my recommendation to Brenda when she called back moments later, attempting to smooth over our last phone conversation and to let it be known that she was coming to visit me tomorrow. Surprisingly, Brenda consented to go home with relative ease but was only willing to do so after I was released on bail.

John possessed a skilled knack in calming my agitation from the phone fiasco with Brenda, though not enough, as I was still in deep thought over the matter when Frank arrived at our door, forcing a painted smile on my face. Frank expressed a joyous greeting while insisting I go with him to talk with a fellow inmate. He could not contain his excitement as we headed to the backdoor toward the clinic, where he said, "You are getting out of here!"

Before I had a chance to ask Frank what the hell he was talking about, he quickly went on to explain what sounded suspiciously like the inner workings of Roberto's involvement. Frank was informed by an inmate who was contacted by someone from the outside of the prison, attempting to contact me with information concerning my release. If that doesn't sound extremely shady, I don't know what else would!

We ended up stopping next to the fence separating the prison from the unruly side across from the clinic where we met an older inmate who definitely looked to have more rough miles on his face than Frank's and an authoritative demeanor suggesting he had been a long time resident of the prison. The non-English speaking man relayed his message through Frank, though it was pretty much a carbon copy of what I already heard during my walk here, but with one exception that he would let Frank know when contacted again with more details.

As quick as my reluctant excitement emerged, it vanished just as fast, though Frank's had not. While walking back to the cellblock, he adamantly reinforced his first statement of my impending freedom. I would like to divulge more info on this very bizarre encounter, but that's all I have been given. Many questions that were never answered!

After dinner, I was sitting on the milk crate watching David and Adrian standing at our cell door involved in a transaction with a younger-looking guard, who was apparently paying off his weekly café tab by handing Adrian cash one bill at a time while counting the amount paid thus far. Adrian continued to receive the bills with his left hand then placing them on the stack of bills in the palm of his right hand, who was apparently watching the guard focusing on the wad of cash in his own hand and not was being dished out to Adrian. With one swift motion, when the guard handed Adrian fifty pesos, he quickly stuffed the bill in David's rolled-up shirt sleeve, then resumed accepting money as if nothing had happened.

David stared at Adrian with total disbelief, then at me as if to say, "What should I do?" We looked at each other, not sure if what we witnessed was a joke or pure thievery. What was David to do, keep quiet and become an accessory, or pull the bill out of his shirt and start laughing? I guess that all depends on the type of relationship they had with the unsuspecting guard, friend, or foe. Neither of us spoke a word while waiting to see how it all played out.

When the guard finished paying his tab, Adrian did a quick recount of the stack of bills and with a look of guiltless man politely said, "You're short fifty pesos," (I assume) then hastily started searching his body as if to say, I don't have it while lifting up shirt revealing no pockets to hide the missing loot.

Adrian performed the part flawlessly, as the confused guard reluctantly handed over another fifty pesos ($2.90) displaying a perplexed expression while recounting the bills remaining in his hand, wondering where the misplaced fifty pesos disappeared to, then soon walked away none the wiser. I don't know if Adrian offered David a cut from the heist, but I honestly don't think he would accept any of the money and willingly involve himself in Adrian's thievery.

Adrian wasn't the only recipient of extra cash placed in the palm of his hand. Today was payday for the café's crew, which involved Emilio divvying out cash to each of the men, excluding the two newcomers, as John and I have yet to be assigned a chore in the café's daily operations. Although I would be hard-pressed to accept any money from Emilio. I feel indebted to him for allowing my encroachment into their minimal space, and wholeheartedly guarantee John would share in my sentiment!

It was after eight o'clock when I made a phone call to my sister Maribeth who lives in Florida to give her a quick update on my situation and most importantly verify no more money was to be extracted from her, in the event Roberto starts requesting for more; which he had already tried to do with her. What an asshole! Even though our conversation was brief, it was truly a relief and a pleasure to hear her voice and the opportunity to personally thank her for all the invaluable support; Maribeth is indeed Frank's counterpart, *she gets shit done!*

In order to kill time until lights out, I put on headphones and listened to music, ate some munchies reflecting on the day's events while jotting down notes of importance.

Time to lay my head down and gaze upon the majestic stars till tranquility cleanses my troubled mind.

Day 25 in Country

Thirteenth day in prison

A drastic decline in the population of Lucy's relatives must have subconsciously eased my trepidation from sleeping in the patio, due to feeling well-rested and eager to start my day with a morning walk. Within a few minutes into my walk, while avoiding the chilly shade, I was joined by Carlos, who inadvertently increased my stride to keep up with his pace, though I honestly didn't mind; I just need to acquire an appropriate pair of shoes for walking.

Carlos greeted me with a distressed expression while voicing a concern, "Where were you yesterday? I tried to find you to play some chess."

I politely replied, "I was busy all day. If you want, we can play later today."

It may sound peculiar, but Carlos' inquiry brought forth a profound moment of clarity. I was sought out yesterday by a fellow English-speaking inmate wanting to involve me in stimulation, interaction, and *entertainment*, all three of which I had been deeply occupied in for most of the day.

In retrospect of my dire struggles when first arriving here, stripped of my pride, dignity and basic human needs, when freedom wasn't plausible, the most important thing to me at that moment was having water to drink. When that need was met, my next concern was food consumption, followed by the ability to sleep. Lastly and eventually, the least concerning, my safety. I never expected entertainment would be on my list of priorities in a Mexican prison or positioned at the top of the chart with great importance!

Upon completion of an invigorating walk followed by a wave hello to the doctor as he walked past me, I entered the cell to enjoy some breakfast and wait for Brenda's promised arrival, which ended up being sometime after ten o'clock.

Brenda's first task upon her arrival was usually to covertly hand me two hundred pesos along with a handful of change, but today she defied prison security once more and smuggled in an SD card containing some of my music, though it was all for not, for the card wasn't compatible with David's crude music devise. Speaking of defying prison security, Brenda informed me she snuck a visitors pass out of the prison during her last visitation and even though she was successful, the fear of getting caught later with it in her possession created an extreme amount of paranoia, inciting her to hide the pass in a Burger King's parking lot, buried under some rocks underneath a light pole. *Seriously*, I can't make this shit up! It's good to know I'm not the only person keeping my options open for an escape.

Brenda voiced concerns of the guards wanting her to carry a wallet while entering the prison, so as not to appear she was attempting to smuggle items within her pockets (too late) therefore after returning from a quick trip to my cell, I handed her a wallet Frank gave me days prior.

The wallet was crafted by weaving together used strips of foiled lined potato chip bags, only revealing the foil side of the bag for the esthetics. His thoughtful gesture was a bit unnecessary, for I already have a wallet that I seldom carry. The day after Frank gave me the gift, I noticed the roaming vendor in the yard selling the exact

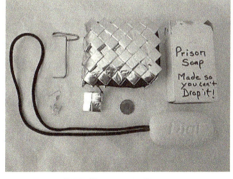

B&E tool, Wallet, soap from my sister Debbie, butterfly earing, Mexican coin

same item, making me consider maybe Frank bought the wallet instead of crafting it himself since he doesn't appear to be an arts and crafts kind of guy. Although, he could have mistakenly omitted the word "had" while handing me the wallet and said, "I made this for you," instead of "I had this made for you." The latter fits Frank's character.

Moments into our visitation, I grabbed John's attention as he walked by our table and introduced him to Brenda, then asked if he could better explain to her the legal definition for my "Abbreviated Process." By having John talk to Brenda, I figured she would have a much better understanding of what was transpiring and more inclined to gain optimism with my case than if I were giving her the info. As expected, John was very informative, providing a quick synopsis of what the "Abbreviated Process" meant for me and relieved some of Brenda's trepidation concerning my impending release.

Soon after John left with our appreciation, Frank showed up and joined us at the table. His demeanor was out of kilter and unlike his natural display of contentment, revealing an urgency not to spend any more time in prison. With a dejected somber tone, Frank started questioning us for instructive guidance in finding and acquiring a good lawyer for his legal matters. I get the impression his altered contentment was brought on by how expedient my criminal case was progressing in only two weeks, compared to the poor souls stuck in here for months and some for years without justification, giving him false optimism for his own predicament. Sadly, I wasn't much help as the best advice given to him was to talk to John for the best way to approach the process, though maybe ten years too late to prove one's innocence.

Days prior, while reflecting over Raúl's discouraging situation, I questioned John for his thoughts pertaining to Raúl and Frank's legality concerning their imprisonment; he said there was hope for Raúl, though sadly none for Frank.

Despite Frank's unresolved dilemma, his spirits were slightly raised when Brenda told him the lotion that he wanted was at the inspection area, but she couldn't find the oil he wanted in any of the stores she visited. Frank was very grateful as he stood up from the table to retrieve his gift and was in a much better mood compared to his arrival and just before walking away, asked the standard question, "DYNA?"

"Yes, there is a treat I would like to have." I figured it would be the perfect opportunity to utilize Frank, to accompany me to the farmers market being conducted within the two security gates next to the courtyard. I wanted to see if any of the vendors carried vanilla extract, in order to add flavor to my pancakes. As expected, nobody had any, but of course, Frank rectified the problem by placing an order from one of the vendors.

Since it was Saturday, the courtyard began filling up with families toting coolers and bags of food, preparing for their all-day visitation. This sparked my interest in ordering lunch for us, though Brenda wasn't very hungry and only wanted french-fries with a lemonade. While quietly sitting there eating my cheeseburger and fries, Brenda became annoyed when she pointed out a female visitor wearing the same type of clothing she was denied entry for on an earlier visit, intensifying her annoyance of another day displaying her birthday suit while other women are allowed to enter the prison unmolested.

Apparently, Brenda's elevated aggravation wasn't purely directed toward others, as she looked at me with a vexed stare and said, "So are you going to wish me a happy birthday?"

Oh no! It was Brenda's fifty-fourth birthday. Of the few birthdays, anniversaries, and special occasions I failed to remember over the many years without a justifiable excuse, excluding worthless holidays, today is one of those moments which shouldn't require one, yet I received the strong impression one was needed or at least a huge apology.

What was my response to her sadden question? "Who fucking remembers?" I'm too damn analytical, realizing there is absolutely nothing I can do or say that will alter a past event, be it ten years or ten seconds, it's all the same. Why do humans feel the need to sensationalize being twenty-four hours older than yesterday? All I do know is I instantly became upset from distressing my vulnerable sweetheart and completely lost my appetite, looking down at my meal searching for an appropriate response, though none materialized.

I consciously made the decision not to reveal my well throughout birthday arrangement awaiting our arrival back home, wanting her to be completely surprised with the prearranged antics of, "Let's make a deal" involving her present hidden among the envelopes. My spur of the moment decision to keep her present a secret may have been a bad judgment call. Nevertheless, I engineered the plan well over a month ago, so can one honestly say I forgot, or just postponed Brenda's aging process? There wasn't much spoken between us afterward as Brenda's early departure had me going back to my cell, feeling dejected from disappointing her.

While entering the café, I smelled a familiar odor one would not associate with an indoor living environment. Accompanied by a shower of sparks falling to the floor in front of Adrian's bed, an inmate was welding metal brackets high up on the wall in front of the bathroom. Come to find out, Emilio hired a couple of inmates to weld a bed frame six and a half feet off the floor in the hallway, which would allow people to walk underneath it in gaining access to the patio while adding another bed for some lucky bastard who was sleeping on the hard concrete floor.

While standing there, diverting my eyes away from the intense flashing light, I turned toward John, who was captivated with the glowing embers spraying the area and asked, "Who is that for?"

He looked at me with a big grin and said, "Who do you think?"

No reply was needed or expected, as John had seniority over me by only three nights and a great deal of respect to go along with the privilege. We stood there, shaking our heads with disbelief making comments on the duo's work practices, wondering how they kept the cell from catching fire, as not all the bedding was removed from the two lower beds that were getting bombarded with tiny balls of fire.

The thought of having a welding machine in our cell without the supervision of a guard had me revisiting Emilio's (my) escape plan. If one were to turn the welding machine to the highest setting, it would be quite easy using a welding rod to cut through a piece of rebar in the patio's ceiling, as I have done it before on a job site.

When the sparks had settled, John and I made our way into the patio where I noticed six roach-motels atop the deep freeze that John had acquired: cool! Did I create a movement in maintaining a bug-free environment? Let hope so!

I don't know who initiated our discussion concerning Brenda. Either way, I ended up confiding in John of my "Let's Make a Deal" surprise, looking for reassurance from his opinion if I had technically missed her birthday, also we revisited the idea of sending her back home sometime soon. Once again, it was very uplifting talking with John, as usual, his calm, collective approach only used logic and common sense in our discussion void of decisions based on emotions. John's technique in combating issues indeed reminds me of my older brother Tom, who is also a compulsive intellectual thinker and can relay that into speech, unlike myself, who can ponder great thoughts but have difficulty expressing them in discussion with precise clarity.

If nothing else was gained from our discussion, at least I walked away with some comfort, thinking, John needs to start charging me for therapy sessions. Although sharing my story by putting it into text has been the best therapy of my life, giving me clarity and direction!

John's free treatment session must have been successful because I attempted to relieve some tension by having a birthday cake made for Brenda, which would only be the second one she ever received for her birthday. I shit you not! Guess who gave the very first birthday cake to her when she was forty-eight years old? I'll give you one guess. The moment she bent over to blow out the fiery-furnace and kept her hair from catching fire, I failed to know she had been deprived of what many spoiled Americans take for granted, as tears of joy assisted in dowsing the flames. If I had known it was her first birthday cake, my attempt at being funny from the greeting written on the cake would have been put on hold, maybe.

Prior to that year Brenda and I witnessed an amusing story of a woman who relayed what she wanted to be written on a cake to a baker, I think it was at Walmart store where high school education is optional. The instructions were as follows, "Happy Birthday," and underneath that, "Micky." (recipient's name is unclear) However, when the customer received the cake, it read, "Happy birthday and underneath that, Micky." No kidding!

Therefore, I thought it would be funny to duplicate the message and replace "Micky" with "Brenda," knowing she would be familiar with the implied amusement. Oddly, it required a great deal of explaining to the baker confirming the peculiar message was completed wrong the correct way. Unlike five years ago, today's cake will not display any comical relief in its message.

So! Where was I to find a cake from within a Mexican prison on a Saturday afternoon? I'll give you two guesses. No, not Frank! While in the bakery the other day purchasing pastries, I noticed some cake pans on a shelf; though it's a damn shame, the light bulb over my head didn't come on while I was in there, avoiding Brenda's displeasure today.

I kindly asked David to assist in my endeavor but having him accompany me to the bakery felt a little strange, for I have only seen him out of his cage twice. My quest went by flawlessly as David was able to articulate what I wanted to the staff members, and surprisingly we left the building shortly after with an order placed for a double layer *heart* shaped lemon-flavored cake for sixteen bucks, pay half now and a half at pickup, ready in a day and a half, though no candles this time.

On our way back to the cell, Carlos caught my attention and requested to play some chess, so I quickly retrieved my chess set from the café, soon returning to tutor the eager student who is lacking retention and will undoubtedly fail my class. But first, I must return to the café in search of a missing black pawn. I can't believe the brand-new game is already missing a piece, where in the hell could it be? Maybe hiding in purgatory with the elusive king. No luck in my search, therefore I kidnapped a pawn from the café's set, which looked ridiculous placed next to its counterparts as it was four times smaller, though much more appropriate than a tortoise.

Carlos failed to make the grade and retain my undivided attention during our game, yet not all my attentiveness was lost, as Emilio was sitting at a table across from ours in the company of some eye candy wearing a cute dress; *no*, not his daughter! The taller one, my archenemies pretty spouse. Once again, no greeting was exchanged between the four of us, making me wonder why.

During our chess match, I exchanged a greeting with Raúl of, "Hey, what's up" as he walked by our table. As Raúl stood slightly off in the distance watching us play, I felt a little bothered by his presence as a trace of sorrow and guilt emerged within my heart, sensing that I had abandoned our friendship by interacting with others who are more capable and willing to participate in likeminded activities.

After completing a couple of games, I let Carlos and Hector use my chess set, while I hung around for a while watching them play, but I quickly lost curiosity in the duo who kept making bad moves followed by no one capitalizing on them, which had me holding my tongue from advising Carlos what to do as it would have been bad etiquette. When I could no longer be witness to the lack of sound strategy, I headed back to my overcrowded home away from home and hoped the agua bill had been paid, also a glowing pilot light for an early evening shower.

Luckily, the bathroom was fully functional, leaving me without a story to tell, except for one minor detail. It was made apparent after toweling off that I forgot to grab a clean shirt, which under normal circumstances would be unnoteworthy, but not today. I was apprehensive in exiting the bathroom without wearing a shirt, not for being self-conscious, but toward reactions from the guys, as I have yet to witness anybody in our cell, or this side of the prison shirtless, unusual as it may sound, so I had no idea what to expect.

By the time I exited the bathroom, Emilio had returned from his playdate, and as I entered the hallway, he made some sort of gestured comment toward my physique. At first, I took offense as I may not appear to be muscular. I'm in good physical condition with absolutely no body fat and can hang a fourteen-foot-long sheet of drywall on a wall by myself while holding it with one arm and swinging a hammer with the other. After quickly questioning John with a raised tone for Emilio's remark, I learned his animated gesture wasn't derogatory toward my physique, just an amiable observation of my slightly toned torso.

To remove any doubt of physical ineptness, I reached up over my head and clutched the angle iron supporting John's new elevated bed and performed a one-arm pullup. A byproduct of hanging drywall for thirty years and the last half of those years, I have been a one-man crew, as employees were a big pain in my ass! Now that I was finished making a spectacle of myself, it was time to go directly to my stash of clothing and conceal the awkward rarity of a half-naked white man in the café's cell.

My time spent here has been long enough for me to notice that the prison serves pizza once a week. I was skeptical in trying some until I witnessed a few eager guards flocking to the large flat top wagon and gathering slices of pizza, as the kitchen staff was rolling the cart to the serving area. It was the only time I observed guards helping themselves to prison food, therefore, while in the courtyard during lunchtime, I took a chance at trying some pizza and grabbed three pieces for my dinner tonight. Even though making good use of the microwave, it only slightly enhanced the flavors taste to well below average.

Despite my comfort food being disappointing, I knew of four roomies who were quite pleased with their meal as they sat at the patio table, devouring their food from a Styrofoam takeout box, acquired from a restaurant from outside the prison. I don't know who delivered their Saturday night dinner, or any of the logistics involved, only that I was envious at their enjoyment and wished I had known beforehand we were allowed to order takeout food. Wonder if Dominos will deliver to a prison?

Toward the end of the evening, I concluded most of my time sitting in the patio writing down notes, working on the Word Seek and eating cookies while listening to the beat of the drums of in the distance that seem to be louder than previous nights. John was the only other person in the room and was sitting across from me in Frank's chair reading a book, making our quiet downtime more pleasurable until I broke the silence by jokingly mentioning that the chanting inmates need to learn a new beat and change their rhythm. Little did I know that my insignificant wisecrack was undoubtedly going to be one of the catalysts driving the passion in my heart to share my story with others.

John Moreno protest banner

I waited for a witty remark from John, but his response was far from humorous. He lowered the book to look up at me then referred to the beating drums with a demeanor of a proud and humbled man, "That's for me." It was at that exact moment when I was made aware that the sounds of the beating drums were coming from outside the prison, and the frequent rallying protesters Brenda mention were all for the unjust imprisonment of John. This latest bit of intel explained the chanting and rhythmic drums I have been hearing lately, a byproduct of John being the Chief of the Lakota Sioux tribe with many supporters.

When the drums were briefly silenced, a protester started voicing their outrage through a bullhorn, which encouraged John to relay their boisterous speech to me. I can't possibly remember what he said, as my mind was overrun with amazement, trying to process the magnitude of sitting next to a man of great importance. This has amplified my respect for his unique character! Soon as the bullhorn went silent along with the cheering crowd and the beating of drums resumed, John revealed info to me pertaining to his legal battle, of which I have researched to help clarify my factual interpretation.

John's legal troubles soon began after filing multiple lawsuits against Mexico Retail Properties (MRP or MIRA) and Black Creek Group (BCG), based out of Colorado, claiming the developer was displacing local fisherman, illegally using town water and destroying environmentally sensitive areas in Todos Santos, Mexico. BCG managed 2.5 billion dollars within Mexico in conjunction with MRP controlled by Mr. Pivero, a brother-in-law of a former president of Mexico, Mr. Gortari. The mega-developer was in the process of building 4,472 homes and two hotels in the small town of Todos Santos and, by doing so, were destroying the beach in which local fishermen have been using for their livelihood for hundreds of years.

When John attempted to prevent the developer from overwhelming Todos Santos with unethical practices, both he and client were thrown in prison with denial of bail. The charges were based on falsified documents from a previous court case they were involved in years earlier, accusing them of ignoring a court order in relation to the Todos Santos development, apparently designed to silence John and put an end to his efforts in continuing with the lawsuits against BCG and MRP. Even though a judge acknowledged the evidence was forged, he still proceeded to deny John's bail for two months.

Four days after John was arrested, a federal judge confirmed that the fisherman had the right to protect their traditional fishing ground (beach) against the threat of displacement. This development fell on deaf ears as John had to fight the local judicial system every step of the way, due to the staggering number of falsified documents, corrupt high-ranking government officials and bribable judges. Fortunately, John had all the evidence to prove his innocence and displayed strong confidence toward his victory, which was going to require a lot of time and patience to complete the process.

Upon listening to John's arduous battle that lay ahead, my problems seem to be much less worrisome, for I was well aware of the sacrifice of being away from his family, compelling me to console him with a few comforting words to conclude our discussion. "Remember, change starts with only one man, don't give up the good fight!"

Moments later, while I was in the other room, David commented with disbelief toward John's diligent devotion, questioned his sanity then adamantly whispered, "I wouldn't have done what he did for others, to end up in prison!" Nor would I, but that's what differentiates John from the rest of us, for I would complain about those greedy, corrupt assholes and do nothing, while John is a man of actionable integrity and passionately fight against injustice!

The clock on the wall revealed it was time to hit the sack and prepare for another peaceful night in the cool outside air, but while heading to the patio, an eruption of joyous cheering throughout the cellblock rang out. Oh no, soccer again! Reluctantly I was forced to embark on a journey back to my old friend the milkcrate and impatiently wait for the completion of the game. Due to the late-night event and proximity of each game I have been hearing lately, it suggests that it was soccer finals, and the inmates were watching a recording of the game, or it was being transmitted from a different time zone or country.

The thought of joining the guys in the patio to partake in the visual stimulation never crossed my mind, for I'm not a big fan of grown men being carried off the field by a stretcher crying like just been shot in the leg; "I'll give you something to cry about!" A frequently used quote by my dad.

When the first hour of waiting for the game to be over began to head into the second hour, I abandoned all hope of sleeping with a thousand squashed soles in the graveyard and grudgingly laid my head down in front of old resting place, tossing and turning past midnight. As it turned out, I wasn't the only creature awake; a brown cat scampered into one of the cells across the hall, most likely as a scavenging pet with the freedom to come and go at will.

Day 26 in Country

Fourteenth day in prison

Four hundred-eighty minutes in the patio, or three hundred-sixty minutes of sleep in front of the door? Without a doubt, I prefer the former!

During my morning walk with Carlos, I once again agreed to play chess with him after breakfast and told him to get me when he was ready. Later, when he came calling, I retrieved the chess set and headed toward the door. Emilio revealed a mischievous grin while conveying something to John, who instantly yielded a smile on his face and said to me, "Are you missing a chess piece?"

I wondered how in the hell Emilio knew about the missing piece. Other than Carlos, Adrian was the only other person who knew I was missing a pawn, as he helped in the search for it yesterday. As I hesitated in responding to John's inquiry, Emilio's grin transformed into a sinister smile while raising up his right arm, dangling a black pawn from his fingers. Well played! I should have suspected I was being pranked when the pawn came up missing, also need to realize I'm up against a fellow jokester who is willing to participate in pranking antics.

The expression on Emilio's face was of pure enjoyment while revealing he was the prankster who caused my frantic search for the missing pawn, becoming even more amused after divulging the caper was committed in the presence of his accomplice wife.

Yesterday when I placed the chess set on the table in the courtyard to retrieve some pizza from the cart and take it to my cell, Emilio took advantage of the opportunity to swipe the pawn from the box using his family man status to shield him from suspicion. Which might explain their avoidance of a greeting and eye contact while only sitting four feet away from my table being suspiciously unsociable.

After replacing the recovered pawn with its tiny counterpart in the box and the laughter died down, I headed to the courtyard with Carlos. Despite improved gameplay, he still gets the queen involved too early in the game and has no chance of winning, even though he once again voiced excited optimism in defeating me.

During our match, my jaw dropped in utter disbelief while observing an activity I would have *never* imagined witnessing in prison, an unescorted inmate carrying a half section of an extension ladder!

I had a running list of things needed to assist me in a successful prison escape:

No evening bed check.
English-speaking inmate familiar with prison layout and operations, plus good rapport with guards.
Communication with someone outside of the prison.
Cellphone.
Money.
Passport.
Visitors pass.
Welding machine.
Ladder.
Weapon.

Oh, wait! I do have access to all that! How am I still here in prison?

Approaching my cell after finishing one game of chess with Carlos, I was once again greeted by Mini-Me's, "Open the window!"

I heard sounds of an electric razor coming from the bathroom, where a few of the men were in the process of getting prison-style haircuts by an unfamiliar inmate. Even though John was a customer of the barber, he kept his ponytail away from the sharp scissors, but was greeted with a few laughs while exiting the bathroom for an improperly trimmed beard, though didn't appear to be bothered by the slip of the razor and displayed a sense of humor toward the mishap.

Even though today was a no-show for Brenda, which was much more beneficial to her welfare than it is to my own, I was visited by the lawyer John contacted days ago after I had the misfortune of meeting Roberto. Because of recent developments of an optimistic outcome in my criminal case, I had John relay my apology to his lawyer friend that his services wouldn't be required, concluding our short encounter in about thirty seconds.

Soon after returning from the meeting room, wasting a lawyer's valuable time, I had the displeasure of getting ensnared in David's discussion regarding religion. I fail to understand how David could have the characteristics of an introvert and repeatedly initiate dialogues over such controversial subjects, yet here we go again! Despite hearing many variations of religious beliefs, I respectfully gave David the benefit of the doubt he might indulge me with a tale of his theory of which I have not yet heard.

I politely listened to his spiel for about one minute, soon to realize his spoken words were heading directly to a nonsensical ideology that everything happens for a reason, yet still fails to rationalize why clergyman molest little boys! At that moment, I suddenly interrupted David to prevent him from continuing, then quickly rambled off my zealous spiel, "I don't agree, I believe everything is based on chance and timing!"

Vague as it may sound, it forces the listener to stop and *think* of the implications; for example, "How does a tree grow from a rock?" If I had to explain it, some would not understand or agree, "Chance and timing!" My short rant was scaled down in the presence of John, recognizing his spiritual beliefs would completely differ from ours, of which I acknowledged by telling David, "We should stop talking, so John doesn't think we are idiots."

My remark confirmed John was actually listening to us talk while reading his book because he closed the book and began addressing me with his tribal beliefs. Unlike David, I intently listened to John with anticipation of learning something new and respected his intellectual ability to carefully choose his words. I found it particularly refreshing he never used words like religion, god, angels, or belief, also never claimed to know, or have all the answers, unlike every other religious fanatical on this planet! "What do all religions have in common?" They all think they are correct!

Our discussion surprisingly concluded with the partial agreement after I converted his spiritual theory into a scientific interpretation. Here is my take on the matter; DNA (deoxyribonucleic acid) has a memory, not of a conscious state, but of a biological one, which has been given to us by our parents and will be handed down to our offspring, therefore scientifically we technically continue to exist after death. John's message was all life continues in one-way shape, or form after death. Is that not what I just said?

Our second questionable agreement was of a force, or energy descending from the cosmos, which has a profound effect and alter us to some degree; of what is unclear. Also, completely plausible as radiation, gravity, magnetism, and many more invisible powers have huge impacts on our daily lives. My only question to John was the powers he was referring to being produced naturally or an unknown entity; his belief suggests the latter.

Please keep this in mind; a man's intelligence may not prove he is always correct, especially from misinterpreted information that has been handed down over thousands of years. Case in point: Try playing the child's game, "Telephone line," a game that consists of a group of children sitting in a circle. The chosen person to start the game whispers a phrase into the ear of the person sitting to their right, who then whispers the relayed message to their neighbors' ear and so on until it reaches the last player in the circle. The game concludes by comparing how different the first person's statement is to the last person. How can somebody hold faith in a spoken phrase from decades ago when history tends to be written by the conquerors of past battles?

My strong personal belief from observing society and thinking for myself is that nobody can truly claim to have all the answers; also, we are all a bit insane, or at least one trip short from laying on a couch listening to a psychologist confirming we are an irrational species and quite *crazy!* For those who refuse or deny my assessment of humankind, are most likely to be the ones teetering toward insanity.

While I was walking past the bathroom, I heard Emilio taking a shower, sounding like he was having way too much fun to be in there all by himself, as he repeatedly kept singing, "My lady, I love you!" My first response to shut him up was to turn off the bathroom light while banging on the door, but that is what he would expect me to do. So to think outside of the box, I retrieved a glass and filled it with cold water from the chest cooler, went to the kitchen and climbed up on the rickety plank that held the hot plates, to reach a small opened window eight-feet off the floor that was directly above the bathrooms shower, then without saying a single word, dowsed the unexpecting vocalist with the cold water.

Even though my stealthy attack was executed in complete silence, Emilio knew the delinquent responsible for the chilling prank as he instantly cried out, "*Sonnof beech, my lady!*" This gave John and David a good laugh as they were witness to my antics while bracing the chair that I used to support one of my legs. Funny as it was, now I must be on guard waiting for Emilio's inevitable retaliation.

During the next couple of hours, I hung out in Lucy's patio, playing various games with a few of my roomies, accompanied by the usual comedic banter and continued sarcasm, creating a mini-vacation of entertainment. When the fun and games were over, and the losers walked away in shame with the big L, my attention focused on the unprepared dinner sitting in the fridge.

A few days ago, Brenda brought me a pound of hamburger meat, which has reached its expiration date and needs to be cooked today. My plan to make cheeseburgers was motivated by the homemade BBQ grill sitting in the courtyard and the bag of charcoal underneath the microwave shelf in our cell. I questioned David for the protocol on the use of the grill, he told me the grill belonged to Emilio, and I could retrieve it to use in our kitchen; an in cell outdoor BBQ grill, how cool is that! Now I can eliminate attracting attention to this white boy cooking food in the courtyard and simplify the process by avoiding multiple back and forth trips to the cell, what a relief!

The burgers made here are pretty good, but they are preformed frozen patties having no comparison in taste to fresh meat grilled on an open flame dripping with juices, giving me great anticipation in completing my first prison meal cooked on a grill.

Upon further inspection of the hamburger, my excitement quickly transformed to concern toward the age of the meat, as it appeared to be discolored and smelled slightly questionable. If I were back home, there wouldn't be any hesitation in throwing the meat outside in the woods to feed the array of wild animals who frequently show up at our home during the night. A benefit of living deep in the wilderness, so much, that our county of 640,000 acres has a population of only eight people per square mile, awesome for solitude and escape from society's dysfunction!

Because of my high hopes in wanting to grill burgers and the uncertainty in the quality of the meat, I had David smell it to get his opinion on whether it was safe to eat. He thought it was okay. Even though I didn't require David's help, he took it upon himself to start preparing the grill, which almost had me saying, "Thanks, but I can get this." Yet I did need some lighter fluid. I was made aware that the prison doesn't allow flammable liquids, so David doused some paper napkins with vegetable oil and sugar, placed them under the charcoal, then proceeded to strike a wooden match to the napkins, producing hot coals in about ten minutes.

After receiving a chemistry lesson from David, I prepared the three hamburger patties for the grill and soon began smelling the enjoyable aroma of grease dripping onto hot coals, while totally disregarding the possibility of a rancid cow. With the acquisition of hamburger buns and cheese from within the café and David's involvement in preparing hand-cut French fries, I was able to enjoy the success of a tasty burger cooked on a grill. I offered David a burger, but he politely declined by choosing to cook a frozen patty and take advantage of the hot coals, though was his refusal directed toward politeness, or concerns over the meat's expiration date?

After dinner, while standing in front of the chest cooler, observing the café's activities, my idle hands led my deviant mind to think of a mischievous prank. During countless hours of observing the café's daily operations, I noticed when the guys wanted to unlock the door they rarely look at the key before retrieving it and blindly reach around the side of the shelf to grab it; obviously, the key has been kept in the same place for a long period of time. With the recognition of their habit, I tied a three-foot piece of string to the keyring and position it so only a small portion of it was visible, then sat down on my crate and waited for an unsuspecting victim to grab the key. It wasn't long before when Adrian blindly reached around the corner, grabbed the key, then headed toward the door as the string became taut it suddenly halted his forward progress. A baffled Adrian looked at the key then around the room for an explanation of why he was holding a tethered keyring, though none was given; as an audience of one, I was the only person in the room who recognized what happened and entertained by Adrian's perplexed expression, who never received an explanation.

While sitting there, I took advantage in one of the few moments John wasn't reading a book, or involved with legal matters of his own, or with others, by asking him to write down the complete names of our cellmates in order for to correctly transfer them to my notes. After John gladly obliged, I informed him of my plans to assign a title, or nickname to each of the men and while mentioning he was going to be referred as the "Brains of the outfit," he immediately disagreed with a stern, "*No, no,* David is the brains, the café was his idea!" Along with all the functioning details of operating a business from within a prison cell.

I took John's recommendation under advisement and eventually replaced David's title from Mr. Hospitality in my rough draft. After some contemplation about what each cellmate signified to me and not how they were perceived to each other, a reversal of my decision was made to replace "The brains of the outfit," with "Mr. Hospitality" a much more appropriate title for David which truly comes directly from deep within my heart!

As another evening drew near the seven o'clock lockdown, John was primping in the bathroom, getting ready for his extracurricular activity with his lovely wife in the all-night not so luxurious prison hotel. Upon exiting the bathroom all fresh and clean, John kindly offered his bed to me, then quickly packed a bag and headed to the door with a joyous eagerness to leave the cell. If one wishes to have a distraction-free evening of intimacy in a foreign land, just sign up for the Mexican Dizney Land package, tickets can be purchased at the nearest military checkpoint.

When it came time to utilize John's elevated bed, my attempted slumber was short-lived by the lack of airflow. The bed was only two feet from the ceiling, laying on a narrow bed placed in the corner of cinderblock walls. I could feel the pressure of confinement while my eyes were shut. Within ten minutes, I climbed out of the cave-like structure, clutching my pillow while dragging a blanket behind me, only to grudgingly end up at the dreadful cell door because soccer had once again denied my preferred option of sleeping in the patio. *Damn it!* Now I suddenly had a disheartening feeling regarding where to sleep, as the only two options are unacceptable!

Day 27 in Country

Fifteenth day in prison

Oh no! Three o'clock in the morning, deep pain in my stomach suddenly awakened me! My first reaction from this familiar nauseating discomfort was to lay perfectly still in a fetal position while hoping the agony would subside enough, allowing me to fall back to sleep. Regrettably, I quickly realized that wasn't going to happen, as my stomach felt like the slightest movement would suddenly induce vomiting. Just thinking about the ramifications began to make me more nauseated and knew a quick trip to the bathroom was inevitable, though the activity required in getting there would surely induce the pain-full spewing of the contents from my stomach. So now it's a matter of timing, of how long it will take to reach the toilet twelve feet away, and the longer I lay there thinking about it, the shorter my reaction time will end up being.

My decision to go to the bathroom ASAP was undeniably the correct judgment call, despite the action prompting an undesirable reaction! Shortly after praying to the porcelain god, I instantly had to prepare for the explosion that was about to discharge south of the border, so while keeping my unwanted dinner projectiles on target, I quickly and carefully removed my underwear. While spitting out the last mouthful of residue, I immediately had to get off my knees to do a swift about-face and take a seat. It was extremely CLOSE! Nevertheless, there was no time to claim victory in the maneuver I just accomplished, as I suddenly had to choose the option of letting my north orifice control the high ground and vomit into the sink while allowing the south orifice to control the low ground. Fortunately, I didn't have to ponder over this strategy for very long.

There were moments of brief cease-fires between the battling North and South, allowing me just enough time to reposition my forces and have the option of which orifice had priority in hovering over the toilet.

I was astounded that my aim was true in this disturbing conflict between the opposing forces as absolutely no carnage had spilled off the battlefield onto the bathroom floor! For the moment, this epic battle was over, but not the war, as there were many more gut-wrenching skirmishes throughout the night, which kept me retreating to the trenches. The pains intensity temporarily decreased after each bathroom trip, though only lasted for fifteen minutes before returning with a vengeance!

My first explosive visit to the bathroom must have awakened David and Adrian, who shared concerns over my severe queasiness and offered Adrian's bed for the night, due to it being conveniently closest to the bathroom. I don't remember saying a single word to David as I promptly collapsed on Adrian's bed and ceased any further motion. I honestly can't recall ever feeling that sick in my entire life, even worse than the few times having the flu, of which I yearned to feel that good!

I'm a complete opposite of a hypochondriac and prefer not taking any drugs, or make frequent trips to a clinic, my motto is; "Take medicine to feel better in a week, or don't take any medicine and feel better in a week." However, I started to get worried there was something really wrong with me, as the pain's intensity hadn't subsided in the last two hours, which had me eyeballing the hallway for the last fifteen minutes in hopes of getting a guards attention, so I could go see a doctor. By now, it felt as if I had waited too long for receiving help as the fear of having a real medical emergency while being caged in the middle of the night scared the living hell out of me!

Unbridled fear drove my weakened body to retrieve the translation book, then to the door to lay on the concrete floor to wait for a guard to pass by while keeping one arm extended partially through the bars to assist in getting their attention if I were to pass out. At about the time I thought of waking up a cellmate for help, a guard happened to be walking by, I raised my hand to grab his attention then attempted to search through the book for "Doctor" with no success, for I had neither the strength or cognizance to do anything but lay my head back down to the floor. The guard could see I was in a world of pain and said, "Clinica?" (clinic).

With a faint sigh of relief, I said, "Si" (yes). When he soon returned with a medic, David crawled out of bed and relayed my symptoms to the medic, as well as the correct amount of medication I should take, one pill for the pain, and the other to settle my stomach.

After the medic left, I headed back to bed with some help from David and grabbed a small bucket to place next to the bed just in case I couldn't make it to the bathroom in time. I was very disappointed with the medic's lack of concern by only prescribing some pills, which failed to work. I truly felt the need to see a doctor, especially after making another trip to the toilet, attempting to unload more vile fluids from my body that no longer existed.

One hour after roll call, I sat up on the edge of the bed with my feet on the floor, thinking I might actually get up to join the living, but that's all the energy I had and found it exhausting just sitting there. After telling David the hamburger gave me food poisoning, I flopped back down and joined the dead, which involved a lot of tossing and turning in pain as the cell was too noisy for sleeping.

Motivation to emerge from my coffin at noon was brought on by Frank's voice at our door, he learned I had been stuck in the cell for nine hours in suffering agony and was agitated while proclaiming, "I would have taken you to the clinic sooner if I had known!" I think Frank was specifically perturbed toward my cellmate's lack of initiative for my welfare, as he insisted with a raised voice, "I'll take you to go see the doc right *now!*" I couldn't agree more! And away we went.

The doctor was busy upon our arrival, so without delay, Frank acquired a place for me to lay down in the examination room, then went back to talk with the doctor. Just as I began to fall asleep, he returned with the doc who performed a quick examination consisting mainly of Q&As. Frank recommended I get an injection for a quicker recovery, of what drug eludes me, he also indicated that the doc would need three hundred pesos upfront to purchase the medications from a pharmacy outside of the prison and would be back later to give me the shot.

While the doc was out and Frank busy taking care of errands, I took advantage of the quiet solitude for an uncomfortable booze nap on the examination table, which went surprisingly well until I reluctantly woke up from a deep sleep when the duo entered the room forty-five minutes later. After dropping my pants and getting an injection in my rump, Frank took me to a private cell in the clinic where I would be away from my noisy roommates and allowed me to get some undisturbed sleep. He proceeded to point out the accommodations of a handicap cell containing a large shower, bathroom, and bed. Despite my following Frank around the cell displaying a minuscule interest in the amenities, I truly didn't give a shit as the mystery injection was effectively relieving my agony as my only objective was to close my eyes in the horizontal position soon as possible.

While sitting on the edge of the bed with overpowering anticipation of collapsing on the mattress, Frank eagerly continued to be accommodating by retrieving water, pillow and a blanket, then exited the room and left the cell door open, while leaving me with his trademark query, "DYNA?" Where in the *hell* would I be without Frank, or access to money?

My unconsciousness was cut short when Frank returned and startled me with an announcement of, "Someone is here to see you!" For a brief second the thought of continuing to lay in bed would be much more favorable than getting out of it to greet a visitor, although when I rolled over to see Brenda standing in the doorway, my ambition abruptly altered to be more hospitable as I greeted my sweetheart from the comforts of the bed. I imagine our unique encounter and Brenda's access deep within the prison, could have only been made possible by Frank's accomplished talent, which felt very odd to me that our unsupervised (no guard) rendezvous seemed to be a typical event in this prison.

After informing Brenda of my unconfirmed food poising, she went to go use the bathroom. I used that moment to give Frank the other half of the money for Brenda's heart shaped birthday cake and had him retrieve it from the bakery. As with the presentation of the butterfly earrings, the sentiment of the special gesture while handing her the cake felt as if it were more meaningful to me than it was to her, but in her defense, she has been struggling much more than I during our stay in Mexico. Shortly after Brenda took two bites of the cake, we laid down in the bed together for some essential spooning, soon falling asleep within the comforts of each other's arms. "Shoulders for pillows, lay your head down and dream."[33]

We had been enjoying our peaceful slumber for about thirty minutes, when we were awakened by Frank's voice informing us visiting hours for the clinic was over, which by then I was feeling much better and decided it was time to head back to my cell and try to eat something. We grudgingly crawled slowly out of bed and began to exit the cell, where I offered Frank half of the cake because Brenda didn't like the flavor and refused to take it with her. Frank eagerly accepted the offer, then after retrieving a paper plate, began cutting the cake with a plastic spoon while expressing enthusiasm that his birthday was within a few days of Brenda's. How convenient is that?

How ironic, I acquired a birthday cake for Brenda, of which she did not eat, half that I don't feel like eating and neither did my cellmates, who had fears in eating anything brought into our cell in the wake of my sudden illness and unbeknownst to me, Emilio's recent minor ailment of stomach issues. In all probability, a hungry cat will be eyeballing a bird feasting on half of my discarded, thoughtful gesture.

Upon entering my cell, David approached with concern about the status of my illness and questions related to the doctor's visit. While relaying a synopsis of what transpired, his facial expression of an inquisitive stare quickly morphed into pure disbelief, when I displayed the piece of paper listing the medications while mentioning the doc charged me three hundred pesos for the prescription. David responded with an agitated tone, "What, *reeeally!*"

After confirming my statement, he became outraged and began relaying his boisterous displeasure to Adrian, who spoke not a word

---

[33] Mark Knopfler song.

as he listened with a concerned stare. When David finished with his rant, Adrian instantly revealed a familiar perturbed expression I recognized from his little chat with Raúl, then exited the cell in a heated rush and voiced his displeasure to the guard operating the security door, in order to gain entry into the corridor leading to the offices.

I wasn't quite sure why it was such a big issue in getting overcharged for some medicine, especially when it was very effective in relieving my agony, though my assumption was totally incorrect. David informed me that the doctor is not supposed to charge for a prescription, implying I have been taken advantage of. This is one of those fine examples when "Assumption is the mother of all screw-ups," as there was a significant discrepancy in the definition of "prescription" between David and me. He was under the impression the doc charged me for the exam and the service of filling out paperwork, allowing me to obtain the medicine. Though I referred to prescription as having the medication in my possession. With some back and forth clarification between us, we eventually came to an understanding of what actually transpired in the clinic, regrettably by then it was already too late as reports of accusation spread throughout the prison like wildfire, soon finding myself standing in front of the captain in his office along with Frank and David.

Oh shit! "What we have here is a failure to communicate!"[34] I felt a strong sense of guilt for partially creating the animosity between Frank and David and knew where this train wreck was headed upon entering the office, therefore before anybody said a word and began arguing, I instantly started apologizing with a sincere tone, revealing it was all a big misunderstanding and my fault. After explaining how our predicament escalated out of control and repeating myself with more apologies, Frank spoke up in an elevated tone and said, "That's why some people should mind their own business!" To my surprise, that was the extent of our encounter, with more apologies addressed to the captain while exiting his office.
Even though I can't verify if somebody gave the doctor a stern talking to, by questioning his ethics, I can say it's very probable, do to his

---

[34] *Cool Hand Luke*, movie.

arrival at my cell door thirty minutes later returning 160 pesos from the 300 I gave him for the medicine. It's a shame I will never know who or what altered the doc's conscience!

When I entered our cell, John addressed me with translated concerns from Emilio, who wanted to share his prebiotic pills and bottles of electrolyte infused drinks with me. This is when I found out Emilio had stomach problems though his illness appeared to be much less severe than mine, for he did not display any signs of being sick also wasn't spending his day in bed. Unlike myself, who after eating a light meal and a couple sips of the electrolyte drink preceded by a prebiotic pill, I concluded the rest of my day lying in Adrian's bed. The hiatus from my thoughtful roomies wasn't because I was tired; it was toward the slight queasiness that suddenly flared up that felt less prominent while lying down, though sleeping was not an option due to the café's noisy activity.

I was rolling around in bed, still trying to find comfort when my name was called out at 8:15 p.m., followed by "Your lawyer is here!"

My usual reaction to the arrival of a lawyer is well received, but what worried me, what was so important to motivate a late-night visit from a lawyer? Since it was well past lockdown, John was my only logical choice in escorting me to the meeting room, which he willingly obliged without hesitation, I eagerly followed him outdoors, with no time to dwell over what waits for me.

Our late-evening trek through the corridor area was completely void of activity, revealing a calm ominous feeling and with previous trips to the meeting room, my anticipation of new information sparked nervous energy, although just the thought of having John by my side added some solace to my anxious mind, again.

Upon entering the room, we saw Karla and Angelica standing there. John and Karla exchanged pleasantries then discussed the reason for the after-hours visit. After they spoke a few words, John suddenly displayed a big smile and looked at me with amazement and said, "You are getting out of here!"

"*What?*" was all I said.

As Karla raised her arm up, clutching release papers in her right hand, John joyously replied, "Yes, you are free to leave!"

Uncontrollable tears instantly began rolling down my sobbing face, as I exchanged rejoicing hugs with everyone and extended a very appreciative gesture to Karla. I was in utter disbelief as unbridled emotions hampered my ability to speak coherently.

While they were revealing details, I was able to calm down enough to ask John, "When do I get out?"

He said with a big grin, "*Right now!*"

I couldn't believe it. "Now?" Just like that, I was free to go!

Along with all the excitement in the room, John revisited a statement he made to me days earlier of my impending release and said with a delighted smile, "*I told you so!*" I was truly touched by John's empathy that he held for my fortunate news.

My unstable emotions were exacerbated by thinking I could go home to the States, not realizing I was only out on bail, though quickly learned of my misguided thoughts when John relayed the three conditions for bail.

I couldn't leave the city.

I had to submit 20,000-peso deposit within three days.

I needed to establish an address in La Paz.

Despite sounding childish, my first concern addressed to John upon listening to the condition of not being allowed to leave the city, was would I be able to visit a beach, which was strange to ask, considering La Paz is butted up against the Sea of Cortez.

As I began to calm down and the tears were wiped away, John started relaying detailed information pertaining to my approaching court date, which was expressed with a positive outcome as Karla and the prosecuting attorney were close to finalizing an agreement in reference to my Abbreviated Process. He also said that Karla wanted to push the trial date back a couple of weeks in order to proceed straight to the Negotiation Hearing and eliminate going to trial; by doing so, we would avoid going to court on two different occasions; which was agreeable by me. As our brief encounter came to an end, Karla displayed a big smile as she handed me the official documents allowing me to exit this amusement park a free man, then conveyed through John that she had to finalize some paperwork in the office of the prison, which would take about thirty minutes. I gave Karla an affectionate hug goodbye and a kiss on her cheek, of which I have never done before with a nonrelative while expressing a passionate "*Mucho gracias!*" Then thanked Angelica along with a hug goodbye, just before John and I headed back to our cell.

As we were standing in front of our cell waiting for the guard to unlock the door, Raúl was amongst a few of his totem pole constituents when he referred to our late-night activity, inducing my enthusiastic response, "I'm getting out of here!" Unfortunately, our further comments are a faded memory, though I can't forget his distinctive smile displaying genuine happiness for me as I entered the cell for the very last time!

Soon upon entering the cell, John made the announcement to the men of my release, which instantly unleased joyous excitement throughout the room, then he relayed pertinent information to all the inquisitive staring eyes. I was at a complete loss of what to do first, or how to conduct behavior toward this uniquely strange experience, which took me a moment to gather my thoughts in order to proceed.

With subdued excitement, I gathered my personal items from the two milk crates under Mini-Me's bed and stuffed them into plastic grocery bags, though not all items would be leaving the prison tonight. I decided to give David the three remaining Frisbees and the Word Seek book.

He responded in the same manner from the first time I gave him a Frisbee, with pure amazement, "*reeeally*, how much?" After I eagerly insisted David could have them for free, he replied, "Reeeally, Dennis, you are the man!"

The next offering was made to Adrian of my Nalgene bottle that Brenda brought me, which inscribed the phrase "Never give up." I had David translate the quote and encouraged Adrian to apply it while playing chess. My finale charitable deed was to leave behind most of my food products, delighting a few of my future ex-roommates, particularly David, Pablo, and Jose, who were having a struggling verbal match over who was to claim each food item. I found their antics quite entertaining, watching grown men behave like children bickering over food that was meant for everybody; failing to recognize that this would be my final amusing moment within their cell.

Even though being packed and ready to leave, I still had to wait another thirty minutes for prison officials to clarify Karla's documentation, while doing so, I sat one last time on my Mexican lounge chair patiently watching for the arrival of my gatekeeper, also exchanging a few more words with Raúl from across the hall. While quietly sitting there, the pillow under my derriere suddenly triggered the realization that I wouldn't be able to covey my profound admiration to Frank or tell him goodbye. It truly saddened my heart and evoked a strong urge that Frank's items needed to be returned to him, i.e., chair, sleeping mat and contraband (pillow), so I pleaded for David to make sure his stuff was returned.

Around nine thirty I saw a guard approaching with a keyring in his hand and knew it was time for me to leave, so I stood up and began saying my goodbyes by giving each of the men a firm handshake, a one-arm embrace along with an earnest gratitude for all they have done for me. After exchanging my farewell with Roseudo (Mini-Me), I said, "I'm going to miss you most of all, scarecrow!" In hopes, John would relay the translated meaning of "The Wizard of Oz" to Roseudo after my departure.

While shaking John's hand, I said with a heartfelt sentiment, "I feel honored to have known you!" To my surprise, he returned the kind gesture, which truly meant a lot to me, as I have tried to conduct myself with respect toward others while in this adverse environment.

My spirits were dampened while saying my goodbyes to the men, feeling like it wasn't fair that I was leaving so soon after my arrival, compared to others who will still be unjustly stuck in captivity. The strong emotional bond I felt for the men compelled me to return their kindness by acquiring something special for them while I was out of the prison, so after exchanging an emotional interaction with John, I asked, "What do you and the guys need?" John looked at me with heartfelt sincerity and said, "Never forget us!" I made a promise to him and myself while raising my left hand, clutching the notebook containing my cherished memories and voiced to the whole room with passionate conviction, "*I won't!*" I ambitiously left the cell with somber smiles and stares from my brothers upon my back, soon disappearing down the corridor to freedom!

Before leaving the area, I requested to the guard that we go to the captain's office first, where I could call Brenda and have her pick me up. It might have raised suspicion from the prison staff if I called her from within our cell, exposing the fact that myself or cellmates possessed a phone if Brenda had arrived before I was actually released. Upon entering the office, I found out where the café's meat cleaver spends its time after business hours, hanging out amongst fellow alloys in the arsenal placed in a pile atop a desk. The impressive conglomerate of metal implements was an oddity to witness inside a prison; there were at least forty items consisting of kitchen knives, hammers, saws, and other potentially dangerous objects buried within the unorganized pile.

It's apparent from my late-night observation that this side of the prison had an honor system allowing certain prisoners the use of treacherous metal objects during the day, only if they promise not to partake in any rebellious, or illicit activity with said implements while in their possession and return them every night. An honor system that seems to be working exceptionally well, until it *doesn't!*

My phone call with Brenda was brief with, "Hey Candy Pants, it's me, come and get me."

She was slightly confused while responding in total disbelief, "You want me to pick you up right now?" After confirming my request, she followed with, "I'll leave as soon as I get dressed, bye!" Was I just talking to a naked woman?

My final destination was the same office that processed me upon my arrival into this prison, yet this trips stopover destined to my unknown resting place is a more pleasurable experience this time around. As with any amusement park exiting is always more expedient than entering, and after handing office personal my "get out of jail free" documents, signing some forms and retrieving my personal items, they proceeded to cast me out from their care into the ominous night with much less importance than when first arriving here fifteen days ago!

There was no jubilant reception waiting for me as the prison gate slammed shut behind me, only met by the silence of the darkened city street completely absent of activity, so after standing around for a few minutes staring down the empty street, I placed my pillow and folded blanket on a sidewalk step and sat with eager anticipation of Brenda's arrival. The excitement of being a free man soon dissolved after sitting there for twenty minutes that turned into thirty, and as boredom emerged, the only person aware of my plight was a guard wearing a black uniform brandishing a machine gun lurking in the dark shadows of the trees next to the prison wall.

When thirty became forty minutes, boredom was replaced with concerns of Brenda's impending arrival as I started thinking about possible scenarios of what could have gone wrong. Fortunately, the pondering was short-lived when five minutes later at ten thirty she pulled up alongside me in a rental car. While opening the door, I hesitated before getting into the car, for something possessed me to stop, turn around and whistle extremely loud, then yell out, "*I am John Moreno!*" The shout out was aimed toward my brothers, as their outside patio was only one-hundred feet away and knew they were able to hear my final passionate departing farewell; only to be quickly scolded by Brenda who reprimanded my obnoxious behavior; setting the tone for the duration of our fifteen-minute drive to a condo, she acquired for the week.

What a great relief to be out of prison, but felt it lacked the euphoria one would expect from a free man; I don't know why? Mostly likely from a combination of deep emotions hindering my enjoyment. First of all, my reunion with Brenda was anticlimactic, and soon upon our arrival at the condo, she disappeared into the bed while I took a shower, where I stood under the water sobbing in fear that our relationship was damaged beyond repair due to resentment involving her in this Mexico fiasco. Second, slight guilt for abruptly leaving my brothers in arms so soon. Thirdly, some sort of strange effect of Stockholm Syndrome, from abandoning special friendships I didn't know could exist in prison in such a short amount of time. No matter! Deep emotional wounds will heal in time, just hope I can live with the scars they leave behind!

With a moment to reflect on the past seventeen days and toward Frank's statement, "They call this prison Dizney Land," I thought about the correlation between the two separate entities and recognized many similarities that were oddly spot-on:

Must travel a very long distance to get there.
Parking is always more atrocious on the weekend.
Entering is never worth the price you pay.
Enter through a security gate monitored by security personal.
The area surrounded by a wall and towers.
Sensory overload upon entering.
Being watched by security cameras.
Not quite sure what to do first.
Venders are walking around trying to sell worthless crap.
Somebody is always cleaning the area.
Food venders with limited seating.
Birds were looking for a free meal.
There is a shirtless mouse.
Must keep a close eye on your personal possessions.
Surrounded by people who don't speak your language.
Food is substandard.
Low budget movie show.
Concerned parents are eyeballing their roaming children.
Eventually, start noticing familiar strangers.
Sounds of screaming off in the distance.
Somebody has the misfortune of vomiting.
Chances are you will have the scariest ride of your life.
Extreme boredom while waiting for the next moment of stimulation.

There are people who really want to go there but can't and others who wouldn't be caught dead there but are forced to go there anyway.

At the end of the day, when you are tired and had enough of the exhausting experience, all you want to do is quickly find the exit and go *home!*

Now I've had the luxury of experiencing Disney Land in Florida and the La Paz prison in Mexico, though only one of them is truly worth writing an incredible story about!

At the conclusion of this late Monday night, the enjoyment of being out on bail would not go unpunished, as the amount of time required to complete the judicial process proved to be more taxing than imprisonment itself. But for the moment, I was free to explore the beachfront of the Sea of Cortez and not spend any more time in that dysfunctional Mouse House, or so *I thought!*

Day 28 in Country

First day out of prison

It may sound really strange, but one of the first things I did upon waking up this morning after sleeping in past eight o'clock for the first time in sixteen days, was to find the Sudoku puzzle that I was working on back in the jailhouse and examine the puzzle to confirm if my memory was correct; no it wasn't, I inverted two numbers.

After eating breakfast, I contacted Karla sometime after nine o'clock to gain information required in paying my bail that was due within three days. She informed me that I was to go to the judicial office to retrieve a document that would allow me to deposit the bail money in a government bank. So our first task for the day was to gather 20,000 pesos to pay my bail, or book a flight home and leave my truck behind avoiding the risk chance of receiving dire news at my next trial, though paying the $1,176 bail money is well worth staying in the country for a while to retrieve all the expensive gear from within my truck. I wouldn't mind abandoning the truck and gear here in Mexico by refusing to pay the bail and just leaving the country ASAP, but all our gear is worth more than the value of the truck; also the reassurance of receiving the Abbreviated Process and just paying a fine encouraged me to stay in the country.

We had enough cash on hand to pay the bail, but a trip to a bank was necessary in order to exchange some of our US currency for pesos and acquire extra cash for living expenses to help avoid credit card surcharges, therefore our first destination this morning was to a bank. A task that sounds simple to perform yet proved to be quite arduous, as the nearby bank was located within an array of buildings that had little to no available parking, requiring us to navigate through the vast amount of one-way streets in search for a place to park, while agonizing with the prolific traffic and unfamiliar rules and laws of city street parking. Also hindering our undertaking was that, by law, we were only allowed to exchange three hundred dollars a day for pesos and limited on the amount of money we could withdraw from an ATM each day. This apparatus clearly not designed for people who are Spanish illiterate, requiring us many failed attempts before eventually receiving our cash.

Our next daunting task was to locate the judicial building that was clear across town, involving more misguided directions on where to go, aggravation brought on by going the wrong way, many U-turns resulting in aggressive driving and searching through the crowded streets for a parking space to eliminate a long hike to our destination. Upon retrieving the document from the judicial office with the help of Hector; the same young man who retrieved Brenda's blanket while we were in jail, we headed to the government bank that was located in the town square near the same area of the town in which we just came from.

Retracing our tracks through the town in search of the bank should have been a simple task; unfortunately, our journey to the judicial building wasn't a direct route where we probably ended up driving five miles for a two-mile trip, consequently leaving us with an inaccurate memory on how we reached our destination. Even though we obtained directions from Hector and the almighty Google for the location of the government bank, we were still unable to locate it, even with a more thorough search by walking around the town square area, confirming that the all-knowing Google was once more incorrect. With my elevated frustration at its breaking point, we were forced to return to the judicial office and ask Hector for a more accurate location, though upon returning to the town square forty-five minutes later, I found the bank by pure accident while driving around in a perturbed frenzy.

There was no time to celebrate in discovering the elusive bank, as there was nowhere to park and once again found ourselves driving around for a parking spot, an ordeal hampered by the abundant one-way streets and curbs painted red marking the no-parking areas.

Once inside the bank, the frustration continued, with a clerk who strung us along for fifteen minutes of not knowing how to proceed with our unique request before realizing the form was missing a key signature, requiring us to make a trip back through town and return to the judicial office.

Familiar confusion in the judicial office had us exiting the building empty-handed, as we were to return tomorrow morning and obtain the proper signature from the staffer who had gone home for the day. Day 2 of my exodus from the mouse house was a complete duplication of yesterday's fiasco, as we had to wait a long time at the judicial office for them to draw up a new document before returning to the bank. Unfortunately, more delays were implemented by the bank teller, by conferring with a fellow staffer and making phone calls regarding our documentation, then informed us that Mexican law prohibits a non-resident of Mexico in depositing 20,000 pesos in a government bank regardless of what form we may possess. Therefore, you guessed it! A trip back to the judicial office was necessary to find out what our next course of action would be, luckily a more proficient route has been engraved in my memory expediting our drive time but was soon disappointed upon our arrival when we were told to go to the courthouse tomorrow with our lawyer and pay my bail there. It appears that everybody involved thinks they know how to handle our situation, but honestly, nobody has a clue on how to proceed, and only after much debate with others does progress slowly evolve. Who would have thought unloading a big wade of cash in Mexico would be so challenging?

If our day wasn't frustrating enough, Roberto and his sidekick—both of whom were completely unaware of my release on Monday—tracked us down via the phone and without asking volunteered our services to transport them all over town to take care of some errands; apparently, they returned their rental car early due to their lack of funds. I say, "bullshit!" At noon we ended up eating lunch at Applebee's, where I inquired to Roberto about retrieving my truck. He said, "No problem," and that I should talk to Karla tomorrow while paying bail. To promote his true character, Mr. Succubus (Roberto) made no attempt to help pay for the lunch and only scrutinized the amount of tip I was to leave for the waiter. What a cheap asshole!

Fortunately, my encounters with Roberto were minimal as he departed from La Paz a few days after my release from prison but did so without telling us he was leaving and only found out about it when he informed Brenda that he left her release documents from jail at the front desk of their hotel. I become very irritated, trying to figure out what Roberto did for me that required paying him 5,000 dollars!

The next day (Thursday) Brenda and I went to the courthouse across from the prison, where we have to sign in at the security checkpoint, fill out the information on a sign-in sheet to receive a visitor's pass, then walk through a metal detector and have our handheld items sent through an X-ray machine, all in the presence of an armed guard brandishing a shotgun. After waiting fifteen minutes for the proper personnel to arrive, I lost my chance at skipping bail by initiating the process requiring completion of an abundant number of forms in triplicate and signing legal documents that secured myself a receipt by relinquishing $1,176 dollars.

Soon after watching a staff member tuck the cash into a large manila envelope, I asked Karla about retrieving my truck today. Moments later, Karla, Brenda, and I went outside and walked over to the jailhouse, where hopeful anticipation was quickly greeted with familiar disappointment. The presence of a lawyer by my side proved to be irrelevant, as the office personal insisted that Karla retrieve a signed form by the prosecuting attorney relinquishing my truck. Oh shit, here we go *again!* Hop back in the car and head to the judicial building (Karla's office), but departing from this side of town to our frequent destination is not yet familiar to me, inducing stress and bickering between Brenda and myself on how to get there.

I failed to mention that every time one of us must enter the judicial building, it always required standing in line, relinquishing our identification, and signing in to receive a visitors-pass, all without the benefit of a translator. A procedure that is not very inconvenient unless nothing gets accomplished while doing so; for instance, now, as Karla had no luck contacting the prosecuting attorney, and maybe she would find something out on Monday. Today is Thursday, the madness continues!

Balandra Mushroom rock

Obviously, nothing was going to get accomplished for the next three or four days. Therefore, Brenda and I escaped the stressful insanity by driving 15 km outside of town to explore the Balandra beach on Friday and do some snorkeling along the seashore. During the weekend, we extended our relaxation by going for walks on the beachfront, watch TV, went to Applebee's for dinner that sucked ass and went atop the roof of the condo to watch the majestic sunsets and tranquility over the Sea of Cortez.

Day 34 in Country

Seventh day out of prison

Because of the proximity of Applebee's to our condo and its familiarity with the locals, Brenda and I used it as a convenient place to meet Irving, my public defender who I met in the jailhouse. He informed us that the truck title and registration needed to be translated into Spanish by a state registered translator before the prosecuting attorney could confirm that the truck was legal and that I was the owner. We were given a phone number by Irvin for someone who could translate the documents for us, but they were too busy and couldn't help us; luckily, they supplied us a number to call who could translate the documents in a *week*.

After agonizing over the thought of waiting a week for a translator and realizing we were desperate for professional guidance and a personal translator who was readily accessible, I decided to hire a competent lawyer the next day. While in prison, John gave me two of his associates' phone numbers, Victor and Marco, who worked at the law firm that I could call for help, so I utilized John's offer and called Victor for an appointment to see him Tuesday afternoon. Even though their law firm was only ten minutes away, it took us thirty stressful minutes to locate their office and another fifteen minutes to confirm we were at the correct place, as nobody was there or answering the phone; hell, I think the GPS was also unsure of our location.

Eventually, Marco arrived with apologies that he was delayed by the court and could not answer the phone; no matter, I was just relieved to be at the correct building and in the presence of John's associate. Marco looked to be forty years old, with an average height and build, a beard, and mustache. He was very mild-mannered and spoke little broken English, making it difficult for us to have an in-depth conversation. Fortunately, I was able to conduct a proper dialogue when Victor and John's sister Mary arrived at the office moments later, though Victor's English was only slightly better than Marco's, as opposed to Mary, who could converse in English as efficiently as John. My recollection of Mary's features eludes me, as having only one encounter with her while sitting next to her on the office couch without direct eye contact toward each other, though I do recall she was slightly older than John, amicable and helpful with translations.

Before an explanation was given for our presence, an exchange of friendly chitchat was conducted between the five of us, creating a very relaxed atmosphere and relieved the stress I have been enduring for a week.

After learning of Mary's relation to John, I instantly became intrigued with enthusiasm and revealed to her that I stayed in the same jail cell with John, igniting stories between us of "It's a small world after all." After revealing to Mary that I lived in Missouri, she eagerly responded, "Oh, we used to live in Missouri and visited Elephant Rocks state park with our parents when we were kids!" A familiar place, as I too have made frequent trips to the unique park and only live about an hour and a half away. Most likely John and I have stood upon the same giant boulder atop the hill, although our quest to reach the summit surely was not for the same reason; mine was to look upon the valley below and ponder its beauty, his was to climb up and say, "Mommy, daddy look at me!" Though I must admit, I too searched for recognition of my achievement.

Another similar thing that John and I share, is having a parent and grandparents from Polish descent, for which is assumed because of his mother's madden name Rutowski.

Through Mary's translation, I told Victor we needed a lawyer to help with procedures and legal advice, retrieve my truck from impound and get access to a personal translator. After Victor and Marco had a short discussion concerning the legality of my case and what would be involved, Mary informed me that it would be 17,500 pesos ($900) to hire them. As soon as I willingly accepted, the duo instantly started asking questions relating to my case, debated among themselves on how to proceed, made phone calls, started making copies of all the legal documentation we had in our possession and contacted a translator. They were busy as bees and quite impressive, all without receiving cash from me for three days!

My amazement was elevated when they found a state registered translator who could translate my truck title, registration, insurance and the receipt for the purchase of the 9mm gun in a day or two; oddly enough it was the same lady who told us over the phone yesterday that she could do it in a week. Adding to my astonishment, they had also acquired her to be my personal translator, but the big surprise was when they revealed her identity as Angelic, the court-appointed translator! How cool is that?

Angelica said for $250, she could translate the documents that I had in my possession and start translating the ones I didn't have by getting them sent to her by E-mail from the US, though eventually needed the original documents for legal verification. I might have responded to Angelica's instructions by saying, "No problem," but a problem would surely ensue, as the truck title and gun receipt were overnighted by mail a few days later, but it took TEN days to reach my possession. Unbeknownst to me, Brenda had her daughter place a bottle of iodine tablets in the same package with the documents, which ended up getting held in customs as contraband. The stress created from that action was insane, requiring three days of many frustrating trips back and forth to the post office, DHL offices and customs office trying to track down the package; unnecessary trips that were brought on by misinformation given to us by staff members working at the various offices. The only reason we were finally able to get the package sent through customs after many failed attempts was by asking Angelica for help, who convinced the customs office to remove the iodine tablets from the package before sending the package on through.

Like a fool, I believed our stressful trips to the post office were over, but on June 19 Angelica informed us that the prosecuting attorney wanted the truck title Apostilled (a government authentication of a document) from a US agency. Regrettably, we didn't receive the title from the customs office until June 25, so we had to wait six more days before I could mail it back to the States to an agency who could Apostille the title, which took ten days to finally reach John's law office. Speaking of the Pony Express with a broken leg, my sister (Debbie) from Michigan mailed me a letter that took thirty days to reach me. Welcome to fucking Mexico!

During the many weeks that Brenda and I had to deal with the countless difficulties that arose, the amount of anxiety between us was getting out of control, so much, that every damn time we climbed into the rental car, an argument or disagreement soon ensued! *For a fact*, I felt less stress within the confines of prison walls!

On one occasion, while we were making one of our many trips to a bank, there was nowhere to park the car, so Brenda told me to park in the no parking area; being submissive and avoiding another disagreement, I reluctantly pulled up to the curb. Soon as we crossed the street, I glanced back at the truck and noticed a policeman was already writing me a parking ticket, who must have been lurking on the sidewalk as there wasn't a police car anywhere in sight.

I ran across the street in hopes of stopping the officer from completing the ticket, but it didn't matter as he continued writing the ticket while I stood there, pleading my case. Shortly after, another policeman arrived and said something about going to an undisclosed location to pay the fine and pointed toward the two policemen who were across the street. At that moment, Brenda had returned to the truck asking what the officer said; soon as I relayed his undescriptive instructions, she instantly became agitated, refusing to follow them across the street, then she had me hand them our lawyers' business card for them to call Victor. The two officers studied the card, exchanged a few words to each other, then handed it back to Brenda and said, "You are free to go."

Our encounters with corrupt policemen that were easily influenced by lawyers continued to plague us, from a policeman who pulled me over for not completely stopping at a stop sign; a violation I'm indeed guilty of frequently executing, by regarding stop signs as a suggestion and only come to a complete stop when there is traffic or a cop present. *However*, I'm a law-abiding citizen compared to

Mexico's drivers; except for tourists, I have not witnessed anybody come to a complete stop unless there was traffic, even the police here act like the signs are a suggestion. La Paz seems to have a stop sign on almost every street corner, so stopping at every one of them is just a big pain in my ass, and to completely stop among these aggressive drivers would ruin their day when they suddenly realize my rear bumper is of hardened steel.

The police officer who pulled us over relayed his limited English rehearsed spiel to us, "You have to pay a one-hundred-dollar fine." After telling him I didn't have a hundred dollars, he informed us there was an ATM machine just down the street where I could get the cash. Back home in the States, I have *never* used an ATM machine and refuse to leave the house without cash in my pocket, so my quick response to the cop was spoken with conviction, "My credit card doesn't work in an ATM machine!"

The determined cop repeated himself as if I didn't understand what he was saying; consequently, forcing me to repeat my statement, but he still failed to comprehend and once again tried to extort money by instructing me to retrieve the money from the ATM. Realizing the cop was incapable of understanding me, or just acting ignorant, I called Victor and handed the phone to the cop, who suddenly aborted his quest to extort money from me and said, "You are free to go."

The fourth time we were instructed to stop by a local policeman, was when I drove slightly past a stop sign to get a visual line of sight down the street that was obstructed by parked cars alongside the curb. A cop who was standing at a street corner yelled out for us to stop, so after stopping in the middle of the street to see what he wanted, he informed us that I didn't stop behind the white line, which was damn near unrecognizable from decades of neglect.

By now, Brenda was all too familiar with Mexico's police procedures, so she instantly became defensive by disagreeing with the cop who was insisting we pull over to the curb; to further his shakedown, but with no success. Brenda said to me, "Screw him, just go!"

So I complied with my accomplice, leaving him standing there in the street arguing with himself, while we drove away in a heated rush and laughing; with no vehicle, or walkie-talkie, what was he to do run after us? Unfortunately, this wouldn't be my last encounter with corrupt law enforcement during my stay in Mexico!

During the time when we were dealing with the truck debacle, I relayed my concerns to Angelica about retrieving my small address book from the truck, for it contained all my passwords and needed to be recovered for obvious reasons. Being a mother, Angelica responded to my inquiry by reprimanding me as if I were a child, "Why do you have your passwords wrote down on paper? I would never do that!"

I may not be the brightest bulb in the pack, but I'm damn sure not an idiot! I told her that all my passwords are preceded by the same six characters, of which are not wrote down, or saved anywhere on this planet, therefore even if somebody should acquire my passwords, they wouldn't have a clue of the first six characters. I think Angelica didn't comprehend my statement or failed to pay attention, as she quickly repeated her reprimand. My suggestion to some of the inhabitants of this world, "*Stop, listen, and think* before opening your mouth!"

Within a couple of days, Angelica arranged a trip to the jailhouse with Irvin (Public defender) and myself to retrieve the address book, while there she mentioned that this would be my last opportunity to retrieve anything from the truck, as it was soon to be towed to an impound lot. Despite Angelica reassuring me that the truck's contents would be secure by the owner of the lot and was responsible for its safekeeping, I still chose not to rely on, or trust a third party in caring for the items in my truck, therefore after getting the address book from the truck, I asked Angelic about retrieving the rest of my gear. With the hope of gaining possession of my truck any time soon fading from reality, I feared that the longer the truck sat in a Mexican impound lot, the greater chance it would be stripped down to a shell when it came time to pick it up.

With the help of Irvin and Angelica convincing the jailhouse staff to release the items from my truck by completing a bunch of paperwork, I was able to reclaim most of the important and expensive items from the truck. Even though we were at the jailhouse well after business hours, there were a lot of employees still working, aid-ing in our effort to complete the process in a timely manner. After a staff member took photos of what I removed from the truck, I loaded up the rental car packing it completely full, giving me great relief of having the gear in my possession; then, I extended much appreciation to Irvin and Angelica before heading down the highway.

Day 48 in Country

Twenty-first day out of prison

Another condition required in keeping my bail secure was to personally sign-in at the courthouse every Monday no later than 4:00 p.m. and continue to do so until my trial date, which involved displaying my passport and posting my thumbprint on the sign-in book next to my signature; confirming I had not violated my parole by leaving town. I completed this task every week with relative ease while we were out taking care of other errands; unfortunately, our plans this Monday were altered which left us with no reason in leaving the condo all day and by doing so, disrupted my routine and not realizing until many hours after 4:00 p.m. that I missed my sign-in at the courthouse.

My forgetfulness raised significant concern for the ramifications of missing a scheduled sign-in and instantly put me into a state of panic. I frantically attempted to call Victor to find out what I should do. Unfortunately, I was unable to reach him, so I immediately contacted Angelica by phone. After relaying my sob story and listening to her scold me for missing the sign-in, she hung up the phone to call Marco and find out how to rectify my problem.

The severity of missing a sign-in was made clear to me when Angelica called back and said, "This is a BIG problem!" The last time I heard those words were at the military checkpoint moments before getting arrested, and you can see how well that worked out for me! After Angelica spoke to Marco, she relayed detailed instructions of what I needed to do and were to be carried out *immediately*. I was directed to go quickly to a designated clinic before it closed and fake an illness in order to receive proof of a doctor's examination and a prescription for medication, then get my prescription filled at a drugstore and retain a sales receipt. Then go to the judicial building tomorrow morning and give the documents to Karla, who would present them to the court; in hopes that I would be excused from accountability in missing my sign-in.

Our late-night frantic search for the clinic left us just enough time to see a doctor before closing time, lucky for me this clinic was still open well past 9:00 p.m. and adjacent to the drugstore with a connecting side door. After standing in a crude waiting area for ten minutes, a doctor emerged from an examination room with a patient, then had us follow him back into the small room where I once again performed as a sick patient complaining of an ailment, though my acting performance had assistance from a supporting actress via the telephone, by Angelica who translated my phantom discomfort to the doctor and request for some medicine.

Soon after the doctor examined me with minimal effort, we left the office with verification of a doctor's visit and prescription in hand, then went next door to the drugstore and purchased some medicine that ended up in the trashcan soon upon completion of our trip, all of which cost less money than my initial visit to the prisons doctor initiated by a rancid bovine.

The next day I went to Karla's office and dropped off proof of my ailment to her secretary, which must have appeared to be legitimate, as I was never notified of any repercussions from missing the sign-in; not sure if Karla was ever aware of my deception, or others involved. Either way, I wasn't about to ask and inadvertently involve her in the deceit.

Throughout the next two weeks, Brenda and I continued to make frequent trips to the lawyer's office, judicial building, courthouse, banks and various drug stores in search of medication to ease Brenda's ailments, of which compounded with her stress contributed to her losing thirty pounds. We also made many trips to Office Depot, where we scanned and copied a multitude of documents to appease the court and the Prosecuting Attorney, utilizing the stores' terminal computers to gain internet access for paying bills, completing legal tasks and printing out more Sudoku puzzles. The abundance of all these arduous tasks persisted in bringing forth most of our stressful moments; fortunately, we once again took advantage of our spare time and incorporated a vacation itinerary from a non-vacation atmosphere, by going to the beach, hikes in the countryside, visiting restaurants and movie theaters; though made the mistake of seeing the movie Wonder Woman without subtitles.

One place, in particular, we frequently visited was a Domino's pizza, where we gained recognition from a young woman working there who always took our order, and even though her English was extremely limited, she was the only employee capable of identifying what we wanted to order. On one occasion I became astonished while waiting to place our order when the friendly woman approached the counter and greeted me by name, then before I had a chance to utter a single word, she established that we wanted a large pepperoni pizza with extra cheese, Pepsi and a bottle of water. Her pleasant recognition of our arrival inspired me to tip her ten pesos. At that moment, it was evident that Brenda and I had been in the country entirely too long, as familiar strangers began recognizing our routine.

The pleasant experience with a Dominos employee wasn't my only encounter with a familiar stranger that brought forth a smile. During one of my trips to the jailhouse in a failed attempt to retrieve my truck, I was walking with Karla and Angelica in the parking area adjacent to the prison, when I heard a loud shout out from atop the guard tower, *"Harry Potter!"*

I instantly recognized the familiar voice, then looked up, extending a wave hello with a big smile and replied, *"Hey Frogman!"*

Karla and Angelica were in total disbelief of my overzealous display toward the boisterous guard, especially Angelic, who commented on my behavior by saying I was crazy. She failed to recognize the pure enjoyment I received from Mr. Frogman's recognition and his handlebar mustache supported by a friendly smile, also will never be aware of what truly transpired between him and I; and if so, she wouldn't understand it.

The next time I saw that distinctive handlebar mustache, was late-night outside of the prisons front gate where I was sitting among a small gathering of people having a pow-wow session in honor for

John when Frogman was among a large group of guards exiting the prison heading toward the parking lot. When we noticed each other at a glance, it was void of our customary loud outburst and only conveyed with a friendly wave hello. As he continued walking by, I suddenly thought about getting his opinion on the kind of prisoner I portrayed, so I quickly grabbed his attention, then enlisted the help of a woman sitting across from me who spoke English and had her relay my inquiry. I expected a humorous reply from the guard, but instead, was disappointed with his lame response, "You were a good prisoner and never caused any problems." Nevertheless, I felt honored!

Another encounter (of many) that made my lengthy stay evident was brought on by the frequent trips to the courthouse, where I would occasionally see the young guard who commented, "Nice vacation," while I was in the courthouse holding cell on the night of my preliminary trial. Our repeated run-ins eventually brought forth a friendly greeting with a handshake and brief exchanges of small talk, which help raised my comfort level throughout this abnormal environment.

From the moment of my release from prison, I possessed an overwhelming urge to buy something special for the men in cell #6 and fulfill my agreement to purchase a radio for Raúl, therefore Brenda and I devoted a couple of days in search for the ideal gift. After searching throughout various stores contemplating what the men would enjoy, I ended up buying a Jenga game at Walmart, a chess book from a local bookstore for Adrian, a small portable

The 'Never give up' puzzle

radio/music player from an electronic store for Raúl and for Brenda and I a thousand-piece puzzle from a large retail store; an unfortunate byproduct of our *lenghty* stay in Mexico. Upon completion of the puzzle weeks later, I used a colored marker to write all the names of the men in cell #6 on the back of the puzzle, along with the quote, "Never give up!" Then delivered it to the prison, in care of David.

I was never certain if my ex-cellmates ever noticed the message on the back of the puzzle, until three years later after sending John an email with a photo of the puzzle's quote. It was very heartening and gratifying to learn that Jose became sentimental when Adrian and John completed the puzzle then revealed the message to the rest of the men.

Days after my release from prison, Brenda downloaded WhatsApp with the translation feature on the phone she purchased in La Paz, allowing us to communicate with everybody involved in our state of affairs, also beneficial in communicating with David, who I regularly kept in contact with during my stay in Mexico. On our first communique, I greeted David with the comical line, "I'm bringing the strippers Monday."

He replied, "Yeah, man!" Followed by, "Everyone says hi. Happy to hear from you. I hope you are doing well and getting home soon."

I arranged to visit him at the prison on Monday, though my visitation would be limited to the outside area where Brenda and I had our five-minute visit at the caged windows.

On the day of my planned visit to the prison, I have yet to purchase the Jenga game, so I bought an assortment of donuts for the men to help relieve the notion that Adrian was the only one who received a gift (chess book). The thought of seeing David at the prison brought immense anticipation, but Mexico has a way of turning optimism into disappointment as it thwarted my first attempt from visiting David; therefore I was only allowed to drop off the donuts and Adrian's chess book, then come back another day after securing permission to see David.

Via the WhatsApp, David revealed he had difficulty obtaining authorization for me to visit him at the prison, so I recommended he ask Frank for help; which of course resulted in me greeting Frank (instead of David) at the caged windows two days later; once again, was there ever any *doubt?* Frank was surprised to see that he had a visitor, since I was the only person to visit him in ten years. After exchanging pleasantries and small talk, I notified Frank of the two boxes of assorted donuts I brought and were waiting to be picked up at the inspection area, one box for him and the other for the captain. I asked Frank to make sure the captain received the donuts with my deepest gratitude for the treatment I received while in prison; it was the least I could do, for I truly regret not being able to personally thank him!

With Frank's masterful ability to bend the rules, I extended my five-minute visitation by asking if he could get David so I could talk to him, who would technically be allowed five minutes to visit me. While waiting for David to arrive, a guard walked over to me and drew attention to his wristwatch, but I just pointed to the window to reveal there was nobody there as if I hadn't visited anybody yet; which worked out well as the perplexed guard walked away without saying a word.

I was at a loss of words when David walked up to the window, greeted me with a smile, and said, "I hate everyone equally." Wasn't sure if he was mocking me, or voicing a statement that we both share toward the displeasure of humanity, either way, his next remark was completely understandable, "Why did you come back here?" No clue of what my response was; nonetheless, in all good conscience, how could I not return to show my respect and admiration toward the men who completely altered my stay in prison!

Most of our conversation is a vague memory, as I found it very difficult to understand, or hear what he was saying do to the rising noise level in the area; which made for an uncomfortable interaction requiring me to lean close to the caged barrier in an attempt to listen with my good ear. As much as I was happy to see David, I became relieved when our five minutes were up, allowing me to finalize our visit by informing him of the gift (Jenga) waiting for his retrieval at the inspection area. David's last response just before walking away to retrieve the gift was spoken with pure amazement as he cried out, "*Reeeally?* You are the man!"

I thought that going to the prison and seeing David would fulfill the desire I held in my heart, however, while walking away from our encounter I felt very dejected from not being able to visit with the rest of my ex-roomies; which brought forth an overwhelming urge to do something more irrational than bringing a gun into Mexico!

The next day, I sent David a text that read, "John, can you see about getting me into the prison this week, thanks."

Their prompt reply of, "Sure thing, looking into it," instantly brought forth an unexplainable joy that would be questioned by others as quite *ludicrous!*

I completely dismissed the regulation of forbidden entry to the prison by a nonresident of Mexico and assumed access would be allowed by a former resident of the prison. Unfortunately, my request proved to be unproductive for John, requiring my return trip to the prison a few days later and enlist Frank's persuasive powers that be. Even with Frank's assistance, there were still repeated trips to the prison, slight confusion at the visitor's check-in and miscommunication between Frank and me, resulting in many days before I was able to finally gain entry and achieve a proper visitation with my comrades.

Even though there were prior trips made to the prison which had me turning away in disappointment, there was one occasion when I became amused by the antics of a guard operating the entry gate. After dropping off a box of assorted cookies at the inspection area for the guys and waiting for Frank to greet me at the caged windows, I noticed Frogman standing between the security gates operating the intercom system. He appeared to be amusing himself by spiritedly speaking into the microphone, and even though I hadn't a clue what he

Prison entrance

was saying, I knew for a fact his entertaining behavior was on my behalf, as his frequently repeated "Harry Potter" during his lengthy chatter. I don't know if I should have been amused or offended, though he did put a smile on my face and etched an unforgettable memory in my mind!

In order to avoid the weekend rush of visitors and lengthy delays, I entered the prison on a weekday, eliminating my wait time in the visitor's check-in area and less time lingering there with nervous anticipation. It never dawned to me the possibility of a strip-search, until I was guided to a closet-sized room where a homo-phobic guard performed an insufficient search; *hell*, I could have portrayed Brenda's profession and smuggled contraband into the prison!

Oddly enough, while greeting David at the metal detector, I had absolutely *no* reservations entering a prison that induced a dreadful night spent in horror. I was so carefree that when we approached my former cage, I cried out, "*Hey*," then clutched the bars on the door and gave it a violent shake.

My assertive behavior might have been tolerated while an inhabitant of the prison but not as a guest, which was instantly made evident by the guard operating the security door who reprimanded me with a verbal command, "*No, no*," then waved his hand back and forth.

When John reacted in the same manner to my outburst, I reluctantly altered my enthusiasm to a lower level to appease the guards' glaring stare.

The guys were surprised to see me standing outside their cell door, particularly Emilio, who responded with an exuberant outburst of my name while displaying a big smile and a wave hello, though sadly, no friendly greeting from Mini-Me, as he recently elected to move to another cell. Since the guys were busy working the lunch rush, David said a few of the men would take turns visiting me, then escorted me to the courtyard where we found an unoccupied table near the big screen TV. David began our conversation in the same manner as when I met him at the caged window many days earlier, by questioning my judgment with a statement, "You are the first person (ex-inmate) who returned here (prison) to visit someone!" His mannerism displayed pure disbelief that I had returned to prison. My questionable actions are truly a struggle between sanity and extreme passion that controls my heart!

While sitting there talking with David about a prison guard who was recently shot dead just outside of the prison along with eight other people, Adrian soon emerged from the cellblock and began to approach us. Before he reached our table, I quickly stood up, took a few steps toward him, extended a greeting with a stern handshake and a smile. Through David's interpretation, Adrian wasted little time in asking if I wanted to play a game of chess, to which I eagerly agreed, prompting him to retrieve the chess game that I donated to Emilio's café.

Adrian and I shared in a gratifying moment when David revealed to me that Adrian had been defeating Chewie and everybody else at playing chess. Even though Adrian had high hopes of defeating me and put up a good fight, the attentive student failed to tarnish this proud teacher's record of 21 and 1 any further. I don't think Adrian was aware that I taught him everything he knows about chess and not everything that I know in the masterful art of playing the game.

During our chess match, there were a few pleasant interruptions from friendly faces walking by, inspiring me to suddenly leave the table to greet them with a handshake; such as Emilio who showed up greeting me with his shit eaten grin while saying, "My Lady," along with his usual humorous vernacular. Another uplifting encounter was when Frank arrived, allowing me the pleasure of a proper greeting free from a caged divider; sadly, Frank was busy and cut our reunion short, leaving with what I thought to be as an incomplete farewell.

A prison visit wouldn't be complete with some type of amusement, of which David soon provided when he returned to the table after trying to rectify an ongoing issue he had with prison staff. Due to David's mattress outliving its usefulness, he requested a new one *many* months ago and was still impatiently waiting for its arrival. He was very agitated while relaying his rant to Adrian, who took an interest in David's predicament by immediately standing up and leaving the area in a heated rush, soon to return with the satisfaction of instantly rectifying David's problem with the acquisition of a new mattress.

This quick-fix only demoralized David even further and responded with his familiar disgust, "Fucking Mexicans!" During that moment of David's grief, I empathized with him and thought about how we both were forced to deal with the dysfunctional circus I call Mexico, but presently I found David's mattress story rather humorous! That poor bastard.

While exiting the prison, I felt immense satisfaction from visiting the men and incredibly proud of having the courage to return to an alien world that so few people would even consider plausible! Even though my return trip to the Mouse house went quite well, I regretted not interacting more with Frank during those fleeting moments in the courtyard. To this day, it still bothers me to think about the missed opportunity to express my gratitude to the man who truly touched my heart! I have a constant struggle between the things I have done (good or bad) and all the missed opportunities that would have altered each outcome.

On July 10, I watched Brenda get aboard a bus to take a two-hour trip to catch a plane back home to Missouri. As much as it saddened me to see Brenda leave, it surely was necessary for her health, my peace of mind, and to eradicate a massive amount of stress for both of us. I don't want to sound cruel, but her ability to process stressful situations was almost nonexistent. Her absence eliminated the anxiety that seemed to be spiraling out of control, particularly while we were in the car driving around town trying to complete all the daunting tasks, which in turn kept my fuse short and quick to anger. It was truly a toxic environment for us both!

Day 65 in Country

Thirty-eighth day out of prison

I have been anticipating today's arrival for *six* weeks, so why am I standing outside of the judicial building fifteen minutes before my trial starts and not at the courthouse?

Yesterday when I was at the lawyer's office, Victor arranged for their intern (Afren) to accompany me to the courthouse and supply assistance if needed. Afren looked to be twenty-five years old, average height and build, polite, clean-cut, and well-dressed. A funny side-note: When Victor first referred to Afren last week, for days, I thought he was saying, "A friend." Afren's English was extremely limited, so we mostly relied on translations through our phone Apps, but it didn't autocorrect our assumption that the other person knew where we were headed. I thought we were to meet Karla at the courthouse, whereas Afren believed it was at the judicial building, who I assumed received more accurate instructions than me, especially when he directed my course of travel to the judicial building.

Within moments of arriving at the judicial building with no sight of Karla and the clock drawing near trial time, I assessed we were at the wrong location and told Afren, "I think we are at the wrong place!" "*We got to go!*" With a heightened fear of being late to my own trial, we retreated to the car at a rapid pace, followed by panic forcing my foot to the gas pedal breaking more traffic laws than usual, then finalizing our trip by trotting from the parking area to the courthouse entrance and quickly scampering up the two flights of stairs.

Upon approaching the courtroom, I received a great sigh of relief when Karla greeted us with information that our scheduled trial time was delayed by a trial that was still in session, giving me ten minutes to sit on a hallway bench composing my thoughts toward the trial. One would think sitting outside a Mexican courtroom facing a five to a ten-year prison sentence that I should be apprehensive, but it was quite the opposite. Knowing that Karla confirmed my Abbreviated Process was agreed upon by the prosecuting attorney and numerous reassurances from everybody involved. I sat there waiting with absolutely no anxiety as if the trial was just a formality in expediting my journey back home, but at the time, I failed to recognize that the judge could overrule the attorney's agreement for the Abbreviated Process and throw my cracker ass back in prison!

During the court proceedings, while Angelica was translating, I became concerned as to the direction of my case and couldn't figure out whether it was being conducted in my favor, particularly when I heard Angelica relay familiar unsettling words that subsequently led to my incarceration. I stayed confused for the duration of the brief trial, only to be relieved of my anxiety when the trial was over, as Karla turned to me with a big smile and a thumbs-up; though did so with a sigh of relief as if she had some doubt of a good outcome. If I had known of her uncertainty, I would have jumped bail a long time ago and gone home!

Rejoicing over my victory was met with bafflement as soon as the judge relayed the conditions of my probation. Even though it is illegal to work in Mexico if you aren't a citizen of the state and are required to get a work visa to do so, the judge ordered that I get a job in the country until the termination of my two-year probation. Also, provide proof of residency for the duration of my probation, accompanied by a document that has my fingerprint on it confirming I'm still in-country, of which must be provided to the court every month for two years. Is it just me, or does that sound totally insane for a nonresident of the country?

I think the judge was delusional expecting me to abide by his peculiar ruling and stay in the country for two years; hell, even Karla, Angelica, Victor, and Marco didn't expect me to stay in Mexico. Even though they never suggested that I leave the country illegally, I received assistance from a few people that will remain anonymous, who established my fictitious place of residency by creating a two-year rental agreement with a third party (intermediary). They also prepared twenty-four duplicate documents stating I had a job in the country, requiring me to sign and leave my ink colored thumbprint on each form, for which I completed in a single seating. One document a month was to be mailed from within Mexico by the intermediary to the court, verifying I was still in the country; for those two services mentioned in keeping my deception up to date, I was to be charged fifty dollars a month by the intermediary.

There were two reasons why I chose to partake in the ruse of being an employed resident in a foreign land and keep my probation requirements current. One was for the misconception that I would be returning to Mexico in the future to utilize our timeshare; the other was due to the amount of time it was taking to retrieve my truck, which has morphed from an arduous undertaking to an enormous irritation! After *countless* weeks of completing the grueling task in acquiring all the required documents for retrieving my truck to appease the Prosecuting Attorney, the SOB just happened to go on a two-week vacation, extending my inescapable reality near its breaking point, which had me desperately rethinking a plan of action toward a final resolution.

Since Mr. Puppet man was making it extremely difficult for me to retrieve the truck, Karla and I decided to procure the truck by taking my case to the judge and have him settle the matter, but getting a court date established in a timely manner was undefined. With the uncertainty of a court date and my approaching drywall job, I said to myself, "Fuck it!" I started planning for a departure from this dysfunctional country!

Since I personally perform 98 percent of the work on the large house that was scheduled for drywall, my take-home pay is quite substantial and would eliminate the financial burden this Mexico fiasco created; minus the five grand I owed my sister for that worthless lawyer (Roberto), as that money would be coming directly from my checking account. Therefore, it made more sense to go home to make money, instead of staying in Mexico and pissing it away daily while waiting for the release of my truck.

Before violating my probation and leaving the country, I needed to claim my 20,000 pesos bail money, a task I dare not assume would be a simple one or completed in a timely manner. As predicted, recovering the bail money proved more problematic than the three days it took to relinquish it; fortunately, my stress factor was severely decreased twofold by the absence of Brenda's worrisome behavior and the proactive assistance from John's knowledgeable law firm.

I was able to allocate the hassle of retrieving my bail money via Victor, who assigned Afren to escort me to the government bank and serve as my translator, a task Afren assumed would be completed with, and I quote, "No problem." Oh, to be young and naïve!

With the receipt of bail payment and passport in hand, Afren and I left the law office at 10:30 a.m. with the courtesy of my rental car and headed to the bank, which was only a ten-minute drive. Due to my recent encounters with corrupt law enforcement, I was diligent in stopping at the posted alto (stop) signs that plagued the city streets, or at least do a quick scan for a police car while performing a slow roll through the intersection. Afren took notice of my timid approaches to the stop signs and began displaying impatience by raising his left hand and waving me through the intersections, a testament that police tend to target tourists and not the locals.

Our arrival revealed we were at the same bank that Brenda and I visited while trying to deposit my bail money, déjà vu. Today's encounter mirrored the one I had six weeks earlier with the bank teller who denied our transaction by informing us we needed the proper documentation from the immigration office with verification from the courthouse before allowing me to receive the money. Before continuing in our quest, we returned to the law office for guidance and verification on how to proceed. Unfortunately, our time spent at the courthouse involved a lot of waiting around, and by the time we returned with the proper form, the bank was closed.

Early the next day, I picked up Afren from the office and returned to the bank along with the correct documentation, where the teller conferred with his supervisor of my request; only to reveal Mexican law prohibits a government bank from relinquishing 20,000 pesos in cash to a nonresident of the country. Huh, who didn't see that coming? Mexico resembles a forthright kleptomaniac who refuses to return my *shit!* What the *hell* is wrong with this country? With accepted disbelief, we traversed back through all the alto signs to land back at the office where Afren notified Victor of our failed effort, though, for some reason, I had no doubt they would eventually find a way to recover my bail money.

I sat on their office couch for about an hour, while Victor and Marco once again worked in tandem, making phone calls and deliberating over ideas in the search for a resolution. They concluded that the most advantageous way of retrieving the bail money was to register Afren as my power of attorney, who would then have the legal right to receive my cash. The *only* downside to this clever plan was the number of days required to complete the process, the pile of paperwork, a trip to the judicial office and courthouse, two trips to the law office preparing documentation for the "power of attorney," pay a minuscule amount of money for said service and trusting someone to receive a large stack of cash in my behalf. What could *possibly* go wrong!

Phase two in the quest of my bail money, mainly consisted of me filling out forms and chauffeuring Afren around town for a multitude of days as he implemented all the interactions with the individuals at our daily destinations; making me feel like a tag-along finding myself not speaking to Afren very much, though I really didn't mind because we were getting stuff done! The lengthiest verbalization between us during the week was held at the courthouse while waiting for the preparation of a document. We talked about wives, girlfriends, and high dollar call girls, also about the seventy-five dollar a week paycheck he received for working at the law office. If you were wondering, it appeared that many items sold in the La Paz Walmart were slightly comparable to a Walmart in Missouri, putting Afren's minuscule income into perspective. Afren's financial hardship was also made apparent by avoiding sending text messages in the middle of the day, waiting until evening when costs were considerably less.

From the moment I inquired about retrieving my bail money, to when Afren placed the 20,000 pesos in my hand took about ten days to complete and was done so with little to no stress or drama, which amazed the hell out of me! Afren and I displayed an extreme amount of patience during the entire process as if our ordeal was standard Mexican procedure and we were callous to all the disorder; but then again, some of my carefree demeanor was supported by a disheartened assumption that led me down a self-indulgent path of pleasure, for which I can no longer avert.

Day 84 in Country

Fifty-seventh day out of prison

With the extensive amount of free time that plagued my final days spent in Mexico, I was once again able to take advantage of exploring the countryside far from the human population. Two of the three exploration trips I embarked on were *entirely* void of people. In a country infested with 126 million inhabitants, I found myself quite fortunate experiencing the unique landscape in its unadulterated form.

A unique feature in the mountains

My first journey took place just outside of town amongst the arid landscape, where the days' temperature was so intense that my dorsum's (top of the foot) felt the heat radiating from my boots forcing my occasional retreats behind the north side of large boulders to get relief from the relentless sun. I hiked a couple of miles through a barren valley surrounded by hills that had been scarred by weather for millennia, leaving behind a few cavernous features that were large enough to traverse through. One of the most impressive landscapes required a treacherous and lengthy trek to the top of a hill, where I eagerly explored the honeycombed hillside in search of more unique features.

DIZNEY LAND by Way of Military Escort

Fake cave art

LaPaz in the far backdrop

Further into the exploration, I was amazed to find a small cavernous area that had petroglyphs painted on the smooth stone walls, though within a millisecond, I became baffled over the authenticity of the very crude paintings. It appeared that an ill-equipped artist attempted to depict Mayan drawings to lure unsuspecting tourists and fatten his wallet, which was almost comical as the paint couldn't have been more than twenty years old.

The locations of my next two destinations were relayed to me by an older gentleman who owned a bungalow in a neighboring town that I rented for ten days. The older gentlemen and his wife were from Germany, friendly, accommodating, spoke English and lived in Mexico, who, were fluent in three languages.

The first location was a unique area consisting of a dried-up creek bed that snaked through high canyon walls for miles, of which I traversed through and explored

Bell at dusk

remarkable features for about three hours. The second place I went to days later was about an hour away, where I went snorkeling in the Sea of Cortez in an area that had exceptional aquatic wildlife, along with the absence of other swimmers. The cove where I did most of the exploring was fascinating, but the area toward the open sea is where my adrenaline began pumping, due to the rough waters crashing against large boulders along the shoreline, making for some unique and exhilarating snorkeling. Another exceptional experience of many in Mexico!

Having Afren as my "power of attorney" sparked my proposal to use him in formulating my plan to return home. Since the release date of my truck was unattainable, and a trial date that hinged on the matter. I was going to have Afren retrieve the truck if it was released before the trial, then with Angelica's approval, have him store the truck at her father's workshop parking area to keep it safe until I returned to Mexico. It was more of a "what if plan," but with *eighty-four* days in the country, I really didn't give a shit; it was indeed time to go home!

It took about a week to transform my escape plan into reality, which only required leaving my signature on one form, obtaining permission from Angelica to store the truck and paying Afren to store all our gear at his house, oh, also put my trust in others!

I overheard someone say that a hardship story can't be true if it doesn't have some shame in it. Well, there is enough shame within these pages to make a believer out of the biggest skeptic, in addition to what is revealed next. First, I must revert to that day when my paradise came crashing down back in April when Brenda blindly accused me of infidelity. That dreadful day has since altered my behavior to a more reserved demeanor, for I constantly find myself avoiding delicate subjects, which might result in an argument between us, though occasionally, we still find ourselves quick to anger over trivial bullshit. The gaps between our moments of intimacy had increased, while the gaps between my depression have decreased, feeling as if I no longer have a pillar of strength to lean upon.

Within days of Brenda's departure from Mexico, I began to dwell over the hostile statement she conveyed over the phone while I was in prison, "I'm going to fucking leave you if you don't do it my way!" Even though my age and life experiences have made me callous to relationship malcontent, I felt severely distressed, wondering how

Brenda could degrade our relationship with such a harsh statement. *Hell*, I can't imagine *ever* saying that to her. Some remarks should never be voiced under duress!

Assuming our relationship was damaged beyond repair, I found myself in an angry depression, not looking forward to returning home and continue to be denied the intimacy and sexual appetite I felt was missing. Therefore, I searched on-line in the promiscuous world of ill-gotten affection to fill the void and take a temporary escape from rationality. After scrolling through a selection of call-girls available in the area, I compiled a small list of potential participants and began making phone calls over the next couple of days for availability.

Before committing to an illegal act while on probation, I went to town and talked to a local street vendor concerning the legality of prostitution in Mexico. The vendor looked to be forty years old, spoke adequate English, had a carefree attitude, displaying an energetic desire to sell his assortment of tacky jewelry, rocks, seashells and shark teeth etc. In order to create a friendly rapport with the sociable man, I approached him with the intent of making a purchase, then listened to his sales pitch for a shark's tooth. After standing there longer than I wanted to and declining to put more worthless crap on a shelf back home, I asked him, "How strict is the law on prostitution here?" He quickly responded with enthusiasm, "No problem, there is a reason why they call this place 'Love Paz,' anything goes!" Then he suggested visiting a pool hall/bar that was down the side street around the corner, where I would find just about anything I desired. *Hell no, I didn't go!* I may lack moral judgment, but I'm damn sure, not suicidal!

My first attempt in acquiring a lady of the evening failed to materialize, due to me contacting someone who was from a town that was nowhere near La Paz, which was made apparent when they contacted me saying they couldn't find the condo. The next day's attempt was more disappointing than the first when my curiosity was ensnared by a voluptuous girl's profile page, despite her requesting payment prior to the meeting and wanted the funds deposited into her personal account. Due to being unfamiliar with SOP in Mexico concerning prostitution, I thought prepayment might be a common practice, even though it seemed suspiciously like a scam. Unfortunately, rational thinking was completely obstructed by desperation, sadness, and the pure pleasure of fulfilling man's *repressed* animal instinct, resulting in me standing outside of Applebee's for thirty minutes waiting for my absentee date to arrive, only to soon realize this gullible fool was taken for $150. Oddly, I wasn't too upset, by sending the mystery participant a text that read, "Well played!"

Undeterred by the recent setback, I returned to the condo and searched through the profile pages for women who didn't demand prepayment. Ultimately that night, I was able to secure a pleasant rendezvous with a very young woman for an hour and a half, who, upon her departure, agreed to see me again, resulting in four more visits during the last three weeks of my stay in Mexico. My fleeting experience with the petite young lady (Karen) was comparable to an addictive drug, with side effects of immense anticipation prior to her arrival, followed by extreme depression upon her exodus and immersing deeply in thought of when I would be able to once again satisfy my addiction! Yet no matter how much I increased the dosage, it was *never* enough to fill the void!

Day 92 in Country

Sixty-fourth day out of prison

Many days before my scheduled flight back home, I made arrangements with Afren to drop off all my gear at his house on the day prior to my departure. While heading to his residence, I made a conscious effort *not* to exceed the speed limit, with the fear of getting pulled over by corrupt police who could hamper my exodus on the day before escaping this country. Even though it truly pains me to drive slowly while watching cars pass me by, I kept the speedometer a couple miles under the posted speed limit to eliminate the possibility of blue lights flashing in my rearview mirror.

    I became more reassured that the police wouldn't pull me over by witnessing the high rate of speed at which other cars were passing me; however, no sooner than that thought crossed my mind, I heard that distinguishable sound of a police siren behind me. *You must be freaking kidding me!* How in good conscience could the cop single me out after I was just passed by a speeding vehicle? To my amazement, the friendly cop greeted me with a handshake, but it failed to disguise his true character. He pointed to the posted speed limit sign located two hundred feet further down the road, then spoke in broken English, "You were speeding." He was referring to the sign that displayed a reduced speed limit, of which I obviously hadn't reached yet; so, what justified him in pulling me over?

    I wasn't about to argue with the *asshole*, so I instantly grabbed the phone and attempted to call a lawyer, but to no avail. Then I called Angelica and explained what happened before handing the phone to the cop. Despite being absolutely in the right, Angelica once again implemented her motherly duties by reprimanding me, as if I were guilty of speeding; mimicking the time I informed her of my stop sign incident with the policeman standing at the corner, when she lectured me for not stopping and said, "I always stop at stop signs!" Deja Vu, I was ostracized for Angelica's failure to listen to the specifics of my narrative. There is an adage that goes, "If a tree falls in the forest and there is nobody around to hear it, does it still make a sound? Of which I have modified, "If a man is all by himself in the forest, can he still be considered *wrong?*

How appropriate that my last day spent in Mexico concluded in the same manner as it began ninety-two days ago, by getting pulled over by the police who declined to charge me a fine, making me wonder if our first encounter with the police back in May was a result of dishonest cops who noticed we were tourists. A valuable lesson to remember—don't worry so much about confrontations with Mexico's police and focus more attention on avoiding the military at all costs!

While accepting that my moral compass was fragmented and the overwhelming urge to sustain my addiction, I picked up the phone and called Karen to schedule a visit on my last night spent in Mexico, though I was only able to leave her a voice mail. After watching the clock for two hours waiting for a reply, I grew impatient with the fear of not fulfilling my anticipation that was set in motion; therefore, I contacted Afren to help with an alternative plan of action.

Weeks ago, while Afren and I were waiting at the courthouse for a document, he oddly brought up the subject of prostitution by mentioning that for 4,000 pesos ($250) he could get me a girlfriend for an hour and a half if I so desired, followed by displaying a photo of her.

I think I responded with "Huh," while ogling the pretty woman's photo and thinking her price was high compared to the 1,500 pesos Karen was charging; I suppose the inflated cost reflected a cut for Afren.

Recognizing that Afren had connections with promiscuous women, I called him to attempt to secure myself a date and negotiated a more acceptable price of 3,000 pesos, though the reduced price was only agreed upon when Afren informed me that it would require a different girl who wasn't as pretty. Afren had to make a phone call to confirm an eight o'clock availability and price, but he failed to call me back in a timely manner, which in the meantime, Karen called me back and said, "I can see you tonight."

Unsure if Afren would be able to secure me an engagement, I told Karen that I was out of town and couldn't see her until eleven o'clock. *However,* only moments later, Afren called me back to confirm the eight o'clock appointment. *Oh no,* what have I done? Am I so desperate for affection that I didn't have the audacity to cancel one of the playdates? Maybe I should have scheduled both rendezvous at the same time and see where the party took us, besides draining my wallet.

Proper etiquette dictates from revealing the details of my sexual exploits; therefore, I will only divulge what happened moments before Karen left my bungalow, of which I found quite amusing. It's related to what transpired with my prior guest three hours earlier when we used our phone APPs to translate our conversation for about an hour that wasn't deleted. Karen and I also utilized the APPs, but with less frequency as she had a slight grasp for the English language. While we were standing in the kitchen finalizing our late-night business transaction, something possessed her to write down her real name (Elizabeth) on a piece of paper, then used a magnet to stick it to the refrigerator door.

While she was doing that, I picked up the phone to voice a comment, but by accident found myself scrolling down the screen that displayed the conversation with my previous guest. Elizabeth (Karen) caught a glimpse of the screen long enough to read the incriminating phrase, "Can I take a shower with you?"

She instantly replied with lighthearted conjecture, "Are you cheating on *me?*" then laughed and said, "No, I'm kidding!"

I was totally speechless at her comment! What could I have possibly said? "Elizabeth, you are not the only person who requires at least two showers tonight." Just thinking about her insinuation was quite humorous and put a smile on my face, although my delighted smile soon transformed into a sadden one while exchanging our finale goodbyes.

On the ninety-third day spent in Mexico, is when I finally journeyed back across the border at an altitude of thirty-thousand feet and headed home to a slightly less dysfunctional country, but it was by no means the end of the hardship story that was soon to erupt!

My arrival into St. Louis was met with a non-jovial welcoming from Brenda and her daughter Summer, who used her van to pick me up from the airport. Few words were spoken between us while heading to a Cracker Barrel restaurant for dinner and even less interaction once we were inside sitting at a table.

An explanation for the ominous silence was soon made crystal clear when Brenda spoke not a word while having me read from a printed-out sheet of paper that was copied from our online chat eight years prior through E-Harmony. She had highlighted a quote I made that read something about how I despised infidelity, in reference to my ex-wife (Helen). *Busted.* If our relationship wasn't already shattered, it sure in the hell is *now!*

On previous occasions when accused of adultery and the truth was rejected, I was quick to anger which added fuel to the heated argument, but this time I had absolutely no right to utter a single word, as the damage has been done and besides, nothing could be said or done that would have altered my unscrupulous activities. My silence was broken when a lawyer sat down at our table and handed me a paper, which read that I was to relinquish ownership of our house and forty acres by signing it over to Brenda. I adamantly refused to sign the form and only agreed to do so after receiving the half of the purchase price I paid for the property.

As soon as the lawyer left with apologies from Brenda for wasting his time, Summer and Brenda walked away from the table in a heated rush and by the time I caught up with them, they were already in the van and had locked the doors. I pleaded for them to at least let me retrieve my stuff from the van but soon found myself staring at the taillights as they quickly drove away, leaving me stranded in St Louis at nine o'clock at night.

Brenda obviously had a well thought out plan of action before I even set foot in the country and did so without the use of hysterical behavior; which consequently had me calmly standing in the middle of a Cracker Barrel parking lot with only my phone, wallet, and the realization of, "Don't fuck with a scorned woman!"

Unbeknownst to me, Brenda had linked her electronic devices to the cellphone and laptop I was using to scroll through profile pages and corresponding with promiscuous women. She was witness to my activities from day 1 and never revealed it during our many phone conversations. Worse yet, she was aware of my intent many days before committing my first self-indulgent act, also acquired voice messages I exchanged with the girl who scammed me.

Even though I totally accepted that our relationship had been terminated, I possessed an extreme desire to personally apologize to Brenda for devastating her world and explain that I thought our relationship was nearing its end; therefore I waited for a taxi for over an hour to take me on a two-and-a-half-hour taxi ride home. By the time I reached the house, the lights were off, and the door was locked; also, the hidden house key was missing, so to avoid a confrontation at two in the morning, I attempted to sleep in a patio chair while agonizing over another fine mess I have created.

The ramification of my actions became more upsetting when I found that all my personal items had been boxed up in the garage and realized Brenda was extremely determined in kicking my dumb ass out of the house. Though almost as devastating was when I learned that my forty-page rough draft had gone missing and I was led to believe that Summer had thrown them in a fire, along with the first page of my translation book that had names written in it of the men in cell #6. I can't be one hundred percent sure who actually tossed the pages in a fire, or if it was even true, but I couldn't force myself to press Brenda for the truth, as it would most likely enrage me even further!

Eventually, weeks later, when all the crying, screaming, accusations, assumptions, arguments, and more crying had dissipated, Brenda and I were civil enough to accomplish a calm discussion concerning our future together. I can't speak for Brenda, but I concluded that the success of a relationship requires two people; all the blame shouldn't rest on the shoulders of one individual. To this day, we are still together, but with a slight sense of frailty that was once foreign to our relationship.

Even though I'm not proud of laying in the arms of other women and it may sound morally wrong to admit, but I'm damn sure not ashamed and don't feel the need to justify my actions to others! For those who insist on riding an ethical high horse, realize some solicit yourselves out for monetary gain during your daily routine that could be considered more unethical than prostitution.

The Reentry

In the first week in October, Karla sent me an e-mail confirming a court date for October eighteenth to request retrieval of my truck. Brenda and I made a return trip to a land that brought forth many conflicting emotions but did so with more patience and a better understanding of what was to be expected with Mexico's dysfunctional inner workings.

Our first task for the second day in the country was going to a bank and exchange some cash for pesos, but it didn't open till 9:30 a.m., so we went to a McDonald's for breakfast and killed some time, but it too had trouble getting out of bed and didn't open till 9:00 a.m., breakfast at nine? Oddly, we found ourselves sitting in the car waiting for one establishment to open its doors so we could wait there for another to open.

Due to the locality of the bank and familiarity of the area, we frequently utilized it to obtain cash during our previous stay in the country. The front part of the building contained three ATM machines in a small lobby separated by the main entrance of the bank, with large plate-glass windows spanning the front wall facing the street. I made a note of this because, on our latest visit to the bank, we noticed there were three bullet holes in one of the glass panes, a testament to the violence in Mexico and legitimacy of my brother's (Tom) statement made to me years ago.

Tom had a Mexican employee who revealed to him stories of criminal activities. Thugs would scout out banks searching for repeat customers who routinely partook in transactions involving a large amount of cash, then use that information to devise a plan to rob the unsuspecting victim at a later date. This bold tactic forced patrons of banks to alter their routine by visiting different banks at alternate times and days, although it by no means deterred customers from going to banks or places where cash exchanged hands, as there were always long lines of people waiting to complete their transaction.

After acquiring some funny money from the bank and securing a small Airbnb in town, Brenda and I went to the lawyer's office to discuss legal matters concerning the truck and what was to be expected in court. We also had them contact Karla to confirm the start time of the court proceedings. It was a pleasant surprise and great relief to see John sitting in his office chair and not on the edge of Mini-Me's bed, enjoying his freedom after sixty-two days of incarceration. Since he was swamped with work, our short conversation was mostly limited to the business at hand, though I was informed he was still fighting an arduous uphill battle with corrupt officials, which persisted many months after I had gone home for the second time!

Due to all the legal documentation we possessed regarding my truck, Karla was quite confident the judge would release it without hesitation; but unbeknownst to her, ignorance of specific bylaws was to her advantage and a huge disadvantage to the prosecuting attorney. Within seconds of the judges opening remarks, he immediately addressed Mr. Puppet by reprimanding him, "You had no legal right to confiscate the defendant's vehicle!" Then went on to say that the prosecuting attorney would be financially required to pay the twelve-thousand-peso storage fee; also, the truck was expected to be in the same condition at which it was obtained. *Hell yeah,* score another point for team worm! Pure gratification arose soon as I witnessed the expression of utter displeasure written all over Mr. Puppet Man's stupid face!

I was torn between two emotions, elation for the return of my truck of which many people back home said would never happen, and pure disgust I held for Puppet Man who unjustly cost me a *massive amount* of money, time, and severe aggravation; *what an asshole!* I should have told him he needs to go back to law school and learn the law before he practices law!

It took five days to complete all the proper work before I was able to retrieve my truck from the impound lot, a task which should have been met with gratification, instead of utter disappointment; though we were able to enjoy two days of playing in the Sea of Cortez in the meantime. I also made a trip to the prison to visit David and drop off packaged dried mangos per his request, sadly, I was denied entry and was only able to see him for five minutes at the caged windows. Even though David was glad to see me and appreciative of the mangos, he once again appeared to be dumbfounded that I returned to the prison; I think he failed to recognize that my presence was to show my gratitude toward him and the men.

It felt comforting when David informed me that Emilio inquired about how I was doing, also that the men enjoyed the Jenga game, though recently had lost interest in the game and didn't play it as much. My warm fuzzy feeling was short-lived when I was denied the opportunity to say hi to Raúl and ask if he was enjoying his radio, because David said Raúl was forced to return to the unruly side of the prison; what a shame!

As our fleeting moment drew to a sober end, I became saddened, realizing it would be our finale goodbye, and I would never see him or the men ever again. But no matter, as David, along with John and I continue to keep in contact to this day! Though I sure do miss the elevated camaraderie all of us shared in cell #6!

On the day Brenda and I were heading to the impound lot, Angelica called to recommend that we do not go by ourselves to retrieve the truck and that she could go with us tomorrow, then with a concerned tone said, "I don't want you thrown to the wolves!" Even though her implication sounded discouraging, it provoked me to go anyway to confirm that the truck was still there, or if it had been stripped down to a shell.

The crude impound lot was a few miles outside of town and looked more like a neglected salvage yard, as opposed to an establishment in charge of safeguarding vehicles. The large property was enclosed by a rickety old fence as its security, housed a rundown shack for its office and had a wide variety of vehicle parts scattered throughout the area.

After presenting documentation to an employee that I was the rightful owner of the truck, Brenda and I walked around scanning the area for a blue truck, but the relief of finding it was brief when I found that humanity had once again revealed its ugly face by the long list of items that were missing from my truck!

Three months earlier I was under the strong impression from Angelica who made it clear my vehicle would be secured, persuading me to leave the less valuable items in the truck; though she quickly criticized me for doing so, when she found out thieves cleaned out my truck, by saying "I told you the truck wouldn't be safe!" I didn't question her memory, or etiquette while thinking to myself, "You can't argue with ignorance!"

Everything with a slight value was stolen from my truck, including my toolbox, floor jack, tow chain, camp stove, shoes, blankets, pillows, BBQ grill, and tie-downs; *hell,* the thieves were desperate enough to steal a jug of antifreeze, a quart of oil, fuel from a gas jug and all the quarters from the ashtray.

Items missing that I found to be most upsetting, were the jumper cables I made while in the military thirty years ago, some of the contents from the toolbox which have been in my possession since I was in high school and the GoPro camera that we assumed was amongst the gear at Afren's house, forgetting that I hid it behind the Tempurpedic mattress. Fortunately, the most expensive item (the mattress) was left behind, but it was a little unsettling deducing that our truck was used for a low budget rendezvous involving ambiguous activities when we found a tube of red lipstick and eyeliner applicator next to the mattress; *no* it wasn't Brenda's!

Two days later, when I returned with Hector and Victor (instead of Angelica) to help expedite the process, I discovered there were more items left behind by the assailants after I attempted to start the truck. Upon raising the hood to check the battery connection, I realized the thieving bastards had a slight degree of moral principle, as they replaced my good battery with an inoperative one with no water in the core. They also left behind shards of green rubber tubing next to the gas cap, a byproduct from siphoning my gas tank completely dry, though that was by no means the last unwanted gift I received.

After replacing the battery, fixing the grounding cable and putting a couple of gallons of fuel in the tank and a splash of gas in the carburetor, we were finally able to get the truck started; but it ran a little rough and continued to do so during our drive back to the States, which progressively worsened over the next few weeks. Upon further inspection, I realized the truck's fuel pump, rear u-joints, drive shaft, sparkplugs, distributor cap, and rotor cap had been exchanged with parts that had to be over ten years old. I knew for a fact that a confused Mexican Robin Hood had compromised my truck, as I had a complete tune-up prior to making our trip to Mexico.

Brenda and I finalized our LAST day spent in La Paz by completing a few errands, the first of which was dropping off the rental car, where I witnessed a young man involved in a disagreement with the clerk concerning payment for missing hubcaps from his rental car, who was adamant that the car didn't possess hubcaps when he acquired the vehicle. Unlike myself, he was clearly oblivious to the scams of rental car companies in Mexico, where they remove the floor mats, tire jack and hubcaps before you rent the vehicle, then when you return the vehicle days later, they charge you a hefty fee for the missing items.

While waiting there listening to the distraught customer pleading his case, I could not help but display a slight smirk while being amused toward his unfortunate predicament, as I'm all too familiar with getting ripped off while in Mexico! As David would adamantly voice, "Fucking Mexicans!" Some free advice to would-be travelers to Mexico; *always* take a detailed video of your rental car before driving it off the lot!

Our second stop was at Afren's house to retrieve all our gear, where he and I previously took photos of said items after I dropped them off in August to confirm nothing was missing upon my retrieval of the gear. Though it must be mentioned that Afren initiated the photo session and I only mimicked his actions, as the thought of not trusting Afren never crossed my mind.

Our last stop was at a restaurant called Tex Burger, an establishment we frequently visited due to their hamburger meat being imported from the States. I was skeptical upon our first visit to the restaurant, assuming the origin of their meat was from Mexico, and they were merely advertising that it was from the States. A concern brought forth by the disappointing burgers we have eaten while in Mexico; possibly a byproduct of local cattle, I have witnessed to possess little to no body fat, or maybe it's what they are fed. Nevertheless, Tex Burger's inflated menu prices were well worth the cost, as we have yet to experience a bad meal there. Oh, by the way, the waiter who always took our order also became familiar with our preferred meal, to the extent that little to no words were needed in placing our order. It's truly time to go back *home* and remain there!

The Finale Exodus!

Our early morning departure from La Paz was the launchpad that propelled us out of the country at a land speed record in only one day, putting my tally of hours spent in Mexico at 2448, equivalent to 102 days or, 146,880 minutes, all because of a *five-second* blunder!

While driving north at a high rate of speed toward the border, the thought of violating my probation never crossed my mind, not even when we approached the same military checkpoint where I was arrested. I couldn't tell whether the soldiers operating the inspection area were the same ones who found my gun; if so, this time we weren't asked to reveal our passports or get out of the truck, they only raised the camper shell door and did a quick peek inside, then without hesitation waved this lawbreaker on through. It appears that the odds of my recent unfortunate incarceration were truly precipitated by a coin flip (chance and timing).

The only other potential setback that could have arisen during our exodus from Mexico was revealed to us many days after arriving back home while watching a news story involving crime in Mexico. Apparently, criminals found a new way to extract money from tourists, by standing alongside a highway and flagging them down to pull over, as if they were in dire need of aid; then, when the gracious victim stopped their vehicle to see what was amiss, they would get robbed by knifepoint.

This crude but effective tactic was attempted on us while driving through a mountainous area of Mexico far from civilization, where three middle-aged men were swiftly walking toward the road while yelling and frantically waving their arms motioning for us to pull over. At first glance, I truly thought there might have been an accident ahead of us, and they were needing help, but after taking my foot off the accelerator for a split second assessing the situation and noticing there wasn't a vehicle anywhere insight, I stomped on the gas just as the three suspicious characters drew near our vehicle. Those clueless criminals didn't realize that if this aggressive driver found himself in a vulnerable and dangerous situation, *I would have* used my vehicle as a weapon and run them dumb bastards over, even if it required putting the truck in reverse and chasing them all around the large parking area. *Hell Yes*, I possess that type of split-second decision making that unleashes pent-up rage, especially having the advantage of a two-ton weapon; if you are going to rob me, you better fucking kill me first! *Never* bring a knife to a "truck" fight!

Within a month after returning to the States, I lost contact with David and feared that I would never hear from him again, but about a year later, he sent me an e-mail which only read, "Hello, Dennis, my amigo!!!" Unfortunately, I'm the type of person who adamantly refuses to be constantly enslaved to the cyberworld (I actually have a real-life); therefore, I only check my e-mail twice a month and, in doing so, found his e-mail twenty-one days later on December 22, 2019. Despite immediately sending David a short e-mail translated into Spanish and receiving his quick reply, I was not happy with my e-mail, as I was able to read the translated version of what David received, which contained segments that were nonsensical; nevertheless, David's response didn't make a note of it.

David said he had been out of prison for about two months and was living in Mexico City. Then went on to say, "I lost contact with you because the authorities (prison staff) got stricter. For a year, I stopped having a phone and lost my access to Google accounts. I appreciate that you answered me, we always remember you and how we had fun, despite the situation. Emilio (still in prison) sends his regards." David's e-mail ended with his phone number and a request to receive a copy of my book, which at that moment was far from being completed.

Even though I received great pleasure from David's correspondence to renew our friendship, it lacked an emotional bond that can only be effectively achieved by a phone call, therefore after dwelling over it for a week, I decided to give him a call to carry out a proper and a more in-depth conversation.

I don't know who was more excited the instant David answered the phone, him or me, as I was thrilled to hear his voice and totally amazed that the long-distance connection went through flawlessly. Upon completion of our small talk, I became intrigued after inquiring about his newfound freedom. David was released from prison after serving more than two years as an innocent man who never received a sentence, which consequently allowed him to receive benefits due to the government's unjustly imprisonment. He went on to say that the prison started implementing more stringent regulations along with enforcing former policies, soon after I saw him in October.

The first thing the prison did was construct a boundary fence ten feet from the outside wall of the prison to prevent people from approaching the prison too closely and tossing contraband over the wall. They also shut down the store and restaurants, while throwing all the refrigerators and cooking devices in the trash, not allowing prisoners to cook any meals and only allowed them to possess a few snacks, requiring them to eat meals the prison prepared. During the massive inspections, the guards confiscated all cell phones, TVs, and all other contraband throughout the prison; also, money was no longer permitted. So officially Dizney Land has raised its drawbridge ending an era of which, so few people enjoyed before converting its unique real estate into a bona fide prison. It sounds like the extreme alterations would have been drastic enough to transform my tolerable imprisonment at Dizney Land into a horrendous attraction at a decrepit carnival.

I recognized that incarceration in a Mexican prison could have been exceedingly worse and probably should have, especially hearing stories of US citizens imprisoned in foreign countries who never get released in a timely manner and for some arrive back home unhealthy, dying or lying in a pine box. I consider myself very fortunate to be incarcerated in the La Paz prison after 2016 and before 2018 and *extremely* grateful to the long list of people who helped see me through the difficulties of this self-inflicted hardship! Compared to the other inmates, there appears to be many questionable variables for my preferential treatment and early release from prison for which I cannot answer, such as Roberto's true involvement, the old inmate who had info of my pending release, also the Captain or Warden who oversaw my mini-vacation in Dizney Land.

There is no measure in ranking each person's support who specifically helped me the most, as everybody involved brought something unique to the coalition. Along with the collective force, I was able to scale that mighty wall pretty much unscathed, walking away with a remarkable memory I can truly claim as my own finding it *impossible* to ever forget! To the seven men in cell #6, hopefully, I have impacted some small part of your lives as much as you have impacted mine!

To the following people goes my deepest gratitude. Karla, without your due diligence, there wouldn't be a gratitude list of names, and instead of praising your accomplishment, I would have placed your name atop the disgruntle list. Your ability to use the legal system to our advantage outside the courtroom removed all doubt I previously held for you, for that I do apologize. There are absolutely no words to express my appreciation for the lady who reunited me with my loved ones. Hopefully, my tears of joy, along with the heartfelt hug, were enough to convey my sincere thankfulness to you!

Frank, Mr. Connections. If not for you, I would have never been reassigned to cell #6 and completely missed out at meeting the exceptional men who truly formulated a more tolerable stay in prison for me. There were moments when I felt awkward, excepting the massive amount of assistance you provided, as your level of concern for my wellbeing and commitment to acquiring items was awe-inspiring. Without a doubt, you must have been exceedingly proficient at your previous profession, and prison life may have restricted your wheeling and dealings, it sure as hell hasn't stopped you in any way! The stability of my keystone truly began with you making my endless gratitude unmeasurable, so to you, a special thanks! PS Frank, please apply your extraordinary talent in securing an exit strategy from your Dizney Land!

Raúl, Helping hands. You were the first inmate to approach who was willing to escort me outside of my cell and help with translations. You were undeniably a vital component who broke the ice getting me through those first few days of transition and playing that first game of chess, you undoubtedly opened the flood gates that were to follow. Playing chess with others, dominos, Aggravation game and a lot of interaction between other inmates, resulting in busy entertaining, full days. Thank you for befriending me! Raúl, stay focused on your legal battle!

Emilio, The Boss. You welcomed me into your world with open arms and never made me feel like an outsider, also the more you razzed me, the more I felt at home. Jokes and pranks between two strangers usually take a long time to develop into a level of comfort, though between us, it was only thirteen days, which is quite amazing as there are brothers who don't have that level of the bond after many years. Your animated expressions revealed the whole story, translating all the fun craziness in pure detail, though I can't imagine how much more outrageous our time spent together would have been if we spoke the same language. For the unforgettable camaraderie and elevated theatrics, I truly thank you! Why do we men have more fun when acting like we have a mind of a child? Hey Emilio, you have a hot wife!

David, "The Brains" Mr. Hospitality. Your compassion for my comfort deeply touched my heart, for you went out of your way, making sure I had what was needed or wanted. You eliminated the discomfort I possessed of being an intruder in the limited amount of space within your cell, also letting me use your music and headphones was a temporary escape from the insanity, which *really* let me visit my happy place. For all you have done for me, I deeply thank you! Remember, "You are the man!"

Adrian, The Enforcer. You are freaking amazing! In my entire life, I can only remember one incident when a non-family member looked out for my interest in a hostile environment, and you performed it twice (at least) that I'm aware of. The first moment I witnessed your concern for my well-being certainly meant more to me than you'll ever know, for it gave me total confidence to be out of the cell amongst prisoners without fear for my safety; and in the dangerous prison world that security is priceless. I didn't need to comprehend the Spanish language to appreciate your intent, I read it all over your face as only a brother would have done what you did for me! Also, I received a great sense of pride when you paid attention to every detail on how to improve your ability at playing chess and now are effectively defeating skilled players who once shamed you. "You learn well grasshopper." From one strategic mind to another, I thoughtfully thank you! Don't forget, "*Never give up!*"

Rosendo, Mini-Me. At my family reunions, we had a driven desire to get each other in trouble with our dad, siblings, or relatives, and that is precisely what you did with me. You took the time to treat me like a sibling at a dysfunctional family reunion. Despite giving you an A for effort in trying to burn me, I was wise to your foolery; as a master, I have been playing that game for many years. Getting in trouble from my dad is one thing, but from a guard in a Mexican prison is a fine line I couldn't cross, unless a lot of drinking was involved. I still don't have a clue what you wanted me to call the guards, though I'm sure it would have received a laugh from you and the cellmates. Thank you for including me in the laughter! Don't ever lose your sense of humor or smile. PS: "Open the window!"

Pablo, The Cook. While cooking my meals in the kitchen getting in your way, not once did you display signs of discomfort or loss of patience and appeared you went out of your way not to be in mine. I sincerely hope you were not inconvenienced while I was cleaning the kitchen. Your patience helped raised a relaxed atmosphere of my intrusion, for that my stomach and I thank you very much! Don't forget, "A good day ends with dirty dishes and a full belly."

Jose, The Cleaner. Even though communication between us was very limited due to the language barrier, you still joked around trying to get a smile out of me. I really appreciate your attempt to include me in the daily comical banter, it surely made me feel like one of the guys. Thanks for your acceptance. Keep this in mind, a strong bond between two different cultures starts with just a smile.

John, The Intellectual. You completely eased my level of anxiety every time you spoke to me, and your ability to translate without loss of essential details was priceless. The long list of things you helped me with, explaining prison rules, interpreting jokes and conversations and assisting with legal issues has undeniably been a tremendous fortune. When I was in the dark depths of despair, you brought me back up to the light, with your reasoning and wisdom that is more profound than most people I have met in my life, and consider myself extremely lucky to have met you. I honestly can't thank you enough! John, change starts with only one man, "Never give up the good fight!"

Captain, The Commandant. I must give thanks to your invaluable support, even though I hope this story does not find its way into your possession until you are no longer employed at the prison. Frank may have altered my stay, but he was only following your requested orders, of which is unknown, whether you were obeying a directive from upper command, or took it upon yourself to oversee my welfare. Either way, my extended gratitude and respect surely goes to the man who effectively allowed me to have my cake and eat it too!

Last but not least, Brenda, Miss Amazon. The giver of needful things and my lifeline to the outside world. You endured so much tribulation for my welfare with a conviction that was truly remarkable, all while under a massive amount of stress. If not for you, my journey would have been much more direr, while feeling alone in the company of strangers and forced to be over-reliant upon them. Despite owing you a great amount of appreciation, I sincerely feel you deserve a humbling apology from the man who induced your traumatic incarceration in a Mexican jail, also for breaking your heart; therefore, *please* forgive this imperfect supplier of your grief!

A genuine reflection of my self-inflicted hardships within Mexico was made more evident soon upon re-exposure to the USA's superficial society, where I'm torn between feeling ashamed for being a US citizen and extremely lucky for not living in Mexico. Those days spent in prison and in Mexico have pried open my eyes to see the world for which it has become. Where society and humankind have completely lost sight of what is truly important and will only be self-aware of its foolishness after everything has been stripped away and destroyed beyond recognition. This left me imprisoned in an *insane* world for which I no longer belong! Consequently finding it much easier to escape from a Mexican prison than from societies harsh enslavement.

Do I have regrets for sneaking the gun into Mexico? Hell no; however, in relation to Brenda's hardships, most definitely *yes!* When people ask if I would ever return to Mexico, my response is no, but it's not based on violating probation, or the discouraging fact of spending time in a Mexican prison, it's because I have witnessed firsthand the true Mexico from outside of the condo-walls protection. A country where crime is second nature, corrupt officials and police are widespread, escalating murder rate and getting ripped-off by a wide variety of inhabitants is a common daily occurrence, especially for tourists who can't speak Spanish.

I may have complained excessively toward certain individuals and circumstances while detained in Mexico, but I'm capable of recognizing the only person to blame for my displeasure is myself. While memorialized my unique journey into text, it became a great reliever of hostility I held toward the Mexico ordeal, and the more I wrote, the more I became mildly amused along with feeling extremely privileged in experiencing a life-altering moment, powerful enough to occasionally bring a tear to my eye; I can't explain why, perhaps some type of deep-down emotion caught between lost pleasure and persistent sadness, creating distorted clarity.

Of the hardships that persisted in plaguing my mind, the most upsetting was of a suppressed memory hidden deep within my mind, until it resurfaced while writing about the house fire and those god damn five seconds. While recovering in the hospital defying the grim reapers pursuit for a corpse, I was inadvertently awakened by Helen and a doctor who was in the hallway discussing Christopher's grim prognosis, which immediately propelled her weary body to his bedside and began softly speaking while he laid there in an unconscious state.

Listening to her passionate desperation for his recovery damn near crushed my heart, so I gingerly crawled out of bed, slowly walked across the hall to be by her side, attempting to ease her sorrow. The only thing I remember from that somber moment was speaking to Christopher with confidence that there was no doubt he would soon recover; sadly, an unachievable promise would be my last words spoken to him, "Christopher, when you get better, I will take you to Disney Land." A painful memory that overrides any hardships I accrued while in Mexico; brought forth by the harsh reality of my own confirmation, *"It could always be a lot worse!"*

Christopher, March 2
1988 March 10 1993

Endnotes

For more in-depth information pertaining to John Moreno's arduous plight, please visit: https://truthsantosnow.org and www.patrimonio-film.com THANK YOU!

CPSIA information can be obtained
at www.ICGtesting.com
Printed in the USA
JSHW051940221122
R12102900002B/R121029PG33385JSX00007B/3

9 781648 017872